HOW TO AVOID PRODUCTS LIABILITY
LAWSUITS AND DAMAGES

HOW TO AVOID
PRODUCTS LIABILITY
LAWSUITS AND DAMAGES

Practical Guidelines
for Engineers and Manufacturers

by

Charles E. Witherell

NOYES PUBLICATIONS
Park Ridge, New Jersey, U.S.A.

Published in the United States of America by
Noyes Publications
Mill Road, Park Ridge, New Jersey 07656

10 9 8 7 6 5 4 3 2 1

Library of Congress Cataloging-in-Publication Data

Witherell, Charles E.
    How to avoid products liability lawsuits and damages.

    Includes bibliographies and index.
    1. Products liability--United States. I. Title.
KF1296.W5 1985   346.7303'82   85-15316
ISBN 0-8155-1052-7 347.306382

Preface

Products liability losses are costing industry millions of dollars. They are forcing even some well-run firms to the edge of bankruptcy, and a few of them over the brink. To the executive, products liability may seem unfair and nothing more than a giant conspiracy to pick industry's "deep pockets." But its roots are firmly embedded within the fabric of our social values. It is but a symptom of society's disenchantment with technology and its growing intolerance of the needless loss of human life and injuries caused by defective products.

Contrary to common belief, products-related harm and injuries, with their costly damages, are not inevitable events. Most of these losses are preventable, including the bill for them that industry is now being called upon to pay.

In a very real sense, today's products liability law represents new mandatory engineering standards. It has become a legal duty for each manufacturing executive, manager, supervisor and engineering professional to understand and comply with them. This is as vital to the success and profitability of a manufacturing concern as business competence and technical know-how.

The key to preventing products liability losses lies in developing a positive attitude toward understanding these new standards and in learning how to apply cost-effective procedures for designing and manufacturing products—safe products that can stand the scrutiny of a court and jury. This is the purpose of this book.

The book explains why a products liability crisis developed. It tells how to evaluate your vulnerability; why insurance is not a cure; why products liability is not about to go away; how to devise practical strategies for avoiding these losses while increasing productivity and profitability. It describes the role of new developments like computer technology. And it gives a glimpse of what lies ahead, including trends toward personal liability, effects of tort reforms, and pros and cons of no-fault insurance.

The book traces each step of a product's life, from conception to disposal. It gives liability prevention guidelines for planning and design, for engineering, purchase and procurement, production, packaging, sales, promotion and advertising, service, and customer relations. It is written from an engineer's viewpoint, expressly for engineers. Its contents are timely and apply to all engineering disciplines and firms manufacturing and marketing products today.

Pleasanton, California   Charles E. Witherell
October, 1985

ABOUT THE AUTHOR

Charles E. Witherell is a consulting engineer associated with the Lawrence Livermore National Laboratory, California, in the area of metallurgical integrity and weld reliability for nuclear weapons and advanced energy systems prototypes. He also maintains a private consulting practice, and has been granted over one hundred patents. Educated in engineering, metallurgy, and law, Mr. Witherell is a registered professional engineer in several states including New York and California. He is also a member of The American Welding Society, The Metallurgical Society of AIME, American Society of Mechanical Engineers, American Society for Metals, American Powder Metallurgy Institute, American Society for Testing and Materials, and The Defense Research Institute.

DISCLAIMER

Products liability law is in a continual state of flux and can differ significantly from place to place. No book dealing with so vagarious a subject can offer guidelines for specific situations. General summaries of judicial and legislative law, regulations of government agencies, and other standards affecting liability, are given for purposes of illustration and are not to be considered complete and authoritative. Similarly, the descriptions of prevention practices are not to be construed as solutions to specific problems but are offered solely for purposes of information and education.

Reasonable care has been taken to assure that the book's content is authentic, timely and relevant to industry today; however, no representation or warranty is made as to its accuracy, completeness or reliability. Consequently, the author and publisher shall have no responsibility or liability to any person or organization for loss or damage caused, or believed to be caused, directly or indirectly, by this information. In publishing this book, neither the author nor publisher is engaged in rendering legal advice or other professional services. It is up to the reader to investigate and assess his own situation. Should such study disclose a need for legal or other professional assistance the reader should seek and engage the services of qualified professionals.

Contents

1

A Problem for Industry

AN UNPOPULAR SUBJECT

Most of us would rather not think about it. Even the words "products liability" have a menacing ring to them. They bring to mind reports of how some have become entangled in expensive and devastating lawsuits over injuries caused by their manufactured products. Or, perhaps they recall a personal experience with some phase of a products lawsuit. Either way, the mere thought of products liability threatens our security and peace of mind.

What makes the thought of it disturbing is a feeling of frustration most of us have over it. This is because of a nagging suspicion that it's hopeless to try to prevent it or overcome it. The fact that it's a *legal* matter doesn't help. Products liability involves lawsuits, courts, judges, verdicts, damages and things of that sort. None of us want to face them. Even one of the country's leading jurists, Learned Hand, felt the same way. He once remarked, "I must say that, as a litigant, I should dread a lawsuit beyond almost anything short of sickness and death."

For engineers, products liability means more than just another legal hassle. This one strikes much closer to home. Manufactured products and those who make them are the targets of these lawsuits. Therefore, these problems are particularly significant to us because our personal interests and careers hang in the balance.

Products liability is a legal obligation. Its purpose is to compensate for harm that arises from the existence or use of products. The key word here is "compensate." That means money, and the stakes can be high.

Stated simply, products liability is a mechanism for transferring cash from pockets of product manufacturers to the pockets of injured victims.

1

Although the machinery itself and the power that makes it run come from the law, its purpose today is essentially economic redistribution.

Although most claims are aimed at the product manufacturer, others may be named in a products lawsuit. Besides the manufacturer it may include raw material and component suppliers, wholesalers, distribution and service organizations and others—anyone who handles products commercially. To simplify our discussion, general references to "manufacturer" will be understood to mean anyone in the product manufacturing and distribution chain.

When you stop and think about it, the legal approach seems incredibly indirect and inefficient for accomplishing this purpose. There is no question that a more effective system could be devised today. But the existing one is so well established, with historical roots as old as this country if not older, that we will have to live with the present system until a better one comes along. This does not mean that we should abandon efforts to improve the system. But, for now, our attention should be upon what we must do to live with the system as it is.

Before we can consider how to positively and constructively cope with the problem of products liability, we must understand this awkward economic redistribution process. We must learn the intricacies of the machinery that makes the system do what it is supposed to do. And we must have some idea of how it all came to be put together this way and why. These issues are covered in Chapter 3. It is essential background for the engineer who wants to minimize effects of the products liability threat upon his career and business.

Before we get to that, it is important to have a grasp on why this is such a major problem for industry and why it persists.

THE CRUX OF IT

Until recently, someone seeking compensation for injuries caused by a manufactured product faced a fairly difficult task. For most products, injured victims had to prove that their injuries occurred because of negligence or fault of the manufacturer. But no longer. Recent changes in the law have stripped away most of these requirements. These changes have opened a number of new approaches that make things easier for the injured to be compensated.

One such approach is to bring suit under a concept known as *strict liability*. This allows liability to be imposed upon the manufacturer regardless of its fault. This approach represents the most drastic change in the law in that its objective is not to punish wrongdoers but simply to allow those injured by manufactured products to be compensated by someone having resources to do so.

This does not mean *absolute* liability, where a manufacturer virtually guarantees a product will not cause injuries. While some recent court decisions seem to have approached the threshold separating strict from absolute liability, there still are certain elements that the injured party must prove but most of these involve the product itself.

Other changes include recent compliations of the law of sales covering commercial transactions under the Uniform Commercial Code (UCC) that now provide other alternative routes to compensation for victims of products-related injuries.

Consequently, as it has become easier for victims of products injuries to obtain compensation, so it has also become more frequent for product manufacturers to find themselves implicated in this economic redistribution process.

How does the process get started? On the face of it at least, injured victims—the ones seeking compensation for their suffering or loss—originate legal action by filing a claim or complaint. They're the *"plaintiffs"*. But once involved in a products lawsuit, you quickly learn that the injured victims are not your only opponents. They're not the most formidable ones. It's their lawyers who represent them. These are the ones you and your attorney will be dealing with.

These lawyers are intensely motivated. They act as though they will stop at nothing to win the case for their clients. Why are they so motivated? Their fee-structure, or how they are paid for their services, has a lot to do with it.

Although contingency-structured fees are unethical for engineers, they are an accepted way of life for products liability trial lawyers. This method of payment gives the lawyers a sizeable portion of whatever money they win for their clients. The greater the settlement or the judgment awarded by the court, the more the lawyers get. Current estimates are that trial lawyers get 41 cents from every dollar awarded in products liability judgments.[1]

On the surface of it, it may seem unfair that the injured victim should be required to turn over a substantial portion of his compensation to his attorney. But there are considerations that justify it, or at least make the system seem more reasonable. Probably the most compelling one is that without a contingent fee system it is unlikely that any but the wealthy would be able to afford the highly specialized legal talent that is often needed to recover damage claims in a civil action. Nevertheless, there are abuses of the system and, as always, it is the abuses that get the most attention.

But why focus on products manufacturers? Why should *they* be the ones called upon to compensate these victims of products injuries? Perhaps the most obvious reason is one given by bank robber Willie Sutton when asked why he robbed banks. He said, "Because that's where the money is!"

If you think this may be stretching things a bit, hear what Justice Traynor said in an early products liability court decision:

> Those who suffer injury from defective products are unprepared to
> meet its consequences. The cost of an injury and the loss of time or

> health may be an overwhelming misfortune to the person injured, and a needless one, *for the risk of injury can be insured against by the manufacturer and distributed among the public as a cost of doing business. (Escola v. Coca Cola Bottling Co. of Fresno)*[2] (emphasis added)

Courts have said that manufacturers should be responsible because they are the ones that create products. This is how the court explained it in a later landmark products liability decision:

> We need not recanvass the reasons for imposing strict liability on the manufacturer. The purpose of such liability is to insure that the costs of injuries resulting from defective products are borne by manufacturers that put such products on the market rather than by the injured persons who are powerless to protect themselves. (*Greenman v. Yuba Power Products Inc.*)[3]

At first, this sounds fairly logical, but did you catch the suggestion that the product user or consumer is somehow subject to attack by these inanimate objects? It's as if manufactured products had minds of their own or were under the control of some diabolical force. If you detect hints of warfare going on, you're beginning to get the idea of what this is all about.

An undercurrent of hostility runs all through products liability. This whole business is charged with emotion. And it's understandable since these are *personal* injuries and losses that we're dealing with. The emotional response may not be altogether spontaneous and unintentional though. It serves the purpose of the proponents of products liability law in generating public sentiment through news media.[4,5] This pays off in increased jury awards and intensified support for pro-consumer legislation and government regulation promoting safety and security for its citizens.

All of this makes an ideal climate for breeding fierce battles: On one side are injured victims and their attorneys, both motivated by the desire to be compensated. On the other side is industry—"big business"—the heavies who, in the eyes of many, are bursting with wealth. And it is wealth derived from making and selling products that sometimes injure people and damage their property. The catalyst that can make the whole reaction go critical, and sustain it, is society's zeal for human rights. In this context, it is the right of individuals to be financially compensated for their injuries and their right to have a safe environment to live and work in.

Lawsuits and court trials are, by definition, adversary proceedings anyway. And, because of its highly reactive ingredients, a full-scale products liability battle can make other industrial struggles like corporate takeovers, strikes, antitrust actions and employment discrimination suits seem mild by comparison.

Do not underestimate its potential danger. Products liability is a hostile force and a major threat to every firm that manufactures and markets products. And this covers a lot of territory: from industrial and consumer products to business products and things that you never thought were products.

So there are many reasons why products liability is a threat to industry. But, considering the magnitude of this threat and the resources that are available to industry to combat it, it is surprising that most products liability contests are as one-sided as they are. A brief look at some of the possible reasons why so many in industry seem to be losing this battle is worth a few minutes of our attention here at the onset.

First of all, industry has been at somewhat of a disadvantage from the start. Practically overnight, products liability law evolved from an obscure legal concept to one of the most devastating threats industry ever had to face. What's more, the "rules" that constitute products liability law were devised by what many perceive to be "the other side." That is, by lawyers, judges and legal scholars; not consensus standards-making organizations having industry representation. Not even by Congress or other elected legislatures. All this happened without the usual rule-making proposals, public and industry hearings and announcements of intentions that serve to give advanced notice of pending legislation.

Secondly, it is an unfortunate fact of life that technical people have never warmed up to legal issues. Even after two decades of living under the threat of products liability, many in industry are still unaware of what the law requires and the potential danger of remaining uninformed.

One reason for this is that much of today's products liability law stemmed from the *common law*. This is law that is created by decisions of judges. Such judge-made law is real law, binding and valid. But it's not found in neatly compiled documents like those formulated by legislative bodies. A search on your own to find out what the law of products liability is can be elusive and exasperating. You have to read through a series of law cases and lengthy judicial decisions to find it. Even then, it's subject to jurisdictional limitations, legal interpretations and overruling or modification by subsequent decisions.

Nevertheless, from what we do know and read, some aspects of products liability law do not seem fair or just at all. We have read about massive cash judgments and penalties charged against some large, respectable and well-run firms. Because of products lawsuits, some of them have been forced to the edge of bankruptcy and a few over the brink. We cannot help but wonder if there is something wrong with our legal system.

There are other reasons for our questioning the fairness of the system. For example, products liability law is heavily weighted against the manufacturer in favor of injured victims. This is not just suspicion, it is admitted policy. The manufacturer may be entirely without fault, but nevertheless must pay. Frequently, it must pay for injuries caused by misuse of or continued use of old worn-out equipment; sometimes equipment that had been improperly modified or incompetently repaired, and perhaps time after time.

The nature of the products liability situation today prevents our remaining neutral to it. For, to choose to ignore it is an affirmative decision for liability exposure. This is because the new products liability law has created obligations that constitute personal duties and responsibilities. They are unavoidable and non-delegable. We ignore them at our peril. We don't have the option to turn them over to specialists and forget them. We *have* to become personally involved.

It goes beyond this too, for the law affecting responsibility for injuries and damage caused by products has created an entirely new legal *environment* to work in. It permeates every task we undertake, every decision we make, every word we write and conclusion we formulate.

TYPICAL REACTIONS

Depending upon our individual differences and backgrounds, we will react in various ways to these circumstances. Our attitudes toward this problem influence our response to it and this governs our vulnerability to products claims and lawsuits. In questioning a broad cross-section of people in industry during the past several years, I have found a widespread tendency for engineers to view products liability as some incomprehensible and hostile force they have no control over. Therefore, they decide to ignore it. They feel partly justified in taking this position since they believe the products liability threat is only a temporary scare; like a storm that will soon blow over. But indications are that it's not about to go away.

Another common reaction is to turn the whole matter over to specialists, admitting our limitations in comprehending products liability issues and assessing our exposure to the risks. Since there are experts like lawyers and insurance companies around who understand these things, it seems plausible to let them handle it. This response "feels" right and appeals to our sense of good management. Besides, it gets us off the hook right away. This reaction, too, can be a mistake because it overlooks the personal responsibilities implicit in new products liability laws. If you wait until it's time to call in insurers and legal counsel, it's too late to start thinking about preventing claims, lawsuits and their damages.

Liability insurance is no panacea either, because many costs associated with products lawsuits aren't covered. The increasing number of deductibles and exclusions in industrial liability policies makes the insured manufacturer a self-insurer for much of its coverage. And, for some manufacturers of high-risk products, it has become difficult to buy insurance at any price.

Intuition tells us that, somehow, a nation whose resources are so intimately tied to its manufacturing industries cannot tolerate such a crisis to continue. This attitude leads to hopeful expectation of an imminent solution, from somewhere. Such optimism has been fueled to some extent by reports that Congress is considering products liability reform legislation. This government involvement was prompted largely by pressure from industrial interests. Many would like to believe that once some kind of reform legislation is passed the heat will be off. But, as we will see later, none of the proposed reforms advocate an upheaval of the now well-established products liability law. Their principal goal is to unify products liability law, not abolish it.

Then there are some who over-react to this threat. They have an obsessive fear of becoming enmeshed in products liability litigation. Paranoia can be as potentially damaging as ignoring the problem altogether. It makes manufacturers reluctant to develop certain types of products and even withdraw existing liability-prone lines from the market. Such an attitude can stunt a firm's growth and stifle progress; particularly for the very product lines that most need innovation for increased reliability and safety.

These negative reactions to the products liability threat are common and they seem completely reasonable and justified. But they are deceptive because they are based upon flawed rationale. This makes the threat all the more insidious.

Industry can criticize the courts for making manufacturers bear the brunt of compensating victims of products injuries. It can deplore products liability law and its costs and damage to respectable firms. And it can lobby for legislation to relieve injustices in the system. But these do not address the immediate problem, which is how to minimize effects of this threat that—right now—is facing us, our companies and the security of our employees.

NOT HOPELESS

Fortunately, avoidance of products lawsuits is not an unattainable goal. What's more, the key to unlocking the products liability trap which industry is in lies in its own hands. Industry may not have been responsible for its plight, it may not have seen it coming and there is probably nothing it could have done to prevent it, anyway. But the problem is here. It's up to us to put aside negative thinking and learn how to cope with it.

This is where this book comes in. It is about products liability *prevention*. It is aimed at the engineering professional and its purpose is to show how to avoid products lawsuits and their adverse economic consequences. This is its only goal.

There are a number of things this book will not do. Since it's not a law book, it won't make you an expert on products liability law. It doesn't get into details of lawsuits. For example, there are no sample dialogues between attorney and expert witness. No step-by-step trial procedures. And the book isn't a how-to-do-it-yourself substitute for competent legal counsel. None of that, because these things won't help you to *prevent* claims and lawsuits.

Once you're into a lawsuit and are concerned over trial tactics, courtroom procedure, and things of that sort; you have passed the point where the material presented here can help much—at least in *that* litigation. What you need then is a good defense attorney who will try to minimize your losses.

The book does include some guidelines on defense strategy, but these are basically preventive measures. They are aimed at building a basis for negotiating early and favorable settlements of claims that may be filed in spite of all the precautions and preventive steps. But the prevention strategies described here will do the most good before a claim is filed because their emphasis is upon more responsible *engineering* and not law.

For this reason, you will not find a collection of product failure analyses. They have their place and can make interesting, even entertaining, reading but their value in keeping you out of products liability difficulties is limited. Sometimes, they can have the opposite effect. This is because we all have an irresistable urge to take short-cuts, to try to guess from an *abbreviated* version of someone else's case how a court might react to our own particular situation. It can lead to wrong impressions and a false sense of security.

Law students learn law through reading cases—judicial decisions of appellate courts. But there, the emphasis is on law. It takes intensive analyses of hundreds of similar cases to catch the dominant thread running through them all. Excerpts of leading judicial decisions are included in this book to illustrate fundamentals of products liability. For our purposes of liability prevention, technical details behind the individual cases are not as important as the holdings of the decisions themselves.

The point is that you don't have to be, and shouldn't try to be, a law expert to avoid lawsuits any more than you have to be a medical doctor to keep healthy. Engineers who aspire to become so well versed in law that they will be able to cleverly maneuver a path through the legal maze with immunity to products lawsuits, without readjusting their engineering attitude to conform to the law's requirements, are headed down the wrong road. There are just too many legal pitfalls, innovative approaches and procedural loopholes available to the opposition.[6] Trial lawyers make a career out of it. Give up the idea of trying to outwit them. A much more effective approach is to spend available time and energy designing and making safe products—defensible products that can survive the scrutiny of a judge and jury.

The beginning chapters describe the products liability crisis itself. They explain where it came from, why it developed as it did when it did. It's important for the practicing engineer to know this because ability to develop preventive strategies depends upon an understanding of what we're up against. Oliver Wendell Holmes, Justice of the U.S. Supreme Court a few generations back, described the importance of this understanding when dealing with the law:

> [T]o know what [the common law] is, we must know what it has been, and what it tends to become. . . . [I]ts form and machinery, and the degree to which it is able to work out desired results, depend very much upon its past.[7]

If you must live with some potentially damaging force or within some threatening environment, it pays to learn all you can about it. This is fundamental in any adversary situation. The higher the stake and greater the potential damage, the more thorough the understanding should be.

So far, we have considered the products liability problem strictly from the viewpoint of the engineer, product designer and manufacturer. From this perspective, products liability law may seem irrational, unjust and unfair; more a curse than anything else. But there is another side to the story, one we cannot ignore.

That other side is the viewpoint of the product user and consumer. These are our customers and prospective customers. From *their* point of view, the new products liability law is something entirely different—a blessing. Intelligent supporters of products liability law are firmly convinced that it is altogether reasonable. They see it as a long-sought-after answer to a longstanding problem. It is essential in maintaining our equilibrium and a proper perspective to resist the temptation to casually dismiss adherents of this position as kooks and rabble-rousers. They are society—the public— and they represent the majority in this country and the majority position on these issues. They have more clout than all the engineers, manufacturers and trial lawyers put together.

So, it is important for us to take a look at the problem from this other side of the fence, because what we see can make us re-evaluate and revise our attitudes. The small amount of effort it takes won't be wasted. These issues are discussed in some of the later chapters.

The methods and approaches this book offers for avoiding products liability lawsuits are not revolutionary or novel. Many firms have proven their value in minimizing claims and lawsuits. These are organizations that correctly approached the products liability threat as they would any other potentially damaging situation. They took time to analyze the problem, thoroughly and objectively appraised their exposure to it, and organized a workable strategy to counteract it.

The procedures presented here have been gleaned from over three decades of personal experience in industrial product development, particularly in analyzing metallurgical and materials-related problems, studying failures, learning what makes them occur and how to prevent them. Over the years I have observed a striking similarity in the kinds of conditions and circumstances that precipitate failures—all kinds of failures. This is independent of the specific product, structure or material. These observations are relevant in liability prevention programs and have been incorporated into the material covering prevention practices and strategies.

Fundamentals of a proper approach to products liability prevention do not differ much with the product, its size, complexity, or market. And these practices are not difficult to incorporate into the framework of an existing sound management system. Of course, no single strategy or method will work for all organizations and product lines. Each company must tailor its own program to fit its own needs. But the prevention program need not be complicated or cumbersome since these principles are fundamental to the successful operation of any firm; whether the stated goal is liability avoidance or the manufacture of reliable products.

While most principles and techniques described are straightforward, this book offers no quick-and-easy cures to products liability problems. Products liability affects every segment of the company and all its employees and is one of the most complex, misunderstood, and potentially damaging threats facing industry today. Success in avoiding it can only come through an enlightened and dedicated management and workforce; relentless determination to design, manufacture and market safe, quality products; and resourceful application of *all* the tools at our disposal.

It is important to keep in mind, throughout, that products liability law is not a science or technology. Our legal system can never be as responsive as a finely tuned machine, electronic circuit or chemical process. Its laws can never be as concisely expressed and reliable as those we work with in engineering. And the outcome of even the best-prepared legal exercise may never be as satisfying as that of a well-planned and executed engineering experiment.

Contrary to popular conceptions of law gathered from novels and television drama, law seldom deals with absolutes of right and wrong. It cannot be counted on to be predictable, consistent and fair. Sometimes it's not even just. The real world of law is unaccustomed to sharp contrasts and incontrovertible relationships. Supreme Court Justice William O. Douglas described it this way:

> [T]here are few areas of the law in black and white. The greys are dominant and even among them the shades are innumerable. For the eternal problem of the law is one of making accommodations between conflicting interests.... This is why most legal problems end as questions of degree. (*Estin v. Estin*)[8]

Before we move on I must reassure you that the objective of avoiding products liability is not a hopeless one. It is well within our grasp and control. But it may not come easily. Nevertheless, the dividends that accrue from having an effective liability prevention program in place are truly impressive and worthy of serious consideration and all the effort we can put into it.

An effective prevention program cannot help but make an organization more productive and profitable. The firm will project a public image of a responsible manufacturer, sensitive to the needs of its customers and society. Channels of communication within each division and from division to division will become clearer and more efficient. Employee morale will improve because there will be less worry and paranoia over threat of lawsuits. What is more, everyone in the organization will cultivate a more responsible attitude and keener sensitivity to the problems confronting modern society. And isn't this what engineering professionalism is all about?

REFERENCES

1. *New Life for the Liability Limiters*, Fortune 44, (November 14, 1983).
2. *Escola v. Coca Cola Bottling Company of Fresno*, 24 Cal.2d 453, 150 P.2d 436 (1944).
3. *Greenman v. Yuba Power Products Inc.*, 59 Cal.2d 57, 27 Cal. Reptr. 697, 377 P.2d 897 (1963).
4. Cairns, J. and Dickson, K.L. (eds.), *The Environment: Costs, Conflicts, Action*, Part V, "The Environment and the News Media" 131-50, Marcel Dekker, Inc., New York, NY (1974).
5. Gunningham, N., *Pollution, Social Interest and the Law* 30-34, Martin Robertson & Co., London (1974).
6. Philo, H.M., 2 *Lawyer's Desk Reference* 660-62, 6th ed., The Lawyers Co-operative Publishing Company, Rochester, NY 14694, and Bancroft-Whitney Co., San Francisco, CA 94107 (1979).
7. Holmes, O.W., *The Common Law* 1-2, Little, Brown & Company, Boston, MA (1881).
8. Douglas, William O., Associate Justice of the United States Supreme Court, in *Estin v. Estin*, 68 S.Ct. 1213, 334 U.S. 541, 92 L.Ed. 1516, 1 A.L.R.2d 1412 (1947).

2

A Threat That Cannot Be Ignored

INDUSTRY'S PREDICAMENT

A Serious Situation

Products liability is but one approach in the legal solution of the problem of responsibility for civilly-inflicted injuries.[1] *Civil* injuries are those resulting from non-criminal acts. This is the province of a classification of common law known as "torts." It deals with losses that arise from unreasonable interference with interests of others. Although most elements of products liability are traditionally rooted in torts, the law of contracts is also frequently involved. We are not concerned here with all civilly-inflicted injuries. Our interest is confined to injuries and damage traceable to manufactured products placed into the stream of commerce by manufacturers and merchants for the purpose of making a profit.

Even within these limits, a report by the National Commission on Product Safety as early as 1970 estimated that each year in the United States more than 20 million people are injured in the home by consumer products; 110,000 are permanently disabled and 30,000 are killed. In terms of medical care and economic loss, its estimated annual cost exceeds $5.5 billion.[2] This study did not include data on certain classes of products such as food, drugs, cosmetics, motor vehicles, cigarettes, insecdticides, firearms and others. And it did not include workplace product accidents, estimated at 7 million annually. The total number of product accidents occurring annually in the United States is believed to exceed 30 million injuries, at an annual cost to the nation of $20 billion.[3]

It is obvious that such a condition did not develop overnight. It has existed and has been increasing for years but only recently have we become

12

aware of it. Our awareness has been sharpened during the past decade or so by a number of things, like accelerating development of products liability law and increasing government involvement in such matters as environmental quality, industrial safety and product integrity. Through creating new quality standards along with accountability and enforcement provisions it has imposed personal obligations and legal sanctions upon those working in manufacturing industries.

But these awareness-sharpening events did not create the products liability crisis. They are merely reactions; reactions to changing circumstances in the world around us, changing social values, and the public's diminishing tolerance for the mounting toll of product accidents. In a later chapter we will consider the evolution of products liability law itself and how industry came to play a leading role. While the law of products liability may be what concerns and threatens us at the moment, it is not the cause of the crisis. It is important to make this distinction because it can affect our approach to liability prevention and the usefulness of preventive measures in keeping us out of trouble.

Like other major crises and calamities, products liability had many interrelated, overlapping and convergent causes. The more dominant ones are worth considering here; as they are still at work shaping the law of today and the requirements we will have to live with tomorrow.

Contributing Factors

Relationship Between Product User and Product Maker. Only a few generations have passed since the product user dealt first-hand with the product maker. The buyer personally knew the baker, weaver, farmer, cooper, smith, wheelwright and other craftsmen who made articles he bought. These circumstances permitted the buyer to visit the craftsman's establishment where he could inspect the ingredients and raw materials, the component parts, the joints and fasteners, and could specify changes to suit his particular requirements and budget. To a certain extent the buyer played roles of designer, specifier and inspector of the products he bought.

The law of *caveat emptor* (let the buyer beware) that developed around such transactions reflected this face-to-face situation. The buyer knew how the product was made and what went into it at every step of its construction. He had the opportunity to inspect it before accepting and paying for it. The law expected the buyer to have his eyes open and assure himself that what he was buying was what he needed and wanted. Once he bought it, the law offered little remedy for failure of the product to fulfill its function or for correction of defects that might have been detected earlier.

Tours through museums of early Americana confirm the stark functional simplicity of most early products. Nearly everyone could comprehend how the things worked, had fairly complete knowledge of materials of construction and could discern quality workmanship. This was true not only for household and farm implements but industrial and business products as well. Exceptions in the law to the rule of *caveat emptor* were few. They were recognized mostly for classes of products that were beyond the purchaser's ability to inspect or verify their safety or suitability for consumption. Such products were drugs and medical prescriptions, food and drink.

In recent times there have been vast changes in every aspect of the products-purchase transaction. The consumer no longer knows the maker of his products. His only association with the manufacturer is through vague recognition of a trademark or advertising slogan identified with the product. He deals with a retailer; merely the last in a long chain of strangers in a multi-layered distribution network. And he is unfamiliar with the materials of construction, how or where the product was produced or its principles of operation. Under these circumstances it is simply no longer reasonable to hold the buyer responsible for assuring quality and suitability of products bought; for he is, in fact, powerless to do so.

Technological Sophistication. Only a generation or two ago, most product users knew how their products worked. They could tell whether they were made of metal and frequently which kind, or if they were made of wood or one of the few man-made materials then available. They were familiar with basic mechanical principles and had a fairly good appreciation of how things were constructed.

All this has changed. Our most simple and common everyday products defy a layman's understanding. Even government-mandated lists of ingredients in prepared foodstuffs defy comprehension. In a way, the buyer-user has been forced to accept the manufacturer's claims of its quality, suitability and value, or do without the product. Admittedly, today's product user is better off than his predecessor of a few generations ago. His life-style is vastly superior, life and even work is easier, more comfortable and enjoyable. This is largely due to technological advancements.

The consumer obtains these product-benefits simply through exchanging money for a manufactured article that performs some previously difficult or distasteful task; for a device that entertains him; for an attractively packaged product that promises to improve his appearance, comfort or well-being; or that tastes good. The purchaser's expectation of satisfaction from exchanging money for the product is based largely upon trust; trust in the advertiser's promises and manufacturer's claims. As we will see later, consumer expectation is a criterion of key importance in evaluating a product's propensity for harm.

Product Dependence. Manufactured products have become indispensable to us. Our food, clothing, housing, labor-saving appliances, transportation, entertainment and health care are all manufactured products or are heavily dependent upon them. It is inevitable that such increasing dependence upon a proliferation of manufactured products, and our almost uninterrupted physical contact with them, increase the probability of injury or harm when products fail, are defective or contaminated, or do not meet our expectations for them.

Intensified Industrialization. Increased dependence upon manufactured products has created huge markets and entirely new industries. New plants are built to refine and process new materials, new machines are developed to do it more efficiently, and satellite industries spring up to service them. Our economy feeds upon industrial growth. But economic constraints and the need for profitability demand high efficiency and productivity at minimal costs. These requirements conflict with the needs for worker and user safety and environmental quality.

Increasing industrialization also requires increased transportation and storage of large quantities of raw materials, chemical feedstocks, and other physical resources; production of fuels and conversion of their energy into power; and disposal of by-products and effluent created by these operations. With all of this accelerated activity there is an increased potential for harm.

Failure Inevitability. Practically speaking, the concept of "zero defects" in manufactured products is a myth and an unattainable goal. This is particularly so as constraints of efficiency and profitability dictate most of industry's decisions. Even in the virtual absence of such constraints, as in our nation's space program where no expense is spared to assure trouble-free and fail-safe operation, failure of components, entire systems and their backups has been commonplace. It has caused injury and even death and has plagued the program from the start. It still does.

As products become more sophisticated and complex and as materials and components are pushed nearer their limits, frequency of failures must increase. Inevitability of failures and our increased dependence upon products make resulting harm and injury a practical certainty.

Gravity of Harm from Product Failure. The combination of growing dependence upon increasingly sophisticated products that offer improved performance also increases the seriousness and extent of harm resulting from failures or defects. They all go together. Newspapers continually confirm this; whether the failure is of a jumbo jet aircraft, a jumbo oil tanker, a widely-prescribed pharmaceutical, a pesticide plant, a nuclear-powered generating station or a high-rise hotel.

"Throw-Away" Philosophy. With increasing technological sophistication it becomes impractical to repair many products and their components. Most "repairs" today are limited to replacement of the faulty part or assembly with new parts. Plug-in or snap-in modules are extensively used in complex electronic and electromechanical systems. This saves the expense of prolonged service calls requiring diagnosis and disassembly and minimizes downtime of expensive equipment. For many moderate to low-priced products, cost of repair frequently exceeds the price of replacement. The pricing structure for spare parts in many industries adds further incentive for replacing failed or faulty components with new.

With increasing popularity of the expendability concept,[4] there is an accompanying need to avoid unnecessary costs associated with over-design. The temptation is to design the component to function no longer or better than it has to. Anything more represents wasted money. This prompts increasing use of marginal materials, low safety factors and shorter design-life cycles. Consequently, reliability drops and failures are more frequent. Harm can result when attempts are made to "push" the product to perform beyond its intended limit or life or when inadvertent flaws shorten the life of components having little design margin.

Society's Disillusionment over Technology. It is probably no coincidence that threats of products liability arose against manufacturers during the very same period that saw the public grow disillusioned over technology and its promises of utopia.

Over two decades ago Rachel Carson viewed our technological age as "an era of specialists, each of whom is unaware of or intolerant of the larger frame . . . an era dominated by industry, in which the right to make a dollar at whatever cost is seldom challenged."[5]

Several years later, the same tone was echoed by a Yale law professor: "Technology and production . . . are mindless instruments; if undirected they careen along with a momentum of their own . . . pulveriz[ing] everything in their path." In another indictment of industry he says, "It is the worst of all possible worlds: uncontrolled technology and uncontrolled profiteering . . . immensely powerful and utterly irresponsible."[6]

In 1976 Florman[7] saw the anti-technology movement still gaining momentum. He characterized it as "a swing toward a fierce abhorrence of technology." Proponents of this movement have adopted what he calls a "doctrine that holds technology to be the root of all evil."

Engineers can no longer ignore this tide of distrust of technology that is sweeping our country. For, if we choose not to heed it, it can drown us. The threat of products liability is but one wave of the tide. We can be certain more will follow.

An analysis of society's increasing distrust of engineering and technology lies beyond the scope of these discussions on products liability prevention. Yet, this sentiment fuels the fire we feel at our feet. Society has come to regard technology as a hostile giant bent upon converting our world's resources, its beauty and the very biological environment that sustains its life into profits for feeding the insatiable greed of heartless industrialists. Our sophisticated technology has far outstripped society's grasp of it. This ignorance breeds skepticism, fear, hostility and inferences of personal threat. These make fertile ground for consumerism, class-action suits and litigation as a vehicle for exercising human rights.

Who's to blame for all this? It is easy to blame reactionists, critics and consumer-activists, even lawyers and politicians. But *are* they to blame? No; they are merely sounding boards echoing society's sentiments and, more than that, its demands. As much as we dislike what we see and feel, I am afraid that once we sincerely and honestly evaluate the situation from every side, we must conclude with Pogo, "We have met the enemy, and he is us."[8]

In a recent address, Admiral Hyman G. Rickover said:

> The impact of technology on individuals and society is profoundly affected by the attitude of the public and its leaders toward technology ... what [it] is and what purpose it should serve.... Unless it is made to adapt to human interests, needs, values, and principles, much harm will be done.[9]

Alarms warning of impending harm are being sounded loudly and clearly across this country. So far, we have dismissed them as the clamour of uninformed agitators and revolutionaries. But perhaps it's time we started to pay attention to what they are saying. We may not agree with it or its rationale, but the message is being "bought" by the public and it has begun to affect our livelihood and careers. Our cause is not hopeless but it won't be easy to regain the public's trust. It will take much well-directed effort and time to turn the tide around.

Government Regulation. Political response to pressures for "relief" by consumers and society has spawned an array of legislation that has created regulations such as the Occupational Safety and Health Act; Environmental Protection Act; Consumer Product Safety Act; Federal Food, Drug and Cosmetic Act; Federal Insecticide, Fungicide and Rodenticide Act; Federal Hazardous Substances Act; Flammable Fabrics Act; Poison Prevention Packaging Act; Toxic Substances Control Act; National Traffic and Motor Vehicle Safety Act; Federal Caustic Poison Act; and others.

These regulations have established a comprehensive set of standards for a wide spectrum of manufactured products. It's not difficult to see how evidence of their violation would be construed by courts as negligence and disregard for the safety and welfare of society.

ECONOMIC IMPACT

Costs of Satisfying Claims

It is impossible to know the full extent of the direct economic impact of products liability upon industry. This is because payment figures are not readily available for most products cases—those settled out of court. Even a good proportion of those tried in court to a verdict are not available either, because of the large number of courts and jurisdictions in the country and the lack of a systematic mechanism for collecting and reporting the information. Nevertheless, some information is available and offers insight of the economic impact of products liability:

Insurance Statistics. For a 34-week period of 1976 and 1977 alone, a group of 23 insurance companies reported that for over 20,000 products liability claims filed, over two-thirds or 14,000 were settled.[10] Average payment per settlement was $19,000.

In another study[11] two surveys, four years apart, covering strictly "large-loss" claims of $100,000 or more, were conducted among 11 insurance companies. While such claims are reported to represent only about 1% of all products liability claims, they account for about half of the total products liability payments.

The number of incidents prompting such claims reported for 1975 and 1979 is shown in Figure 2-1. There is more than a 100% increase in the four years. Average economic loss per bodily injury claimant (payment plus insurer's cost for handling claim) also more than doubled; see Figure 2-2. Requests for punitive damages for the same period were up nearly eight-fold, as shown in Figure 2-3. Figure 2-4 shows that the manufacturer of the product is the one most frequently targeted in products lawsuits. Figure 2-5 shows, perhaps contrary to expectations, that business and industrial products are involved most of the time—nearly four times as often as consumer products.

All but four of the incidents reported in the 1979 large-loss claims study involved a lawsuit .Two-thirds were settled before trial; another 17% were settled during trial and only 13% were tried to verdict.

Jury Verdict Reports. Studies of jury verdicts for jurisdictions reporting data give another view of the magnitude of the problem.[12] It is important to keep in mind that these represent less than 15% of all products liability cases.[13] Figure 2-6 shows the trend of verdict averages from 1971 through 1982. Products cases lead all other liability situations in the number of verdicts *exceeding* one million dollars, with 258 jury verdicts of this magnitude reported for this period. The 12-year trend for number of verdicts exceeding a million dollars is shown in Figure 2-7.

Hidden Costs

The most obvious result of an adverse products lawsuit is a decrease in the company's cash. Not all products lawsuits threaten a firm's viability, but some do. It all depends upon the firm's size, its assets, the number of claims and the amount it must pay. Of course, it is the massive awards that make headlines and these are what come to mind when we think of products liability. But this represents only part of the cost of products lawsuits. Although the final cash settlement or judgment for damages has the most obvious financial effect and is a serious one, it's not the only one.

Long before that negative cash-flow shows up on the defendant company's books, there probably had been a steady drain on its resources for some time. Perhaps for several years since the suit began.

To maintain its competitive position, every company must continually monitor its activity. It must evaluate its line of products and their positions

Figure 2-1: Incidents Generating Products Liability Claims
Exceeding $100,000

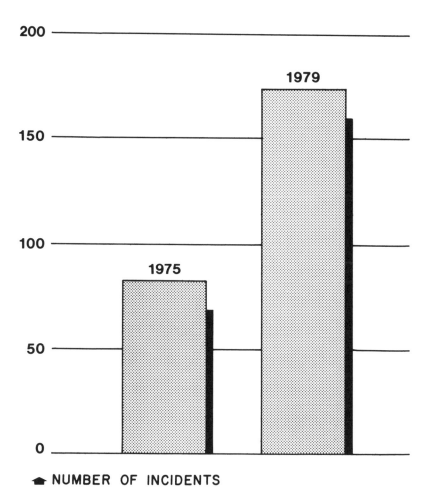

Figure 2-2: Economic Loss per Bodily Injury Claimant for Products
Liability Lawsuits
(Claims Exceeding $100,000)

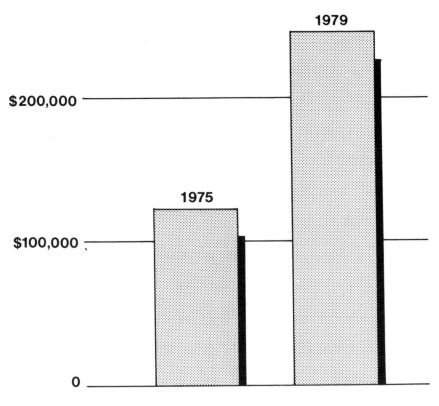

AVERAGE ECONOMIC LOSS

Data: Alliance of American Insurers

Figure 2-3: Requests for Punitive Damages in Products
Liability Lawsuits
(Claims Exceeding $100,000)

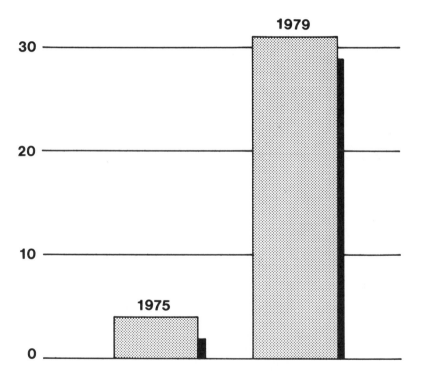

REQUESTS FOR PUNITIVE DAMAGES

Data: Alliance of American Insurers

Figure 2-4: Defendants of Products Liability Lawsuits
(Claims Exceeding $100,000)

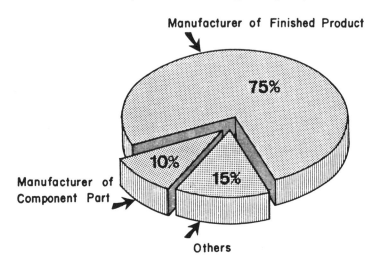

Data: Alliance of American Insurers

Figure 2-5: Kinds of Products Involved in Products Liability
Lawsuits
(Claims Exceeding $100,000)

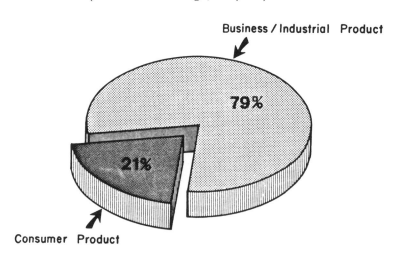

Data: Alliance of American Insurers

Figure 2-6: Average Jury Verdicts for Products Liability Lawsuits

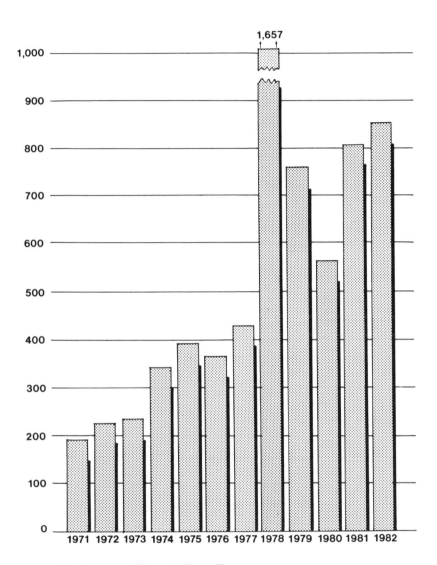

AVERAGE JURY VERDICT
(in thousands of dollars)

Data: Jury Verdict Research, Inc.

Figure 2-7: Products Liability Lawsuit Jury Verdicts Exceeding
One Million Dollars

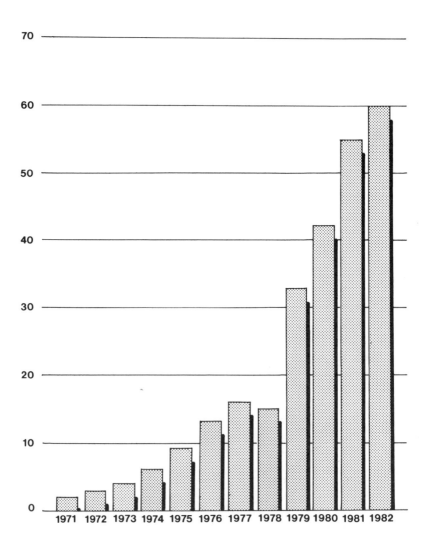

◆ NUMBER OF VERDICTS EXCEEDING
ONE MILLION DOLLARS

Data: Jury Verdict Research, Inc.

in the marketplace, its research and development commitment, its capital expenditures, its advertising approach and budget, its business projections and a host of others. It must be alert to any changes that might affect its strength and vitality. And it must be ready to readjust priorities and resource allocations accordingly.

No company can do everything it would like to do or even all it feels it should do. Resources are always limited and compromises are inevitable. Everything it does must be cost-effective. Each product in the line, each department and each division must pay its own way and earn its keep or be pruned away. It's a cold, cruel and often heartless world when it comes to competing for a company's limited resources. And, in general, the tighter its controls, the more ruthless its decision-maker, and the more cost-efficient the company is, the more likely it will be healthy and profitable over the long haul.

It is against this background that we must assess the effects of products lawsuits. For, here, a major "project" of sorts suddenly materializes and demands priority attention. There is no control over its timing; it cannot be worked into the firm's docket of other projects and programs as schedules permit, and it is always unwelcome. Procrastination can be costly, though. A company has no choice at all but to divert whatever resources it takes to answer the claim and defend the suit. And the quality of its defense is usually directly proportional to the resources it commits to the task.

Someone usually raises the question of insurance: Isn't this the purpose of having liability insurance; to avoid all this disruption and expense? Certainly, liability insurance is essential and no firm should be without it in this litigious environment. But even the best of policies does not cover everything. There are exclusions, deductibles and limitations written into every policy. Also, insurers need information before they can help. In fact, a promise to provide whatever help and information are required by the insurer to handle the claim or defend the client is almost always a contractual condition of the insurance policy.

Most insurance representatives are capable and many are technically knowledgeable. But they cannot defend a client without guidance and assistance. And only the company that made the product in question can provide that help. Much of it will be routine; retrieving such things as records and files, design sketches, stress calculations, shop drawings, manufacturing procedures and inspection charts, qualification sheets, purchase requisitions and specifications, approval forms, change orders, correspondence and shipping documents.

The list is virtually endless. Someone must locate and retrieve these, perhaps photocopy them and maintain the file (sometimes it's an entire library), interpret them, resolve discrepancies and explain the records policies, its documentation process and retention system. Company employees must be diverted from productive work to find and provide this information for the insurer and legal counsel and, later, opposing counsel and its experts.

Someone, either within the company or hired from outside, must evaluate the evidence and reconstruct the incident reported to have caused the injury or damage. This means surveys and tests; all kinds of them. Every scrap of evidence and each particle from the failed product is scrutinized and catalogued. These steps are too important to be delegated to outsiders without close supervision of company representatives. So, knowledgeable technical people within the company become involved at each step of these tests, evaluations and reconstructions. This, too, diverts company re- sources—sometimes its best people—away from existing work schedules.

As you can probably guess, all of this examining of records and evaluating of evidence and test results requires countless hours on the telephone, writing reports, attending meetings, briefings and conferences. Up to this stage, these are mostly internal meetings and discussions with the firm's own legal counsel and insurance representatives. Not only do these activities absorb the time of principals directly involved, but also that of clerks, secretaries, typists and machine operators. Sooner or later, practically everyone involved in making the product is drawn into the suit in some way.

So far, we have considered only preliminary stages of *in-house* investiga- tion. This is done to assemble available facts on the history of the product in question, its origin and design, how the design or concept evolved, how the product was manufactured, of what materials, how it was inspected and to what standards, and all the rest. Then the facts surrounding the reported incident are studied and evaluated to determine if the product was responsible and, if so, in what way. Is it a one-of-a-kind "fluke" that somehow got through the inspection system or does it represent a defect inherent in the entire production run, product line, or in the company's operating policies?

These are crucial questions to answer, because it makes a great deal of difference if the company is facing an isolated product that is out-of-spec, or one of possibly thousands that is within internal manufacturing standards but somehow caused an injury anyway, and might do so again, and again. It takes time and experienced people familiar with the product, the manu- facturing steps and the company's policies and operations to make these determinations and to furnish this and other necessary information to those who need it.

If the claim matures into a full-blown lawsuit there will be many more demands upon the company and its people. This is because the opposing attorney representing the injured party must be given access to all information pertinent to the product and incident. Usually, what is or is not pertinent is up to the opposing attorney to decide and the defendant company can be ordered by the court to furnish it. This intensive digging and sifting of records, data and facts is a legal process of inquiry known as *discovery*. Both sides are involved. The point of it all is to characterize the case; to give each side the opportunity to size it up and get a grasp of how solid or weak its position is. It is usually in the interests of both sides to settle as soon as possible.

During the discovery process there are additional demands made of the company and its employees. One of these is in the form of *interrogatories*. These are long lists of questions that deal with every imaginable aspect of the company, its products, employees and many things that may seem wholly irrelevant. These require careful and thoughtful attention. They cannot be answered hastily because they become permanent legal records and can strongly influence the outcome of the case. So it takes a lot of time to make sure they are done right.

There is another demand for various employees, both inside and outside experts and witnesses to participate in *depositions*. These proceedings resemble a court, but without judge or jury. They, too, are fact-finding exercises and are usually conducted in the office of one of the attorneys. Depositions are sworn testimony, recorded, later transcribed word-for-word by a court stenographer, that become part of the permanent court record. Attorneys for both sides are present and free to question the one testifying. The scope of questions and subject matter addressed in these proceedings can be extremely comprehensive. Obviously, preparation for and participation in these depositions consume time and energy of company employees. It is time and energy that otherwise could be spent pursuing the company's primary business objectives.

All this activity—the inquiring, collecting and reviewing of information—is driven by the desire on the part of both sides to reach an early settlement. This continues, as it is said, right up to the courthouse steps. Negotiations continue even beyond that. Sometimes the parties settle during the trial and may do so up to the moment the jury returns a verdict. Only a small percentage of products liability cases ever go all the way to a verdict. Most are settled at some stage before.

The point of bringing up these details here is to show that actual cash payment made to settle the claim or satisfy the judgment of the court represents only a fraction of the total cost of a products lawsuit. In addition to costs of employees' time and other out-of-pocket expenses, there is the cost to the company of deferring activity on its mainstream programs. This may delay a project or product introduction long enough to give the competition a lead. Its costs to the company in lost profits or opportunities may never be fully known.

The costs do not stop there. Pressures of a flood of claims or even a single protracted lawsuit requiring participation of company employees in tedious fact-finding sessions, conferences, and court appearances, plus media coverage that may not present the firm in a favorable light, can be demoralizing to everyone—management, employees and stockholders.

Such loss of "spirit" is difficult to assess, but it can adversely affect productivity at every level of the company and tarnish its reputation.

Unpredictable Consequences

News reports have also made us aware of the recent surge in medical malpractice claims and awards. Although this is a major concern for medical practitioners and their insurers, the individual nature of most medical treatment usually limits the source of malpractice claims to one injured party per incident. Contrast this with the potential for damage from a single *product* failure or defect that can affect hundreds, thousands and, conceivably, even millions, as the consequences of that defect and its potential for causing injury are multiplied by the number of products sold.

There is virtually no limit to the number of claims or their economic implications. A few recent examples will show how extensive and costly products liability can be and the bizarre and unpredictable situations that can develop:

Asbestos-Related Injuries. Manville Corporation's recent experiences show the extent to which products liability can threaten the viability of even a large company.[14,15] Estimates are that Manville faces between 30,000 and 120,000 lawsuits over injuries claimed to stem from exposure to asbestos many years before. Considering that the average estimated cost of disposition of each lawsuit is $40,000, the total cost of this litigation is between $1.2 billion and $5 billion.[16] The prospect of such massive settlement costs, in view of a net worth of $1.1 billion, prompted Manville in August 1982 to seek protection under Chapter 11 of the federal Bankruptcy Code.

This use of Chapter 11 by an otherwise financially sound company to afford shelter from a flood of products claims has, understandably, been the subject of extensive debate and judicial scrutiny. The situation raises complex questions and issues that are not readily answered. It dramatically illustrates how extensive a company's loss can be, how exposure to risks years before can suddenly develop into a crisis and how unpredictable latent biological reactions to a substance can have major and drastic consequences. It also points up another important element of the direct economic impact of products liability: A large potential for loss can develop over a *single* product or substance.

Tragic Effects of Factory Malfunctions. Of potentially equal magnitude to the Manville Corporation's plight is the more recent occurrence in Bhopal, India, where a pesticide plant owned jointly by Union Carbide Corporation and an Indian subsidiary leaked a toxic gas during the night. The lethal cloud spread over the city of nearly a million, adjacent to the plant, killing over 2,000 people; injuring 150,000; and affecting nearly a quarter-million residents.[17,18]

It is still too early to assess its financial impact upon the company, but business news publications reported that within a week or so after the disaster the company had lawsuits seeking damages exceeding the company's net worth.[19].

A few weeks before the India disaster, hundreds of people were killed and thousands injured when a Mexican liquefied natural gas (LNG) plant near Mexico City exploded.[20]

These are but two of the more dramatic examples of how the viability of even large corporations can be seriously threatened through the failure or malfunction of operating equipment or some safety feature.

Toxic-Shock Syndrome. In 1980 the federal Centers for Disease Control reported that a rare but possibly fatal disease, toxic-shock syndrome, was connected with the use of tampons.[21] By the end of 1982 about 1,800 women had filed claims against tampon manufacturers.[22] Although the full impact of these claims is not yet known, indications are that it will be costly. It is estimated that one tampon manufacturer alone faces more than $4 billion in damage claims.[23]

In April 1982 a federal jury in Iowa awarded $300,000 in compensatory damages to the family of a woman who died of toxic-shock syndrome.[24] A few months later a California jury awarded a toxic-shock victim $500,000 in compensatory damages and $10 *million* in punitive damages.[25] In December 1983 the U.S. Court of Appeals for the Eighth Circuit affirmed the Northern Iowa District Court's decision in the first case (the $300,000 award).[26] Appeal of the California case is pending. This may be only the beginning of litigation arising from one widely-used product.

Diethylstilbestrol (DES). From 1947 to 1971 diethylstilbestrol (DES), a synthetic estrogen, was manufactured and marketed by 150 to 300 companies in the United States for preventing miscarriages. Several million women used the drug. In 1971 medical research showed incontrovertible causal connection between occurrence of cancer in young women and use of DES by their mothers while pregnant. Estimates of cancer rate in these daughters ranged from one in 250 to one in 10,000; in either event, an unusually high rate.

Because of the generic nature of the way DES was marketed and the long period of latency before the onset of cancer, it was impossible for these women to later identify the manufacturer/s of the drug taken by their mothers. Under traditional rules of law, the burden of such proof had always rested upon the party claiming injuries and failure to prove who manufactured the drug defeated the claim.

The situation presented plaintiffs' attorneys with a tremendous challenge: Injuries of a large number of innocent victims were gravely serious and their origin undisputed; yet, existing law offered no remedy. One or more of a known group of pharmaceutical manufacturers made the drugs that caused the injuries. The question was which one; for this was essential for litigation under existing law. In response to the challenge, plaintiffs' attorneys devised a number of ingenious approaches for fixing liability upon these manufacturers. Some of them have been successful.

In a precedent-breaking decision a few years ago, a California court imposed liability upon eleven companies representing a "substantial share" of the DES market. The liability of each was declared by the court to be in proportion to each company's share of the market.[27]

In this decision the court removed from the shoulders of the victim the traditional burden of identifying the manufacturer of the offending product. Instead, the court placed upon the manufacturer the burden of proving it did not supply the product that caused the injury. This, in effect, makes a manufacturer an insurer of its own and all generically identical products made and sold within its industry.[28]

While the remedy was devised specifically for innocent victims of DES, there was no suggestion in the court's decision that this *market-share liability* concept should be confined to that product. Note this excerpt:

> In our contemporary complex industrialized society, advances in science and technology create fungible goods which may harm consumers and which cannot be traced to any specific producer. The response of the courts can be either to adhere rigidly to prior doctrine, denying recovery to those injured by those products, or to fashion remedies to meet those changing needs.... [B]etween an innocent plaintiff and negligent defendants, the latter should bear the cost of injury. (*Sindell v. Abbott Labs*)[29]

At about the time this case was decided, a New York court similarly found a manufacturer liable to a DES victim, but on somewhat different grounds.[30] In that approach the injured party filed suit against only one of the manufacturing companies, the single largest supplier of DES. The plaintiff's argument hinged upon the manner in which the various manufacturers collaborated in formulating the drug, preparing standards, conducting tests, and other steps in obtaining approval prior to marketing the drug. The suit claimed this collaboration (or "concert of action") constituted joint activity that led to the injury.

Under a concept of *parallel behavior*, adapted from antitrust actions, one of several parties acting in the same way with similar objectives and outcome may be held responsible for what others may have done. By this theory, where all participants are "jointly and severally" liable, one manufacturer—the market leader in this case—could be made 100% liable (for $500,000 in damages). This argument was upheld in this New York case even though the manufacturer possessed only 45% of the market, and even though it may not have produced the actual medication that led to that particular injury.

During the few years after the California decision based upon the "substantial share" theory was reached, courts in other jurisdictions rejected similar arguments by attorneys representing DES victims. However, plaintiffs' attorneys have persisted in pursuing these concepts and, recently, a few courts have adopted them in DES cases. Although courts differ somewhat in their legal reasoning, the effect has been the same: liability for the manufacturer and compensation for DES victims.[31,32] The rationale for these positions is described in this excerpt from a decision by the Wisconsin Supreme Court:

> [A]s between the injured plaintiff and the possibly responsible drug company, the drug company is in a better position to absorb the cost of the injury. The drug company can either insure itself against liability, absorb the damage award, or pass the cost along to the consuming public as a cost of doing business. We conclude that it is better to have drug companies or consumers share the costs of the injury than to place the burden solely on the innocent plaintiff. Finally, the cost of damages awards will act as an incentive for drug companies to test adequately the drugs they place on the market for general medical use. This incentive is especially important in the case of mass-marketed drugs because consumers and their physicians in most instances rely upon advice given by the supplier and the scientific community and, consequently, are virtually helpless to protect themselves from serious injuries caused by deleterious drugs. (*Collins v. Eli Lilly & Co.*)[33]

With adoption of the parallel behavior concept in products cases and the implication that this and similar concepts could apply to products beyond DES, the door may be opening to a new wave of ominous consequences for manufacturers of generic products.[34] While the future of industry-wide liability is yet uncertain, one thing is sure; these approaches are bound to be aggressively pursued in future cases by zealous plaintiffs' attorneys.

Tris (2,3-Dibromopropyl) Phosphate. Standards issued in 1971 and 1974 under the Flammable Fabrics Act required children's clothing to be flame-resistant. Most polyester, acetate and other synthetic fabrics and blends could not meet requirements unless chemically treated. "Tris" proved an effective flame retardant chemical, was not expensive, showed no allergenic reactions and became widely used throughout the garment industry.

Soon after, the chemical was suspected of being harmful, and later tests on animals confirmed its carcinogenic characteristics. Projected lifetime cancer incidence from wearing Tris-treated clothing ranged from one in 200 to as high as one in 60.

In April 1977, the Consumer Products Safety Commission (CPSC) cited the federal Hazardous Substances Act in banning the use of Tris and required manufacturers of the chemically-treated clothing to repurchase the garments from retailers. Estimates are that 18 million garments were involved. Later that year a federal court overturned the CPSC ban on procedural grounds.[35] Garment manufacturers sued the government for $30 million in damages, but in November 1983 a U.S. Court of Appeals dismissed the claims.[36]

While the suit against the government was pending, Congress provided the garment manufacturers a remedy under Public Law 97-395, signed by President Reagan in December 1982. This measure authorizes federal compensation for losses resulting from the 1977 CPSC Tris ban incurred by manfacturers, processors and distributors who had treated children's clothing in compliance with the earlier flammability standard.

Other events were compounding the situation. For a time it appeared that passage of the remedial legislation was questionable (President Carter had vetoed a similar bill). While the legislation and the manufacturers' suit were pending, a number of manufacturers attempted to secretly divert government-banned Tris-treated garments back into retail outlets.[37] There have been a number of convictions. Some have resulted in jail terms and heavy fines.[38,39]

This example illustrates the complexity of products liability issues: Here we have a federal standard enacted to reduce one hazard (clothing fires in small children) and it merely introduces a more serious one, cancer. Then, during the switch in the government's signals, clothing manufacturers attempting to comply with the flammability standard become subject to losses of millions of dollars. For a time, they appear to have no remedy. Out of desperation, a number of them attempt to minimize their losses through illegal diversion of affected clothing back into retail channels. This subjects them to severe penalties and jail terms.

Such an incredible and improbable series of events defies the imagination. With society's increasing concern over product safety, prompting increasing legislation, more of these situations can be expected.

PRODUCTS LIABILITY: CURSE OR CURE?

Engineers, or for the moment at least, the companies that employ them, are the targets of products liability lawsuits, so it is only natural to regard this matter negatively, acknowledging it to be the personal and business threat that it is. Certainly, we must do everything we can to minimize our exposure to it. Even so, it is a mistake to regard products liability as some totally evil and destructive force, utterly without merit. For if we do we will close our minds to its origins and its purpose and what it has to say. We will take the attitude that the less we see, hear and know about it the better. This can lead us to become one of its most vulnerable targets.

To a manufacturer, products liability appears to be nothing more than a giant conspiracy to pick industry's "deep pockets" and destroy its businesses. Some see it symptomatic of disintegration of our legal system. Others point to its inflationary character, its tendency to stifle technological progress and the unfair advantage it gives foreign competition.

But to supporters of products liability, it is something entirely different. They see it as saviour for thousands of victims of products injuries; a means for preventing accidents and reducing the exorbitant costs to the nation in terms of personal safety and loss, restricted activities, medical care and the resulting loss of on-the-job productivity. The common theme running through all products liability legislation, judicial decisions and commentaries is accident prevention, safety and the welfare of society. Surely, these are worthwhile goals.

While we dislike the prospect of increased government regulation, we must realize that all of us are better off in many ways because such regulation exists. When we visit foreign countries, particularly those of the Third World, we suddenly miss it. We become apprehensive over basics taken for granted at home: quality of food and drinking water, safety on the road, competence of medical practitioners, and many other matters. We are free of these basic concerns here in the United States largely because of government controls, standards and regulations, even though we are constantly exposed to potential harm.

Each day we drive small, light, fuel-efficient cars at high speed only a few feet from massive trucks hurtling down the road with tons of frequently hazardous cargo. We routinely take airline flights in bad weather and through crowded skies. We seldom give a thought to the possibility of contaminated water, diseased meat or tainted food. We purchase prescriptions and over-the-counter drugs without worrying over the possible harm they could do to us if a mistake was made in their formulation. We use high-speed elevators to whisk us up into high-rise buildings as readily as we step up onto a curb. And we almost never consider the possibility of structural overload or fatigue failure of some critical component of our automobiles as we drive down crowded highways and take sharp turns at high speed. All this freedom from worry, and so much more, is possible through government regulation, whether we care to acknowledge it or not.

Need for product safety suddenly is driven home whenever we have some manufactured article fall apart in our hands and injure us or a member of our family. We tend to take it as a personal affront. We feel victimized and wronged, and insist upon someone making it right. This is especially so for products that seem to be poorly constructed, are of questionable or marginal design or carelessly assembled—where a little care or expenditure of a few more pennies could have averted the problem.

It pays, from time to time, to put ourselves in the position of one of the victims or loved-ones of someone who has been killed or seriously injured by a defective product, a dangerous drug or the careless neglect of some professional who was well-paid for services rendered incompetently. It makes us place things in perspective, and see things as trial attorneys convince juries they are.

In the following excerpts from the 1970 *Final Report* of the National Commission on Product Safety, note the dominant theme of product safety and accompanying responsibility of product manufacturers that runs throughout:[40]

> Manufacturers have it in their power to design, build, and market products in ways that will reduce if not eliminate most unreasonable and unnecessary hazards. Manufacturers are best able to take the longest strides to safety in the least time. . . . The law [therefore] has tended in recent years to place full responsibility for injuries attributable to defective products upon the manufacturer. . . .
>
> But beyond his liability for damages, a producer owes society-at-large the duty to assure that unnecessary risks of injury are eliminated. He is in the best position to know what are the safest designs, materials, construction methods, and modes of use. Before anyone else, he must explore the boundaries of potential danger from the use of his product. He must be in a position to advise the buyer competently how to use and how to maintain and repair the product.

The same tone is found in a 1957 comment:[41]

> [T]he manufacturer is in a peculiarly strategic position to improve the safety of his products, so that the pressure of strict liability could scarcely be exerted at a better point if accident prevention is to be furthered by tort law.

And it is found in a concurring opinion expressed by Justice Traynor in an early (1944) landmark products liability case:[42]

> [P]ublic policy demands that responsibility be fixed wherever it will most effectively reduce the hazards to life and health inherent in defective products that reach the market. . . . Those who suffer injury from defective products are unprepared to meet its consequences. . . . However intermittently such injuries may occur and however haphazardly they may strike, the risk of their occurrence is a constant risk and a general one. Against such risk there should be general and constant protection and the manufacturer is best situated to afford such protection. (*Escola v. Coca Cola Bottling Co. of Fresno*)

Finally, listen to the strong words of a trial lawyer explaining the purpose of products liability law: "The social purpose of tort law is accident and injury prevention. . . [W]hen we fail . . . we move to the secondary purpose, compensation for the victim. The injury or death . . . in all probability occurred because the law historically gave legal license to kill and maim."[43]

The same lawyer sums up his assessment of industry's attitude: "It is an inevitable conclusion of tort attorneys that the defendants did not know about safety, did not care about safety, did not do anything about safety. This should be the theme of such litigation."[44]

Is products liability law a curse or a cure? The answer will differ with which side of the courtroom you are on. If it is *your* company's resources, *your* company's deep pocket that is being tapped to compensate victims of injuries claimed to have been caused by *your* allegedly defective product; products liability law will seem to be a curse. Under these circumstances, it is easy to ridicule and be suspicious of the claims of injured victims. Shakespeare said, "He jests at scars, that never felt a wound."[45]

But, if it is *your* child that has been permanently disabled by someone else's manufactured product and you are seeking compensation for medical care, physical therapy, medication, rehabilitation training and perhaps psychotherapy—to say nothing of your desire for assurance of continued financial support for the child as he or she faces a competitive world often unsympathetic to disabled accident victims—it is, indeed, another matter. Any law that now makes such compensation possible, when only a few years ago such a remedy would have been inconceivable, will be viewed as a boon for mankind, a godsend.

The answer to the question, "curse or cure?" is perhaps most eloquently answered with one of my grandmother's expressions from another generation, "It all depends upon whose ox is gored."

REFERENCES

1. White, G.E., *Tort Law in America—An Intellectual History*, Oxford University Press, Inc. (1980)
2. National Commission on Product Safety, *Final Report* (June 1970), presented to The President and Congress. National Technical Information Service, Springfield, VA 22161. (The National Commission on Product Safety was established by U.S. Congress under Public Law 90-146, 90th Congress; S.J. Res. 33, November 20, 1967.)
3. Keeton, W.P., Owen, D.G., and Montgomery, J.E., *Products Liability and Safety, Cases and Materials* 2, The Foundation Press, Inc., Mineola, NY (1980).
4. Packard, V., *The Waste Makers* 41-52, David McKay Company, Inc., New York, NY (1960).
5. Carson, R., *Silent Spring* 23, (1962), (Fawcett Crest Edition; January 1964) New York, NY.
6. Reich, C.A., *The Greening of America* 7, 110, Random House, Inc., New York, NY (1970).
7. Florman, S.C., *The Existential Pleasures of Engineering* 45-56, St. Martin's Press, New York, NY (1976).

8. Kelly, W., *Pogo: We Have Met the Enemy & He Is Us*, Simon & Schuster, New York, NY (1972).

9. Rickover, H.G., *A Humanistic Technology*, presented in the Distinguished Lecture Series at the University of California, Lawrence Livermore National Laboratory, Livermore CA (December 15, 1983).

10. *Insurance Services Office Product Liability Closed Claim Survey: A Technical Analysis of Survey Results*, Insurance Services Office, 17 Water Street, New York, NY (August 30, 1977).

11. Dewey, C.G., Alliance of American Insurers, Chicago, IL, personal communication (February 23, 1982), and *Highlights of Large-Loss Product Liability Claims*, Alliance of American Insurers, Research Department, 20 North Wacker Drive, Chicago, IL 60606 (August 1980).

12. Personal Injury Valuation Handbooks, Current Award Trends, *Injury Valuation Reports in the Continuing Jury Verdict Research Project*, Nos. 258 (1982) and 280 (1984), Jury Verdict Research, Inc., 5325 Naiman Pkwy., Suite B, Solon, OH 44139.

13. O'Connor, J. and Gallagher, D.C., *Defending Nationwide Litigation*, For The Defense 22 (May 1982).

14. Maxwell, N., Hill, G.C., and Joseph, R.A., *Manville's Big Concern As It Files Chapter 11 Is Litigation, Not Debt*, The Wall Street Journal (August 27, 1982).

15. *Manville's Bold Maneuver*, Time 17 (September 6, 1982).

16. Maxwell, N., *Manville's Costs Could Exceed $5 Billion in Asbestos Suits, Study It Ordered Shows*, The Wall Street Journal, p. 14, col. 1 (September 15, 1982).

17. Hall, A., *The Bhopal Tragedy Has Union Carbide Reeling*, Business Week 32 (December 17, 1984).

18. Iyer, P., *India's Night of Death*, Time 22-26, 31 (December 17, 1984).

19. Dobrzynski, J.G., Glaberson, W.B., King, R.W., Powell, W.J., and Helm, L., *Union Carbide Fights for Its Life* (Cover Story), Business Week 52-56 (December 24, 1984).

20. The New York Times, p. 1, col. 6 (November 20, 1984).

21. *A Verdict on Tampons*, Time 73 (March 29, 1982).

22. Darlin, D., *Lawyers Who Won Verdicts in Rely Trials Are Selling Their Evidence Angering P&G*, The Wall Street Journal (December 20, 1982).

23. Rotbart, O., *First Toxic-Shock Verdict Might Be Costly for P&G Despite the Jury's Mixed Decision*, The Wall Street Journal (March 22, 1982).

24. *Kehm v. Procter & Gamble Mfg. Co.*, No. C-80-119, U.S. District Court, Northern Iowa (April 21, 1982).

25. Dolan, C. and Ingrassia, P., *Toxic Shock Victim Wins $10.5 Million In Decision Against Johnson & Johnson*, The Wall Street Journal (December 24, 1982).

26. *Kehm v. Procter & Gamble Mfg. Co.*, 724 F.2d 613, U.S. Court of Appeals, 8th Circuit (1983).

27. *Sindell v. Abbott Labs*, 607 P.2d 924, 163 Cal. Reptr. 132 (Cal. 1980), *cert. denied* 101 Sup. Ct. 285, 449 U.S. 912 (1980).

28. Sales, J.B., *Theories of Industry Liability for Product Related Injuries and the Collateral Estoppel Doctrine*, Products Liability Litigation, Course Book 81-4 at Cl-60, Defense Practice Seminar, in Houston, Texas (January 7-8,

1982), Defense Research Institute, Inc., 750 North Lake Shore Drive, Chicago, IL 60611.

29. *Sindell v. Abbott Labs, supra* reference 27.

30. *Bichler v. Eli Lilly & Co.*, 79 App. Div.2d 317, 436 N.Y.S.2d 625 (1981).

31. *Collins v. Eli Lilly & Co.*, 116 Wis.2d 166, 342 N.W.2d 37 (1984), *cert. denied* (U.S. Supreme Court, October 1, 1984).

32. Abel v. Eli Lilly & Co., 418 Mich. 311, 343 N.W.2d 164 (1984).

33. *Collins v. Eli Lilly & Co. supra* reference 31.

34. *A Liability Ruling That Has Business Alarmed*, Business Week 41-42 (February 27, 1984).

35. *Springs Mills, Inc. v. Consumer Product Safety Commission*, 434 F. Suppl 416 (District Court, South Carolina, 1977).

36. *Jayvee Brands, Inc. v. United States*, 721 F.2d 385 (Court of Appeals, District of Columbia, 1983).

37. 9 Product Safety & Liability Reporter (Current Report) 795 (October 16, 1981), and 10 Product Safety & Liability Reporter (Current Report) 64 (January 29, 1982).

38. *United States v. Articles of Hazardous Substances* (No. 78-1066, February 16, 1982) in 10 Product Safety & Liability Reporter (Current Report) 123 (February 26, 1982).

39. 10 Product Safety & Liability Reporter (Current Report) 339 (May 28, 1982).

40. National Commission on Product Safety, *Final Report 1, supra* reference 2.

41. Fleming, J.M., *General Products - Should Manufacturers Be Liable Without Negligence*, 24 Tennessee Law Review 923-27 (1957).

42. *Escola v. Coca Cola Bottling Co. of Fresno*, 24 Cal.2d 453, 150 P.2d 436, (1944).

43. Philo, H.M., 1 *Lawyer's Desk Reference* xiii, 6th ed., The Lawyers Co-operative Publishing Co., Rochester, NY 14694, and Bancroft-Whitney Co., San Francisco, CA 94107 (1979).

44. Philo, H.M., *supra* reference 43, 2 *Lawyer's Desk Reference* 763.

45. Shakespeare, William, *Romeo and Juliet*, II, ii, I (1594-1595).

3

Origins and Causes

CHARACTERISTICS OF THE LAW

Over an entrance to the Yale Law School quadrangle are these words:
THE LAW IS A LIVING GROWTH, NOT A CHANGELESS CODE

Many of those unfamiliar with the law see it as cold, rigid, lifeless, unyielding and uncompromising, beyond any thought of change or adaptability. Yet, no law devised by man for his benefit can ever be fixed and final.

The practical necessity for flexibility in the law is eloquently expressed by Judge Jerome Frank:

> The law always has been, is now, and will ever continue to be, largely vague and variable. And how could this well be otherwise? The law deals with human relations in their most complicated aspects. The whole confused, shifting helter-skelter of life parades before it—more confused than ever, in our kaleidoscopic age.[1]

A legal scholar once described it this way:

> The rules and principles of case [common] law have never been treated as final truths, but as working hypotheses, continually retested in those great laboratories of the law, the courts of justice. Every new case is an experiment; and if the accepted rule which seems applicable yields a result which is felt to be unjust, the rule is reconsidered.[2]

This sharply contrasts with *laws of science*; the laws that engineers are most familiar with. Scientific law is "a statement of a relation or sequence of phenomena *invariable* under the same conditions . . . [a] principle based on the *predictable consequences* of an act, [or] condition" (emphases added).[3] Put another way, "a [scientific] law . . . is the assertion of an invariable association, and the events or properties of other things that it declares to be invariably associated are themselves collections of other invariably associated things."[4] Note throughout these definitions of scientific law the theme of invariability, its changelessness and universality.

Scientific laws are statements of cause and effect: if A is done, then B will follow. We can *count* on these things. We must be able to do so, as laws constitute the keystone of science and engineering. Without them and their dependability, engineering as we know it could not be practiced.

Consider, for a moment, an engineering world whose physical laws had the characteristics of "legal" (common) law. Imagine the chaos there would be if engineering concepts and their mathematical relationships had to be reaffirmed or derived anew for each set of circumstances; if they were indefinite, often illogical, and dependent upon the specific use or application, local conditions and even geographic location! Yet, this is how it is with most common law. Note the stark contrast between the two kinds of law with respect to the traits shown below:

Scientific Law	*Legal (Common) Law*
Independent	Dependent
Universal	Parochial
Immutable	Changeable
Logical	Empirical
Definite	Interpretable

It is important for the engineer to be aware of these fundamental differences between the two kinds of law. Much of the frustration and exasperation that technical people experience with "legal" law stems from misunderstandings over these fundamentals. But the differences *must* exist. As Judge Frank points out, considering the complications and conflicting interests in today's world, "how could this well be otherwise?"

We enjoy definiteness, precision and predictability in scientific laws because they are not devised by man but, somehow, simply *are there* for man to discover and learn to use. Theologians would explain that their characteristics reflect the unchangeable character of their Creator. Laws devised by man are as they are because they reflect his character, temperament and changing needs. Justice Cardozo said the law becomes "whatever the needs of life in a developing civilization require."[5]

As we will discuss later in this chapter, technological developments during the preceding century played a dominant role in the evolution of legal concepts, particularly those of products liability law. They still are shaping this law and what it requires of us; so, in an indirect way, we, as engineers, have had a hand in it. Barry Commoner, in speaking of environmental issues, described this kind of interaction:

> We have become accustomed to think of separate, singular events; each element dependent upon a unique singular cause. . . . [But,] every effect is also a cause . . . in the real world everything . . . is connected to everything else.[6]

Common law has the traits it does out of necessity. It must be flexible and capable of change to suit our changing and developing civilization. Yet, if it is too flexible, imprecise and indefinite, it would be of limited practical use in ordering our affairs. There must be some degree of predictability and stability to it; otherwise we would be unable to conform to the law's requirements and maintain an orderly society. Someone has said, "If a law was applied against me today when I was a defendant; tomorrow, when I am a plaintiff, I shall expect the same judgment."

There is much to be said for fixed standards. Legislators and judges are among the first to recognize this need. A cardinal concept in common law has been the principle of *stare decisis* (let the decision stand). That is, a decision by an appeals court establishes a precedent (or rule of law) that shall be followed thereafter in that jurisdiction when similar fact situations arise.[7] But this does not mean it is chiseled in stone.

A former justice of the New York Supreme Court explained why it cannot be:

> Precedents . . . set the pattern of the common law. But the pattern is never static. It must fit a growing social body and be adaptable and expandable to meet new problems and changing conditions. . . . [When] entirely new questions arise . . . to which prior decisions provide no answer . . . judges must go pioneering on new frontiers.[8]

And a noted legal scholar, William Prosser, has pointed out that:

> [I]t [the principle of *stare decisis*] is not, and never has been, an ironclad and absolute principle, and such precedents may be departed from when the court subsequently concludes that they are unreasonable or out of line with altered social conditions.[9]

So we have a paradox. On the one hand is the practical need of society and business for stability in the law; while, on the other hand, it cannot be so fixed and rigid that it will cease to serve its purpose. Roscoe Pound, former dean of Harvard Law School, remarked: "Law must be stable, and yet it cannot stand still."[10] There must be a continual balancing—an inevitable compromise—of the two sides of the issue: predictability vs. flexibility. With every judicial decision the law is being reformulated. It is an on-going process. But it's seldom sudden, even though the effects of changes upon the unsuspecting may be. The process was described in 1921 by Justice Cardozo in these words:

> This work of modification is gradual. It goes on inch by inch. Its effects must be measured by decades and even centuries. Thus measured, they are seen to have behind them the power and pressure of the moving glacier.[11]

This sounds quite orderly and reasonable. Yet, ther have been a great many changes, in everything, since 1921. And these have affected some of the predictability in the law. At least part of the reason for the liability crisis which industry is facing is traceable to attempts to devise a body of law that more closely fits the needs of society in a highly technological world. This has become increasingly difficult to do because of *accelerating* technology and the volatile reaction of society to it all.

While industry wants (and, until about 1960, it had) stability and predictability in the law, society in its backlash of reaction to technology and in exercise of its human rights is clamoring for change. You can't have it both ways at the same time. The apparent suddenness of the advent of products liability and the economic devastation it has wrought upon some sectors of industry attest to the immense problem of trying to reconcile major opposing interests and achieve the "best" compromise in an increasingly perplexing, complicated and sometimes irrational world.

It is obvious that, of various conflicting interests, the side with the most clout will inevitably win. As far as products liability is concerned, that side is not the side of technology, but that of society. It is indeed unfortunate that there must be "sides" at all. Are not all of us—engineers, industrial executives and other technical people—part of society too? Perhaps we have lost sight of that simple fact somewhere along the way. In my opinion, we will continue to feel the heat of society's adverse reaction to what it regards as "mindless and uncontrolled" technology until industry learns to consolidate its values with society's values. Perhaps the forces of products liability will help achieve that unity.

ANCIENT ROOTS

Why Have Laws?

Since the beginning of civilization, law has existed for the same basic reasons. The purpose of primitive law was strictly a peaceable ordering of society at any cost.[12] Its primary mission was to satisfy society's need for security. After several millenia of evolution of the law its mission remains largely the same. A leading jurist explained it like this:

> The final course of law is the *welfare of society.* . . . When [judges] are
> called upon to say how far existing rules are to be extended or
> restricted, they must let the *welfare of society* fix the path, its direction
> and its distance.[13] (emphasis added)

There are a great many complications muddying our legal waters, but
beneath it all still lies that one fundamental reason for its existence: the
welfare of society. The standard has always been and, for ages to come, will
probably continue to be "the greatest happiness of the greatest number."[14]
Dean Pound, in summarizing his views on "the end of the law," said:

> I . . . see in legal history the record of a continually wider recognizing
> and satisfying of human wants or claims or desires through social
> control; . . . in short, a continually more efficacious social engineering.[15]

Individual interest, no matter how honorable, noble, well-intentioned or
beneficial; if contrary to those of society, must be sacrificed to them. And it
doesn't matter if the "individual" is a person, company, group of companies
or even an entire industry. Abraham Lincoln observed over a century ago:
"With public sentiment nothing can fail, without it nothing can succeed." It
is as true today as it was then.

Despite the apparent simplicity of the law's reason for existence and its
mission, it has never been a simple or straightforward matter to determine
amid myriad choices just what *is* "the best" for society. As civilization grew
more complex, particularly as it became industrialized, what was "best for
the most" at one time or place was not necessarily what it was at another
time or place, especially a generation or more later. It is the ceaseless
striving to determine what is "best for the most" that fills the countless law
books that have been written and compiled since the beginning of recorded
history.

The question is never really settled, because society's needs, wants and
values are always changing. It is not so much that human beings are
unstable and capricious, but because our environment, threats and fears
keep changing. And legal concepts must be continually tuned and re-tuned
to keep in harmony with society's needs.

Origins of Liability

One's obligation to answer for harm done to another has roots as old as
recorded history. Recovered fragments of Babylonian law formulated
within the Code of Hammurabi more than 2,000 years before Christ called
for the death of a builder if a house he incompetently constructed caused
the death of its owner; or the death of the builder's son if the collapse killed
the owner's son.[16] This is, perhaps, the first reference to "products liability"
in recorded history; because it deals with injury not associated with direct
personal contact but injury resulting from a "product" incompetently

constructed. As will become apparent in later pages, this was a remarkably advanced concept considering the date.

Only a few hundred years later Mosaic Law distinguished between accidental offenses and intentional ones and those that could have been averted. It prescribed more severe punishments for intentional assaults and harm due to neglect or failure to exercise care (for example, failure to provide adequate restraint for an ox having a reputation for goring) than it did for unintentional or inadvertent accidents.[17]

This, too, was a highly developed legal concept for the day. But we must keep in mind that these early civilizations were uniquely advanced. The fact that we have written records of their existence attests to it. Unfortunately, human history does not show that man has always built upon past accomplishments and improved himself. There were many lapses and regressions. Thousands of years after Babylonian and Mosaic law had proven beneficial for an advanced society we find a return to crude and primitive concepts.

Nevertheless, no society has ever tolerated individuals doing as they pleased without regard of others or their interests. Supreme Court Justice Oliver Wendell Holmes summed it up well when he said, "Your freedom ends where my nose begins." It is a concept that need not be taught to children, as other children instinctively "teach" it to them the moment one of them acts in disregard of the comfort, wellbeing, or security of another or offends in some way.

The immediate reaction by one wronged is to mete out retribution fitting the offense. We even see it in the animal world. Retribution, of course, does not undo the incident or erase its effect or result. Most of us can recall parents admonishing that "two wrongs do not make a right." Nevertheless, the craving for revenge is virtually spontaneous; it's in our nature. The roots go deep. It's the ancient *lex talionis*, the "eye-for-an-eye, tooth-for-a-tooth" notion from the Mosaic Law.[18] We even find it in children's old Mother Goose nursery rhymes:

> Taffy was a Welshman, Taffy was a thief;
> Taffy came to my house and stole a piece of beef.
> I went to Taffy's house, Taffy wasn't home;
> Taffy came to my house and stole a marrow bone.
> I went to Taffy's house, Taffy was in bed;
> I picked up the marrow bone
> and hit him on the head.[19]

Although, at times, all of us feel compulsion for revenge as a "remedy" for offenses committed against us by others; there is no place for unbridled vengeance in civilized society. It would turn every offending encounter into a brawl and society into a jungle. But there *has* to be a remedy for such offenses; human nature demands it.[20,21]

Long ago, society recognized these conflicting needs and in time devised a legal principle that solved two major problems arising from the propensity of human beings to harm one another. The principle (a) appeased man's instinctive urge for revenge for wrongs committed against him, and (b) did so without disturbing the peace. That legal principle is what became known as *liability*.

In early times it took the form of an obligation for the offender to surrender to the injured party the offending instrumentality, article or implement. Later, in its place, the one charged with the injury was required to simply offer something of value—eventually money—to "buy off" the vengeance of the injured party. An Anglo-Saxon legal proverb stated the options: "Buy spear from side or bear it." In other words, the offender had two choices: buy off the vengeance or end up fighting it out.[22] In the interest of preserving peace and order it was preferable in the eyes of society to reward the offended party, or his family (kin or clan), for abstaining from taking revenge through blood feuds and similar violence.

Today, we take for granted the compensatory function of tort law (the process of economic redistribution mentioned in Chapter 1), but it took thousands of years for this concept to evolve. It might be well, in passing, to note that virtually all our law came to us through centuries of struggling and experimentation. The process is never completed.

Of course, none of our body of knowledge or the accomplishments it has made possible—whether they be in physics, chemistry, medicine, mathematics, engineering or law—came easily. In his excellent book on scientific investigation, Beveridge makes this point:

> Things that are now quite easy for children to grasp, such as the elementary facts of the planetary system, required the colossal intellectual feat of a genius to conceive when his mind was already conditioned with Aristotelian notions.[23]

As difficult as it has been for new scientific concepts to be born; once they have been demonstrated, they become fairly obvious—even to laymen—and they are self-confirming. That is, their validity can be proven through experimentation; anyone can do it with proper apparatus and procedure. This is possible because *scientific* concepts are universal, independent, immutable, and so on. When dealing with scientific matters, you *know* when you have reached your goal because the thing flies, the machine works, the disease is cured, or the substance is synthesized. In this respect, the discovery of scientific knowledge is much more satisfying than the often thankless struggle to devise solutions for legal problems. You never know when the law is "right." This is because law has no absolutes; it can never be *always* right.[24]

It was not until early in this century that monetary compensation was viewed as the purpose of legal actions in tort liability. Before this, the primary purpose of such lawsuits had been to punish the wrongdoer; with payment of compensation merely a by-product of the punitive process.[25] It is worth noting that compensation for the injured individual is not an element of criminal law, since a crime is an offense against the public at large. So far as criminal law is concerned, the victim leaves the courtroom empty-handed.[26] According to White:

> The compensatory features of tort law came to be seen as significant . . . once American society came to be perceived of as an interdependent entity whose members were responsible for one another. If the lives of injured persons affected the lives of others, so that injuries were a social 'problem,' then compensating people for injuries became a paramount policy goal.[27]

The punishment notion in tort law was never abandoned altogether though (see Figure 2-3 of the previous chapter). All that really happened is that the primary emphasis shifted from punishment to compensation. They merely switched positions.

With few exceptions, early civil law did not give much thought to notions of "fault." As already mentioned, its chief concern was to keep the peace and devise practices that would be acceptable by injured or wronged individuals as substitutes for gratifying their passion for personal vengeance.

The reasons for largely ignoring fault are fairly obvious. Only the one charged with the offense and responsible for the injury really knew if the incident was intentional or accidental. And it was unlikely that he would admit intentional harm. Telling the truth did not seem to be a popular concept in early courts. In fact, oaths of slaves were given no credibility at all unless taken under torture or fear of death. Anyway, pleas of innocence by the offender would carry little weight in the eyes of the one who had been injured. Consequently, the major task of the court was to see that no further harm was done; to keep the dispute contained and not let it get out of hand, as it might if those injured were allowed free reign to gratify their passion for revenge.

Accordingly, in early law, all charged with offenses—even if the incident occurred entirely by accident—had an obligation to make restitution to the injured party. In a fragment from one of the oldest recorded cases of English tort law, a pronouncement by the Kings Bench in 1466 stated: "if a man does a thing he is bound to do it in such manner that by his deed no injury or damage is inflicted upon others."[28] Another English court decision three centuries ago made this obligation quite clear: "In all civil [non-criminal] acts, the law doth not so much regard the intent of the actor, as the loss and damage of the party suffering."[29]

This notion of liability regardless of fault or "liability without fault" is today known as *strict liability*. However, the law stated in these old English decisions is more *absolute* liability; where one is virutally a guarantor to the whole world against causing injury. Yet, the history of old English law does not show widespread litigation, as might be expected under such liability rules. Apparently, it was not as "litigious" a society as ours.

There were good reasons it was so. In the first place the law of torts, as we know it today, did not exist. Many "wrongs" had no remedy in a court of law. Also, the law was deeply mired in a morass of forms of procedure.[30] Generally, a plaintiff had no legal remedy unless his complaint fit one of the prescribed, narrowly-defined existing "writs." And not every court would hear every complaint; jurisdictions were limited and legal action was available to only certain classes of people under rigidly defined circumstances—largely fixed by the whim of the king, local magistrate or landowner.

Legal terms mean whatever tradition and custom of the day say they mean. Over the years, much of what has become termed "strict liability" has been an obligation imposed by the law upon those engaged in certain ultra-hazardous acts or situations; an obligation that amounts to a guarantee ("absolute" liability) that they will make restitution for any resulting harm.

The term "strict liability" generally refers to liability that is imposed without regard to *a quality the law regards* as "fault." We will discuss this in greater length later on in this chapter since it is of considerable importance to an understanding of products liability. But, for now, it is important only to realize that *legal* "fault" is not synonymous with moral blame. Legal fault is simply deviation from some agreed-upon standard of conduct that society requires for its protection. If someone's action (or inaction) constitutes such deviation that is wholly unintentional, or even beyond his control, he may be *morally* blameless yet *legally* at fault.[31]

Unfortunately, legal terms do not always mean what they appear to mean, what we think they mean or what they mean in ordinary conversation. When dealing with legal matters, it is risky to ignore the possibility of differing definitions or interpretations of terms that seem familiar. "Fault" is one of these terms.

Early law also did not pay much attention to injuries or harm that resulted from one's *failure* to act. Possibly, the law had enough problems dealing with incidents where harm resulted from overt actions that it could not be bothered with such subtleties as harm caused by *in*action. It is more probable, however, that the notion of imposing liability for *non*-action simply was incomprehensible to early legal thinkers.

Children, even today, often find it "unfair" to be held responsible for something they "didn't do," even if they were supposed to do it. Many adults, as well, have difficulty accepting responsibility for some failure to act. It is a legal notion that, for reasons we can appreciate, did not take hold until late in legal history. Nevertheless, it is a well-established legal concept today.

Even so, imposition of liability for failure to act usually stems from some legally-mandated *duty*—generally a situation where one is regarded by the law as having undertaken a duty to act. Liability is imposed when harm results from failure to respond to that duty or failure to execute that duty in accord with the standard demanded by society. This may seem to be indirect reasoning, and perhaps it is, but the law is full of such rationalizations and fictions as we shall soon see.

Most of the historical development of civil law that we have been discussing so far has dealt with wrongs and injuries committed by one individual upon another through direct personal contact. We noted some exceptions in the earliest recorded history of Babylonian and Mosaic law. But these represented uniquely advanced legal concepts for their day. Aside from these isolated exceptions and harm resulting from selling corrupt food and drink, civil law—until relatively recent times (pre-1800)—did not concern itself much with injuries by "things." That is, unless they were clutched in the hands of human beings when they caused the injuries. Civil liability was confined to harm readily and directly traceable to other people.

REPRIEVE FOR FLEDGLING INDUSTRY

Industrial Revolution Overwhelms Civil Tort Law

Inventions that led to today's sophisticated products were little more than crude contraptions that seldom worked as intended. Their materials of construction were frequently inferior and unproven. Quality standards did not exist. As a result, every encounter in those days with a manufactured device incurred risk of bodily harm to not only the immediate user but bystanders as well. Every industrial operation, whether it was mining coal, smelting iron ore, transporting materials or tending machinery, was hazardous. Personal injury associated with industry and its manufactured products was widespread. Yet, there was little remedy for these injuries and the process of seeking legal redress was so cumbersome that most victims chose not to pursue it.

But during the first half of the nineteenth century, the "forms of action" and writs were giving way to a more accessible and uniform legal system. The combination of a sharp increase in injuries in an expanding industrialized society and a legal system favoring absolute liability created a situation that could have hindered industrialization and the economic growth that went along with it.

"Privity" Rule Insulates Manufacturers

History does not record an epidemic of lawsuits over industrial or product-related injuries. However, concern over this possibility was clearly voiced in an 1842 English court opinion.

The case involved legal action by the driver of a mail coach against a manufacturer and repairer of mail coaches who had contracted with the Postmaster General to keep the coaches in good repair. The driver was permanently crippled when the coach he was driving broke down for lack of repair. The court refused the driver's claim on the grounds that there had been no contractual relationship (no "privity") between the driver of the coach (the plaintiff in the case) and the firm (defendant) that had contracted with the Postmaster General. However, this reason seems more of a smokescreen to obscure the principal concern of the court:

> There is no privity of contract between these parties; and if the plaintiff can sue, every passenger, or even any person passing along the road, who was injured by the upsetting of the coach, might bring a similar action. Unless we confine the operation of such contracts as this to the parties who entered into them, the most absurd and outrageous consequences, to which I see no limit, would ensue. (*Winterbottom v. Wright*)[32]

The court was clearly apprehensive over the potential wave of legal actions that might result (in the words of present-day critics of our legal system: "opening the floodgates to litigation") if the driver had been allowed to recover damages for his injury. We can infer from the court's comments that injuries from mechanical failures must have been commonplace. Considering the increase in the quantity of manufactured goods, the increasing frequency of personal contact with them and production machinery, and lack of quality control as we know it; possibilities for legal action over product failures probably were tremendous.

The decision of the case itself covered a fairly narrow issue: the question of liability for injuries stemming from failure to maintain the mail coach. But the court's position, or "rule of the case," later came to be applied to a broad range of products liability-type situations. It was misapplied to many negligence cases and formed the basis for courts to reject claims against product sellers brought by anyone except the immediate buyer (the one contracted with).[33] Once the immediate buyer (who may have been strictly a dealer and never a user) re-sold the product, the manufacturer/seller was virtually exempt from any future liability stemming from the transaction.

It probably was no accidental blunder that the courts pounced on this decision and proceeded to bend it out of shape to suit their own purposes (to prevent "the most absurd and outrageous consequences"). Their interpretation succeeded in restricting the cast of possible defendants of products liability-types of actions for many years. An extension of the principle of absolute liability to include within its scope injuries from product defects apparently was just too much for the legal system of the day.

Absolute Liability Reserved for Ultra-Hazardous Acts

In America, at about the time this was taking place, there was increasing sentiment tempering the notion of absolute liability that had been the legal rule in civil actions. The substance of that sentiment was that liability should instead be based upon a breach of moral responsibility; that, before being held liable, the one charged with the offense should be found to be "at fault" in some way.[34]

Brash new legal concepts are frequently followed by a series of counter-balancing court decisions that limit the scope and application of the new concepts, or otherwise distinguish fact-situations in which they do and do not apply. Courts soon realized that there were certain activities or conditions that constituted abnormal hazards, even when carried out with the utmost of care. To allow these activities or conditions to proceed with immunity from liability (unless carelessly done) and possibly injure innocent people unaware of such hazards seemed to conflict with the welfare of society.

In 1868 an English court found mill owners who had constructed a reservoir upon their own land liable to a neighboring mine owner who had been damaged when the reservoir broke allowing water to flow into the mine.[35] Although the original "rule" of the case has often been misstated and misapplied, it held that one is liable for harm to another when his activity creates an abnormal hazard, even if the harm was completely accidental.

Shortly thereafter, in America, two states adopted the rule (correctly applied), but a number of other states rejected the rule (in an incorrect interpretation of the original House of Lords decision). Those rejecting it broadened the original rule through eliminating the "abnormal hazard" qualification. In other words, they were stating that they were against holding one absolutely liable for harm that might result from loss of control over something (or anything) he was doing. This apparently deliberate broadening of the rule by several American jurisdictions merely illustrates the strong sentiment that had arisen against absolute liability.

It is significant to note that whether the rule in the 1868 English case was adopted or rejected *in name* by an American court, there had always been, and still is, a general acceptance of its rule: that one is liable when something or some activity deemed ultra-hazardous at the time or in the place where it is done harms another. And this is regardless of the degree of care that might have been exercised throughout (that is, one may be liable even without any fault). Examples of activity for which the rule has been applied include injury resulting from harboring ferocious animals, from blasting operations, crop dusting, and storing flammable materials and creating smoke and poisonous fumes within heavily populated areas.

Both of these legal developments in the mid-1800s, the "privity" requirement and the "fault" requirement, tended to insulate manufacturers and sellers of manufactured products from liability for injuries resulting from their products' existence or use. Many legal experts feel that this effect was no coincidence but deliberately engineered. This being done not only to keep the courts from becoming burdened with an onslaught of products-type injuries that defied the minds and legal system of the day; but to give our developing industrial nation room to breathe, to freely expand, and to bring about the utopia that everyone wanted to believe was just around the corner.

Industry: A "Sacred Cow"

In this connection we must remember that, at the time, technology and scientific progress were viewed as sacred. Its champions—engineers and industrialists—could do no wrong. To recapture the spirit of the time, hear the tribute to the engineer of this earlier day by Herbert Hoover (former President and civil engineer):

> It is a great profession . . . [U]nlike the doctor, his is not a life among the weak. Unlike the soldier, destruction is not his purpose. Unlike the lawyers, quarrels are not his daily bread. To the engineer falls the job of clothing the bare bones of science with life, comfort and hope.[36]

Samuel Florman describes the public's image of the engineer in reacting to those technical marvels of the day: "The conventional wisdom was that technological progress brought with it real progress—good progress—for all humanity, and that the men responsible for this progress had reason to consider themselves heroes."[37]

Against this background, then, it is not surprising for an 1873 New York court, in a case involving an exploding steam boiler, to refuse to hold its owner liable for damage to neighboring buildings; rejecting the 1868 English rule and the notion that industrial equipment such as a steam boiler was abnormally dangerous to society. Note the court's rationale:

> *We must have* factories, machinery, dams, canals and railroads. . . . If I have any of these upon my lands . . . I am not responsible for any damage they accidentally and unavoidably do my neighbor. *He receives his compensation for such damage by the general good, in which he shares* . . . no one can be made liable for injuries to the person or property of another without some fault or negligence on his part. (*Losee v. Buchanan*)[38] (emphasis added)

The rule that emerged and gained essentially universal acceptance in industrial America during the latter half of the nineteenth century is expressed by Justice Holmes in 1881:

> The general principle of our law is that loss from accident must lie
> where it falls. . . . No case or principle can be found . . . subjecting an
> individual to liability for an act done without fault on his part.[39]

By this time vestiges of absolute liability of earlier days had just about disappeared. A few exceptions persisted. But these mostly involved ultra-hazardous situations.

In those days, industry could almost do as it pleased with virtual immunity to liability and lawsuits. Society believed that technical innovations would ultimately lead to unlimited prosperity for everyone, and the law reflected that belief through according industry's interests first priority in what amounted to public subsidy. Interests of the individual—his safety and welfare—were secondary, if they received any attention at all. It was a climate conducive to exploitation of the worker. Everyone assumed the risks of the workplace as a condition of employment with no remedy for injuries or incapacitation from on-the-job accidents. Since there were no incentives for maintaining a safe workplace, issues of plant safety and environmental quality were practically unheard of.

Beyond the immediate confines of industry, the situation was not much different. The only ones who could possibly take legal action against a manufacturer for injuries caused by defectively designed or poorly constructed products were the dealers or distributors who purchased the products directly from the manufacturer. This is because only they had a contractual relationship with the manufacturer and such a relationship, or privity, was an essential condition for sustaining legal action. But these were probably the ones least likely to suffer consequences from product deficiency.

Bystanders injured from product failure were no better off than the "remote" purchaser and user (not having contractual privity with the manufacturer). Neither of them had a legal remedy against the manufacturer for injuries or damage sustained from product failure or defectiveness. The posture of the law at the time with respect to injuries from products is summed up in a 1903 court decision:

> [T]here must be a fixed and definite limitation to the liability of
> manufacturers and vendors for negligence in the construction and sale
> of complicated machines and structures which are to be operated or
> used by the intelligent and the ignorant, the skillful and the incompetent,
> the watchful and the careless, parties that cannot be known to the
> manufacturers or vendors, and who use all the articles all over the
> country hundreds of miles distant from the place of their manufacture
> or original sale. (*Huset v. J. I. Case Threshing Machine Company*)[40]

The "good old days" offered grim prospects for injured people. Industrial big-business was "god" and individuals had to learn to keep out of its path.

COUNTDOWN TO CRISIS

"No Liability Without Fault" Rule Dominates

The notion of absolute liability that had long been the rule in early law was all but discarded in America during the urban growth and industrialization of the post-Civil War period. In its place courts fashioned a set of rules that predicated liability upon a concept of "fault." It would be impossible to overstate the tremendous effect this concept had upon the field of tort law.

Before the fault concept became established and applied in the determination of liability for civil wrongs there was no uniformity among their various classifications. Most of them were simply procedural remnants of the old English court system of writs. The title "torts" was a catch-all term that covered this disorganized hodge-podge of miscellaneous non-contractual offenses that frequently were cause for legal action. In fact, until the year 1859, there was no formal treatise of law in America devoted to the subject.[41] The concept of "fault" and the standards that evolved for determining it were the mortar that eventually cemented the individual and diverse "wrongs" into a respectable monolithic body of law known today as "torts."

As observed earlier, ancient law did not concern itself with intent of the actor, the one charged with causing an injury. It was thought that since no one could know what was going on in the mind of man, debating intent was meaningless and futile. So, early law confined itself to seeing to it that the one who caused the injury or harm, whether it was accidental or not, made some kind of acceptable restitution to the one injured—mainly to keep the peace.

This simple approach avoided the complex and "unknowable" issues of intent, the difficulties in assessing contributory and intervening causes and their effects upon the incident, the entire question of moral blame and the problem of what to do about harm that resulted from someone's failure to act. There was a clean-cut appeal to the absolute liability approach.

Despite its early juristic appeal, this approach became inadequate for an increasingly complicated society, particularly for an urbanized industrial one with its plethora of injury-producing agencies. For many offenses and incidents absolute liability yielded a harsh, often unfair and unjust result. It also placed a heavy burden upon individuals and businesses involved in technical or industrial activity. The solution—virtual abandonment of the principle of absolute liability—soon, however, was recognized as over-reaction in the opposite direction and equally unsatisfactory. Since there had always been at least a taint of moral blame associated with those actions and situations that, in the eyes of the courts, give rise to liability, the search for a common denominator to unify this field of the law logically began there—by following up the thread of blameworthy conduct that seemed to run through the fabric of so many cases.

Legal thinkers of the day soon realized that they were on to something; for, starting with the notion that *some kind* of blameworthy conduct almost always lay at the root of all civil wrongs (torts), it was not too difficult to conceive a set of standards to evaluate tort liability. "Fault" was identified as the common denominator, the catalyst, that enabled the courts to fuse that jumble of disjointed offenses with their individual "rules"—vestiges of a distant past—into a coherent and uniform system of law.

The Negligence Principle

But "fault" is only a notion in a vacuum, a subjective quality. What was needed was the definition of a standard for determining liability based upon this common denominator; a standard that could be applied across-the-board to the entire spectrum of civil wrongs. In time, legal fault became defined as conduct that falls below the standard established by law for protection of others against unreasonable risk of harm.[42] That standard established by law would be dictated largely by the mores of society and the needs of the time—what is the best for the greatest number—and, like all law, would be subject to revision and change.

Failure to live up to that standard was termed "negligence" and this principle became the keystone of tort law. It satisfied the need for unifying cohesion in this branch of law. Besides, it provided a *flexible* standard; one that would always be current and appropriate to the situation at hand because the standard would be whatever the court declared it to be. In other words, liability would be established whenever the court found that one's conduct fell below the standard established by the law; that is, when there was *negligence*. No longer was there any need for inconclusive philosophical debates over whether the defendant was "at fault." If, through applying the standard, he was found negligent; he was, by definition, at fault and therefore liable.

Prior to this time the term negligence had been used mostly to describe failures or omissions and non-action, as when one would overlook ("neglect") some duty or responsibility that would lead to harm. But now it had much broader connotation. Negligence would now exist whenever there was failure to live up to what the law expected for the protection of society. One charged with failure to comply with some legal duty or standard may be morally blameless and it may have been impossible under the circumstances at the time to live up to the standard; nevertheless, before the court, that one would be negligent and liable.

The value of the negligence principle was profound in that it provided a foundation upon which to administer civil justice within a system of law that met the needs of an expanding industrialized society. For the first time, tort law had an *objective* standard—a universal tool—that had virtually unlimited application in dealing with civil wrongs. The rule of "no fault, no liability" that had become law could now apply to the entire gamut of situations that came before the court. It furnished a chromatic scale for civil law upon which could be played any tune in every imaginable key.

The practical usefulness of the negligence principle would be demonstrated over and over again in constructing a rational and coherent basis for solving a problem that had never really gone away: how to shift the loss from those injured to those who caused the injuries. At the same time, its self-regulating character afforded a measure of stability and a means for controlling the expansion of liability and its compensatory function.

"Fault" and "Negligence" Not the Final Solution

By the turn of the century, tort law had become encumbered with a variety of complex mechanisms and philosophical concepts that had arisen in applying the negligence principle within the "no fault, no liability" rule. These dealt with questions of proof, proximate cause, means for defining degrees of negligence, assumed risk, establishing standards of conduct that constituted unreasonable risk of harm, what duties individuals owed one another, the need for balancing interests in situations of shared liability, affirmative defenses to claims of negligence, and others.

In the early 1900s, signs were beginning to appear that the excursion away from the long-standing concepts of absolute liability had begun to turn back. One sign was evident in the increasing number of ingenious devices that courts had concocted for assuring recovery for injured victims under the negligence principle. Holmes' dictum that "loss from accident must lie where it falls" had a simplistic appeal but questionable utility. If it had been useful, then why all the efforts by the courts to fix fault within the ambit of the rule so that losses from accidents could be transferred from where they had fallen to the shoulders of someone else?

The answer to the question lay in the mounting statistics of industrial accidents. The spectre of maimed victims without a remedy was casting a dark shadow across America's industrial scene. The eagerly-awaited prosperity was always just around the corner. In its place were increasing casualties of workplace accidents, industrial disasters, product failures and environment disregard. Big business and its industrial base were no longer infants that needed to be subsidized by the public to survive. They were now mature and well established, notorious for their wealth.

The common law rules of "privity" and "no liability without fault" had served their purpose but were no longer appropriate. The days when a product purchaser/user dealt face-to-face with the manufacturer were long gone. So were the days of simple and obvious products. There now were increasing layers of product distribution and dealer networks insulating the ultimate product purchaser from the manufacturer. Industrial catastrophes were frequently responsible for widespread devastation, involving many who had not even been vaguely aware that a hazard lurked nearby.

It does not take much contemplation to appreciate that society's tolerance was wearing thin. A few legal scholars began to speak out in condemnation of industry's free hand:

> To encourage commerce and industry by removing all duty and incentive to protect the public is to invite wholesale sacrifice of individual rights on the altar of commercial greed. . . . It would appear to be high time to consider whether this price is not too high to pay for industrial expansion, and whether those who profit by the operation of a business should not bear at least the burden of exercising reasonable competence and care therein . . . it cannot be to the interest of any community to encourage carelessness and disregard of human life and property therein.[43]

Workmen's Compensation: A Step Toward Strict Liability

The time was right for the pendulum to start its swing back toward strict liability. It received its greatest thrust in that direction through passage of the workmen's compensation acts. Legislation passed in 1908 granted coverage for federal employees. This was followed only two years later in New York by the first state workmen's compensation statute. By 1921 nearly every state had passed similar legislation.

Through *legislation* (not through evolution of common law processes) the burden of worker injuries was instantly passed from the shoulders of employees (who previously had been forced to assume these risks) to the shoulders of the employer. The employer was expected to distribute the cost of this burden over all its operations, as overhead.

To assure existence of funds so that the injured would be compensated, insurance was compulsory throughout industry. Ultimately, the costs associated with this were to be passed back to the public through price increases. This legislation by-passed the legal system in that questions of negligence, or who was at fault in any given incident, disappeared. If a worker was injured on the job he was entitled to financial compensation of a prescribed sum fixed by the kind and severity of the injury. To obtain this, however, the worker had to relinquish his common law right to sue his employer. But it was a prompt, guaranteed payment; no lawsuits, no hassles, no expense. By this legislation

> the human accident losses of modern industry are . . . treated as a cost of production, like the breakage of tools and machinery. The financial burden (of injuries) is lifted from the shoulders of the employee, and placed upon the employer, who is expected to add it to his costs, and so transfer it to the consumer. . . . [It] is thus a form of strict liability.[44]

Workmen's compensation legislation was one of those few events that, at the time, would have been difficult to criticize. Everybody seemed to gain and nobody seemed to lose. Even employers who had to foot the bill gained because the legislation created incentives (through insurance premium costs) for improving workplace safety, decreasing accidents and lost time and increasing productivity and morale.

Of course, it was not a perfect system as the compensation payment usually represented a compromise; a certain payment of a nominal sum now, in contrast to an uncertain amount—most likely, no recovery— through the expense and prolonged ordeal of court action. Besides, some classifications of employees were not covered and the injury had to be purely accidental. Yet, overall, the worker had a remedy although, in some cases, a limited one; whereas previously there was essentially none.

While, of itself, workmen's compensation legislation was a significant benefit to society; it had a strong influence that extended well beyond its immediate scope. That is, it had a conditioning effect upon the public; it demonstrated the appeal and acceptability of a nationwide mechanism for transferring hardships and losses from a relatively small group of people least able to bear them to another much larger group more able to bear them. Workmen's compensation provided everyone employed with a working model of machinery that seemed to accomplish something that was beneficial to them personally. It nudged the public toward expanding this social benefit through imposing the principles of strict liability upon manufacturers of defective products that cause injuries.

The tempering of what are regarded as hard rules of law frequently begins with citing "exceptions." As these gradually increase in number, they tend to undermine the old concepts. Once this occurs it is a fairly simple matter for a court or legal scholar to redefine a "new" rule (in reality the old rule so riddled by exceptions and patched over with qualifying substitutes that it takes on an entirely new identity and character). Exceptions to the contractual privity and "no liability without fault" rules had existed for some time. These, and new ones that were added, played a significant role in the softening, and eventual dissolution, of these general rules as far as liability for defective products was concerned.

Exceptions to "Fault" and Privity Rules

Manufacturer Liable for Poison Drug. In a case decided in 1852 a drug manufacturer mislabeled a poison as a harmless drug.[45] It was sold to a pharmacy who sold it to a customer whose wife became poisoned from taking it. In a lawsuit *against the manufacturer* the court held it liable on the grounds that it had a duty, not only to the immediate buyer (the pharmacy); but also to those who were the intended consumers of the product, to avoid the creation of a dangerous condition. Through its negligence it endangered human life. This decision clearly was contrary to that of the 1842 English mail coach rule that had become the pole star of the contractual privity doctrine for manufactured products.

The holding of strict liability in this poison drug case was not fundamentally different from those involving conduct of ultra-hazardous activities. In both situations those held liable may not have been consciously aware of the specific outcome of their activity (that certain people would be seriously injured or killed). Yet, they were made strictly liable; that is, they were liable for the outcome despite the existing privity and "fault" requirements of civil law at the time.

Courts Find "Implied Warranty" in Food Sales. Much later, in 1913, another exception to these requirements also was made in a case involving a restaurant owner who sued a meat packing plant for damage to his business and reputation when customers became ill from eating contaminated meat he had served them and made it known publicly. The restaurant had not purchased the product directly from the packing plant but through a distributor; nevertheless, the court found the meat packer liable:

> Plaintiffs have been injured. No other person or firm had an opportunity to check the offensive package after it was sealed and sent on its way. Right and reason demand that any party injured shall have a right of recovery *against the first offender* without resorting to that circumlocution of action against intervening agents. . . . (*Mazetti v. Armour & Co.*)[46] (emphasis added)

Here, the court declares that "right and reason" must prevail over any attempt to impose a requirement of contractual privity upon the right to recover. This case is a key one in the evolution of the strict liability law of today because it was among the first where a court said that an *implied warranty* of fitness for consumption extended beyond the immediate party to a transaction. A "fiction" perhaps, but this decision and similar ones that followed began to erode away the old privity and fault rules even if, at the start, it was for a narrowly-defined class of products.

This decision is mentioned here because it was a significant departure from the rule of contractual privity then in vogue. However, the public (and the law) never had much sympathy or tolerance for sellers of bad food. As early as the thirteenth century there were statutes against selling "corrupt victuals." So, while the 1913 decision was important as a precedent in cases to follow, it merely restated a well-established rule that society strongly resents attempts to sell it contaminated food. (This sentiment probably has something to do with the fact that defectiveness of food is not always immediately obvious, particularly if it has been processed in some way.)

Privity Abolished for "Inherently Dangerous" Products

Only three years after the 1913 defective food case was decided in the state of Washington, a landmark decision in New York eliminated the privity requirement for negligence actions for injuries caused by "inherently dangerous" products.[47] Although the language of the decision hinged upon the inherent danger issue, this qualifying classification disappeared in a few years as other jurisdictions following the case loosely interpreted its decision.

In that case, a man who purchased a new automobile from a dealer was injured when one of its wheels, made of defective wood, splintered while he was driving the automobile down the road. He sued the manufacturer of the automobile. The automobile manufacturer had not manufactured the wheel but had purchased it from another supplier and was unaware of its defective nature. Apparently, the automobile manufacturer had installed the wheel on the automobile without conducting its own in-house inspection. In deciding against the automobile manufacturer the court said:

> If the nature of a thing is such that it is reasonably certain to place life and limb in peril when negligently made, it is then a thing of danger. Its nature gives warning of the consequences to be expected. If to the element of danger there is added knowledge that the thing will be used by persons other than the purchaser . . . then, irrespective of contract, the manufacturer of the thing of danger is under a duty to make it carefully. . . .
>
> [T]he presence of a known danger, attendant upon a known use makes vigilance a duty. We have put aside the notion that the duty to safeguard life and limb, when the consequences of negligence may be foreseen, grows out of contract and nothing else. We have put the source of the obligation where it ought to be. We have put its source in the law. (*MacPherson v. Buick Motor Co.*)

With regard to the fact that the automobile manufacturer did not make the wheel, the court said:

> We think the defendant was not absolved from a duty of inspection because it bought the wheels from a reputable manufacturer. . . . It was not at liberty to put the finished product [the automobile] on the market without subjecting the component parts to ordinary and simple tests. . . . The obligation to inspect must vary with the nature of the thing to be inspected. The more probable the danger the greater the need of caution. (*MacPherson v. Buick Motor Co.*)

In time, the rule of the case spread to all classes of products. This extension of the rule was not as drastic as it may seem at first; because, if a product injured someone, it was not difficult to find some quality in its "defectiveness" that made it "inherently dangerous" and, therefore, within the scope of the original rule of the case. Thus, this decision removed the requirement of contractual privity that, since 1842, had stood in the way of injured victims' recovery for negligence of remote manufacturers (those not dealt with directly).

Strict Liability for Breach of *Express* Warranty

Up to this time, courts in a few jurisdictions and for a few exceptions had set aside the requirement that, to sustain legal action, the injured party had to have dealt directly with the product manufacturer (in "privity" of contract). One of these situations was the sale of bad food or mislabeled drugs where the courts said there was an "implied warranty" of fitness by the manufacturer. Another was "inherently dangerous" products. However, courts were slow to abolish the privity requirement for most other products. The feeling was that sales of products were contractual dealings, face-to-face, and the creation by the courts of some fictitious warranty that had not been contemplated or intended by the parties to the transaction was outside their rightful province.

Nevertheless, in a 1932 decision, a court in the state of Washington eliminated the requirement for contractual privity in cases where the injured party claimed that an *express* warranty had been made ("expressed," or affirmatively communicated). The case arose when a driver lost his eye when the windshield of an automobile he had purchased shattered when struck by a pebble. The automobile manufacturer had claimed in an advertisement that the windshield on this model was "shatterproof." The court concluded in its decision against the manufacturer:

> It would be unjust to recognize a rule that would permit manufacturers of goods to create a demand for their products by representing that they possess qualities which they, in fact, do not possess, and then, because there is no privity of contract existing between the consumer and the manufacturer, deny the consumer the right to recover if damages result from the absence of those qualities, when such absence is not readily noticeable. . . .
>
> [The plaintiff] had the right to rely upon the representations made by [the defendant] . . . relative to qualities possessed by its products, even though there was no privity of contract between [them]. (*Baxter v. Ford Motor Co.*)[48]

The holding of the case is important because it has been widely followed and because it said that manufacturers of products are *strictly liable* (no need to prove negligence) for claims that turn out to be false when made to the public through advertising, literature or messages printed directly on the product or its package.

As significant as these developments were in clearing the way for injured plaintiffs to recover from "remote" manufacturers for certain classes of products and situations; it still was necessary for most product injuries for the injured party to prove the defendant negligent before the court could hold him liable. Such proof was usually very difficult to establish; frequently it was impossible.

A 1940s Preview of Today's Liability Law

In 1944, a California court decided a case involving a waitress who had been injured when a bottle of carbonated beverage exploded in her hand, severely injuring her. The decision in the case against the beverage bottling company called upon the doctrine of *res ipsa loquitur* (the thing speaks for itself) to supply an "inference" of negligence which, at the time, was necessary for imposing liability upon the defendant. Although the decision of the case itself, in favor of the injured waitress, broke no new legal ground; it included a statement by one of the judges that would generate considerable attention and debate for the next several decades.

In a written concurring opinion, Justice Traynor had this to say about the need for proof of negligence in defective product cases:

> I concur in the judgment, but I believe the manufacturer's negligence should no longer be singled out as the basis of a plaintiff's right to recover in cases like the present one. In my opinion it should be now recognized that a manufacturer incurs an absolute liability when an article that he has placed on the market, knowing that it is to be used without inspection, proves to have a defect that causes injury to human beings. . . . Even if there is no negligence, however, public policy demands that responsibility be fixed wherever it will most effectively reduce the hazards to life and health inherent in defective products that reach the market. It is evident that the manufacturer can anticipate some hazards and guard against the recurrence of others, as the public cannot. Those who suffer injury from defective products are unprepared to meet its consequences. The cost of an injury and the loss of time or health may be an overwhelming misfortune to the person injured, and a needless one, for the risk of injury can be insured by the manufacturer and distributed among the public as a cost of doing business. It is to the public interest to discourage the marketing of products having defects that are a menace to the public. If such products nevertheless find their way into the market it is to the public interest to place the responsibility for whatever injury they may cause upon the manufacturer, who, even if he is not negligent in the manufacture of the product, is responsible for its reaching the market. However intermittently such injuries occur and however haphazardly they may strike, the risk of their occurrence is a constant risk and a general one. Against such risk there should be a general and constant protection and the manufacturer is best situated to afford such protection. (*Escola v. Coca Cola Bottling Co. of Fresno*)[49]

At the time they were made, these comments were to be more prophecy than compelling law. In 1944 neither the real world nor the world of legal philosophers was quite ready to accept these doctrines.[50] Yet, Justice Traynor, in one comprehensive stroke blazed a trail that would lead to the products liability law we have today. In a few decades, these somewhat revolutionary notions would become widely accepted law in the United States.

There were several points of major significance in Traynor's statement. One was that product-caused injuries were a matter of public concern, affirming the increasingly popular sociological notion that when one of us is hurt, we all suffer. Secondly, he advocated doing away with the burden the injured party had for proving the defendent negligent before recovering for his injuries. Third, he saw the law as a mechanism for economic redistribution in compensating victims of accidents that had been caused by defective products. Then too, he sounded a note heard only faintly before but one that would become a dominant tone in the years ahead; that the public has a *right* to recover, a *right* to be compensated for injuries caused by defective products.

"Implied Warranty" Spreads Beyond Food and Drugs

Courts had been reluctant to extend the notion of implied warranty beyond drugs, food and drink. But during the early 1950s the concept began to spread to other products, starting with animal food and products for personal grooming such a as soap, cosmetics and hair care formulations. In 1958 a Michigan court even held a cinder block manufacturer liable on implied warranty (without contractual privity and without need to prove negligence) when a user's house collapsed.[51]

In an attempt to shield themselves from the growing threat of liability for products injuries, it had become standard practice for manufacturers to include disclaimers of liability for personal injury within their contracts of sale. Disclaimers are contractual denials made in an attempt to avoid liability. By this means, legal action for damages for personal injury from a defective product would be defeated in court when the defendant could produce a disclaimer signed by both parties. (This amounted to the buyer contracting away his legal rights, as pointed out by the court in a 1960 New Jersey decision.)

That lawsuit was brought against an automobile dealer when a steering defect in a new automobile caused it to run off the road out of control.[52] The resulting accident totally destroyed the automobile and seriously injured its driver, the buyer's wife. Although the purchaser had signed a sales contract containing a disclaimer against liability for injuries resulting from mechanical defects, the court allowed the injured plaintiff to recover:

> The language [in the contract's fine print, which included the disclaimer] gave little and withdrew much. In return for the delusive remedy of replacement of defective parts at the factory, the buyer is said to have accepted the exclusion of the maker's liability for personal injuries arising from the breach of the warranty, and to have agreed to the elimination of any other express or implied warranty. An instinctively felt sense of justice cries out against such a sharp bargain. . . . the disclaimer of an implied warranty of merchantability by the dealer, as well as the attempted elimination of all obligations other than replacement of defective parts, are violative of public policy and void. (*Henningsen v. Bloomfield Motors, Inc.*)

During the few years before this case was tried there had been a growing trend for courts to impose liability upon manufacturers of certain types of products for injuries to those outside the circle of the privity relationship. The basis for this had been a concept, fabricated by the courts, that implied warranties of fitness for intended use "traveled with" the products. But this case, once and for all, abolished the privity requirement and held that implied warranties extend to any foreseeable consumer or product user:

> [W]here the commodities are sold such that if defectively manufactured they will be dangerous to life or limb, then society's interests can only be protected by eliminating the requirement of privity between the maker and his dealers and the reasonably expected ultimate consumer. In that way the burden of losses consequent upon use of defective articles is borne by those who are in a position to either control the danger or make an equitable distribution of the losses when they do occur. (*Henningsen v. Bloomfield Motors, Inc.*)

By this time, most of the former obstacles to holding the manufacturer strictly liable for injuries due to defective products had been removed. Contractual privity, a tenacious principle that for so long had defeated claims of injured victims who had had the misfortune of not dealing directly with the manufacturer, had gradually been worn away. The first assault was through creating an exclusion for ultra-hazardous activity, for drugs and food and drink; later the exclusion was extended to include other products "inherently dangerous" or that involved intimate bodily contact. Then, in 1960, the New Jersey court held that implied warranties ran to any reasonably expected ultimate consumer of a defectively manufactured product.

The basis for these exclusions to the "privity" requirement was the concept of implied warranty—purely a figment of the court's imagination. However, any attempt to contract away this illusory figment was declared void and in violation of public policy. One by one, previously formidable barriers to strict liability for injuries caused by defective products had been taken away. The long-sought-after goal of strict liability was now directly ahead and clearly within reach. It was only a matter of time until that doctrine would be formally proclaimed.

Manufacturers Strictly Liable for Defective Products

Only three years after the New Jersey case eliminated the privity requirement through announcing that "implied" warranties ran to any forseeable user, a California court declared that warranties need not even enter the picture.

A man had been injured when a combination power tool that he was using as a wood lathe failed to restrain a block of wood being turned. The block struck him in the forehead, seriously injuring him. He sued both the dealer and the power tool manufacturer (his wife had purchased the tool from the dealer).

The suit faced a number of legal obstructions. One of them was failure of the injured user to give the manufacturer timely notice of the "breach of express warranty." He claimed the manufacturer had committed this breach in failing to provide a safe power tool despite assurances in its advertising brochures of suitability for a variety of woodworking applications. In declaring the manufacturer *strictly liable* for the injury, the court said:

> [T]o impose strict liability on the manufacturer under the circumstances
> of this case, it was not necessary for plaintiff to establish an express
> warranty. . . . A manufacturer is strictly liable in tort when an article he
> places on the market, knowing that it is to be used without inspection
> for defects, proves to have a defect that causes injury to a human being.
> (*Greenman v. Yuba Power Products, Inc.*)[53]

This court decision transferred the subject of products liability from the sphere of the law of sales, with its warranties, contractual requirements for privity and notice of breach and other hindrances to an injured plaintiff's recovery, and placed it on its own footing—strict liability.[54] This, of course, did not abrogate the earlier approaches of negligence and breach of warranty that became stepping stones to strict liability. These are still useable legal principles and are commonly stated in products liability cases, but they are less direct and usually more difficult to pursue. Although the California decision was binding at first only in that state, a great many other states soon followed it. Strict liability for injuries caused by defective products is now the dominant rule in most jurisdictions in this country.

In tracing the development of products liability law, as we have, it should be obvious that its roots lie deep in legal history. Although the principles of strict liability for product-related injuries may have become accepted law in most states in only recent years, they have been standing in the wings for a long time—in a way, they never really left the legal stage. While strict liability may be a "new" concept to industry, it is far from new to the world of law. All of this should tell us that, in one form or another, it's probably here to stay.

A LOSS-SHIFTING MECHANISM BREAKS DOWN

Products-Related Harm—A Matter for Courts

From a practical point of view, our legal system is cumbersome, with its assortment of courts, rules, jurisdictions and procedures that, to a great extent, are ghosts of the past. An attempt to use such a system to solve a widespread social problem created by modern technology seems to be an inappropriate and inefficient way to handle it. One of the reasons why the law has become the primary vehicle for solving products-related-injury problems has been the taint of moral blame on someone's part that has always been associated with harm sustained by one at the hands of another.

Our nature craves the satisfaction that comes from finding out who's to blame, who's at fault, and seeing to it that they "pay" for it. These are needs that are best handled by a legal system; a forum for hearing both sides of a matter, for reaching an impartial conclusion, and that has machinery for enforcing the judgment and assuring it will be carried out.

However, many hurts in life are inevitable, unavoidable and "go with the territory." Then too, we tend to bring some difficulties and harm upon ourselves. There is usually no incentive for attempting to correct those kinds of wrongs because we cannot identify some specific individual (other than ourselves) as the cause. We do seem to get satisfaction from talking about the weather, the economy, taxes, poverty, crime and the other deplorable but largely uncontrollable hostile forces in the world. But when it comes to harm that is reasonably traceable to a specific individual, situation or object made by someone (we call such harm "wrongs"), *then* we feel we have an opportunity to set things right. Then we have a specific target to aim at.

But not all morally reprehensible behavior, or behavior that produces harm, is considered a "wrong" in the eyes of the law. For example, the law imposes no obligation on anyone to rescue a drowning person even though one may be within arm's reach of a life preserver and could easily toss it out to the victim. We have no legal duty to feed a starving neighbor, to come to his aid or even phone the police when we see him being beaten by thugs, or to save his wandering child from tumbling off a precipice. Yet, the law chooses to regard some kinds of behavior that are detrimental to others as legal wrongs for which we incur liability—a legal obligation to make restitution for those wrongs.

Accompanying the rise of industry with its machines, chemicals, steam boilers and other potentially injurious agencies arose a new kind of harm or wrong; the kind that occurs when some manufactured product becomes an instrumentality for harm or injury or when these things get out of control. It was only natural for complaints of such harm to be brought to the courts, a legal system and forum that already existed and was accustomed to administering justice for other kinds of wrongs.

As discussed earlier, much of the "justice" function of the legal system has been eclipsed by movement of the law toward strict liability for injuries caused by defective manufactured products. The thrust of the movement, pure and simple, has not been to see to it that justice is done but to secure financial compensation for injured victims.

Admittedly, in every lawsuit there still are shadows of the old emotionally-charged "pleadings" that allege the blameworthy nature of the defendant's conduct as lying at the root of the plaintiff's injury. And plaintiffs' attorneys do their best to cast the defendant in as bad a light and with as black a hat as they can find to make him appear a "bad guy" in the eyes of the court and jury.

Awarding "punitive" damages (as punishment for civil offenders) is far from an outmoded practice. Yet, most of the traditional courtroom appeal to the emotions is needless dramatization when the plaintiff's action is brought on the basis of strict liability. Theoretically, at least, there's no reason for the "good-guy/bad-guy" syndrome in a strict liability case. But perhaps the human psyche has not developed (matured?) as quickly as products liability law and still needs to find someone at fault and to gratify its revenge through making him pay. This may lie at the root of why, despite the remedy of strict liability that is now available in most jurisdictions in this country, so many products liability lawsuits still are brought on negligence and breach of warranty or combinations of old principles.

Loss-Redistribution Through Insurance

Over the past several decades the law has been relentless in its search for a rationale for shifting losses stemming from injuries and other damage caused by manufactured products. Its goal is to transfer losses from the shoulders of those least able to bear them (the victims) onto the shoulders of those best able to bear them (the manufacturers).

What are being shifted, though, are not really "losses." One cannot really transfer an injury or harm to someone else. And why would one want to? During its development, the law has moved well away from requiring "an eye for an eye." This "remedy" was never of any *material* benefit to the injured party. We have learned to measure a victim's loss in terms of money and have imposed liability for such loss in terms of an obligation to pay him money. Of course, this does not restore the victim to his original pre-injury condition and it is not, in a true sense, a remedy; but it probably is the next best thing to it. What this all boils down to then is simply a process of economic redistribution.

The notion of having a large number of people periodically contribute relatively small sums of money to a pool of funds to pay the legal obligations of a few is nothing new. Liability insurance of various sorts had been known and used since the early 1800s. Justice Holmes, in 1881, detected a trend in legal thought in the direction of a concept of nationwide insurance to compensate victims of industrial and products-related accidents. He had this to say about it:

> The state might conceivably make itself a mutual insurance company against accidents, and distribute the burden of its citizens' mishaps among all its members. . . . The undertaking to redistribute losses . . . offend[s] the sense of justice.[55]

To understand Holmes' contention that existence of liability insurance violated his sense of justice, we must appreciate a basic difference between *liability* insurance and *accident* insurance. Accident insurance pays the victim; liability insurance pays the perpetrator or alleged wrongdoer. Liability insurance indemnifies the *insured* for obligations imposed by the law for compensating victims of injuries, or at least to the extent of the agreed-upon policy limits.

Early criticism of liability insurance for industrial accidents and those caused by manufactured products centered about a concern that substitution of "professional litigants" (insurance companies) for actual wrongdoers would encourage antisocial conduct.[56] That is, if insured, one might be tempted to become careless and irresponsible about the safety of others. This is a largely unfounded fear today, however, as a record of irresponsible behavior is reflected in higher insurance premium costs and even cancellation of coverage altogether.

As importance of the punitive function of tort law faded somewhat and compensatory aspects became more dominant, the concept of indemnification of the defendant by outsiders has become less offensive to the sense of justice, and even quite acceptable. In fact, it is not difficult to argue that the very existence of insurance makes it easier to satisfy today's objective of tort law: compensation for the injured.

At the other side of the coin were concerns over possible effects the existence of insurance might have on the verdict. It was reasoned that the court and jury would be less reluctant to impose damage costs upon a defendant who was indemnified by an insurer than upon one who was uninsured and might be financially ruined by the need to pay the costs out of his own pocket. Such a situation would conflict with the original premise that injuries of the few (unable to bear the costs) would be compensated from pooled contributions of the many (able to bear the costs).

There is little doubt that knowledge of the existence of insurance can have a very real effect upon the outcome of a trial. Such an effect is probably unavoidable, despite usual attempts by courts to prevent disclosing the existence of insurance to the jury. The judge certainly is aware of it (from pre-trial conferences) and the jury will presume that a large manufacturing company is insured, even if the court is successful in preventing plaintiff attorneys from revealing it during the trial.

Prosser expressed concern over the potential prejudicial effect of insurance coverage:

> What insurance can do, of course, is to distribute losses proportionately among a group who are able to bear them. What it cannot do and should not do is to determine whether the group should bear them in the first instance.[57]

The existence of liability insurance also has a motivating effect toward early settlement of a lawsuit. This is usually in the interests of everyone concerned, but may not always be. Insurers are running a business. Like all businesses, their objectives are to make a profit. This means, among other things, avoiding prolonged (and expensive) disputes. There is always the inevitable tradeoff: pay a given sum in settlement now and be rid of the case for good, or take a chance that through holding out until later the plaintiff may be willing to accept less. Generally, insurers consider it advantageous to settle early and this is what they usually do. This may not be in the best interests of the insured manufacturer, however.

Throughout the development of legal concepts that created today's products liability obligations, there had always been an unquestioned presumption of availability of liability insurance at an affordable price. The crux of the presumption was that, although the courts were bent upon fashioning a body of law that would make industry financially responsible to compensate victims of product-derived injuries, this requirement would create no real hardship for any individual. Industry could simply buy insurance to cover the costs. These costs could be buried in the company's overhead and passed back to the public through price increases. In theory it was considered a neat idea. This concept is clearly described by a California court in a case referred to earlier:

> The cost of an injury and the loss of time or health may be an overwhelming misfortune to the person injured, and a needless one, for the risk of injury can be insured by the manufacturer and distributed among the public as a cost of doing business. (*Escola v. Coca Cola Bottling Co. of Fresno*)[58]

Since insurance companies are in business to make profit, they must be concerned over how much they are paid to assume the risks they do in the policies they write. If paid too little, they lose money; if they ask to be paid too much, they won't be competitive and people will take their insurance business elsewhere. It is a market like any other and there are many firms competing for the business. Their fees, or premiums charged for coverage, must be arrived at through a careful balancing of various factors, many of them unknown. Prediction of future events becomes a very critical ingredient in setting premiums; yet, insurance companies are not clairvoyant. Therefore, they depend heavily upon statistics. It is said that while insurance companies do not know exactly *who* will die tomorrow, they do know exactly *how many*.

Their ability to predict the future with reasonable accuracy comes through computations based upon past history and estimated effects of other factors. The longer the history and the more stable the loss situation (whether it be deaths, accidents, storms, building collapses, fires or some other catastrophe) the better insurers can predict the future; or, more specifically, quantitatively determine their exposure to risk and what their probable payout will be for losses they have insured against.

What can upset all of this are unanticipated occurrences—unusually severe storms, unprecedented catastrophes and epidemics. Even then, insurers use various reinsurance techniques to spread the economic effects of such events over a large number of companies.

Signs of Overload Create Panic

Until about the mid-1960s the field of liability insurance of manufacturers was fairly stable and predictable; but once the concept of strict liability caught on, the insurance industry was hit with a sharp increase in the number and value of claims. (See Figures 2-1 through 2-7 of Chapter 2.) This called for drastic adjustment in the rate structure for products liability coverage. But, since there were no precedents for such a deluge of claims insurers faced some real unknowns. Without past history to guide them, statistics were worthless. Rate-setting became a game of intuition and pure guesswork.

Obviously, they had to increase premiums and take a hard look at policy coverages. The outcome was predictable: there were significant increases in premiums, decreases in coverage, increases in deductibles and exclusions and, for some "target" industries, cancellation of liability coverage outright.

Many panic-stricken insurers over-reacted to the epidemic of products lawsuits and claims; some probably under-reacted and lost money. Manufacturers complained of increasing costs of insurance premiums and, in some cases, unavailability of liability coverage. Insurers complained that they were losing money. It was a chaotic and unhealthy state of affairs for everyone, insurer and manufacturer alike.

In 1976 the President's Economic Policy Board established an Inter-agency Task Force on Product Liability to investigate "the crisis" that had developed. Its study found that the larger the manufacturing firm the more likely it was to be hit with products liability lawsuits. It confirmed that there had been a sharp increase in the dollar-value of products claims. From 1971 to 1976 the claims per firm surveyed climbed in value from $434,000 to more than $3.5 million. New claims per firm increased in number 130 percent during the period. The study also found that although from 1965 to 1974 liability claims increased 1,300 percent, the Consumer Price Index had risen only 56 percent.[59]

Products liability problems had also taken their toll from manufacturers in creating new business risks. In testimony before the House Small Business Committee in April 1977, 21.6 percent of the manufacturers said that they were not insured because of excessive costs of coverage or because coverage was not available.[60] One company out of three reported the need to raise prices on at least one line of products as a direct result of increases in insurance rates. Products liability problems had led one out of six manfacturers to abandon at least one product line. The same group reported that sales volume from 1970 through 1976 increased 162 percent but premiums for products liability coverage during the same period went up 945 percent.

Some industries were hit harder than others. Machine tool builders, for example, experienced an average increase in products liability insurance premiums from $10,000 in 1970 to $140,000 in 1979.[61] From 1970 to 1977 some manufacturers had average cumulative premium increases as high as 5,000 percent.[62]

Perhaps the best that could be said for the products liability insurance situation at the time was that it was unstable. Many called it a crisis unprecedented in business history; particularly those manufacturers facing the prospects of increasing numbers of liability claims without insurance coverage.

The creators of the intricately-devised system for shifting such losses apparently had not anticipated the possibility of a breakdown of one component in the system essential for it to work—insurance coverage. The loss transfer cycle—injured victim/manufacturer/insurance company/ manufacturer/public—cannot work if the insurer/manufacturer link in the circuit fails. Most likely, it had been assumed that laws of supply and demand would continue to operate in the products liability field. In the long run, they probably will prevail. Yet, there has been an interval of instability brought about by an overload on the intricately-devised loss-shifting system that has affected the vitality and morale of our nation's manufacturing industry.

What Caused the Overload?

One of the underlying causes for the insurance crisis is the fact that products manufacturers no longer confine operations to the limits of a single city or geographical area. Most manufacturers of any size today do business in all 50 states and in hundreds of foreign countries. While this represents a significant change from what the scope of manufacturers' markets was one or two hundred years ago, we are still operating within a system of common law *procedures* that has not changed much during that same period.

The common law system developed around disputes between individuals and local situations. It didn't matter much if a court in a neighboring territory or jurisdiction did not hold to the same rules or interpretations of them. But with increasing need for courts to consider problems that cross jurisdictional boundaries has come a need for greater uniformity in at least certain fields of law that cannot be geographically limited.

This century has seen unification of law in a number of commercial areas. As early as 1896 the National Conference of Commissioners on Uniform State Laws enacted the Uniform Negotiable Instruments Law and, in 1906, the Uniform Sales Act. These were followed by other uniform laws relating to commercial transactions. These "acts" were widely accepted although not collectively adopted by all states. These were forerunners of what is now the Uniform Commercial Code (UCC).[63] Every provision of the UCC is not uniformly accepted in every jurisdiction of the United States, even today, but it has extremely broad acceptance. Many of its provisions impinge upon products liability and these issues will be discussed in greater detail later. The UCC is but one example of many codes that were enacted to meet a need for uniform law to facilitate commercial business transactions.

Even in areas of the law where there is no uniform national code, courts do not operate in disregard of laws of other states or jurisdictions. While decisions by courts in other states are not necessarily binding, they can have a persuasive influence and are commonly cited by attorneys whenever there are no cases "in point" within the jurisdiction. Despite this general tendency for uniformity, unification within the common law system is a slow process and is never achieved, or really ever comes close, because everything is in a state of flux.

Consider, now, the difficulty facing courts across the country over how to decide products liability cases. In just a few years there have been dramatic changes; changes of a magnitude unprecedented in the history of law. These changes have taken place state-by-state. Considering the relatively short time since the concept of strict liability in tort was first applied to products cases, it is remarkable that there is as much unity in products liability law as there is. Nevertheless, there are gaps. Not every state has had an opportunity to apply many of the new concepts, so it is not known how these states stand on the question.

What we have today in this country has been referred to as a "crazy-quilt" of laws and rules. One of the incentives for the federal products liability legislative reform measures that have been brought before Congress is the need for unity in this law. We will discuss some of these issues in a later chapter. Our immediate concern is how this disunity has contributed to the problem, particularly with respect to the availability of insurance at an affordable price.

To begin with, in many jurisdictions it is difficult to know the standing of the courts on various products liability questions. There may simply have been no opportunity for the courts to make a decision on the issues and it is, therefore, not known how they might decide. This creates uncertainties over the law for not only manufacturers located within these jurisdictions but also for users of products sold there. And the products sold there may have been produced elsewhere and shipped in.

But, more than that and against this background of uncertainty, how are insurers to assess their exposure in accepting products liability risks? There is little wonder that the question of insurance is as shrouded in uncertainty as it is. It is evident that there can be no real stability in the liability insurance market until there is greater unity among the states on these questions. No doubt, it will improve in time, either through federal legislation or through broader adoption of the new concepts.

The trouble with the latter is that the upheaval in products liability law is still underway, it's still unsettled. It is too soon to tell where it may ultimately lead as there are too many complicated issues clouding the crystal ball. Meanwhile, manufacturers must operate their plants and market their products and do so without unreasonable risk. While it is essential to have insurance coverage, we must have more than that to minimize risks; for, how can insurance purchased within such an unstable climate offer any long-term freedom from loss? This is why products liability prevention should be the cornerstone of every company's risk control program.

Since the initial impact of the insurance crisis several years ago, Congress has taken some action to relieve the insurance availability problem. In 1981 Congress passed the Risk Retention Act (Public Law 97-45) making it possible for small businesses to self-insure through purchasing insurance as a group at more favorable rates.[64,65] There are as yet no reliable indications of how many manufacturers have taken advantage of this legislation or its actual benefits.

There has been considerable debate over what influence the availability of affordable liability insurance has had upon the situation. Again, it probably depends upon whom you ask. A manufacturer within a target industry who has been through a few lawsuits, and has just had his liability insurance policy canceled, certainly will have a different view of it than an insured manufacturer free of claims and threats of suits. The difference lies in their ability to shift liability losses off their own backs and onto someone else.

Then there is the question of whether existence of insurance coverage in itself creates an attractive target for lawsuits. No reasonable, clear-thinking attorney will waste time and money pursuing a civil action against an uninsured defendant who does not have the financial resources to pay damages. If we proceed a bit further down this line of reasoning we will reach a point where it would appear that liability insurance is *a cause* of the products liability crisis. But this argument does not stand up very long because, insured or not, large corporations would still have sufficient financial resources to make them worthwhile defendants and targets of lawsuits. In fact, this was reflected in the findings of the 1977 study by the Interagency Task Force on Product Liability.[66]

Liability insurance, its availability and affordability, certainly have played a role in creating a crisis over products liability; but probably not as dominant as many believe. Nevertheless, it seems clear that these factors have been a contributor to the *panic* that has been generated over products liability. While no manufacturer today can consider itself immune to products lawsuits, an effective cure for panic and paranoia is to know that your products are well made and safe to use and that there is a comprehensive and well-organized liability prevention program in place.

REFERENCES

1. Frank, J., *Law and the Modern Mind* 6, Anchor Books edition, (1963), Doubleday & Co., Inc., Garden City, NY (originally published by Brentano's Inc. in 1930).
2. Smith, M., *Jurisprudence* 21, Columbia University Press New York, NY (1909).
3. *Random House Dictionary of the English Language* 812, Unabridged Edition, Random House, New York, NY (1969).
4. Campbell, N., *What Is Science?* 49, Dover Publications, Inc., New York, NY (1921).
5. *MacPherson v. Buick Motor Co.*, 217 N.Y. 382, 111 N.E. 1050 (1916).
6. Commoner, B., *The Closing Circle; Nature, Man and Technology* 7, 8, 20, Alfred A. Knopf, New York, NY (1971).
7. Prosser, W.L., *Handbook of the Law of Torts* 188, Fourth Edition, West Publishing Co., St. Paul, MN (1971).
8. Peck, D.W., *Decision at Law* 3, Cornerstone Library, New York, NY, a Division of Pocket Books, Inc., New York, NY (1961).
9. Prosser, W.L., *supra* reference 7.
10. Pound, R., *Interpretations of Legal History* 1, The Macmillan Co., New York, NY (1923).
11. Cardozo, B.N., *The Nature of the Judicial Process* 25, Yale University Press, New Haven, CT (1921).
12. Pound, R., *An Introduction to the Philosophy of Law* 12, 32-34, Yale University Press, New Haven, CT (1954).
13. *Id.* at 65-66.
14. Prosser, W.L., *supra* reference 7 at 14-16.
15. Pound, R., *supra* reference 12 at 47.
16. Driver, G.R., and Miles, J.C., *The Babylonian Laws*, 2 Vols. (1952, 1955).
17. *Exodus* 21:1-23:9, *Deuteronomy* 22:1-25:19.
18. *Exodus* 21:24.
19. Newbury, J., publ., *Mother Goose Rhymes* (1765).
20. Cohen, M.R., *Reason and Law* 52-54, The Free Press (1950), Collier Books Edition, New York, NY (1961).
21. Holmes, O.W., *The Common Law* 2-38, Little, Brown & Co., Boston, MA (1881).
22. Pound, R., *supra* reference 12 at 74.
23. Beveridge, W.I.B., *The Art of Scientific Investigation* 142-43, Vintage Books, New York, NY (1957).
24. Smith, M., *supra* reference 2.
25. White, G.E., *Tort Law in America—An Intellectual History* 62, Oxford University Press, Inc. (1980).
26. Prosser, W.L., *supra* reference 7 at 7.
27. White, G.E., *supra* reference 25 at 231-32.
28. Anonymous, Y.B. Edw. IV, f.7, pl.18 (King's Bench, 1466).

29. *Lambert v. Bessey*, T. Raym. 421, 83 Eng. Rep. 220 (1681).
30. Maitland, F.W., *The Forms of Action at Common Law*, Cambridge University Press, London (1962).
31. Kionka, E.J., *Torts in a Nutshell* 35, West Publishing Co., St. Paul, MN (1977).
32. *Winterbottom v. Wright*, 10 M.&W. 109, 152 Eng. Rep. 402 (1842).
33. Bohlen, F.H., *Studies in the Law of Torts* 76-80, The Bobs-Merrill Co., Indianapolis, IN (1926).
34. *Brown v. Kendall*, 60 Mass. (6 Cush.) 292 (1850).
35. *Rylands v. Fletcher*, L.R. 3 H.L. 330 (1868).
36. Hoover, H.C., former President of the United States, quoted by R.L. Smith in Alpha Sigma Mu Lecture, *Engineers in Turmoil*, ASM News 4-5 (January 1983).
37. Florman, S.C., *The Existential Pleasures of Engineering* 3-10, St. Martin's Press, New York, NY (1976).
38. *Losee v. Buchanan*, 51 N.Y. 476 (1873).
39. Holmes, O.W., *supra* reference 21 at 94-95.
40. *Huset v. J. I. Case Threshing Machine Company*, 120 F. 865 (8th Cir.) (1903).
41. Hilliard, F., *The Law of Torts or Private Wrongs* (2 vols.), Little-Brown & Co., Boston, MA (1859).
42. American Law Institute, *Restatement (Second) of the Law: Torts* Section 282, American Law Institute Publishers, St. Paul, MN (1965).
43. Bohlen, F.H., *The Basis of Affirmative Obligations in the Law of Tort*, 53 University of Pennsylvania Law Review 209, 280-285, 289-310 (1905).
44. Prosser, W.L., *supra* reference 7 at 530-31.
45. *Thomas v. Winchester*, 6 N.Y. 397 (1852).
46. *Mazetti v. Armour & Co.*, 75 Wash. 622, 135 P. 633 (1913).
47. *MacPherson v. Buick Motor Co., supra* reference 5.
48. *Baxter v. Ford Motor Co.*, 168 Wash. 456, 12 P.2d 409 (1932).
49. *Escola v. Coca Cola Bottling Co. of Fresno*, 24 Cal.2d 453, 150 P.2d 436 (1944).
50. Prosser, W.L., *The Assault Upon the Citadel (Strict Liability to the Consumer)*, 69 Yale Law Journal 1099, 1120-21 (1960).
51. *Spence v. Three Rivers Builders and Masonry Supply, Inc.*, 353 Mich. 120, 90 N.W.2d 873 (1958).
52. *Henningsen v. Bloomfield Motors, Inc.*, 32 N.J. 358, 161 A.2d 69 (1960).
53. *Greenman v. Yuba Power Products, Inc.*, 59 Cal.2d 57, 27 Cal. Reptr. 697, 377 P.2d 897 (1963).
54. Prosser, W.L., *The Fall of the Citadel (Strict Liability to the Consumer)*, 50 Minnesota Law Review 791 (1966).
55. Holmes, O.W., *supra* reference 21 at 96.
56. Prosser, W.L., *supra* reference 7 at 543.
57. Prosser, W.L., *supra* reference 50.
58. *Escola v. Coca Cola Bottling Co. of Fresno, supra* reference 49.
59. U.S. Interagency Task Force on Product Liability, *Insurance Report*, U.S. Department of Commerce (1977), available from National Technical Information Service, Springfield, VA 22161.
60. Rosenberg, M.H., *Prospects for Federal Legislation on Product Liability*, Proceedings, PLP-78 at 145-51, Product Liability Prevention Conference, Philadelphia, PA (August 21-23, 1978).

61. *Product Liability Gets New Options*, Business Week, August 31, 1981.
62. *Congressional Record*, S.403, 95th Congress, 1st Session, (1977).
63. Stone, B., *Uniform Commercial Code in A Nutshell* at 1-8, West Publishing Co., St. Paul, MN (1975).
64. *Supra* reference 61.
65. Barrett, E.T., *Commerce Secretary Announces Administration Endorsement for Product Liability Self-Insurance Bill*, Proceedings PLP-79 at 43, Product Liability Prevention Conference, New York (October 22-24, 1979).
66. *Supra.* reference 59.

4

Your Vulnerability

THE COURTS: AN UNINVITED BUSINESS PARTNER

Accessibility to Company Information

When a need arises for increasing staff or replacing someone, we search for the "right person" with considerable thought and care. There are sound reasons for doing so; for there is too much at stake to act hastily or thoughtlessly. The higher the level of the position's responsibility and the broader the access to company information, the greater the attention we give to recruitment and selection.

The process can take months and a lot of money to fill high-level positions carrying authority that can affect the viability of the company and its destiny. It can involve a selection committee working with executive search consultants, innumerable interviews and painstaking series of decisions to narrow the choice to that one of the dozens of qualified candidates who most closely matches the organization's requirements. The time and effort expended in such searches are considered justified since we are extremely selective about whom we trust with decision-making responsibilities and access to corporate information.

Yet, whether we realize it or not, every manufacturing company in today's business world is vulnerable to suddenly finding itself in intimate "partnership" with someone that it does not know, did not choose, and one it would not have chosen if it had desired a partner. It is one that does not have the firm's interests at heart at all; in fact, its purpose is downright hostile and subversive to the company's objectives.

No executive in his right mind would even momentarily consider such an absurd possibility, let alone tolerate it. Nevertheless, every manufacturer and product marketing and sales organization is living under the constant threat of acquiring such an unwanted, uninvited and unwelcome partner. That "partner" is a civil law court and jury.

It may be a shock to realize that virtually everything the company has and does is subject to their relentless scrutiny. Of course, the court and jury are not the only ones with this access; they are merely the ones at the end of the line. Once a company is a named defendant in a products lawsuit, it can expect a horde of perfect strangers to descend upon its operations. Before long, they will become constant companions, though altogether unwanted. These people are attorneys, insurers representatives and outside experts. Under today's liberal rules of full disclosure governing legal discovery, their access to the company is practically unlimited.

Sooner or later in the lawsuit, everything will be dragged out into the light, sifted again and again, handled, scrutinized and gone over with the proverbial fine-toothed comb: files, records, documents, letters, internal memoranda and notes; sketches, engineering drawings and product specifications; manufacturing standards, tolerances and formulations with complete lists of ingredients; names of suppliers of raw materials and component parts; test data; laboratory reports; purchase specifications and requisitions; customer complaints; sales orders and figures; service histories and user comments; personnel records; advertising literature, brochures and operating manuals; pricing schedules; financial statements; patents and much else, including investigations of the personal affairs of employees, questioning competitors and former (perhaps disgruntled) employees.

It's not an attractive prospect. The scope of the discovery process in civil cases during post-Watergate years has become extremely liberal. Its purpose is to assure that nothing significant to the outcome of the case is overlooked. This principle is summarized in the following statement by the United States Supreme Court:

> The very integrity of the judicial system and public confidence in the system depend on full disclosure of all the facts within the framework of the rules of evidence. (*United States v. Nixon*)[1]

In the spirit of this comment, the Federal Rules of Civil Procedure spell out the scope of legal discovery in more detail:

> Parties may obtain discovery regarding any matter, not privileged, which is relevant to the subject matter involved in the pending action, whether it relates to the claim or defense of the party seeking recovery or to the claim or defense of any other party, including the existence, description, nature, custody, condition and location of any books, documents, or other tangible things and the identity and location of persons having knowledge of any discoverable matter. It is not ground for objection that the information sought will be inadmissible in the trial if the information sought appears reasonably calculated to lead to the discovery of admissible evidence.[2]

In discussing legal rules that create products liability, our emphasis has been upon how they have become threats to manufacturers. This is consistent with the theme and targeted readership of this book; however, it is worthwhile noting that discovery rules apply to both sides. Not only can these liberalized discovery rules make life difficult for a defendant manufacturer in providing a plaintiff attorney with a mountain of material with which to wage an offensive campaign; but they can be a tremendous advantage in erecting a strong defense as well. They allow the defense the same opportunity to get facts surrounding the plaintiff's claims, such as how he may have misused the product, his history of litigation, complete medical details of his injury, and anything else relevant to the case.

The excerpt from the Federal Rules of Civil Procedure states that courts may agree to regard certain matters as "privileged." This provision allows for exclusion from discovery of trade secrets, confidential research, profit margins and other commercially sensitive information.[3] Nevertheless, courts tend to look with suspicion upon any such requests for privileged status and they must be convinced that denial of discovery access is justified. Exclusion is not granted automatically upon request.

As might be expected, there are various undesirable consequences in store for defendants who thwart discovery processes and attempt to withhold facts, evidence and access to relevant information.[4] It is not beyond the realm of possibility for a court to enter a default judgment against a defendant who fails to comply with discovery requests.[5]

It is well to note, however, that every state does not follow the federal rules governing discovery and evidence, although many do. The trend is in the direction of full disclosure and it is prudent to assume that this is the climate that will be facing future litigants in civil actions.

How Would It Appear to a Court and Jury?

Now, to bring all of this down to matters of practical everyday concern, it is useful to stop to consider how everything in a firm's records (and other "discoverable" things within the purview of the liberalized rules) would appear in court when presented—not by a friendly public relations director—but by an opposing attorney. This examination is not confined to documents, but includes products, components, manufacturing procedures, as well. They are subject to review, dissection and analysis by opposing attorneys and experts they have retained. Needless to say, none of this will be seen in its most favorable light; it will be presented and examined out of context and probably without an opportunity for the defendant to explain apparently "incriminating" entries and practices.

What is even more disturbing is that many of those reviewing what is presented in court and are drawing conclusions about it will, in all likelihood, not be professionally competent to do so. We are not talking about testimony of expert technical witnesses here, but about the weighing of that testimony and all the evidence and from it drawing conclusions. It is almost certain that those making these decisions will be unfamiliar with technical matters and have no knowledge of engineering or manufacturing operations. We can expect that the members of the jury will have been chosen in such a way to exclude technically competent individuals who may understand the details of what the defendant is trying to present. This exclusion of technically competent people is done deliberately, and permitted by the court and the procedural rules of civil actions, to avoid prejudices and other bothersome obstructions to the opposing attorney in constructing his argument and presenting his case. He needs docile folk who accept at face value what they're told, not technical specialists accustomed to deferring decisions until they have considered every possibility from every angle and reaching conclusions through scientific reasoning.

It is always a useful and enlightening, but sometimes frightening, exercise to occasionally take a few steps back from the intricacies of our daily grind and to look at what we design, write and do from the standpoint of a court and jury. In other words, to ask ourselves how it all would appear to a jury of laymen, completely unfamiliar with technical matters; but a jury nevertheless charged to examine everything related to the manufacture of some product that is claimed to have caused someone's injury.

It would even be rewarding to strive to make such a court-perspective review a routine part of everything we do. With a little practice, it can become automatic. Such an exercise, as simple as it is, can be of immense help in avoiding a possibly embarassing situation when we may someday be called into court to explain something we wrote, did or said (or didn't write, do or say) perhaps in all innocence at the time, but that now makes us appear careless, negligent or unconcerned over the safety of users of our products.

Obviously, the need for such an objective evaluation (by someone "standing in the jury's shoes") extends beyond individuals. What is required is for *everyone* in the organization, individually and collectively, to develop this kind of thinking. No one individual can create, produce, and market a given product. It is a team effort. So, too, are responsibility for prevention of claims and, when the inevitable claim is filed against the company, responsibility for defense.

But a strong defense position is not something that can be brought about at will or by corporate edict after a claim is filed. It's too late then. A strong defense must be built item-upon-item, task-by-task, and day-by-day, over a period of time. The court must see a consistent pattern of good habits, not a spasmodic twitch of response to a fleeting sense of guilt in a half-hearted attempt to hide a shabby track record of neglect. The spirit underlying effective products liability prevention is an attitude of individual concern and responsible behavior that must pervade the whole organization from top to bottom. It must become a way of life. When it does, no manufacturer need fear products claims; for he knows that when the day of reckoning comes and the company is called before the court and all its deeds are spread before the unsympathetic scrutiny of a court and jury the company can stand proud, confident that it has nothing to hide and can defend its actions and products from a position of strength. It's something money cannot buy.

INDUSTRY'S NEW "ENGINEERING STANDARDS"

A Need for Standards

Most development engineers regard standards as a necessary evil. The work of design and development of structures, processes and products is personally satisfying to engineers, even if it takes years of painstaking computations, tests and evaluations of prototypes. The reward lies in the successful achievement of the program or project objectives and that satisfaction makes all the toil worthwhile.

As exhilarating as engineering achievements can be, a successful development eventually leads to the mundane task of preparing specifications and standards for what was developed. If it is to have any practical utility; if others are to ever use the concept, formula, product, process or technique; the thing must be defined, and to do that a whole array of limits must be defined.

There are all sorts of limits: limits on dimensions, weights, materials, compositions, properties, costs and many others. Of course, research or development engineers know some of these already since logical and organized experimentation demand rigid adherence to control of variables. Yet, many variables that must be addressed in commercialization of an innovation may never have had to be considered during its development. Far too many creative young engineers have become disenchanted when post-development-triumph turns to the need for defining for a cold and skeptical outside world what they had perfected within the comfortable surroundings of the laboratory. In many respects, this end of the development stage is far more difficult, costly, time-consuming and frustrating to the engineer than the experimental work itself.

One of the traits "that separates the men from the boys" in R&D is not necessarily technical competence but ability to foresee the need for defining the end-product in terms of feasible and cost-effective commercialization, including compliance with existing standards. Sometimes standards must be revised or new ones written for a new product. Many technically excellent products have never left the laboratory because during their development someone failed to consider these factors adequately. This is one of the major responsibilities of the R&D Director; to make certain potentially good products don't die during adolescence or early adulthood because they were not properly prepared for the real world.

Whether engineers like working with standards or they don't, it is an essential part of an engineer's life. Without standards, an engineer's work becomes indistinguishable from that of a shadetree tinkerer. Engineering without standards is inconceivable; in fact, organized civilization without them would turn to chaos. Each dimension and instrument reading we make must be backed up by a standard or the data are worthless. Without design and production standards the manufacturer could never assemble a product profitably or manufacture it in quantity. And without quality standards, the market would not accept it. Juran[6] identifies six general purposes or "bases for regulation" or reasons for standardization: metrology, interchangeability, technological definition, safety and health of the citizenry and of the state, and economics.

In recent years we have become engulfed by a proliferation of standards. To illustrate, the computer-produced Index of U.S. Voluntary Engineering Standards[7] lists over 20,000 standards that have been developed and published by some 360 engineering organizations in this country. This listing includes only trade association and voluntary consensus industry standards; it does *not* include military, government and individual company standards. The Department of Defense Index of Specifications and Standards (DODISS), alone, lists over 40,000 MIL-specifications.

The American Society for Testing and Materials (ASTM) has more than 7,500 published standards in its 66-volume Annual Book of ASTM Standards. These have been prepared by 140 main technical committees comprising about 2,000 subcommittees and sections. Its current membership is nearly 30,000 organizations and individuals.[8]

It has been estimated that there are now well over one million published engineering standards in use in the United States and the number is increasing every day. This is an inevitable result of the interplay of the various "Factors Contributing to the Products Liability Crisis" described in Chapter 2.

Without doubt, it is an overwhelming task for an engineer to keep pace with the flood of standards and their amendments. This difficulty, however, does not relieve engineers of the responsibility to assure that their products comply with them.

Clearly, there is a growing and critical need for manufacturers (or someone) to devise methods for dealing with this profusion of standards; to identify those pertinent to specific manufacturing operations, product lines and markets; to monitor developments in the area; and to permit their easy access and prompt retrieval. Computer technology certainly exists for doing so, but no comprehensive system has yet been developed.

Standards Compliance and its Effects

A good many engineers today feel that if *they* have difficulty in keeping up to date on standards developments, then plaintiffs' attorneys—not trained in technical subjects—must be completely snowed under by the blizzard. They reason that, if so, it is extremely unlikely that an attorney will find, let alone recognize the relevance of, some obscure specification that the manufacturer himself may have overlooked in designing, manufacturing and marketing his product.

This is risky reasoning. In the field of tort law there are increasing numbers of plaintiffs' attorneys with high levels of expertise in various technical specialties. Some of them have engineering degrees or medical degrees in addition to law degrees and some have these specialists on their staff. And, for those without personal expertise, there are comprehensive guidebooks for plaintiffs' attorneys, updated annually with cumulative supplements available on subscription that contain extensive lists of current sources of technical information including names and addresses of experts covering the entire spectrum of specialties involved in products lawsuits.[9]

Some attorneys practice nationwide with offices in principal cities, representing an array of specialized technical expertise and regional familiarity. In addition to this, groups of plaintiffs' attorneys have organized informational pools permitting their members to share data on "target" products, manufacturers and their previous litigation experiences and defenses.[10,11] Some of these groups are becoming highly sophisticated in their development of software for computerized information storage and retrieval through multi-access data bases and user-equipped telephone modems.[12,13]

The point of all this is that we must assume that, by whatever means, an opposing attorney is familiar with current standards covering the products in question, with all their nuances and weaknesses, and probably has hard copies of relevant specifications and knows how they apply to the case at hand. It is not beyond the realm of possibility that the plaintiff's access to technical information, including pertinent safety standards, and his understanding of them could be more complete than that of the manufacturer-defendant. This gives him an unhealthy advantage over the manufacturer-defendant, no matter how solidly the manufacturer believes in the attributes of his products.

It is worth mentioning that even if a manufacturer could be 100 percent certain that his product and everything connected with it satisfied every relevant technical specification and safety standard, he still could be held liable for a product-caused injury. There are a number of ways this might occur.

One is through the plaintiff bringing suit under the concept of strict liability. Later in this chapter we will see how a strict liability action looks at *the product* and its defectiveness; not at the manufacturer and his conduct. If the court finds the manufacturer's product defective and that its defectiveness caused the plaintiff's injury, it is useless to insist that the product met every existing specification and standard. The court's reply to such a statement would be that the injury proves the inadequacy of existing standards. Hear what one plaintiffs' attorney has to say about voluntary industry standards:

> Standards and codes represent a low-level consensus of these combined interest groups: industry, unions, insurance, government, users, suppliers, etc. . . . Lawyers must use standards and codes to recognize and prove liability and ridicule the standards which are much less than due care.[14]

The National Commission on Product Safety in its *Final Report* sounded the same note:

> Since approval of a voluntary standard requires a consensus of those concerned, the participating manufacturers tend to agree on safety levels that are least costly and troublesome. . . . If a manufacturer fails to meet standards his own industry considers minimal, the evidence should be conclusive proof of fault. If a product does meet the industry standard, this evidence of due care may be rebutted by proof that the entire industry has been lax. Safety standards of industry . . . seldom satisfy objective requirements and are promulgated largely without effective consumer participation.[15]

This is a succinct description of the weight the law gives code compliance by a product manufacturer: failure to meet them is presumptive evidence of negligence but full compliance does not confer immunity to liability. It is well for the engineer to also keep in mind in this context the fact that most engineering codes and even government standards represent *minimal* standards. Responsible design and construction call for substantially more.

There have been a number of court decisions against defendants despite their conformance to all existing codes and standards in the manufacture of their products. It is worth examining the court's reasoning on some of the key cases as these represent the law in most jurisdictions.

A landmark case in 1932 involved a boiler explosion injuring people and causing property damage in the vicinity. The defendant manufacturer showed that it had complied with all existing codes and safety practices; nevertheless, it was held liable. In its decision the court said:

> The fact that it was not the practice of tube manufacturers generally to use these tests [metallographic evaluation of microstructure of the steel], and that such an examination is not incorporated in the specifications of the American Society of Mechanical Engineers, or required or provided for in the Wisconsin Boiler Code is certainly strong evidence against the position taken by [professors of metallurgy testifying during the trial for the plaintiff]; but it does not dispose of their evidence as a matter of law. The fact that the custom of manufacturers generally was followed is evidence of due care, *but it does*

*not establish its exercise as a matter of law.*Obviously, manufacturers cannot, by concurring in a careless or dangerous method of manufacture, establish their own standard of care. (*Marsh Wood Products Co. v. Babcock & Wilcox Co.*)[16] (emphasis added)

And, in another frequently-cited decision, Judge Learned Hand in the same year clearly pointed out that standards established by the law must supersede and overrule industry's standards:

There are, no doubt, cases where courts seem to make the general . . . [industry practice] the standard of proper diligence. . . . a whole [industry] may have unduly lagged in the adoption of new and available devices [or practices]. *It never may set its own test,* however persuasive be its usages. *Courts must in the end say what is required*; there are precautions so imperative that even their universal disregard will not excuse their omission. (*The T. J. Hooper*)[17] (emphasis added)

While compliance even to "the letter of the law" in legislated standards does not confer immunity to products liability, it does at least provide some evidence that the manufacturer exercised due care. While we may safely assume that *failure* to comply with some federal, state or industry product standard is undesirable, it is worth considering its consequences and the extent of the liability exposure it incurs. As we will soon see, product safety statutes provide penalties for their violation and this, in itself, constitutes liability of a sort. However, in the context of the larger issues of products liability that we are concerned with here, failure to comply with legislated standards has more serious implications than liability for payment of the fines imposed for statutory infractions.

In a legal action, evidence of a manufacturer's violation of product safety statutes does not automatically confer liability for harm or injuries from the existence or use of the product, although it may. It all depends upon the product and the statute. Obviously, if a product is made "defective" through violation of some statutory standard, and its defectiveness is the cause of the injury or harm, the manufacturer may be held liable. But, in the strict sense, the products liability in this instance flows from the product's defectiveness and not from the statutory violation. The point is that a product is not *necessarily* "defective" because it represents a statutory violation.

There are a number of roads leading to products liability. One of them is through defectiveness in the product itself. Another is through proof of negligence of the manufacturer, and this is where statutory violations can open the door to trouble.

Inanimate products do not violate statutes and laws; people (and manufacturers) do. So failure of a manufacturer to comply with existing law (federal or state legislation or municipal ordinance) covering his product may be construed as evidence of negligence or lack of due care.[18-21] Legislation enacted to protect the public from certain hazards establishes standards of care that create *duties* of due care for manufacturers and others in the product marketing and distribution chain. If someone is injured and the injury is traceable to violation of a legislated standard, it is not difficult for a court to find that the manufacturer's breach of his duty of due care caused the injury and, therefore, that the manufacturer should be liable for those injuries.

It was stated in a court decision many years ago that:

> Negligence is the breach of legal duty. It is immaterial whether the duty is one imposed by the rule of common law . . . or is imposed by a statute. . . . The only difference is that in the one case the measure of legal duty is to be determined upon common law principles, while in the other the statute fixes it, so that the violation of the statute constitutes conclusive evidence of negligence, or, in other words, negligence per se.(*Osborne v. McMasters*)[22]

In evaluating exposure to products liability it is important to consider legal implications of one's actions broadly. This requires not only a comprehensive understanding of the principles of common law but also a working knowledge of statutes that apply; for there can be synergistic relationships between the two that can create a degree of liability that, for all practical purposes, may be considered absolute.

Courts and Legislatures as Standards-Makers

So far in this discussion, we have been dealing with the need to comply with relevant industry and government standards. Compliance with them is expected by the law of prudent and careful manufacturers but compliance does not immunize against liability. The preceding excerpts from court decisions plainly state that while industry is expected to develop standards, these do not overrule in a court of law; for "courts must in the end say what is required."[23]

What we have, then, are independent "standards-making bodies" spread all across this country—the courts of civil law—that are fashioning engineering codes for industry. These are true codes as they deal with the product's design; its composition, construction, safety, and reliability; risk-benefit assessments, profit incentives and every aspect of communication between manufacturer and product user or consumer, and the manufacturer's duties to them. It even dictates what its duties are to those who may not even know of the product's existence but may still be affected by it or its existence.

Besides the courts, there are a great many government agencies having power conferred by Congress or state legislatures to similarly make standards that industry must follow.[24-26] The consequences of neglecting to conform to these court-made and government-made standards are no less serious than are failures to conform to industry's engineering standards. In some respects they can be more damaging to the company, since most of industry's standards include built-in redundancies, cross-checks and compliance audits (for example, proof tests, trial runs, safety factors, provision for automatic sensors and feedback controls). These features act as safeguards against inadvertent omission of critical details.

"Non-industry-developed" standards (those developed by courts and government agencies) have no fail-safe provisions. It is up to each manufacturer to, first, keep abreast of the existence of these standards and their requirements; and secondly, to devise and implement its own system of audits, controls and fail-safe procedures. Methods for achieving this are covered in subsequent chapters of this book.

As we review standards that have been set by courts and legislatures, particularly those devised by courts, it is important to recall the fundamental differences between scientific law and "legal" law already noted. We cannot expect court-made standards to be as logical, predictable, factual and technically competent as the engineering standards we deal with each day. They are not "consensus standards" by any stretch of the imagination but a product of adversary proceedings, conceived in a climate charged with human emotion. And they are retrospective, not prospective. While successive revisions of engineering standards may build on experiences gleaned from past events, they are intended primarily as guidelines for future action. But court-made standards deal with past events, usually isolated occurrences.

Court-made standards even differ on how facts are judged in arriving at a conclusion. Engineers familiar with statistical bases for establishing scientific certainty will be confused over civil law's basis for reaching decisions. It only requires "a preponderance of evidence" for drawing conclusions and reaching a decision. "More likely than not," or 51 percent certainty, is all that's needed. This difference has bewildered many technical experts when testifying in court on their certainty over some conclusion they have drawn. Attempts to apply scientific reasoning and concepts of certainty to courtroom testimony in a civil case can be confusing at best, and sometimes disastrous when plaintiffs' attorneys seize upon the witness' bewilderment over the "certainty standard" as an opportunity to create in jurors' minds doubts about the validity of the testimony.

Before we examine specific legislated and judicially-created standards that affect manufacturers' products liability, it is worthwhile to briefly compare the two sources of these laws or standards.

Judicially-Enacted Standards vs. Legislated Standards

Traditionally, the United States is considered a "common law jurisdiction" whose laws stem primarily from court decisions. Any law student will attest to the need to study and brief hundreds of cases—the written decisions of appellate courts that constitute this nation's common law. Nevertheless, in actual practice, legislative or statutory law—that contained in statutes or "acts" of legislatures—often dominates many legal issues. All legislatures create laws, from local government ordinances to acts of Congress. Of most significance to products liability are laws enacted by Congress (including those enacted by federal agencies under Congressional authority) and by the state legislatures.

Much controversy has arisen over the question of which law has precedence; common law or that enacted by legislatures. There have been many views on it. For our purposes, perhaps the best explanation is that given by a federal court in a 1968 decision involving a question over whether or not the National Traffic Safety Act, a "legislated" law, superseded common law principles on the same general subject:

> It is apparent that the National Traffic Safety Act is intended to be supplementary of and in addition to the common law of negligence and product liability. The common law is not sterile or rigid and serves the best interests of society by adapting standards of conduct and responsibility that fairly meet the emerging and developing needs of our time. The common law standard of a duty to use reasonable care in light of all the circumstances can at least serve the needs of our society until the legislature imposes higher standards. (*Larsen v. General Motors Corp.*)[27]

As may be inferred from the tone of this excerpt from the court's decision, legislatures and courts are reluctant to countermand or rescind common law rules. The key phrase in the above excerpt is "supplementary of and in addition to the common law." Unless clearly stated otherwise, legislation does not cancel established common law principles. Also, courts have determined that federal legislation will preempt other state laws only when local rules frustrate the full effectiveness of federal law or when compliance with both is physically impossible. This should be kept in mind when encountering any real or apparent discrepancy upon comparison of products liability law of a given jurisdiction with federally legislated acts.

At first, it would seem that legislated law, statutes and acts, would be preferable over court-made (case-derived) law in that they would be easier to apply. Case law originates from actual disputes between individual plaintiffs and defendants and fact situations peculiar to them. Legislated law, it would seem, would have broader application and, therefore, be more useful. In some respects this is true but a good many disputes have arisen over "legislative intent"—or what the legislature really had in mind when it created some act. Remember that most questions must be answered, not by the legislatures that created the law, but by the courts. It's their job to interpret the law and apply it to the situations that come before them.

So the thrust or meaning of some legislated act simply comes down to how it is interpreted by courts. There are a good number of legislated acts that, through a series of exceptionally broad (or narrow) interpretive court decisions, now are applied to situations that were far from the minds of the original legislators. Yet, they serve the needs of justice, and persist. No matter how lucidly and carefully drafted, legislated laws are seldom the "last word" on the subject. And it is only after new legislated acts have come before the courts that we can know with any degree of certainty what their probable impact will be. If the first courts to decide a case on the basis of a given legislated law hold to a narrow interpretation, that interpretation sets the stage for others to follow. In other words, those initial interpretations constitute legal precedents for subsequent cases and these are largely independent of actual legislative intent, whatever that may have been.

There are other factors to consider in comparing common or judicial law with legislated law. Judicial law is a composite of court decisions stemming from individual disputes, past occurrences and usually involves issues of limited application to other situations. One of the functions of legislated law is to bridge gaps in common law that exist because of this characteristic of judicial decisions applying to specific fact situations and to provide continuity between peaks of judicial precedent.

By its nature, judicial law looks backward to some past situation. Its holdings are tailored to fit *that* case. Legislated law, on the other hand, looks forward in contemplation of situations that are predictable and plausible, but yet to occur. Also, judicial law is bound to the doctrine of *stare decisis*. As noted earlier, this provides some measure of stability and predictability through avoiding sweeping changes in one step; it accomplishes changes gradually through a series of small steps and over a period of time. Legislatures are not so constrained but theoretically are free to enact whatever degree of change they deem society requires at the time they enact the law.

In this country, legislated law is usually the product of a complicated and involved process and not simply the outcome of a pronounced edict. Most federal legislation is preceded by a series of proposals with notices published in the *Federal Register*, preliminary studies, hearings that consider the interests of all concerned, presentation of expert testimony and evidence, a series of committee and sub-committee recommendations and drafts of bills. These may be followed by more hearings, debates and modified drafts and this may go on for months and even years before it all matures into a final legislated act. As a result of attempts to satisfy all concerned interests, most enacted legislation is a compromise of the original objectives. Sometimes the final bill bears little resemblance to early drafts.

Legislation tends to have more uniformity than law deduced from judicial decisions made within given jurisdictional boundaries. This is because legislation represents an amalgam of current interests, is more specific, predictable and concise. During the preliminary stages of the lawmaking process, those who will be most affected by it usually have an opportunity to have a voice in it and, later, all have advanced notice of its enactment.

Considering the potential that exists for gross disparities between judicial (common) law and legislative law, the two are generally in remarkable harmony. Perhaps this is because of the leveling influence of courts through exercising their prerogative of interpretation. Differences do exist and disputes arise but these are most frequent in the fringe areas, seldom on fundamental issues.

Legislation Affecting Products Liability

Does Not Rescind Industry Standards. It should be recognized at the outset that *any* failure to comply with relevant existing codes and standards is regarded by courts as evidence of lack of due care. Such evidence is difficult, if not impossible, to refute and will weigh heavily against the defendant in a products liability action.

In the discussions that follow, we will be emphasizing the effects legislation has had upon creating products liability standards for industry. However, such emphasis should not be construed to mean that these are more important than engineering standards developed through trade associations or voluntary consensus standards-making organizations (like SAE, ASTM and ASME). Many legislated standards, at all government levels, have adopted such industry engineering standards as are pertinent and have incorporated them into their standards. Therefore, there is some overlap through reference to existing engineering standards; but for a full picture of what the law requires it is necessary for the engineer to become familiar with the legislation itself. This is in addition to whatever engineering standards or portions of them that might be incorporated through reference.

The subject of standards governing products liability is a complex one, it's not easily mastered and takes considerable attention to maintain awareness of changes and their implications. But avoidance of products lawsuits and their consequences requires a good working knowledge of these standards; at the very least, a familiarity with those pertinent to one's particular line of products and their markets.

In a number of respects this is a new requirement for engineers. I say "engineers" because the breadth and depth of today's standards influencing products liability require each individual associated with the design, production and marketing of the product to be familiar with the standards; the responsibility can no longer be shifted over to the Quality Control department, legal counsel or someone or other group in the company.

Also, it is a new requirement from the standpoint of information sources that must be consulted. Most engineers have little idea of where to locate copies of government regulations affecting the products they deal with and practically none know how to find the common law requirements (a later chapter gives recommendations on locating these materials). This has traditionally been regarded the sacred province of the firm's attorneys and legal counsel; the presumption being that only they are qualified to read and interpret the law.

There is no suggestion here that a firm curtail contacts between legal counsel and its staff; quite the opposite. In today's litigious climate the need for frequent communication with legal counsel is even more acute than ever. What is suggested, however, is that the frequency of contact that is typical of most engineering staffs in our manufacturing industries is far less than it ought to be.

Besides this, engineers must change their attitude with respect to delegating "legal matters" to lawyers. The legal blinders we all have should be removed. The legal climate we are working in today makes it essential that all become acquainted with the fundamentals of what the law expects of us and our products, how to find that law, and how to keep informed of changes and their effects on what we do, make and say.

In the descriptions that follow, space does not permit more than a cursory summary of the more relevant legislated acts. These summaries are not intended to be exhaustive or complete in any sense, but are included to alert the engineer to some of the more significant legislation affecting products liability. Our attention will be generally confined to federal enactments, but it should be mentioned that some states have passed their own regulations covering specific types of products. It is left to the reader to peruse the references and determine his state regulations for himself; for each product-market combination is unique, and so is every company, its vulnerabilities and, sometimes, the requirements of its legal jurisdictions (locations where it transacts business).

Since, because of the wide diversity of engineering disciplines and responsibilities represented by our readers, we must deal in generalities; it is strongly recommended that study of supplementary materials include discussions with the firm's legal counsel or others acquainted with the local law and the company's products. This is necessary to determine how to most effectively satisfy requirements for a *specific* product line and markets while minimizing liability exposure. In fact, it is desirable for all engineers to devote some time to formal study of these subjects. If they are not offered in engineering school curricula (as they should be) they can be found in university extension programs, seminars, workshops and individual-study courses.

Warranty Legislation. *Early Concepts.* A warranty is simply a promise that something is true. Its use in commercial transactions probably predates recorded history. The proliferation of products and their makers during the Industrial Revolution brought into use various identifying imprints such as merchant marks, watermarks and hallmarks. Primarily, these identified the maker but also were useful in identifying the level of quality of the merchandise.

Mere stamping or marking of a product carried with it a promise of some level of quality or distinctive characteristic and it offered the purchaser assurance that the item or material was backed by the integrity of its maker and afforded traceability through the mark to the one who made the product. Even today, we frequently judge a product by the "mark" of its manufacturer (by brand names, trademarks, logos, symbols, etc.). Besides identity of the firm these marks represent value, prestige, or some unique quality. This is evident from the furor that can occur over trademark infringement and counterfeiting of products such as jewelry, toys, aircraft parts, and even designer clothing.

Early warranty law developed around the need to enforce promises made regarding quality of products or merchandise; whether the promise was expressed directly or implicitly by use of a mark or some other means. A cause of action at common law was based upon failure of the product or manufacturer to live up to the promise.

For various reasons, these concepts—fairly advanced for their day—gave way to the rule of *caveat emptor* (let the buyer beware). By the nineteenth century the buyer had the burden of inspecting and checking the product before buying it. Once the buyer judged it acceptable at the agreed-upon price and bought it, there was no recourse for failure of the product. The buyer accepted all risks.

An exception to the general rule of *caveat emptor* could be made, however, through specific agreement between the parties: an express warranty that modified the general rule. But this was regarded as part of the purchase contract and to this day warranties are frequently considered to be subjects for contract law and not tort law. Later, the concept of implied warranty evolved for certain types and classes of product, or wherever the application of *caveat emptor* was inappropriate because the buyer was incapable of inspecting and judging a product's quality or suitability (generally food, drink, and drugs, as discussed earlier).

The Uniform Commercial Code. The English Bills of Exchange Act by Parliament in 1882, followed by the English Sale of Goods Act in 1893, codified warranty rules then in existence. No doubt, this influenced passage of the Uniform Sales Act in the United States in 1906. It was adopted by some 40 states. Then, in 1957, the commissioners on uniform state laws drafted the Uniform Commercial Code (UCC).[28] Although, when and as-drafted, the UCC did not have the authority of law in any jurisdiction; its provisions have now been adopted by every state. There have been several modifications since its enactment and various states have made minor changes. But, with few exceptions, it is considered the uniform law of sales in this country.

The entire UCC is a formidably massive document contained in over 700 pages. As might be expected, the Code has created a great volume of literature that discusses it and comments on it. The Code covers the spectrum of details surrounding sales, including sales contracts, payment, shipment and storage of goods under contract and financing of sales transactions. However, the scope of the Code is confined to sale of goods and products. It does not include the purchase of professional services, although some services involve use of products and this could bring such transactions under the province of the UCC.

Our interest from the standpoint of products liability is primarily confined to only a few pages of Section 2 of the Code that deal with express and implied warranties.[29]

The UCC says that express warranties are created by affirmations, promises, descriptions and samples that are given or represented to the buyer while negotiating the sale.[30] The seller need not use specific terms such as "warranty" or "guarantee," or even intend to create a warranty, for one to exist.

The Code provides some leeway in allowing for sales talk or "puffery" in statements of opinions or value without creating an express warranty; that is, unless the statements were made as an inducement for the purchaser to buy. Obviously, it could be difficult after the fact for the seller to prove to the court's satisfaction that they were not made as inducements to buy, or that there was no intention to make such statements part of the transaction and that they should therefore not be construed as express warranties.

Despite this apparent loophole, it is advisable to play it safe and assume that all affirmations of facts, promises, or descriptions of goods, whether in words (directly to the buyer or indirectly through advertising) or through submitting samples or models, create express warranties under the UCC.

The significance of it all to products liability is that, if someone is injured through failure of a product to meet the seller's affirmations or promises, that failure constitutes a breach of express warranty and gives the injured party a cause of legal action against the seller. Such affirmations, promises or representations create liability that is virtually absolute and, therefore, deserve a good deal of caution. It is important to realize that we are not necessarily dealing with product failure due to defective design or manufacture; but with failure of the product to live up to the promises and affirmations of the seller, and regardless of whether such a product could live up to those promises.

In the previous chapter we saw how the concept of implied warranty played a key role in the development of products liability law. In contrast to express warranty, implied warranty does not require any affirmations or statements to have been made.

Section 2-314 of the UCC states that an *implied warranty of merchantability* exists in all sales where the seller is a merchant of goods of that kind.

The language defining "merchant" is deliberately specific to exclude, for example, occasional sales by individuals or incidental sales by plant owners of surplus or used equipment. The warranty implied is that the goods are of a quality that is fit for the *ordinary* purposes that such goods are used for. This is not very definitive and its precise meaning is left to the courts to interpret and determine for each situation. Obvious examples of unmerchantable products would be fuel additives for improving engine efficiency that corroded fuel lines, clothing flame-retardants that proved carcinogenic, and a food grinder that contaminated food with metallic particles.

What the Code has established is a minimum standard of quality for virtually all goods sold in business transactions. Fitness for "ordinary purposes" can be lost through defects that make the product dangerous to use, or through some quality or characteristic that causes damage or renders the product itself worthless. Such lack of fitness for ordinary purposes constitutes a breach of implied warranty and grounds for liability for damage traceable to that breach.

The previously discussed section of the UCC covers implied warranties of merchantability of fitness for *ordinary* purposes that are customary for products of that kind. Another section of the Code holds that an implied warranty of fitnesss for a *particular* purpose is created where the seller at the time of the sale has reason to know the specific purpose intended for the goods being purchased and that the buyer is relying on the skill or judgment of the seller in selecting or furnishing goods suitable for that particular purpose.[31]

A qualifying distinction, and an essential element in the creation of implied warranty of fitness for a particular purpose, is the buyer's reliance upon the seller's judgment or skill. Again, a breach of implied warranty would exist if the product proves to be unfit for the purpose. This would constitute grounds for the seller's liability for resulting harm or injury.

Note that an action for liability could be sustained against the seller (but probably not the manufacturer, unless it is the seller) under this rule even if there is no defect in the product. Once the seller who knows the buyer's intent for the product recommends a product that is unsuitable for the purpose, and knows the buyer is relying on his skill and judgment, he is liable for harm that may occur. This is despite the seller's best intentions, honest and sincere belief and self-confidence. Under these circumstances, the seller incurs liability that is virtually absolute and makes him a guarantor against harm.

The UCC recognizes that situations arise where it might be desirable to sell products without warranties. This could involve a sale of products that are used, worn, and "seconds" or inferior in some way. Section 2-316 of the Code permits the seller to disclaim warranty by a conspicuous written statement that must mention "merchantability." All implied warranties may be excluded through statements like "as-is" or other terminology to make the buyer aware that there are no implied warranties connected with the sale. As with most apparent loopholes in the law, here too there are some limitations. That is, despite the disclaimer, the seller may still be held liable if the court considers the disclaimer "unconscionable" as, for example, a disclaimer of responsibility for consequential damages for *personal injuries* associated with the use of a consumer product.[32]

Magnuson-Moss Warranty Act. The stated purpose of this 1975 legislation is

> [T]o improve the adequacy of information available to consumers, prevent deception, and improve competition in the marketing of consumer products ... [through providing] minimum disclosure standards for written consumer product warranties ... [and] minimum Federal content standards.[33]

The principal intent of this Act is to improve *consumer* protection, as in the late 1960s there was increasing evidence that the provisions of the UCC (intended primarily for *commercial* transactions) left consumers at a disadvantage.

Its scope covers tangible personal property normally used for personal, family or household purposes. Products that may be used for both personal and commercial purposes are defined as consumer products. Within its defined scope are separate items of equipment attached to real property, such as air conditioners, furnaces, siding, roofing and storm windows.[34]

Among its provisions are full and conspicuous disclosure in simple and readily understood language of the terms and conditions of consumer product warranties. Its subject matter includes names and addresses of all parties, identification of the products or parts covered, a description of what the remedy will be in the event of failure of the items covered to conform to the warranty, what the consumer's obligations are and what steps he should take to obtain performance of the warrantor's obligation, the time limitations that apply and information on legal remedies.

In addition to these provisions, this legislation and its amendments also specify pre-sale availability of terms of sale, the distinctions between "full" and "limited" warranties, warranty terms and format, service contracts and insurance, remedies for settlement of disputes, and policies on the legislation's implementation and enforcement.

While this legislation does not require warranties to accompany the sale of consumer products, it does impose specific duties and liabilities on those who do offer them. Its principal thrust is to eliminate the practice, detrimental to interests of consumer-purchasers (and allowed by the UCC), of embedding fine-print disclaimers of implied warranties within the fabric of written warranties.[35] It prevents sellers from using the subterfuge of warranties to strip away from unwary purchasers their rights to implied warranties that are available at common law.

Of course, the motivation for the seller to eliminate implied warranties is to avoid liability. As discussed in the previous chapter, these issues played a significant role in the development of the rule of strict liability, as two principal cases arose over attempts to avoid liability for injuries through disclaimers and notice requirements in written warranties.[36,37]

Notwithstanding provisions of this Act, the seller is still free to disclaim implied warranties through simply withholding a written warranty or service contract altogether. Also, even where a written warranty is given, the Act allows sellers to limit their liability for consequential damages stemming from breach of implied warranty if a written statement to this effect is *conspicuously* displayed on the written warranty.

Nevertheless, manufacturers and sellers should understand that courts are inclined to set aside (ignore) disclaimers that they regard as unconscionable or violations of public policy. The message to remember about disclaimers is that they are a poor substitute for making quality products. The only circumstances where their use may be above reproach are possibly transactions between commercial buyers and sellers who are able to bargain on equal footing and where both are fully acquainted with a product's construction, its attributes, functions and limitations. Yet, once a product leaves a commercial environment and exposes the public to risks of injury because of poor or marginal quality, the disclaimer that permitted the product to enter the marketplace will again be open to question.

Product Safety Legislation. *Consumer Product Safety Act.* This legislation had its beginnings in 1967 in the National Commission on Product Safety. In creating this Commission, Congress and the President declared that "the American consumer has a right to be protected against unreasonable risk of bodily harm from products purchased on the open market for the use of himself and his family."[38] Its mission was to:

> conduct a comprehensive study and investigation of the scope and adequacy of measures now employed to protect consumers against unreasonable risk of injuries which may be caused by hazardous household products . . . [and] to consider the identity of categories of household products . . . which may present an unreasonable hazard to the health and safety of the consuming public.[39]

In its report of June 1970 the Commission concluded that:

> The annual cost of the Nation of product-related injuries may exceed $5.5 billion . . . The exposure of consumers to unreasonable consumer product hazards is excessive by any standard of measurement. Because of the inadequacy of existing controls on product hazards, *we find a need for a major Federal role in the development and execution of methods to protect the American consumer.*[40] (emphasis added)

As a result of this study, Congress concluded that there were an unacceptable number of consumer products that presented unreasonable risks of injury and that the public should be protected against these risks. It found that complexities of consumer products and the diverse nature and abilities of consumers using them frequently resulted in their inability to anticipate risks and to adequately safeguard themselves. Existing federal authority for protecting consumers from exposure to such risks of injury was viewed as inadequate, as was control by state and local governments.

In response to the Commission's recommendation for the creation of a federal agency to regulate the safety of consumer products, Congress in 1972 enacted the Consumer Product Safety Act (CPSA) establishing the Consumer Product Safety Commission (CPSC).[41] The purposes of the Act are to protect the public against unreasonable risks of injury associated with consumer products; to assist consumers in evaluating the comparative safety of consumer products; to develop uniform safety standards for consumer products and minimize conflicting state and local regulations; and to promote research and investigation into the causes and prevention of product-related deaths, illnesses, and injuries.[42]

Several existing legislated acts formerly under the jurisdiction of other government agencies were combined within CPSC authority. These are the Federal Hazardous Substances Act,[43] previously under the Food and Drug Administration; the Poison Prevention Packaging Act,[44] previously under the FDA and the EPA; the Flammable Fabrics Act,[45] previously under the Commerce Department and the FTC; and the Refrigerator Safety Act,[46] previously under the Commerce Department.

The provisions of the CPSA exclude certain classes of products. These are: motor vehicles and related parts and equipment (under the National Highway Traffic Safety Administration); aircraft and related equipment (under the Federal Aviation Administration); tobacco and tobacco products and firearms and ammunition; pesticides; food, drugs, medical devices and cosmetics (under the Food and Drug Administration); boats (under the U.S. Coast Guard and Department of Transportation); and products that are not considered "consumer products" (see reference 47 for CPSA definition). The CPSA also excludes certain product *hazards* (not necessarily specific products) that are adequately controlled under the Occupational Safety and Health Act, the Clean Air Act, the Atomic Energy Act, and the Radiation Control for Health and Safety Act.

To carry out its purposes, the Act empowers the Consumer Products Safety Commission with broad authority. Among its functions are the collection, study and dissemination of data and information on causes and prevention of death, injury, and illness associated with consumer products. It may study and investigate injuries and resulting economic losses and conduct research investigations and tests on the safety of consumer products.

It may promulgate safety standards and requirements covering product performance, warnings and instructions for preventing injury. "Imminently dangerous consumer products" (those that present imminent and unreasonable risk of death, serious illness, or severe personal injury) may be seized and banned and the manufacturer prevented from stockpiling such products.

Manufacturers of products subject to CPSC standards may be required to issue certificates of conformance to testing programs prescribed by the CPSC. Manufacturers, distributors or retailers of products presenting "a substantial product hazard"[48] may be ordered to give public notice of the condition and to so notify those who received or purchased such products. They may be ordered to make these products comply with the applicable rules, repair the defect, replace the product, or refund the purchase price.

The CPSC has authority to enter and inspect a manufacturer's premises and product-compliance-related documents. It may refuse admission into the country any imported products that fail to comply with its rules. And it may order any person to submit written reports and answers to questions it may prescribe, and require by subpoena the attendance and testimony of witnesses and production of all relevant documentary evidence.

The Act declares that it is unlawful to manufacture for sale, distribute or import any non-conforming or banned consumer product. It is also unlawful to refuse or fail to permit access to or copying of records, to fail to establish or maintain records, to fail to make reports or provide information, to fail to permit entry or inspection of premises or to fail to comply with any rule or request for relevant data or information.

Violators are subject to civil penalties not to exceed $2,000 for each violation with violations of respective sections constituting separate offenses with respect to each consumer product involved. The maximum civil penalty for any series of violations shall not exceed $500,000.

Any person who knowingly and willfully violates acts prohibited under the CPSA after receiving notice of non-compliance from the CPSC is subject to criminal sanctions and shall be fined not more than $50,000 or be imprisoned not more than a year or both. In addition, any individual director, officer or agent of a corporation who knowingly and willfully authorizes, orders or performs any of the acts or practices constituting in whole or in part a violation of acts prohibited under the CPSA and who has knowledge of notice of non-compliance received by the corporation from the CPSC shall be subject to the same penalties.

Besides these penalties, U.S. district courts have jurisdiction to restrain violation of acts prohibited by the CPSA; restrain any person from manufacturing for sale, offering for sale, distributing in commerce, or importing into the U.S. a product in violation of orders issued in connection with products declared to be substantial product hazards; and to restrain any person from distributing in commerce products that do not comply with a CPSC rule.

The Commission established the National Electronic Injury Surveillance System (NEISS) to assist it in collecting and assembling data on deaths, injuries and illnesses associated with consumer products.[49,50] The reporting system collects reports of injuries from the emergency rooms of a nationwide sample of currently 73 (originally 119) hospitals. These reports include information on the patient's age, sex, location of the injuries to the body, treatment given and the consumer product involved.

Various computerized indices are generated from the data to show frequency and severity of injuries associated with (but not necessarily caused by) various consumer products. The results are interpreted to determine priority of attention required by the CPSC.[51]

Although the CPSC has been in existence for more than a decade, its progress in standards development would seem to be slow. To date it has developed 11 standards[52] and issued 5 product bans[53] under its authority of the Act; besides numerous standards under authority transferred to CPSC to establish standards for products under the Federal Hazardous Substances Act, the Flammable Fabrics Act, the Poison Prevention Packaging Act and the Refrigerator Safety Act.

The reasons for this apparent inaction in standards development are primarily budget-related. Considering its broad charter and practically limitless scope in the field of consumer products (estimates are that the CPSC has jurisdiction over more than 10,000 products); its resources are extremely limited, with a fiscal year 1985 budget of $35 million.[54] Its experiences in developing the existing standards have demonstrated that it is a costly, time-consuming process. In the future, the role of the CPSC in developing its own standards may well diminish in favor of other more cost-effective functions such as its surveillance, product monitoring, data collection and information dissemination activities.

One of the responsibilities of the CPSC is to "assist public and private organizations or groups of manufacturers, administratively and technically, in the development of safety standards and test methods."[55] Since the nation's voluntary standards-making network is well-established, cost-effective, efficient and successful; it makes good sense to keep it intact. Constructive guidance made available by the CPSC to the existing standards-making bodies would appear to serve all interests. For example, the CPSC, from its national vantage point and injury information clearinghouse function, is in an excellent position to identify deficiencies in existing industry standards and the need for new ones, and to pass this information on to industry.

The provisions of the CPSA furnish incentives for manufacturers to respond voluntarily in improving the safety of their products. The required procedures for manufacturers to follow upon discovery of the existence of a problem with one of its products that could constitute a "substantial product hazard"[56] create incentives for the manufacturer to voluntarily institute a product coding system, a record-keeping system and a safety assurance program. This is preferable to facing the consequences and sanctions of a CPSC violation.[57]

It is quite possible, then, that the principal contribution of the CPSC in carrying out the Act's provisions will be to serve as an incentive for manufacturers to voluntarily conform to the new product safety standards the public demands. If so, it will be a major contribution in helping manufacturers avoid products lawsuits.

Other CPSC-Administered Acts. In its legislation that created the CPSC, Congress transferred to the Commission authority to administer four previous product safety statutes.[58] These acts are briefly described in the following paragraphs. These descriptions are included mainly to give the reader who is perhaps unaware of the comprehensive scope of product safety standards legislated by the government in recent years some insight into their extent. Keep in mind in reviewing these provisions that the CPSC is concerned primarily with consumer and consumer household environment and the non-industrial and non-technical public at large. Most of these legislated acts had their origins in legislation enacted many years ago and embody those provisions and various amendments.

Federal Hazardous Substances Act—This legislation is intended to regulate the existence, and particularly the introduction into commerce, of "hazardous substances." This means substances that are toxic, corrosive, irritants or sensitizers, flammable or combustible, or generate pressure through decomposition, heat, or other means, if such substances may cause substantial personal injury or illness from handling or use or from ingestion by children.[59] It may also include toys or articles intended for use by children and that present an electrical, mechanical or thermal hazard.[60] The Act excludes substances and materials regulated by other legislation or government agencies such as pesticides subject to the Federal Insecticide, Fungicide and Rodenticide Act; foods, drugs and cosmetics subject to the Federal Food, Drug and Cosmetic Act; and certain fuels and tobacco products.

The Act recognizes the need for and usefulness of most hazardous substances and prescribes requirements for labeling them and informing the public of their hazardous nature. A substance whose packaging or labeling violates such requirements is termed a "misbranded hazardous substance," which makes those responsible for such violation subject to various penalties.[61] However, certain classes of hazardous substances may be declared "banned hazardous substances." Such a classification may be given to a substance when, despite cautionary labeling, the degree or nature of the hazard involved in the existence or use of such substance in households is such that protection of the public health and safety can be adequately served only by keeping such substance out of interstate commerce channels.[62]

Requirements for cautionary labeling for hazardous substances are spelled out by the Act and require prominent, conspicuous and legible statements of: the name and place of business of the manufacturer, packer, distributor or seller; the common, usual or chemical name of the hazardous substance or of each component that contributes to its hazard; the signal words "*danger*" on extremely flammable, corrosive or highly toxic substances, or "*warning*" or "*caution*" on other hazardous substances; an affirmative statement of the principal hazard involved; precautionary measures to be followed; instruction for first-aid treatment, handling and storage and statements advising it be kept out of the reach of children.[63]

Violations of provisions of the statute are considered misdemeanors and subject to fines of up to $500 and/or imprisonment for up to 90 days. For offenses committed with intent to defraud or mislead, or for second and subsequent offenses, penalties of up to $3,000 fine and/or imprisonment for up to one year may be imposed.[64] Provisions for premises entry, inspection, access to records and material samples and for seizure of misbranded or banned hazardous substances are similar to those of the CPSA.

Specific standards defining hazardous substances, labeling requirements, test methods for determining their hazardous nature and prescribed requirements for particular products are contained in Hazardous Substances Standards.[65]

Poison Prevention Packaging Act—This Act gives the Commission authority to establish standards for the special packaging of any household substance if it finds that such packaging is required to protect children from serious personal injury or illness resulting from handling, using or ingesting such substance. For the purposes of the Act, "household substance" means any substance customarily sold for consumption or use by individuals in or about a household and which is a hazardous substance (as defined by the Hazardous Substance Act); a food, drug or cosmetic; or household fuel stored in portable containers.[66]

Various considerations apply in determining the need for enactment of such packaging standards, such as technical feasibility, practicability and suitability; their reasonableness, scientific, medical and engineering data on the packaging itself and hazards involved; manufacturing practices of industries affected; and nature of the household substance.[67]

Poison Prevention Packaging Standards specify substances that must be specially packaged, the effectiveness of the packaging and testing procedures for determining its adequacy and compliance.[68]

Flammable Fabrics Act—This statute authorizes the Commission to prescribe flammability standards that may be needed to protect the public from the hazards to life, health and property caused by dangerously flammable products.[69] The legislation originated in the Federal Trade Commission in 1953. Declaration of failure to conform to its flammability standards was regarded an unfair method of competition and a deceptive act or practice in commerce.

This Act prescribes Flammable Fabrics Standards for textiles and vinyl plastic film for clothing and other wearing apparel, particularly clothing and sleepwear intended for children and surface flammability of rugs and carpets, mattresses and mattress pads.[70]

Provisions for enforcement and penalties for violation generally follow those of other CPSC-administered acts.

Refrigerator Safety Act—This legislation creates authority for enacting standards for devices to permit opening household refrigerator doors from the inside. Its purpose is to enable the door's latching mechanism to be readily released by a trapped child to permit his escape.[71] The standard specifies detailed requirements covering release forces; effects of age and wear on the ability of the device to function; protection against adverse effects from condensation, defrosting and spills, and test procedures.

Radiation Control for Health and Safety Act. This Act is administered by the Bureau of Radiological Health of the Food and Drug Administration (FDA) within the Department of Health and Human Services.[72] Its purpose is to establish and implement an electronic product radiation control program to protect the public health and safety.

It grants authority to develop and administer performance standards; plan, conduct, coordinate and support research, development, training and operational activities to minimize emissions of and the exposure of people to unnecessary electronic product radiation; to maintain liaison with other government agencies and industry organizations on present and future potential electronic product radiation; to study and evaluate emissions of, and conditions of exposure to, electronic product radiation and intense magnetic fields; to develop, test and evaluate effectiveness of procedures and techniques for minimizing exposure to electronic product radiation and to coordinate these efforts with other federal agencies.[73]

The term "electronic product radiation" means ionizing or non-ionizing electromagnetic or particulate radiation or sonic, infrasonic, or ultrasonic wave emitted from electronic circuits of products.[74] This definition includes the entire electromagnetic spectrum of radiation of any wavelength (gamma rays, x-rays, ultraviolet, visible, infrared, microwave, radiowave and low-frequency radiation) as well as charged particles such as protons, electrons and alpha particles having sufficient kinetic energy to produce ionization or excitation.[75]

Specific examples of electronic products which may emit x-rays and other ionizing electromagnetic radiation are television receivers and other cathode-ray-tube (CRT) equipped devices and x-ray machines (medical, dental, industrial). Examples of products which may emit other wavelengths of electromagnetic radiation include welding equipment; tanning lamps; black light sources; infrared dryers, ovens and heaters; diathermy units;

microwave ovens; radar devices; signal generators; cauterizers; lasers; vibrators; sound amplifiers; ultrasonic cleaning and nondestructive testing equipment.[76]

Radiation Control Regulations include recommendations and precautions in the use of such equipment; labeling; performance and documentation requirements; procedures for reporting discovery of defects and failure to comply; manufacturers' obligations to repair, replace or refund purchase price; inspection methods; enforcement provisions and penalties for violation.[77]

Food, Drug and Cosmetic Act. This 1938 legislation gives the FDA authority for interstate commerce regulation of foods, drugs and devices, and cosmetics.[78] The FDA had its start as early as 1906 and today includes various bureaus with specific authority such as the Bureau of Radiological Health, mentioned before. Scope of operation and standards-making authority of the FDA are very broad and its regulations create many obligations that can lead to products liability.

These standards exist to protect the public from the potentially harmful effects of adulterated, substandard and contaminated food, drink, medicines and drugs, including mislabeled drugs. It represents one of the earliest fields for legislation of product safety standards; consequently, these standards and standards-making functions and the need for compliance and their enforcement are well established and accepted in this country.

Beyond immediate and obvious food articles and constituents, there has been an increase in the use of chemical food additives, preservatives, dietary supplements, colorings, flavoring, thickening and emulsifying agents and others. These are deliberately added to food products to offer some benefit, feature or sales appeal. The quality and suitability of such additives are of concern to the FDA.

During growing, harvesting, production, manufacture and packaging, foods and their ingredients are subject to inadvertent contamination from many sources. Within its authority are development of procedures for detecting the presence and measuring the levels of such contaminants; standards establishing tolerance thresholds for them; requirements for labeling and packaging; investigations of the suitability of new drugs and approving them; and many other functions.

National Traffic and Motor Vehicle Safety Act. Authority for this legislation is with the National Highway Traffic Safety Administration (NHTSA), under the Department of Transportation (DOT).[79] Its purpose is to reduce traffic accidents, deaths and injuries to persons resulting from traffic accidents. This is done through establishing safety standards for motor vehicles and equipment in interstate commerce and through undertaking and supporting safety research and development.[80]

Motor vehicles played a dominant role in the evolution of products liability laws. It is not surprising in view of their increasing complexity and degree of technological development, their widespread use and indispensability in this country, their performance capabilities and propensity for causing injury, their adoption as a lifestyle element, and other factors. A recent report released by the Insurance Institute for Highway Safety showed motor vehicle crashes to be the leading cause of unintentional death, with 45,000 to 53,000 deaths annually and 4 to 5 million injuries.[81] A significant percentage of this country's workforce is employed by firms that in some way are related to the production, distribution, sales, servicing or use of motor vehicles. Since motor vehicles continue to be prominently involved in products liability disputes, it is to be expected that they are the subject of comprehensive federal standards.

As defined by the Act, "motor vehicle safety" is performance of motor vehicles and their equipment in such a manner that the public is protected against unreasonable risk of death or injury in the event accidents do occur.[82] Motor vehicle safety standards shall be practicable, shall meet the need for motor vehicle safety, and shall be stated in objective terms.[83]

In prescribing standards, relevant available motor vehicle safety data shall be considered, including results of research and development, testing and evaluation activities conducted under the Act. Also, the standards-making process shall consider whether the proposed standard is reasonable, practicable and appropriate for the particular type of vehicle or equipment it is prescribed for.[84]

As with most other product safety legislation provisions, this act prohibits the manufacture, sale, delivery and importation of substandard products and imposes civil penalties and fines for violations ($1,000 fine for each violation, counting each vehicle or item of equipment as a single violation, for a maximum penalty of $800,000 for any related series of violations).

The legislation authorizes fact-finding and data-gathering inspections and investigations; provides for access to manufacturers' premises; requires manufacturers, dealers and distributors to make and maintain records and reports; and authorizes inspections of such documents. Under the Act, manufacturers have an obligation to notify owners of motor vehicles having safety defects and, for some unsafe conditions, it may order vehicle recalls.

To assist in fulfilling its objectives, the NHTSA maintains a number of offices and facilities, including a Safety Research Laboratory and offices of Vehicle Safety Research, Crash Avoidance, Standards Enforcement, Crashworthiness, and Defects Investigation.

Workplace Safety Legislation. *Workmen's Compensation.* Although not intended to be a standards-making law like others we have been considering, this legislation has had significant effects upon products liability and is worthy of some attention here. In Chapter 3 we saw how workmen's compensation legislation created a no-fault system of compensation for employee injuries and incentives for improving workplace safety.

Through this legislation, workers injured on the job obtain a prompt and certain although nominal compensation in exchange for voluntarily relinquishing their common-law rights to a legal remedy.

In the early 1900s this option was a welcome alternative to pursuing a lengthy, costly and usually fruitless quest for compensation through the court system. However, in recent years, workmen's compensation has lost much of its early appeal. At present there is considerable dissatisfaction over insufficiency of compensation amounts—many unadjusted for effects of inflation—and their restrictions and ceilings tied to local wage levels. Increasing attention by news media to large liability settlements and jury awards given injured victims has also played a part in creating dissatisfaction with the "token payments" available under workmen's compensation.

The injured employee has not been content to simply settle for workmen's compensation when other routes to larger compensation are available through products liability litigation. For example, many workplace injuries involve use or operation of manufactured machines, tools and equipment. Although workmen's compensation rules prevent an employee from suing his employer, they do not prevent the employee from suing the manufacturer of the machine, tool or equipment that may have caused or contributed to the injury. Through such so-called "third-party" action the injured employee has available to him the whole spectrum of remedies of modern products liability law. These represent substantial improvement over nominal sums provided under workmen's compensation. Accordingly, product-related workplace accidents and inadequacies of workmen's compensation increase the industrial product manufacturer's vulnerability.

Of course, the procedures for pursuing legal remedies for injuries occurring within a workmen's compensation environment are far from straightforward. And the outcome is subject to jurisdictional rules. Also, there are complications over possible contributions that the employer might have made to the occurrence of the employee's injury. There are a number of ways this may happen. Modification and abuse of the product, or removal of safety features, are examples. And there is genuine concern over making a product manufacturer bear the entire cost of an injury when the employer may have contributed to the offending product's defectiveness. Legal entanglements that can result do not have uniformly accepted solutions.

There are signs that courts are becoming more sympathetic to the plight of the injured worker and inadequacies of workmen's compensation as a remedy.[85] They are becoming more inclined to favor devising a way to give him adequate compensation, even if it means drawing the employer (as a co-defendant with the product manufacturer) out from under the shelter of immunity offered by workmen's compensation laws into a scheme for apportionment of damages awarded in products liability actions.[86]

It is not too difficult to see how an employer's compliance with other relevant workplace safety standards could have a significant effect upon his exposure to liability in such employee lawsuits for compensation for workplace injuries.

Occupational Safety and Health Act. This 1970 federal legislation has had profound effects upon legal obligations of employers and manufacturers of industrial products as well as the public. It is but one more indication to those concerned over their vulnerability to products liability of how extensive is society's consciousness of and dedication to the cause of product safety.

This act, administered by the Occupational Safety and Health Administration (OSHA), affects the safety of some 60 million workers. By now, virtually everyone in a position of responsibility for other employees has become acquainted with some aspect of OSHA. Its purpose stated in the preamble to the Act is

> To assure safe and healthful working conditions for working men and women; by authorizing enforcement of the standards developed under the Act; by assisting and encouraging the States in their efforts to assure safe and healthful working conditions; by providing for research, information, education, and training in the field of occupational safety and health.[87]

Section 5 defines "duties" of employers and employees under the Act:

> (a) Each employer—(1) shall furnish to each of his employees employment and a place of employment which are free from recognized hazards that are causing or are likely to cause death or serious physical harm to his employees; (2) shall comply with occupational safety and health standards promulgated under this Act. (b) Each Employee shall comply with occupational safety and health standards and all rules, regulations, and orders issued pursuant to this Act which are applicable to his own actions and conduct.[88]

Its provisions authorize access (through employer consent or warrant) to places of employment for compliance inspections and investigations, and require employers to make and maintain various records regarding activities related to the Act, including reports on work-related deaths, injuries and illnesses. It spells out certain rights of employees to request OSHA inspections of their workplace, to observe the employer's monitoring of employee exposure to toxic substances and to be informed of individual exposure levels. Such employee instigation of complaints or participation in OSHA workplace investigations and hearings cannot be grounds for dismissal from employment or for employer's disciplinary action.

Penalties prescribed for violations can include fines and jail terms and

> U.S. district courts shall have jurisdiction upon petition . . . to restrain any conditions or practices in any place of employment which are such

that exists which could reasonably be expected to cause death or serious physical harm immediately or before the imminence of such danger can be eliminated through any enforcement procedures otherwise provided.[89]

That is, the law gives federal authority to shut down operations deemed immediately dangerous to employees until the employer complies with the law.

Under the Act, The National Institute for Occupational Safety and Health (NIOSH) was established under the Department of Health, Education and Welfare as a research data-gathering and standards-writing arm of OSHA.[90] Its mission does not include standards enforcement. OSHA has issued a fairly large number of standards and has incorporated various national standards into its rules.[91] These include specific occupational safety and health provisions contained in standards issued by such organizations as the American National Standards Institute (ANSI), the National Fire Protection Association (NFPA), the American Society of Mechanical Engineers (ASME), and Underwriters' Laboratories.[92]

Despite the array of federal legislation that has been enacted in recent years, there is traditional reluctance by the federal government to enact legislation that usurps authority from states. Accordingly, OSHA has provisions whereby states may, and are encouraged to, assume full responsibility for occupational health and safety.[93] OSHA standards in this regard are to be considered *minimal requirements*. OSHA-approved state rules can supplant basic OSHA rules, but their safety requirements must be equivalent to or more demanding than OSHA's.

This means that mere familiarity with OSHA requirements for a given product could be inadequate, as a state where the product is sold may have tighter requirements, making it a violation (illegal) to sell the product that just meets OSHA's (minimal) standards. It is therefore essential for manufacturers to be fully knowledgeable of all regulations affecting their products in every jurisdiction where they will be sold or used.

Common Law Requirements

Judicially-Created Standards. Although legislated standards such as those just examined have had a pronounced effect upon liability of product manufacturers and others in distributive channels, products liability critics usually focus upon the common law rules that have come into being during the last few decades. There are various reasons for this and we briefly touched on them in an earlier chapter.

It is ironic that manufacturers vehemently hostile toward common law product standards can find *legislated* product standards tolerable, and even quite acceptable. And this is so despite the fact that many legislated standards are more demanding and restrictive than those evolved through common law. In fact, manufacturers are now lobbying in Washington *for* federal products liability legislation (!) with the hope that some kind of reform legislation will diminish the threat. Such willingness to trade a problem you know for one you don't know is not always the best approach; for sometimes you simply end up with one more problem than you started with.

Much of the difference in acceptability between judicial law (common law) and legislated (statutory) law probably is related to comprehensibility of law-making processes. Practically everyone is familiar with federal and state statutes and local ordinances and how they come about. In an indirect sort of way all of us have had a hand in making them through our election of "lawmakers"—senators, congressmen and local officials. We therefore feel some allegiance toward and personal responsibility for laws these elected representatives enact.

Laws or standards created by judges remain a mystery to many. Even the fact that decisions by appellate courts *are true law* is not well understood or accepted. Not only are common-law-making processes obscure to many people, laymen unfortunately cannot easily find the actual written laws that affect them. So it is not difficult to see why laymen regard common law rules with skepticism and distrust—sometimes to the point of ignoring their existence or giving up entirely, and mentally (if not actually) turning the whole business over to lawyers. Nevertheless, the manufacturer and engineer are responsible for knowing their requirements and complying with them.

The description in Chapter 3 of how products liability law developed in conjunction with society's changing needs and values provides a solid foundation for a discussion of standards created by that law. Again, a word of caution in dealing with common law or judicially-created rules: resist the temptation to make the standards, rules and definitions fit rigid molds. Engineers and technically trained people are most prone to this error. It is important to remember the fundamental differences between legal law and scientific law outlined in the previous chapter. We are not dealing here with precise definitions and "go/no-go" gauges.

In contrast to legislated acts that are relatively rigid and definite (although also subject to revision and amendment), common law is a "living growth." Its nature has been compared to a flowing river—always there, but always different from day to day. It is a good practice to try to understand the spirit, or motivation, behind legal decisions, with less attention to details surrounding them. Like the river, direction of flow is not all that difficult to determine, and neither is its breadth or depth. So it is with the law.

The law's message to product design engineers and manufacturers is clear, whether it is spoken in the precise words of the statute or in the often-shrouded language of judicial decisions: there is no tolerance in today's society for dangerously defective products. Products liability laws are society's backlash to the increasing toll of victims of injuries from manufactured products and modern technology. Society is telling industry, through the law, to clean up its act or suffer financial consequences. Of course, there's more to it than that, but this is the core of its message.

In the next few pages we will be examining standards imposed by two common law causes of action: *negligence* and *strict liability*. Of the two, strict liability applied in the field of manufactured products is the more recent development. Its principles represent dramatic departures from previous concepts of manufacturers' liability and, since it offers injured plaintiffs easier access to compensation, it constitutes a major threat to the product manufacturer. However, negligence is far from an obsolete concept and it deserves close attention.

A third category of products liability action is *misrepresentation*, often tied in with *breach of warranty*. The "standards" aspects of these concepts have already been covered under our discussion of legislated standards earlier in this chapter. Before the trend during the past few decades toward government legislation in the products field, legal actions for misrepresentation proceeded on common law (generally, contract law) grounds. However, with passage of warranty legislation, particularly the Uniform Commercial Code (UCC), the standards that apply in most jurisdictions now are found in these statutes.

Negligence Standards: The *Manufacturer* On Trial. In early times before industrialization, legal remedies for harm or injuries caused by another generally were restricted to those stemming from definite, but wrongful, acts. The law offered little recourse to victims of injuries that resulted from one's neglect to carry out some obligation correctly or carefully, not to mention injuries that resulted from total failure to act.

Need for a legal remedy for harm caused by one's neglect to act in a proper manner evolved from transactions with merchants or others professing to be experts or possessing a certain level of competence in providing personal services.[94] In these transactions, potential users or customers were solicited by merchants through explicit or implicit representations of competence that were intended to assure the public of confidence in their abilities or in the quality of services being offered. In early recognition of today's principles of negligence law, reliance by the user or customer upon such representations was viewed as creating legal obligations for those offering the services to render them competently. Careless, improper or incompetently rendered services became grounds for legal action for negligence. The notion of liability for failure to act came later.

With the advent of mechanical devices and machinery, people soon became accustomed to earn their livelihood with them and to depend upon them. Such dependence often led to personal injuries when the contraptions, commonly devoid of safety features, failed or broke or were used by inexperienced people—frequently children. But, at the time, knowledge of strength of materials and ability to properly refine them were lacking; product quality standards were non-existent; performance limits were seldom even given a thought by the manufacturer or user; and product failures and injuries were understandably commonplace.

Legal action toward the manufacturer of the offending product based upon "fault" could not proceed very far because the crude state of technical knowledge did not offer much basis for showing improper design or incorrect use of materials. For example, it was inconceivable that a manufacturer could be responsible for brittle fracture of a previously sound steel wagon axle that, in the technical vernacular of the day, suddenly and mysteriously "crystallized." How could the manufacturer of the axle, let alone the manufacturer of the wagon, have been at fault? Besides this, since the one injured probably had no direct dealing or transaction ("privity") with either one, he was out of luck anyway.[95]

We must realize that the law is a product of many concurrent forces and events. We cannot consider legal developments without considering technical developments, sociological developments, economic developments, political developments and the elusive, indefinable but pervasive *zeit geist* (the "spirit of the time"). The concept of negligence in tort law, like all law, become "whatever the needs of life in a developing civilization require."[96]

Before the early 1800s "neglect" and "negligence" meant little more than failure or omission to act or perform some duty or task. Even today, apart from legal issues, we use these terms to describe forgetfulness, inattention, unconcern, indifference, disregard, or even continued procrastination of an obligation, responsibility or duty. Development of negligence in tort law has altered and expanded the legal definition of "negligence" to mean more than this. In tort law, negligence, stated simply, is behavior that creates unreasonable risks of danger to others. What determines this behavior is important to product manufacturers; for negligence is one of the principal causes of action in products liability, if not the dominant one.

The principle has had remarkable vitality for a long period of time and there are a number of reasons for this. Negligence furnished tort law with a flexible and timeless standard; one that would always be current and applicable because it set a standard that was whatever the court said it was. By now it is a well-established, widely applied and accepted concept, even by laymen. Through news media, novels and television courtroom drama we have become familiar with the term and its application in a variety of legal situations.

Because negligence carries with it the notion of some kind of blameworthy conduct, or fault, plaintiffs' attorneys find it easier to use as the basis for a plaintiff's injuries than the use of more recent and somewhat abstract concepts, such as strict liability. It apparently seems fairer to juries of laymen to award damages to a victim of someone's negligence than it is to award damages merely for the sake of compensation, or because our benevolent society feels that "someone" should pay, regardless of fault. It is probable that negligence and its standards will be around for a long time.

To understand the obligations created by products liability negligence law, we must become familiar with a number of terms or concepts which constitute standards of behavior. These elements and how they are classified and defined differ among authorities, but all generally agree upon their content. This subject has filled a great many lawbooks and legal commentaries over the years and there are numerous complex issues and side-issues involved. Our limited treatment here cannot hope to do any more than summarize principal elements and provide awareness of duties and responsibilities the law imposes on those who design, manufacture and market products.

The elements described in the following paragraphs not only constitute standards by which a manufacturer or engineer may evaluate his conduct, but they are the same elements that an injured plaintiff must prove in sustaining legal action for negligence against a product manufacturer. Unfortunately, it is not possible to define tort negligence strictly through an examination of its individual elements. It is a little like attempting to characterize properties of a chemical compound through studying the properties of its individual elements such as carbon, oxygen and hydrogen. The compound is more than the sum of its parts. But we can only understand the concept of negligence when we have defined its constituent elements and how they interact to comprise the whole.

Legal Duty of Care. Negligence is a matter of *conduct.* It is conduct regarding specific individuals and circumstances and it has nothing to do with morality, ethics or fairness. For the good of society, the law imposes certain duties of care upon each one of us. These duties constitute legal obligations to conduct ourselves in some acceptable manner for the benefit of others.

These duties are not founded upon inherent human rights but are merely creations of the common law to enable courts to impose liability when duties are shunned or breached. The notion of duty simply furnishes a fulcrum for the legal lever of the law. The duty is not absolute and well-defined or predictable; and it will vary with the circumstances. We must remember that negligence is a fabricated concept fashioned by courts of law to enable them to administer justice. We must, for now, accept their fabrication at face value since it accomplishes a useful purpose and has withstood the tests of time.

The legal concept of duty of care, or due care, is not limited to products liability or even to the broader field of tort law. The concept is widely used to set limits for behavior in many fields of law. A step outside that limit or boundary (a breach of the duty) exposes one to liability. As new hazards and risks arise, or are invented through technological advancements, the law responds by creating new duties and erecting corresponding behavioral limits, or by adjusting existing ones. It's all for the ultimate good of the greatest number. It is never final or fixed and, typical of common law, these duties and limits can differ from one place (legal jurisdiction) to another.

The duty of care created by law also is selective; that is, it does not extend to everyone, everywhere and under all circumstances. Its extent, depth and breadth depend upon the particular circumstances or the situation. As mentioned earlier, not all behavior that harms people creates liability. The issue in a lawsuit usually hinges on the question of whether, in the eyes of the law, the defendant owed the plaintiff a duty. If the court finds that no duty was owed, other facts have little significance; for without a duty owed the plaintiff—regardless of the defendant's negligent actions or omissions or their degree—there is no legal obligation.

Another limitation on the scope of liability for harm to another caused by one's actions is *foreseeability* of the risk of harm or injury. Generally the law will impose no duty upon one for avoiding unforseeable risks of injury or toward unforseeable defendants. Therefore, one acting negligently will be held liable only if the consequences of what he did or did not do were "reasonably foreseeable." The law does not impose liability for unpredictable consequences of one's conduct. It is well to note in our context of products liability, however, that the law imposes upon the manufacturer of potentially dangerous products a virtually *universal* duty of care that extends to all of society.[97]

While its flexibility and indefiniteness may seem to make the negligence concept so elusive as to be useless, we should realize that a legal concept must be versatile enough to encompass the spectrum of situations that may arise. In a field that is concerned with conduct of human beings toward one another in a complicated modern society with its widespread use of potentially harmful products, that spectrum covers a practically limitless array of circumstances. So, legal principles must be widely adaptable. Duty of care is but one element in the negligence equation.

Standard of Reasonable Conduct. To satisfy the demand for a standard of conduct that would cover the plethora of fact situations and occurrences, the law created a standard around a fictitious individual known as "the reasonable man," or "a man of ordinary sense using ordinary care and knowledge," or "the average prudent individual." This ideal person sets the standard for us all to follow. The law expects us to behave as if we were standing in his shoes. Using this standard of "the reasonable man," negligence has been defined as

> the omission to do something which a reasonable man, guided upon those considerations which ordinarily regulate the conduct of human

affairs, would do, or doing something which a prudent and reasonable
man would not do. (*Blyth v. Birmingham Waterworks Co.*)[98]

It is truly an ingenious standard, as it is flexible and can be made to apply
to virtually any situation, time, place or person. It is an unwritten standard,
and need not be written, for all mature reasonably intelligent adults carry it
about with them. That is, all of us have basic notions of how a reasonably
prudent individual would be expected to respond to given situations under
particular circumstances. This is the negligence standard the court will
apply to a defendant who owes a duty of care to the plaintiff. If his actions
were what would be expected of a reasonably prudent person under the
given circumstances, he will not be considered negligent. If, on the other
hand, his conduct failed to measure up to what would be expected of a
reasonably prudent person, he will be considered negligent.

The law recognizes the need to consider the particular facts surrounding
the occurrence in question. As Prosser points out, "conduct which would be
proper under some circumstances becomes negligence under others."[99]

The standard also considers the level of skill and expertise of the actor (or
defendant). That is, if the defendent charged with negligence is a member of
a profession (for example, chemist, engineer or surgeon) the standard
applied will be that of "a reasonably prudent (chemist, engineer or
surgeon)". The standard applied will be consistent with the level of
knowledge, skill or special expertise that is commonly possessed by
members of that group or profession. And this standard will be applied if
the defendant *held himself out to be* a member of such a group or as
possessing such expertise even if, in fact, he is proven not to possess such
skills.

It is important to note in these discussions of standards of reasonable
care that an injured plaintiff charging that a manufacturer's negligence led
to his injury must prove that the manufacturer failed in some way to fulfill
the duty owed him. From the plaintiff's side of the fence, this can be
difficult, and sometimes impossible, to prove; since it is the manufacturer
who has access to pertinent evidence, information and facts. This places the
plaintiff at a severe disadvantage. In an attempt to equalize the positions of
the two sides—the manufacturer with all the information on the product
and the injured plaintiff faced with the burden of proving the manufacturer
failed to do something, or did something he should not have done—courts
have fashioned another principle, *res ipsa loquitur* ("the thing speaks for
itself").

What this evidentiary concept does is, in the absence of hard evidence to
support the plaintiff's allegation of a manufacturer's failure to exercise due
care owed him, turn the attention around and focus upon the product. In
doing so it relieves the plaintiff of the burden of proof that the manufacturer
(or actor) was negligent. It does this through permitting admission of

circumstantial evidence that in all probability the injury would not have occurred if the product in question had not been negligently manufactured (that "there is greater likelihood that injury was caused by defendant's negligence than by some other cause.").[100]

In shifting the burden of proof from the shoulders of the injured plaintiff, and attention away from the manufacturer's conduct and over toward the product itself, the outcome approaches that of strict liability—discussed later in this chapter. In fact, one of the reasons for increased use of strict liability and breach of warranty actions in products liability cases is that in these actions the plaintiff is relieved of the burden of proving the manufacturer's negligence.

Causation. Without any reference to legal rules, it should be intuitively apparent that one can only be liable in a negligence action for another's injury or harm if his negligent conduct caused the injury or harm. While, on the surface, this element seems straightforwardly simple; it is not when real-world facts and issues are involved. The subject of causation in negligence actions has been the crux of endless debate for many years.

Most of the problems arise from the law's need to distinguish two classifications or issues of causation. One is called "cause in fact." The other is sometimes referred to as "legal cause," "responsible cause" or "proximate cause." Since both are essential for the plaintiff to prove in establishing the defendant's liability, we will briefly examine them.

"Cause in fact" addresses the fundamental question of whether the defendant's conduct was, as a matter of fact and evidence, a cause of the plaintiff's injury. Recognizing that most accidents, catastrophes and other harmful occurrences can be traced to a number of causes,[101] the question is usually determined on the basis of whether the defendant's negligent conduct was a "material element" or "substantial factor" in the occurrence of the harm. Put another way by some courts, the act or omission would not be judged a "cause in fact" if the occurrence would have taken place without the negligent act or omission (this is the *sine qua non*, or "but for" test).[102] This issue is ordinarily discernible from evidence of the case and is a "fact" question that the court may leave to the jury to determine.

Even though causation is an element that must be proven in establishing liability, causation alone does not determine it. Here we are faced with the synergism mentioned before. Other issues must be considered in determining "proximate cause" or "legal cause." The term "proximate cause" is frequently misleading as the concept has little to do with "proximity" in time or location and it also has little to do with cause. The only "proximity" it really deals with is whether there is "legal proximity", or legally sustainable linkage, between the "cause in fact" and its injurious result. So, in reality, the debates over causation frequently have more to do with semantics than legal principles.

The concept of "proximate cause" is perhaps best illustrated by an example. Consider this hypothetical situation: A switching relay in a central electrical generating station is deficient in its response because of negligent manufacture. Its failure to operate properly during a period of exceptionally high demand causes a momentary sector overload that trips a number of large circuit breakers in a remote substation. This abruptly cuts electrical power to the downtown business center of a major city at rush hour, plunging it into darkness.

Before power can be restored, there are numerous vehicular accidents at intersections from confusion over inoperative traffic signals. The accidents cause considerable damage and some injuries. There are other injuries from people groping about in the dark on streets and stairways, others become ill when confined in crowded elevators immobilized between floors. Merchants in the downtown shopping area report widespread looting during the blackout with losses approaching a million dollars.

All of this is attributable to the power outage. But, even if it is proven conclusively that the negligently manufactured relay was the "cause in fact" of the power failure, it is unlikely that the manufacturer of that relay would be held liable for all the consequences of its failure.

In this example the manufacturer's negligence in making a defective relay was without question the "cause in fact" of all those problems and injuries. But it is most doubtful that a court would find that the negligent manufacture of the relay was the "proximate cause" of those losses and injuries occurring in the blacked-out city.

The task of establishing "proximate cause" starts with the already-established "cause in fact" (if proven) that the defendant's negligent conduct was a substantial factor in the occurrence of the plaintiff's injury; or, without (but for) his negligent conduct the injury would not have occurred. But it is necessary to go beyond that to establish "legal" or "proximate" cause to determine if liability attaches to the "cause in fact."[103]

The quest for proximate cause continues from there and inquires if the occurrence was a natural and probable consequence of the defendant's action and if the outcome was reasonably foreseeable. When pursued to any extent, the issue eventually returns to questions of duty. That is, did the negligent defendant have a duty to protect *this specific* plaintiff or group of plaintiffs against the *actual occurrence* or series of occurrences that resulted from the defendant's negligent act? Because of its pivotal importance many authorities view the issues of proximate cause as the key to a negligence action.

Damages. To sustain a products liability action, it is not enough for a plaintiff to claim negligent conduct that may have been objectionable or offensive. If he has suffered no actual physical harm, injury or loss, there is no liability. There may be other legal remedies for interference with individual rights or interests but, as far as products liability is concerned, proof of actual harm is an essential element in sustaining an action in negligence.

Negligence Standards of Liability. Negligence has been defined in various terms and we have already considered two versions. The American Law Institute's definition, a consensus of the country's leading legal scholars, is conduct "which falls below the standard established by law for the protection of others against unreasonably great risk of harm."[104] With few exceptions, a negligence products liability lawsuit is not so much concerned with the product itself as it is the behavior of the manufacturer.

The elements we have just reviewed represent "test standards" for determining if some particular conduct that already may have or possibly will become associated with someone's injury constitutes legal negligence and, if so, if that negligent conduct incurs liability.

For our purposes in considering how to avoid products liability lawsuits and damages, these test standards are like "spot tests" that metallurgists and other engineers sometimes use to identify metals and alloys. In those tests, drops of various chemical reagents are placed on the clean surface of an unknown metal sample. A series of test indications following a prescribed sequence progressively narrows the possibilities to the actual alloy, or a high probability of it. Of course, whenever the engineer must have documented evidence and assurance confirming the material's identity he would submit the sample to an analytical laboratory that would use more sophisticated procedures in conjunction with control standards. But the chemical spot tests have their place in industry and can be extremely useful.

Likewise, it is advantageous for every engineer involved in design and marketing of products to be able to apply *legal* "spot tests" to evaluate behavior that could constitute negligence and possibly lead to liability. These tests do not require apparatus or reagents and, with a little practice, they can become second nature and help avoid products liability.

Engineers need not become attorneys any more than the field engineer who wants to quickly identify an unknown metal must become an analytical chemist. It is simply that in today's litigious climate we all would do well to develop "tools" of our own for readily obtaining indications of potential liability exposure. When there is an opportunity to do so, it is advisable to confirm the validity of "spot test" indications with legal counsel who are more familiar with the law and its jurisdictional nuances, and have access to "control standards," much like the analytical laboratory.

Legal scholars have identified in the products liability field several categories of negligent conduct that can lead to liability. For the most part, these are simply the more common causes of negligence action for injuries traceable to manufactured products. It is worth remembering in reviewing them that negligence continues to be an extremely comprehensive and versatile basis for legal action. It is less encumbered by definitive constraints, conditions and restrictive requirements than other bases for products liability action. It can be brought against *anyone* who is part of the marketing chain.[105] *Any* conduct that fails to meet the law's standards for the protection of others against unreasonable risk of harm, or that constitutes one's failure to fulfill his duties to others, is grounds for negligence.

This will become more evident in the discussions that follow. For the sake of simplicity, we will consider three classifications of products liability negligence actions. These relate to: what you *do*, what you *make*, and what you *say*:

Design Negligence, or What You DO—Negligence is a matter of conduct and relates to what one *does*. In this discussion of products liability issues, this classification of negligence will center about the manufacturer's management policies, its attitudes, planning, and approach to making and marketing the product—more than about actual production operations. No matter what analytical classifications one uses for the various kinds of activities that may incur negligence, the same basic rule applies to them all: a duty to use the care that a reasonably prudent person (or manufacturer) would use under the circumstances. (Again, the reader is reminded that use of the term "manufacturer" in these discussions is not meant to exclude others in the "marketing chain" who also may be subject to liability for negligence in products actions.)

As we saw earlier, a manufacturer has a duty to exercise reasonable care in manufacturing his product. This means that he must see to it that the product is free of potentially dangerous defects that would present an unreasonable risk of harm to foreseeable users and others.[106] The standard of "reasonable care" is, of course, dependent upon the product, its foreseeable users, its propensity for harm, its usefulness and need, and many other considerations. Nevertheless, the law does not yet demand perfection or products that are accident-proof or foolproof or that will never wear out.[107]

The question of liability of those who manufacture components of products that are later incorporated by other manufacturers into final products is not easily answered because of differences from one jurisdiction to another. It generally depends upon whether the subsequent manufacturer/s would reasonably be expected to inspect and able to discover defects in supplied components or assemblies and whether the component is used as-supplied or is subject to further processing or change.[108] It is considered established law in many jurisdictions that the manufacturer of the final product containing parts supplied by others is responsible for testing and inspecting the components.[109] It is therefore prudent to assume, as some jurisdictions hold, that the (final) product manufacturer is as liable for the existence of defective components in his product as he would be if he made them himself.[110-112]

The most frequent cause for legal action within this category of conduct is allegation of improper or defective *design* of the product. This means that all products of a given kind that the manufacturer made may be identical and conform to the manufacturer's own internal standard, yet are faulty.

The allegation condemns not only the particular product that caused the injury but the entire production of that product. The potential for trouble in having the total population of a given product adjudged defective makes negligent design a particularly serious indictment of the manufacturer.

Besides this, finding such a condition can also help the plaintiff in building his case against the manufacturer. One of the elements that the injured plaintiff must prove in a products liability action against the manufacturer is that the defect that led to his injury existed in the product when it left the hands of the manufacturer. Frequently, after a product has been in use for some time, it can be extremely difficult to prove that some defect existed when the product was first manufactured. The manufacturer, in its defense, could claim that intervening events out of its control had made the product defective. However, if a plaintiff can prove defective *design*, he has already proven that the defect existed when the product left the hands of the manufacturer, making it pointless to argue about intervening events.

For this reason, proof of defective design is a primary goal of the plaintiff in products liability lawsuits, for both negligence *and* strict liability actions. Accordingly, it is critically important for the manufacturer to avoid conduct that could become a basis for proving defective design.

In alleging that negligent product design caused his injuries, a plaintiff is claiming that the manufacturer failed in its legal obligations to provide a safe design. The standard created by the courts for safe product design is described in terms of duty to use such care in designing or formulating the product that it is reasonably safe for intended or foreseeable uses, including reasonably anticipated emergency situations.[113-116] There is also a duty in product design to avoid concealment of dangers that may not be obvious to unskilled users;[117,118] a duty to use materials and components that have adequate strength, durability and integrity for the intended service;[119,120] and a duty to provide safety features which, if absent, would create unreasonable risks or hazards.[121,122] The duty goes beyond that to protect against foreseeable injuries from the product's existence and even probable misuse. This means that there should not be hidden dangers that can injure a user during a moment of inattention or carelessness.

With proliferating legislated standards, statutory requirements and adoption of industry and trade association standards, there has been an increase in products liability cases claiming that lack of compliance with applicable standards constitutes evidence of negligent design or *negligence per se*.[123,124] Compliance with such standards may be considered evidence that the product was designed safely, but it does not confer immunity to liability.[125-128]

Negligence in product design is also created through failure in fulfilling the duty to adequately test or inspect the finished product, its ingredients, components or subassemblies.[129,130] This is especially important for products that present unreasonable risks of harm from characteristics that may be discovered during testing or inspection or where testing and inspection is necessary to assure a safe product.[131] The manufacturer has a duty to see that the inspection procedures used are up-to-date and reflect current knowledge and state-of-the-art.[132] Courts have found that duty to inspect products for reasonably discoverable defects is not confined to manufacturers. Depending upon the product, its characteristics, intended use and foreseeable users, it may extend to others along the distribution chain.[133,134]

An action for negligent design alleging that a product presents an unreasonable risk of danger ultimately must address the question of whether or not the manufacturer's action or conduct constituted reasonable care. The question is usually answered through applying a "cost-benefit" analysis. One of the first concise descriptions of the test in general terms, including admissions of its elusive nature, was by Judge Learned Hand in a 1940 decision:

> The degree of care demanded of a person by an occasion is the resultant of three factors: [1] the likelihood that his conduct will injure others, taken with [2] the seriousness of the injury if it happens, and balanced against [3] the interest which he must sacrifice to avoid the risk. All these are practically not susceptible of any quantitative estimate, and the second two are generally not so, even theoretically. For this reason a solution always involves some preference, or choice between incommensurables, and it is consigned to a jury because their decision is thought most likely to accord with commonly accepted standards, real or fancied. (*Conway v. O'Brien*)[135]

This evaluation balances the probability and gravity of harm expected to result from some activity, course of action or decision, against the burden, or cost, of preventing its occurrence. By Learned Hand's formula, if probability and gravity of the harm (either or both) outweigh the cost of prevention; a manufacturer failing to take action (pay the cost) to prevent it would be considered negligent.[136,137] An obvious example would be failure to specify a five-cent cotter pin to assure the security of a critical bolt that, if its retaining nut vibrated loose, could damage an expensive machine and possibly seriously injure its operator.

In real-world decisions, application of such a formula is not so simple and straightforward. The "burden" of prevention often cannot be expressed in terms of the price of a cotter pin, safety feature, or even a complete redundant system. There are other factors to consider; for example, a choice among apparently equivalent and equally effective (or questionable) preventive measures (the "choice between incommensurables" that Learned Hand spoke of).

Who can predict which one is really best without actual user experience in the field and under a variety of conditions and environments? And should the product's market introduction be delayed to evaluate the relative efficacy of safety measures? Or, perhaps, is a longer testing period needed, or more tests under different conditions more closely simulating actual use? Then there are questions over reliability of new, possibly unproven but more discriminating, approaches to product testing. And will the precautions or safety features that seem to be needed in the product hinder its utility or reduce its sales appeal?

These kinds of considerations and many others even more complex are what makes it difficult to apply the balancing test before bringing the product to market. Yet, it must somehow be done because it must be assumed that a court and jury of laymen will one day apply the test after the fact. Obviously, no rule-of-thumb balancing test can offer factual and direct answers to questions that may not have clear answers, or any practicable or acceptable answer. But they do serve to indicate how courts look at the situation and what they consider significant, although grossly oversimplified.[138]

In summary, then, a "design defect" is a problem that affects the entire production, not simply the individual product that caused the injury. Defects of this kind frequently arise through some unanticipated use for the product, but a use that should have been foreseen. Or, they can arise when a product responds in some unexpected way during its use, is adversely affected by its use environment, or deteriorates prematurely. A manufacturer's failure to keep abreast of new technology, new materials and construction methods and inspection techniques affording a "safer" product also could result in liability for injuries from "defective design."

A manufacturer facing allegations of design negligence can expect a difficult time in court. For a plaintiff attorney, it is only a short distance from defective product design to implications of carelessness and conscious disregard of the public's safety and welfare. This can open the door to punitive damages and possible criminal sanctions under statutory violations. A manufacturer would do well to assure that nothing it does can be construed as design negligence.

Practices within the category of what one does that have led to products liability would include failure to comply with, or indifference to, statutory requirements, industry codes, standards or practices, and user or manufacturer specifications. Other acts that have made manufacturers vulnerable to legal action have been failure to anticipate extent of use and misuse of the product; failure to foresee long-term response of the product to conditions of use, misuse and exposure to various environments; failure to apply state-of-the-art technology in design and manufacture of the product or to incorporate safety features that are in use by others in the industry; and failure to maintain a level of technical competence in both engineering staff, manufacturing labor and service representatives that is consistent with the intended and expected performance of the product and its complexity.

A more general source of difficulty, and one commonly encountered, has been inadequate documentation. This becomes a problem when the manufacturer is faced with the burden of proving that it used due care in designing or making the product or that the product is not defective. A lack of records supporting manufacturers' contentions of due care and responsible conduct will be construed as evidence of failure to meet such standards.

Manufacturing Negligence, or What You MAKE—It is useful to distinguish negligent *design* from negligent *manufacture*. Since negligence in products liability deals with a manufacturer's conduct and since both design and manufacture are conduct related to the product, the reasons for distinguishing the two may not be immediately obvious. But the reasons for doing so concern differences in legal implications and liability. We have already touched on some of them.

The previous discussion dealt with products, though defective and capable of inflicting injury, that were what the manufacturer intended; even if the manufacturer did not intend to make them defective. Whatever they were, the products lived up to the manufacturer's expectations. The negligence was in the manufacturer's standard, plan or design and his policies concerning them.

This classification deals with products that do *not* meet the manufacturer's own standards. This is the occasional product or production run that not only fails the legal test, but also the manufacturer's own test; yet, a product that somehow escapes detection and makes its way into the marketplace.

In contrast to a defectively designed product, or a product having a design defect; one with a *manufacturing* defect or flaw is an isolated bad product among a line of good ones. It differs from the rest of them; whereas a defectively designed product is identical to all the others, and faulty. The injury caused by the product with the manufacturing defect may not be any different from the one caused by the product with the design defect, but the legal implications are not the same.

Manufacturing defects are caused by any number of things: inadvertent error somewhere during production; mixup in material, composition, or part number; substitution of an apparently correct but wrong ingredient; incorrect assembly or assembly in an incorrect sequence; inadequate inspection; or a flawed part or component that inspection did not, or perhaps could not, identify. Although any manufacturing defect having potential for causing injury is undesirable, legal implications are not so drastic as with the design defect.

A product could be defective on both counts—design defect *and* manufacturing defect. It could have been negligently designed and negligently manufactured. This would occur if the manufacturer's standards appeared adequate to him but are inadequate as to the law and a product he makes fails even to satisfy his own inadequate standard.

It is not unusual for a manufacturer to have an occasional product or even some predictable proportion of his production output defective or rejectable in some way. And there is nothing negligent about that (although it may be economically unsound). Our attention here is not so much upon rejects, or products identified during production as faulty, as upon faulty products that are *not* rejected, although rejectable, and end up being sold along with the others. Therefore, the focus in a case of negligent manufacture is upon the manufacturer's quality control, assembly and inspection operations. Are they capable of catching the occasional substandard product? There is some overlap here with the category of defective design; for if quality control procedures are faulty, uncalibrated or obsolete, then negligence runs deeper.

Ordinarily, quality control and product inspection are carried out on a statistical basis. Each individual product is not tested; only enough are to furnish some level of statistical confidence. The same general considerations apply right on down the line to sizing of parts, sampling of raw materials, testing of components and subassemblies, through final inspection.

The question of whether the manufacturer did or did not exercise due care during manufacture of the product relates back to a cost-benefit analysis. Testing and inspection at every step of production are expensive and may not be cost-effective or safety-effective. It is absurd, and suicidal from a competitive viewpoint, to go overboard in quality control such that a product having little propensity for harm is priced out of the market by internal safety checks and intensive inspections. The opposite is encountered more often.

The amount of testing that is required to avoid allegations of negligence depends upon elements of the cost-benefit test: the probability and gravity or seriousness of harm from a defective product must be balanced against the cost or burden of eliminating the hazard or risk. Helicopter rotor shafts demand greater scrutiny and more sophisticated flaw-detection techniques than do pleasure boat propeller drive shafts.

Frequently, problems and costs associated with testing and inspection can be minimized through effective use of specifications. These can range from purchase specifications to in-house production specifications. Specifications place controls on materials, parts and components that go into the product and can lessen demands for testing assembled products. Again, however, use of and conformance to specifications do not relieve the manufacturer of need for assuring that only safe products leave the plant. And the greater the risk of harm the products represent, the greater is the manufacturer's duty to inspect.

Product-related practices that commonly make manufacturers vulnerable to products lawsuits include use or substitution of unsuitable, substandard or questionable materials; unjustified or unsupportable reliance upon quality of parts and components made and supplied by others; use of a design or production technique that is incompatible with the intended or foreseeable use or functions for the product; and existence of preventable danger or risks of harm that outweigh the product's usefulness, social benefits and costs of prevention.

Marketing Negligence, or What You SAY—This category is mainly concerned with a manufacturer's communications to others about its product. Negligence can be incurred not only by what is said and how it is said but also by what is *not* said. So far, we have been discussing negligence that concerns mostly the product manufacturer. But negligence through failure to perform some legal duty to communicate can be charged to anyone in the product marketing and distribution network. This most often occurs through representations of facts that are untrue, particularly those concerning safety of the product or its use.

The law imposes liability for misrepresentation when a foreseeable plaintiff is injured while acting in reasonable reliance upon false or incorrect information given him.[139] Liability is incurred even if the one communicating the false information believes it to be true.[140] Negligence lies in failing to verify accuracy of information given, in attempting to give it at all, or in failing to communicate it adequately or correctly. The test is whether a reasonable individual of ordinary skill and knowledge would have given the information.

If the one communicating the information is an individual having special expertise or holds himself out as possessing such expertise or superior knowledge concerning the product, he will be held to the higher standard of what would be expected of a reasonable person possessing such expertise or knowledge. The same considerations apply to the recipient of the communication. That is, if the purchaser, user or consumer is known to possess some special knowledge or expertise, as he well might in a commercial or professional environment, the defendant's liability exposure diminishes somewhat because the duty owed the knowledgeable professional user is different from that owed the average person having no special knowledge of the product or of its possibly harmful characteristics.

To establish liability on the basis of negligent misrepresentation in a products liability action, an injured plaintiff must show that the statement made by the defendant was not true and was made as an inducement for the plaintiff to change his position (an inducement to buy, for example), that he relied upon the information in good faith and that, through such reliance, he was injured.[141]

It is not necessary that the misrepresentation be made directly, through face-to-face contact, but may be made through advertisements, brochures, product datasheets or other means of communication.[142] Since nationwide adoption of the UCC with its statutory provisions for breach of warranty, most legal actions for negligent misrepresentation are now brought under breach of warranty as provided by the UCC. However, for some plaintiffs and situations in some jurisdictions, an action based upon negligence may offer certain advantages.

An increasingly common basis for products liability negligence action within this category is *failure to warn.* Such action stems from breach of a recognized duty for manufacturers or marketers to warn when a product possesses dangerous characteristics or when there is danger associated with use of the product.[143] Besides constituting a basis for negligence actions, failure to warn is a basis for strict liability action (discussed in the next section). In those cases, failure to warn has been viewed as a "defect" per se.

Strict Liability Standards: The *Product* On Trial. *A Matter of Burden of Proof.* In Chapter 3 we noted distinctions between what is known as "strict liability" and "absolute" liability. Strict liability has been described as "liability without fault." But it is not so much liability without fault as it is liability *without the need for proving* fault. Recall that "fault" here is not moral blame or common notions of fault but behavior that simply fails to measure up to the standard imposed by the law. And, by definition, such failure is negligence.

But *strict* liability is not *absolute* liability, where the manufacturer is virtually an insurer against injury from use of its products.[144,145] Admittedly, there are circumstances created by the manufacturer's representations, express warranties or characteristics of its products, that impose what amounts to absolute liability for product-caused injuries; but these are exceptions.

Strict liability differs from absolute liability in that, for strict liability to attach to a defendant manufacturer, the injured plaintiff must prove that the product that caused his injuries was defective, and was defective when it left the hands of the manufacturer. The principal distinction between strict liability and absolute liability is the burden upon the plaintiff in strict liability to prove defectiveness of the product, that its defectiveness caused his injuries and that the product was defective when it was placed on the market by the defendant.

Strict liability is distinguished from negligence generally by the shift of attention from the conduct of the manufacturer (defendant) to the condition of the product.[146]

> In a strict liability case we are talking about the condition . . . of an article which is sold . . . while in negligence we are talking about the reasonableness of the manufacturer's actions in selling the article. . . . (*Phillips v. Kimwood Machine Co.*)[147]

In strict liability, the plaintiff is not burdened with the need to prove lack of due care by the manufacturer or to prove any privity relationship. Such need for proof of facts concerning a manufacturer's conduct in the manufacture of its product was viewed by the courts as placing the injured (and "powerless") plaintiff at a serious disadvantage in his quest for a remedy or compensation. Among other things that prompted this conclusion was the fact that the injured party is remote from the manufacturing operations and without accessibility to facts and evidence required for such proof.

This has been stated in a California Supreme Court decision as one of the reasons for development of the principle of strict liability in products cases:

> [O]ne of the principal purposes behind the strict products liability doctrine is to relieve an injured plaintiff of many of the onerous evidentiary burdens inherent in a negligence cause of action. (*Barker v. Lull Engineering Co.*)[148]

The rationale that prompted the shift in emphasis from the conduct of the manufacturer to the product itself is well-described in the same California decision:

> [T]echnological revolution has created a society that contains dangers to the individual never before contemplated. The individual must face the threat of life and limb not only from the car on the street or highway but from a massive array of hazardous mechanisms and products. The radical change from a comparatively safe, largely agriculture society to this industrial unsafe one has been reflected in the decisions that formerly tied liability to the fault of a tortfeasor but now are more concerned with the safety of the individual who suffers the loss. As Dean Keeton has written,[149] the change in the substantive law as regards the liability of makers of products and other sellers in the marketing chain has been from fault to defect. *The plaintiff is no longer required to impugn the maker, but he is required to impugn the product.* (*Barker v. Lull Engineering Co.*)[150] (emphasis added)

While the shift in emphasis from manufacturer to product brought about by strict liability represents a major change, legal implications of this shift have been somewhat overstated. Many critics of the strict liability doctrine (generally manufacturers) fail to realize that strict liability is not absolute liability and that it does not provide a free handout to injured plaintiffs. While, in some respects, burden of proof has shifted from injured plaintiff to the defendant manufacturer, the plaintiff still must prove that the product was defective. And, in doing so, such proof is a reflection upon the conduct of the manufacturer.

In other words, the widely-heralded "departure" of products liability law from negligence principles never got very far from the dock. Products do not manufacture themselves. So, while strict liability in its focus on the product offers *procedural and evidential* advantages for the injured plaintiff in pursuing legal action, it is still the manufacturer and its conduct that are under the gun.[151] And it is the manufacturer who will pay the damages if found liable.

In court decisions during the last decade or so since strict liability became widely accepted for products cases, there have been gradual indications of a trend toward a blending of negligence and strict liability principles.[152] Those critics who propose abolishing strict liability for products may not have a full appreciation of this situation. By now, the likelihood of successfully eliminating strict liability principles from products-related tort law is about equal to that of removing already-added leaven from bread dough to keep it from rising.

Essential Elements. The action of strict liability is clearly described in the first decision in this country to recognize the doctrine independent of other legal concepts in a products case:

> A manufacturer is strictly liable in tort when an acticle he places on the market, knowing that it is to be used without inspection for defects, proves to have a defect that causes injury to a human being. . . . To establish the manufacturer's liability, it was sufficient that the plaintiff proved that he was injured while using the [product] in a way it was intended to be used as a result of a defect in design and manufacture of which plaintiff was not aware that made the [product] unsafe for its intended use. (*Greenman v. Yuba Power Products, Inc.*)[153]

Soon after this court decision, the American Law Institute, in its Restatement (Second) of the Law of Torts, incorporated most of these provisions into Section 402A. As mentioned earlier, the Restatements are intended to distill the essence of leading court decisions into a coherent and understandable reference source of judicial law in the United States. Restatements are not statutes or law in themselves and are not binding on any jurisdiction; nevertheless, they are well-respected and persuasive, and many courts adopt their principles verbatim. Since its publication in 1965, the provisions of strict liability in tort contained in Section 402A of the Restatement (Second) have been widely adopted in court decisions throughout the country.

Its Scope—The Restatement limits the scope of strict liability in tort to defendants who are commercial "sellers" (includes manufacturers, distributors and dealers) in the business of selling products such as the one claimed to have caused the harm. For a strict liability action, the product sold must be "in a defective condition unreasonably dangerous" to the purchaser, or user or his property and the product's condition must remain unchanged when it reaches the purchaser or user.[154] The seller's liability is for resulting "physical harm" to the purchaser, user, or his property.

While the Restatement did not offer an opinion on whether injured bystanders were included, most cases decided since it was written have held that they may bring an action under strict liability for products-related injuries. These decisions have indicated that reasonable foreseeability of the bystander and his injury govern whether an action may be maintained by the non-user. A Florida court has said, "This doctrine of strict liability applies when harm befalls a foreseeable bystander who comes within the range of danger."[155]

The Restatement indicates that action for strict liability would apply even if the injured party had no contractual relationship with the seller and even if the seller took every possible precaution in making and selling a safe product.

There has been considerable dispute on the question of who may be liable. From the increasing body of case law on the subject, it can be said that no one in the product distribution chain is immune.[156] Besides the manufacturer, this includes everyone who stands to gain from the sale of products: refiners and converters of raw material, producers of structural members and bulk ingredients, designers, engineers and suppliers of components, assemblers, packers, distributors, wholesalers, marketers, brokers, advertisers, retailers, testers including independent testing laboratories, endorsers and financiers, installers, repairers and servicers, builders and rebuilders, trade associations and anyone else who may have had some commercial dealing with the product.

In this connection it may be useful to review the definition of "manufacturer" given in a Senate bill proposing a uniform product liability law:

> "[M]anufacturer" means (A) any person who is engaged in a business to design or formulate and to produce, create, make, or construct any product (or component part of a product), including a product seller, distributor, or retailer of products with respect to any product to the extent that such a product seller, distributor or retailer designs or formulates and produces, creates, makes or constructs the product before that product seller, distributor or retailer sells the product; or (B) any product seller not described in clause (A) which holds itself out as a manufacturer to the user of the product.[157]

It is beyond the scope of this work to discuss intricacies of transactions that can lead to liability of suppliers of raw materials, ingredients and component parts; effects upon liability of manufacturers who subcontract certain manufacturing or testing functions to others; and whether one, some or all in the distributive chain should be held liable.

Generalizations about relative vulnerability of the large number of potential targets are difficult to make, but there are some practical guidelines. One is the question of who has the "deepest pocket" or the one with the most financial resources. Economic compensation is the theme and goal of products liability; so, of all possible targets for a products lawsuit, the primary ones are those with enough money to pay claims.

This does not mean that these will be the only ones named as defendants. The trend is to name everyone who had any connection with the product, for this is cost-effective to plaintiffs' attorneys. The cost of naming additional defendants is low but the potential it offers for obtaining information that can assure recovery of sought-after damages is high. Often, access to critically needed information to prove defectiveness of the product or negligence of the manufacturer can best be obtained through sources other than the manufacturer.

Another consideration is jurisdictional access. The actual manufacturer of the product may be out of practical reach of the court's jurisdiction. For example, a foreign concern without offices or operations in this country. But possibly the importer, packer, distributor, advertiser, marketer and seller or others involved with the product are all within reach of the court. Obviously, these would become primary targets. There are any number of examples where the "innocent link" in the product distribution chain became the primary target because it had financial resources and the greatest accessibility.

At the other side of the strict liability products lawsuit is the consumer or user, the one who is injured and seeking compensation. The user who becomes injured by a product can be anyone from an innocent and helpless infant to a seasoned professional or industrial expert. Does it make a difference in a products liability action? Knowledge and experience of the user *are* important and can even defeat an otherwise valid products liability claim.

The most obvious valid situation is injury of a child by a defective technically-sophisticated product intended for children's use but that a child could not even begin to comprehend. Such a situation would offer no difficulty. The same conclusion would hold for most injuries of unknowledgeable laymen who have no understanding of the product, its constituents or possible danger associated with its use.

Courts are sympathetic with the layman or ordinary user who is not expected to have any technical knowledge about sophisticated manufactured products, chemicals, pharmaceuticals or machinery. The general public are bargain-seeking, quality-conscious and emotionally conditioned by advertising to expect amazing performance and marvelous benefits from the products they buy. The industrial, professional or commercial product user who brings legal action against a product manufacturer for injuries has a different status and courts take this into account.

Products intended for sole use of professionals and sold through commercial channels have somewhat lesser requirements for instructions, labeling and warning of dangerous characteristics. However, it is possible that others than the ones the products are sold for may come into contact with them and be injured by them. The question over the extent of warning and other duties to professional users usually hinges upon foreseeability of use and misuse and exposure of non-professionals or non-experts to potential hazards associated with the product.

Since our emphasis is upon liability avoidance and the need to know what practices make a manufacturer vulnerable to a strict liability action, it is important to understand how courts have defined some of the key terms concerned with the product itself.

What Is a "Product?"—The term "product" is central to the entire subject of products liability. We use the term to describe the manufactured article or implement that is the instrumentality alleged to be responsible for the plaintiff's harm or injury. But exactly what *is* a "product?" An examination of case law shows an incredible array of things that courts have defined as products.[158] A clue to the breadth of the legal definition of "product" may be found in the Senate bill proposing a uniform products liability law:

> "[P]roduct" means any object, substance, mixture or raw material in a gaseous, liquid or solid state which is capable of delivery itself, or as an assembled whole in a mixed or combined state or as a component part or ingredient, which is produced for introduction into trade or commerce, which has intrinsic economic value, and which is intended for sale or lease to persons for commercial or personal use;[159]

Defectiveness—The principal elements that an injured party must prove in a products lawsuit based upon strict liability principles concern defectiveness of the product and its causal connection to the harm or injury. These same elements are also required in other products liability actions and are fundamental in maintaining a cause of legal action in products lawsuits. Because of its importance in assessing liability exposure and, therefore, preventing it; the concept of product defectiveness deserves some attention.

The Restatement's criterion for strict liability is "a defective condition unreasonably dangerous . . . "[160] As with most straightforward-sounding legal concepts, tests for determining "defectiveness" have generated incredibly intricate distinctions when applied to real-world situations. In fact, a leading jurist has concluded that "no single definition of defect has proved adequate to define the scope of the manufacturer's strict liability in tort for physical injuries."[161]

The several classifications of defectiveness described under negligence standards also apply to strict liability actions. That is, product defectiveness may be the result of improper design, incorrect manufacture, or faulty communication; that is, through what is done, made, or said. Many authorities define product defectiveness in terms of consumer *expectations*. In its interpretive comments following Section 402A, the American Law Institute's Restatement of Torts (2d) indicates that for a product to be "defective" and "unreasonably dangerous" the danger associated with it must be greater than the ordinary user or consumer would expect.[162]

This has been referred to as the "consumer expectation test" and, since it seems reasonable and offers an apparently easy solution to a knotty problem, it has been adopted by a good many jurisdictions. While the criterion of consumer expectation may be convenient for courts to use, it represents a formidable standard for the manufacturer. What this standard says is that expectations of the ordinary user dictate whether the product is or is not "defective" in the eyes of the law. If the danger in the product's use is greater than the ordinary user might expect it to be, it is defective.

Right off, considering the shallow depth of technical knowledge of the ordinary user, this test seems absurd; particularly for complicated "high-tech" products operating under principles well beyond the grasp of the ordinary user. Yet, that ordinary user is the one who determines whether a product is defective or unreasonably dangerous (as when ordinary users are injured and their attorneys cite the "user expectation test" or when they sit on a jury panel).

Of the three bases for product defectiveness standards: negligent design, negligent manufacture, and negligent marketing; negligent or defective design has been the most troublesome for injured plaintiffs to prove (as well as the most troublesome for manufacturers to face). This is largely because of the plaintiff's inferior position with respect to knowledge of technical tradeoffs and information on available design and safety options and their costs. Accordingly, there is not much difference between actions for negligence and strict liability where the plaintiff claims design defectiveness. This is despite the goal of strict liability to relieve the plaintiff of the burden of proof associated with negligence actions.

In examining a "cost-benefit analysis" or test for evaluating whether or not a product constituted negligent design in presenting an unreasonable risk of danger, we noted that this test balanced probability and gravity of harm expected to result from some activity against the burden of preventing it. In a California decision a few years ago, the court defined design defectiveness using criteria based upon *both* consumer expectations and a version of a cost-benefit analysis.[163] Although it is too soon to know if other jurisdictions will adopt this standard or modifications of it, it has attracted considerable attention and, since it blends two well-established liability criteria, it is worth discussing here.

In that decision, the court described its test for determining when a product has a design defect:

> [A] product may be found defectve in design so as to subject a manufacturer to strict liability for resulting injuries, using either of two alternative tests. First, a product may be found defective in design if the plaintiff establishes that the product failed to perform as safely as an ordinary consumer would expect when used in an intended or reasonably foreseeable manner. Second, a product may alternatively be found defective in design if the plaintiff demonstrates that the product's design proximately caused his injury and the defendant fails to establish, in light of relevant factors, that, on balance, the benefits of the challenged design outweigh the risks of danger inherent in such design. (*Barker v. Lull Engineering Co.*)[164]

Under this rule, a product with an alleged design defect that has caused a plaintiff's injury must be scrutinized against a double-barreled standard. For, even if a product did perform as safely as an ordinary user would have expected it to perform when used in an intended or reasonably foreseeable manner; the defendant manufacturer must prove that the product is not defective by applying the "risk-benefit" criteria.

By this decision, the California court has lessened the burden on the injured plaintiff and transferred it to the defendant manufacturer. It did this following the rationale that it is the defendant manufacturer who has the better knowledge of and access to technical information for applying the risk-benefit test, and not the injured plaintiff. Thus, the burden is upon the defendant manufacturer to show that its product is not defective; or, that the benefits inherent in its particular design outweigh its risks of injury.

In diminishing the injured plaintiff's burden of proof of the product's defectiveness in this way, it would seem that the court has achieved what strict liability originally set out to do and, until adopting this composite test, had not achieved in the case of design defectiveness. Of course, the plaintiff still has the burden of proving that the product failed to perform as safely as an ordinary consumer would expect and that the product was defective when it left the hands of the manufacturer and that the defect was the proximate cause of his injury. But this is so for the other strict liability products actions, as well.

All of this is procedural in nature. What matters is how the proof and evidence appear to the court and jury; for these are the ones that determine if the manufacturer is liable. These are the ones applying the standards. To show the extent of the court's evaluation in determining whether a product's design is defective, the court in the decision just cited said that a product may have a defective design

> even if it satisfies ordinary consumer expectations, if through hindsight the jury determines that the product's design embodies 'excessive preventable danger' or, in other words, if the jury finds that the risk of danger inherent in the challenged design outweighs the benefit of such design. (*Barker v. Lull Engineering Co.*)[165]

In its determination mentioned above, the court said the jury may consider such issues as

> gravity of the danger posed by the challenged design, the likelihood that such danger would occur, the mechanical feasibility of a safer alternative design, the financial cost of an improved design, and the adverse consequences to the product and to the consumer that would result from an alternative design. (*Barker v. Lull Engineering Co.*)[166]

In another, more recent, decision a New York court in applying a risk-benefit analysis identified seven factors for determining design defectiveness:

> The question for the jury, then, is whether after weighing the evidence and balancing the product's risks against its utility and cost, it can be concluded that the product as designed is not reasonably safe. . . . In balancing the risks inherent in the product, as designed, against its utility and cost, the jury may consider several factors. . . . Those factors may include the following: (1) the utility of the product to the public as a whole and to the individual user; (2) the nature of the product—that is, the likelihood that it will cause injury; (3) the availability of a safe design; (4) the potential for designing and manufacturing the product so that it is safer but remains functional and reasonably priced; (5) the ability of the plaintiff to have avoided injury by careful use of the product; (6) the degree of awareness of the potential danger of the product which reasonably can be attributed to the plaintiff; and (7) the manufacturer's ability to spread any cost related to improving the safety of the design. (*Voss v. Black & Decker Mfg. Co.*)[167] .

These excerpts from recent products liability decisions in jurisdictions that have played a leading role in development of strict liability tort principles provide a glimpse of how courts evaluate a product's defectiveness. This affords an opportunity to observe the extent of the scrutiny with which a court and jury may one day examine your products, every aspect of their design, cost-risk-benefit tradeoffs and related engineering decisions.

Besides design defectiveness, defects occurring during manufacturing are also obvious causes for strict liability action. Manufacturing flaws present less difficulty in establishing a product's defectiveness than do design defects. The user-expectation test mentioned earlier and described in the Restatement seems to have a dominant position in evaluating such a condition.[168]

Generally though, a manufacturing defect will not be debated and require involved legal analysis. It is relatively easy for the plaintiff to prove that the product is not what the manufacturer intended. In fact, the manufacturer will likely be among the first to admit it and this admission frequently prompts a settlement to be negotiated at an early stage of the lawsuit.

Note that the court decisions we have been examining in this book are virtually all *appellate* decisions—cases that originally were tried to a verdict in lower courts and whose decisions were appealed to higher courts. It is cases that involve unsettled principles, unprecedented occurrences or questionable application of precedents and obscure fact situations that defy early settlement and whose issues persist through the court system to forums of final authority. Remember that only a very small percentage of products lawsuits ever go all the way to a court or jury verdict; most are settled well before that.

The Restatement covering strict liability elements also indicates that a product sold by manufacturers or others who have reason to believe that there is danger associated with a particular use of the product, and sell the product without warning of it, such failure to warn constitutes a defective condition for that product.[169] Failure to warn of danger that might result from use of a product not only is a basis for negligence, as we saw; but also a basis under strict liability for declaring a product defective. Therefore, such a basis for legal action is not confined to jurisdictions that have adopted the Restatement's position, for there is little practical difference between the elements of a lawsuit brought in strict liability for failure to warn and those for one brought in negligence.

Because proof of defective condition is a critical element in a strict liability case, particularly where a design defect is claimed, the defectiveness issue receives the most attention. But the Restatement's criterion for a strict liability action is "a defective condition unreasonably dangerous ... " In other words, proof of a "defective condition" may not be enough. The additional considerations that may be required in establishing whether the product defect also constituted an "unreasonably dangerous" condition are often unnecessary, depending upon the criteria used for defining "defectiveness."

The characteristic of being "unreasonably dangerous" usually stems from some design defect, obscure to the ordinary user, that makes the product dangerous to use; or from failure to provide some safety feature. The question of unreasonable danger is closely tied to the user's expectation and this is a function of the user's knowledge, background and understanding about the product and its use. Ability of a product to inflict serious injury is not the test for declaring a product "unreasonably dangerous," because knives, saws, razors, matches and guns are not considered *unreasonably* dangerous products. Their propensities for harm are usual, well-known and often obvious, and this is the key—how safe does the ordinary user expect the product to be when it is used in an intended or reasonably foreseeable manner.

Determinations of unreasonable danger also involve questions of the amount and degree of *preventable* danger in the product. Knives have to be sharp to cut; their danger cannot be eliminated without making them useless for their intended purpose. So it is with dynamite. It is a dangerous product, but not necessarily defective from the standpoint of a strict liability action. But dynamite that is unexpectedly hypersensitiive to heat, making it unstable and likely to explode spontaneously on a hot day, would be *unreasonably* dangerous, and therefore defective.

A number of considerations must be applied in deciding whether a product is or is not unreasonably dangerous: Does its usefulness outweigh the probability of harm that might occur from its use or foreseeable misuse? Do risks inherent in its use outweigh benefits that accrue from its design, use and existence? Do foreseeable probability and gravity of harm outweigh the burden of an alternative design or other action that would prevent that harm? Is there excessive preventable danger associated with the product or its ordinary or reasonably foreseeable use or misuse?

Among the array of products made and used by modern society are classes of products that simply cannot be made safe for their intended use; yet are useful and even essential.[170] These products have been described as unavoidably unsafe. Some drugs, vaccines and industrial chemicals would be in this class. Although they are unavoidably unsafe they need not be unreasonably dangerous. Duty to warn of the risks would, of course, be crucially important, as would be the effectiveness in communicating the warning, in avoiding action for strict liability under the "unreasonably dangerous" rule of the Restatement.

The need for these legal considerations and balancing tests for proof of product defectiveness may seem burdensome and redundant, but the greater the burden of proof of defectiveness the better it is for the defendant manufacturer. Unfortunately for the manufacturer, however, the trend is toward easing the plaintiff's burden of proof. In fact, plaintiffs' attorneys would like to simplify the criterion of product defectiveness to the question of whether the product caused an injury; if it did, it is "defective."

Their rationale is that the manufacturer should design out all danger. If, despite all design precautions, there still is risk of injury in use of the product; the manufacturer must warn of it and an "adequate" warning will prevent injury. There is no way to know if this definition of defectiveness will ever be broadly adopted, but the trend of some recent decisions in relieving the injured plaintiff's burden of proof is in this direction.

The principal purpose for applying strict liability principles to products lawsuits was to allow *injured* individuals to be compensated without the burden of proof formerly associated with negligence actions.[171,172] Consequently, most strict liability actions involve physical injury or death, although wrongful death is not specifically mentioned in the Restatement. However, the Restatement does address physical harm to property, and strict liability actions have been sustained for damage to property (even the product itself) and other property that may be in the vicinity; although not all jurisdictions allow such recovery on strict liability principles.

Courts have allowed an injured plaintiff to recover economic losses connected with occurrence of the injury, such as lost wages and medical expenses, but they are reluctant to allow recovery of indirect and consequential losses under strict liability principles. Other approaches are available for such losses, however.

A "STACKED DECK" BUT NOT A LOST GAME

The objective in this chapter has been to show how developments in the law during the past two decades have increased vulnerability to lawsuits of manufacturers and others who handle and sell products for profit. Attack can come on any number of fronts. Industry is surrounded on all sides by hostile forces equipped with well-honed weapons that can undermine even the most solid and well-established companies. Unfortunately, it seems unlikely that any kind of counterattack by industry is now possible. The author of the bumber sticker slogan that says "you don't have to be paranoid to know they're out to get you" must have been a manufacturer with products liability on his mind.

Legal principles for the aggression have foundations that were laid long ago and go deep. The heated public sentiment that has created the many-headed monster of government regulation and judicial law, and environment for its nurture and growth, is likewise deep-seated and shows no signs of cooling off. The very lifeblood of American business—technological revolution and product innovation—has borne seeds of causes for products liability action that have sufficient destructive potential for damaging even large firms and entire industries.

Yet, while damage potential is great, disaster is not inevitable. Attempts to turn back the tide of products liability that is running against industry today may be futile, and perhaps the first constructive step to take is to recognize this. Considering the fact that every company has limited resources with many interests competing for them, it is doubtful that attacks upon "the system" through such activities as lobbying for legislative reform will be cost-effective in the long run.

While offensive action against the forces of products liability at this late stage in our history may be ineffective, it is never too late for preventive action and defense. Of course, once an occurrence creating a basis for a products liability claim takes place, it may be too late to implement preventive measures, as far as *that* occurrence is concerned. And certainly, competent legal counsel are essential in defending against the claim and minimizing its adverse effects. Development of an effective defense strategy should not wait until a claim is filed but should be an integral part of a program of liability prevention.

While an effective prevention program should include adequate insurance coverage and availability of and representation by the best legal counsel, it must go further than that. The best defense against the threat of products liability is to prevent claims, to *avoid* it as far as it is possible to do so.

So far in our discussions of vulnerability to products liability, we have considered how new laws have, for all intents and purposes, created new standards for every product manufacturer and others in the product distribution chain. This means that each product we develop, produce, test and sell must be capable of passing not only our own codes, standards and specifications, but also scrutiny of a court and jury, and evaluation based upon *their* standards. As we have seen in this chapter, the legal "standards" and requirements for our products are many, they are complex, and not always consistent with one another. Nevertheless, it is possible to make some summarizing comments about these requirements, duties and responsibilities.

On the one side, the law views the product user or consumer as being at a disadvantage with respect to the seller (including the manufacturer and others connected with its sale and distribution). The disadvantage is in knowledge and understanding about the product, what it is made of, how it is made, how it works and why. Not only is the ordinary user lacking in technical understanding but he would have difficulties in attempting to learn these facts even if he was motivated to do so. He is at a disadvantage as to access to this information, as well.

At the other side, the law views the product manufacturer, distributor, dealer or retailer as a profit-motivated entity that deals in products solely for profit and financial gain. The law recognizes that this motivation has potential for conflict with the welfare of society. That is, what is best for the purchaser of the product is not always best for maximizing profits for the producer. Courts feel that they must equalize the positions of the two parties—the disadvantaged "powerless" individual consumer on the one hand and the rich, powerful and knowledgeable business organization on the other—and do so with the goal of achieving "the greatest happiness of the greatest number," or the welfare of society.

Coincidental with and superimposed upon these conflicting motivations and the law's attempts to equalize the positions of the parties is the increasing concern of society for the plight of its victims of injuries and other harm traceable to manufactured products. So, there has been a trend toward finding a solution to the problem of these victims through economic compensation. This social concern is seen in many other areas: social security, workmen's compensation, Medicare, welfare programs and other government-funded social assistance activities.

The underlying notion is a form of social insurance where all contribute to a fund that may be distributed to victims of various misfortunes in an attempt to avoid isolated pockets of severe economic hardship. Products liability law plays a role in this concept through awarding victims of products accidents financial payment taken from the (presumably larger and relatively inexhaustable) resources of the product manufacturer who purchases insurance for such requirements. The manufacturer can pass its costs back to the consumer through price increases, making everyone contribute a little to the welfare of the unfortunate few.

The law accomplishes these massive and ambitious tasks of equalization and economic redistribution through imposing certain duties and responsibilities upon product manufacturers and others who make, distribute and sell products for profit. These duties have been expressed in terms of standards of care and conduct of the manufacturer and also in terms of product qualities. The purpose of imposing these duties is to prevent harm associated with the use and existence of manufactured products; and the duties are exactly that, not optional practices but mandatory obligations. Incentives for complying with legally-imposed duties are provided in the form of court-ordered sanctions, forced payment of financial damages— both compensatory and punitive—and, for some violations, imprisonment of responsible individuals.

In this context, the "deck" truly is stacked against the profit-motivated manufacturer or merchant and in favor of the product user and consumer. It did not just happen that way; it was made that way, deliberately and on purpose. Quite frankly, the manufacturer has little choice but to learn to comply with the law's requirements, or face an uncertain and insecure future.

The best response a manufacturer can make is to nip products liability in the bud at the earliest possible stage. This may mean re-thinking the entire production operation; it may mean reorganizing the firm; and it certainly will require reviewing policies and practices and formulating new ones, from the top executive level down. These are some of the issues covered in the next chapter.

REFERENCES

1. *United States v. Nixon*, 418 U.S. 683 (1974).
2. 28 U.S.C.A., Fed.R.Civ.P., 26(b) (1), General Provisions Governing Discovery (Scope of Discovery).
3. 28 U.S.C.A., Fed.R.Civ.P., 26(c), General Provisions Governing Discovery (Protective Orders).
4. 28 U.S.C.A., Fed.R.Civ.P., 37, Refusal to Make Discovery: Consequences.
5. *Bollard v. Volkswagen of America, Inc.*, 56 FRD (Federal Rules Decisions) 569 (W.D. Mo. 1971).
6. Juran, J.M., ed. *Quality Control Handbook* 4-22, Third Edition, McGraw-Hill Book Co. (1979).
7. *Index of U.S. Voluntary Engineering Standards*, National Bureau of Standards, U.S. Department of Commerce, U.S. Government Printing Office, Washington, DC 20402.
8. *1985 Publications Catalog*, American Society for Testing and Materials, Philadelphia, PA 19103.
9. Philo, H.M., *Lawyer's Desk Reference*, 6th ed., 2 volumes, The Lawyers Co-Operative Publishing Co., Rochester, NY 14694, and Bancroft-Whitney Co., San Francisco, CA 94107 (1979).
10. Association of Trial Lawyers of America Product Liability Exchange, 1050 31st Street, N.W., Washington, DC 20007.
11. Zackey, J.T., *The ATLA Exchange: Professional Cooperation and Product Safety*, 14 Trial 63 (November 1978).
12. Hayes, S.L., *Computers and Litigation Support*, Law & Business, Inc. (1981).

13. Kinney, E.H., *Litigation Support Systems, An Attorney's Guide*, Callaghan (1980).
14. Philo, H.M., 2 *Lawyer's Desk Reference* 754, 764, 6th ed., The Lawyer's Co-Operative Publishing Co., Rochester, NY 14694, and Bancroft-Whitney Co., San Francisco, CA 94107 (1979).
15. National Commission on Product Safety, *Final Report* (June 1970), presented to the President and Congress, National Technical Information Service, Springfield, VA 22161.
16. *Marsh Wood Products Co. v. Babcock & Wilcox Co.*, 207 Wis. 209, 240 N.W. 392 (1932).
17. *The T.J. Hooper*, 60 F.2d 737 (2d Circuit 1932).
18. Ballway, J.H. Jr., *Products Liability Based Upon Violation of Statutory Standards*, 64 Michigan Law Review 1388 (1966).
19. Bird, R.E., *Federal Hazardous Substances Legislation: Effects on Consumer Protection and Manufacturers Liability*, 13 Boston College Industry & Commercial Law Review 504 (1972).
20. American Law Institute, *Restatement (Second) of the Law: Torts*, Section 288 B(1) American Law Institute Publishers, St. Paul, MN (1965).
21. Sherman, Paul, *Products Liability for the General Practitioner*, 175-86, Shepards/McGraw-Hill, Colorado Springs, CO (1981).
22. *Osborne v. McMasters*, 40 Minn. 103, 41 N.W. 543 (1889).
23. *The T.J. Hooper, supra.* reference 17.
24. Lilley, W. and Miller, J., *The New Social Regulation*, American Enterprise Institution, Washington, DC (1977).
25. Coccia, M.A., *The New Federalism in Products Liability*, 10 Forum 1057 (1975).
26. Byington, S.J., *Public Regulation of Consumer Products and Products Liability—The Interface*, 14 Forum 327 (1978).
27. *Larsen v. General Motors Corp.*, 391 F.2d 495 (U.S. Court of Appeals, 8th Circuit 1968).
28. Uniform Commercial Code (UCC), Uniform Laws Annotated (Master ed. 1976).
29. *Id.* at Sections 2-312 through 2-318, 2-607, 2-718, 2-719, 2-725.
30. *Id.* at Section 2-313.
31. *Id.* at Section 2-315.
32. *Id.* at Section 2-719.
33. Magnuson-Moss Warranty—Federal Trade Commission Improvement Act, Public Law No. 93-637, 93d Congress, S.356, 15 USC 2301-12 (January 4, 1975).
34. *Id.* and Interpretation of Magnuson-Moss Warranty Act, 16 CFR 700, 42 FR 36112 (July 13, 1977).
35. *Supra* reference 33 at Section 108.
36. *Henningsen v. Bloomfield Motors, Inc.*, 32 N.J. 358, 161 A.2d 69 (1960).
37. *Greenman v. Yuba Power Products, Inc.*, 59 Cal.2d 57, 27 Cal. Reptr. 697, 377 P.2d 897 (1963).
38. Public Law No. 90-146, 90th Congress, S.J.Res 33 (November 20, 1967).
39. *Id.*
40. *Supra* reference 15.

41. Consumer Product Safety Act, Public Law No. 92-573, 92d Congress, S.3419 (October 27, 1972), 15 U.S.C. 2047-84; Consumer Product Safety Commission Improvements Act of 1976, Public Law No. 94-234 (May 11, 1976); the Emergency Interim Consumer Product Safety Act of 1978, Public Law No. 95-319 (July 11, 1978); Public Law No. 95-631 (November 10, 1978); Public Law No. 96-373, (October 3, 1980); Public Law No. 96-486 (December 1, 1980); Public Law No. 97-35 (August 13, 1981); Public Law No. 97-258 (September 13, 1982); Public Law No. 97-414 (January 4, 1983).

42. *Id.* at Sect. 2(b).

43. Federal Hazardous Substances Act, Public Law No. 86-613, Sect. 17, 74 Stat. 380 (1960), *as amended* 80 Stat. 1305 (1966), *as amended and renumbered* Sect. 18(b) (2), 83 Stat. 190 (1969), *as amended* 90 Stat. 510 (1976).

44. Poison Prevention Packaging Act, Public Law No. 91-601, Sect. 1-9, 84 Stat. 1670-74 (1970), 15 U.S.C. 1471-76.

45. 15 U.S.C. 1191-1204 (1976), *as amended* 15 U.S.C. 1196, 1202 (Supp. II 1978).

46. Refrigerator Safety Act, Public Law No. 84-930, 84th Congress, H.R. 11969 (August 2, 1956) 70 Stat. 953 (1956), 15 U.S.C. 1211-14 (1976).

47. *Supra* reference 41 at Sect. 3(a) (1): "The term 'consumer product' means any article, or component part thereof, produced or distributed (i) for sale to a consumer for use in or around a permanent or temporary household or residence, a school, in reaction, or otherwise, or (ii) for the personal use, consumption or enjoyment of a consumer in or around a permanent or temporary household or residence, a school, in recreation or otherwise;"

48. *Supra* reference 41 at Sect. 15(a), "[T]he term 'substantial product hazard' means—(1) a failure to comply with an applicable consumer product safety rule which creates a substantial risk of injury to the public, or (2) a product defect which (because of the pattern of defect, the number of defective products distributed in commerce, the severity of the risk, or otherwise) creates a substantial risk of injury to the public."

49. Verhalen, R.D., *The NEISS—What, How and Why*, Proceedings PLP/74 at 119, Product Liability Prevention Conference, Newark, NJ (August 21-23, 1974) IEEE Catalog No. 74CH0911-8R; and *NEISS—Past, Present, Future*, Proceedings PLP/75 at 9, Product Liability Prevention Conference, Newark, NJ (August 19-22, 1975) IEEE Catalog No. 75 CH0986-OR.

50. Hoffman, M.E., *The Consumer Product Safety Commission: In Search of a Regulatory Pattern*, 12 Columbia Journal of Law and Social Problems 393 (1976).

51. CPSC Statement of Policy on Establishing Priorities for Action, 16 C.F.R. 1009.8, issued at 41 F.R. 27960, (July 8, 1976), 42 F.R. 53953 (October 4, 1977).

52. *Standard on Architectural Glazing Materials*, 16 C.F.R. 1201; *Safety Standard for Matchbooks*, 16 C.R.F. 1202; *Safety Standard and Certification Regulation for Omnidirectional CB Base Station Antennas*, 16 C.F.R. 1204; *Safety Standard for Walk-Behind Power Lawn Mowers*, 16 C.F.R. 1205; *Standard for Swimming Pool Slides*, 16 C.F.R. 1207; *Interim Safety Standard for Cellulose Insulation*, 16 C.F.R. 1209; *Safety Standard on Unvented Gas-*

Fired Space Heaters, 16 C.F.R. 1212; *Labeling and Data Submission Requirements for Self-Pressurized Consumer Products Containing Chlorofluoro-carbon Propellants,* 16 C.F.R. 1401; *Standard on CB Base Station Antennas, TV Antennas, and Supporting Structures,* 16 C.F.R. 1402; *Requirements on Cellulose Insulation Labeling,* 16 C.F.R. 1404; *Requirements for Performance and Technical Data on Coal and Wood-Burning Stoves,* 16 C.F.R. 1406.

53. *Ban of Unstable Refuse Bins,* 16 C.F.R. 1301; *Ban of Extremely Flammable Contact Adhesives,* 16 C.F.R. 1302; *Ban of Lead-Containing Paint and Certain Consumer Products Bearing Lead-Containing Paint,* 16 C.F.R. 1303; *Ban of Consumer Patching Compounds Containing Respirable Free Form Asbestos,* 16 C.F.R. 1304; *Ban of Artificial Emberizing Materials Containing Respirable Free Form Asbestos,* 16 C.F.R. 1305.

54. 12 Product Safety & Liability Reporter 78 (Current Report) (1984).

55. *Supra* reference 41 at Sect. 5(a) (4).

56. *Supra* reference 48.

57. Mackay, D.R., *Voluntary Industry Actions,* Proceedings PLP-77E at 27, Product Liability Prevention Conference, Hasbrouck Heights, NJ (August 22-24, 1977).

58. *Supra* references 43-46.

59. *Supra* reference 43 at Sect. 2(f)1(A).

60. *Supra* reference 43 at Sect. 2(f)1(D).

61. *Supra* reference 43 at Sect. 2(p) and (q), Sect. 3-5.

62. *Supra* reference 43 at Sect. 2(q)1.

63. *Supra* reference 43 at Sect. 2(p).

64. *Supra* reference 43 at Sect. 5.

65. Hazardous Substances Standards, 16 C.F.R. 1500, 1501, 1505, 1507-12.

66. *Supra* reference 44 at 15 U.S.C. 1471.

67. *Id.* at Sect. 1472.

68. 16 C.F.R. 1700-01.

69. *Supra* reference 45 at Sect. 1193(a) and 16 C.F.R. 1602.1 (b).

70. 16 C.F.R. 1610, 1611, 1615, 1616, 1630-32.

71. *Supra* reference 46.

72. Radiation Control for Health and Safety Act, 42 U.S.C. 263b-263n (1968).

73. *Id.* at Sect. 263d(a).

74. *Id.* at Sect. 263c(1).

75. 21 C.F.R. 1000.3, subchapter J.

76. *Id.* at Sect. 1000.15.

77. 21 C.F.R. 1000-1005, 1010, 1020, 1030, 1040, 1050.

78. Public Law No. 75-717, 52 Stat. 1040-59 (1938), 21 U.S.C. 301-92 (1976), *as amended* 21 U.S.C. 321, 343, 343a, 352 (Supp. II 1978).

79. Public Law No. 89-563 (Sept. 9, 1966), 15 U.S.C. 1381-1431 (1976).

80. *Id.* at Sect. 1381.

81. 12 Product Safety & Liability Reporter 338-39 (Current Report) (1984).

82. *Supra* reference 79 at Sect. 1391.

83. *Supra* reference 79 at Sect. 1392.

84. *Id.*

85. Steinberg, Robert B., *Liability of Third Party Manufacturers,* 1 Journal of Products Liability 52-62 (1977).

86. *Dole v. Dow Chemical Co.,* 30 N.Y.2d 143, 331 N.Y.S.2d 382, 282 N.E.2d 288 (1972).

87. Occupational Safety and Health Act of 1970, Public Law No. 91-596, 91st Congress, S.2193, December 29, 1970, 29 U.S.C. 651-78.

88. *Id.* at Sect. 5.

89. *Id.* at Sect. 13(a).

90. *Id.* at Sect. 22.

91. 29 C.F.R. 1910.

92. *Id.* at Sect. 1910.268-1910.269.

93. *Supra* reference 87 at Sect. 18.

94. Prosser, W.L., *Handbook of the Law of Torts* 139, West Publishing Co., St. Paul, MN (1971).

95. See references 32 and 33 of Chapter 3.

96. See reference 5 of Chapter 3.

97. *Id.*

98. *Blyth v. Birmingham Waterworks Co.,* 11 Ex. 781, 156 Eng.Rep. 1047 (1856).

99. *Supra* reference 94 at 149.

100. *Giant Food, Inc., v. Washington Coca-Cola Bottling Co.,* 332 A.2d 1 (1975).

101. Bignell, V., Peters, G., and Pym, C., *Catastrophic Failures*, Second Printing (Revised), The Open University Press, New York, NY (1978).

102. Prosser, W.L., *supra* reference 94 at 238-40.

103. *Craig v. Burch*, 228 So.2d 723, 728-30 (1969).

104. *Supra* reference 20 at Section 282.

105. *Hanberry v. Hearst Corp.*, 276 Cal.App. 2d 680, 81 Ca.Rptr. 519 (1969).

106. *Supra* reference 20 at Section 395.

107. *Jamieson v. Woodward & Lothrop*, 101 App.D.C. 32, 247 F.2d 23, *cert. den.* 355 U.S. 855, 2 L.Ed.2d 63, 783 S.Ct. 84 (1957).

108. *Supra* reference 20 at Section 395, illustration 2.

109. *City of Franklin v. Badger Ford Truck Sales, Inc.,* 58 Wis.2d 641, 207 N.W.2d 866 (1973).

110. *Boeing Airplane Co. v. Brown*, 291 F.2d 310 (Court of Appeals, Washington) (1961).

111. *Markel v. Spencer*, 5 App.Div.2d 400, 171 N.Y.S.2d 770, *affd.* 5 N.Y.2d 958, 184 N.Y.S.2d 835, 157 N.E.2d 713 (1958).

112. *Supra* reference 20 at Section 400.

113. *Supra* reference 20 at Sections 395 and 398.

114. *Gosset v. Chrysler Corp.*, 359 F.2d 84 (Court of Appeals, Michigan) (1966).

115. *Putensen v. Clay Adams, Inc.*, 12 Cal.App.3d 1062, 91 Cal.Rptr. 319 (1970).

116. *Reusch v. Ford Motor Co.,* 196 Wash. 213, 82 P.2d 556 (1938).

117. *Grimshaw v. Ford Motor Co.*, 119 Cal.App.3d 757, 174 Cal.Rptr. 348 (1981).

118. *Zahora v. Harnischfeger Corp.*, 404 F.2d 172 (Court of Appeals, Indiana) (1968).

119. *Seattle First Nat. Bank v. Volkswagen of America, Inc.*, 11 Wash.App. 929, 525 P.2d 286, *affd.* 86 Wash.2d 145, 542 P.2d 774 (1974).

120. *Leichtamer v. American Motors Corp.*, 67 Ohio St.2d 456, 21 Ohio Ops.3d 285, 424 N.E.2d 568 (1981).

121. *Pike v. Frank G. Hough Co.*, 2 Cal.3d 465, 85 Cal.Rptr. 629, 467 P.2d 229 (1970).

122. *Richelman v. Kewanee Machinery & Conveyor Co.*, 59 Ill.App.3d 578, 16 Ill.Dec. 778, 375 N.E.2d 885 (1978).
123. *Supra* references 18 and 20.
124. *Orthopedic Equipment v. Eutsler*, 276 F.2d 455, 79 A.L.R.2d 390 (Court of Appeals, Virginia) (1960).
125. *Raymond v. Riegel Textile Corp.*, 484 F.2d 1025 (U.S. Court of Appeals, 1st Circuit 1973).
126. *Jonescue v. Jewel Home Shopping Service*, 16 Ill. App.3d 339, 306 N.E.2d 312 (1973).
127. *Larsen v. General Motors Corp., supra* reference 27.
128. *Rumsey v. Freeway Manor Minimax*, 423 S.W.2d 387 (1968).
129. *Supra* reference 20 at Section 395, comment f.
130. 6 A.L.R.3d 91.
131. *LeBlanc v. Ford Motor Co.*, 346 Mass. 255, 191 N.E.2d 301 (1963).
132. *Edison v. Lewis Mfg. Co.*, 336 P.2d 286 (1959).
133. *Ford Motor Co. v. Zahn*, 265 F.2d 729 (Court of Appeals, Minnesota) (1959).
134. *Reynolds v. Natural Gas Equipment, Inc.*, 184 Cal.App.2d 724, 7 Cal.Rptr. 879 (1960).
135. *Conway v. O'Brien*, 111 F.2d 611 (2d Cir. 1940), *rev'd. on other grounds*, 312 U.S. 492, 61 S.Ct. 639, 85 L.Ed.969 (1941).
136. *United States v. Carroll Towing Co.*, 159 F.2d 169 (2d Cir. 1947).
137. *Supra* reference 20 at Section 293.
138. *Micallef v. Miehle Co., Div. of Miehle-Goss Dexter, Inc.*, 39 N.Y.2d 376, 348 N.E.2d 571, 384 N.Y.S.2d 115 (1976).
139. *Supra* reference 20 at Section 311.
140. *Baxter v. Ford Motor Co.*, 179 Wash. 123, 35 P.2d 1090 (1934).
141. *Supra* reference 20 at Sections 311 and 402B.
142. *Supra* reference 20 at Section 402B, comment h.
143. *Supra* reference 20 at Section 388, comment b.
144. *Supra* reference 107.
145. *Mondshour v. General Motors Corp.*, 298 F.Supp. 111 (Maryland) (1969).
146. *Jackson v. Coast Paint & Lacquer Co.*, 499 F.2d 809 (Court of Appeals, Montana, 1974)
147. *Phillips v. Kimwood Machine Co.*, 525 P.2d 1033 (Oregon, 1974).
148. *Barker v. Lull Engineering Co.*, 20 Cal.3d 413, 143 Cal.Rptr. 225, 573 P.2d 443 (1978).
149. Keeton, W.P., *Products Liability and the Meaning of Defect*, 5 St. Mary's Law Journal 30 (1973)
150. *Supra* reference 148.
151. Herbert, E.R., and Griffin, P.R., *Fault Substitutes: The True Bases for Strict Liability*, 1 Journal of Products Liability 81-92 (1977).
152. Zimmerman, B., *Products Liability: The California Supreme Court's Attempted Balancing Act*, 2 Journal of Products Liability 215-36 (1978).
153. *Supra* reference 37.
154. *Supra* reference 20 at Section 402A.
155. *West v. Caterpillar Tractor Co.*, 336 So.2d 80 (1976).
156. *Carter v. Yardley & Co.*, 319 Mass. 92, 64 N.E.2d 693 (1946).
157. S.44, 98th Cong. 1st Sess., Sect 2(6) (1983), see Appendix.

158. Noel, D.W., and Phillips, J.J., *Products Liability Cases and Materials* 1-5, West Publishing Co., St. Paul, MN (1976).

159. *Supra* reference 157 at Sect. 2(10).

160. *Supra* reference 20 at Section 402A.

161. Traynor, R., *The Ways and Meanings of Defective Products and Strict Liability*, 32 Tennessee Law Review 363 (1965).

162. *Supra* reference 20 at Section 402A, comment i.

163. *Supra* reference 148.

164. *Id.*

165. *Id.*

166. *Id.*

167. *Voss. v. Black & Decker Manufacturing Co.*, 59 N.Y.2d 102, 463 N.Y.S.2d 398, 450 N.E.2d 204, (1983).

168. *Supra* reference 20 at Section 402A, comment i.

169. *Supra* reference 20 at Section 402A, comment h.

170. *Supra* reference 20 at Section 402A, comment k.

171. *Supra* reference 37.

172. *Supra* reference 107.

5

Win—Through Prevention

COMMITMENT COMES FIRST

Real Solutions for Real Problems

It is difficult to generate interest in prevention unless there is a threat of some impending harm that has a reasonably good chance of affecting us personally. For example, people in the United States are not highly motivated toward civil defense. One of the reasons is that we have never had to face an enemy invasion on our mainland or need for evacuating civilian population from our major cities. Therefore, Americans have little motivation toward taking steps to minimize effects of such an eventuality. The prevailing sentiment is that "it can't happen here" so why bother fretting about preventing something that won't happen.

With civil defense, it is not a matter of preventing disaster itself or eliminating its cause, but minimizing harm that will result if it does occur. Products liability is not much different. We probably can do nothing to eliminate its potential or to prevent it from threatening us, but there *is* a good deal we can do to prevent it from ruining our businesses and careers. The old proverb says it well, "You may not be able to prevent buzzards from flying over your head, but you *can* keep them from making nests in your hair."

Unless we appreciate the extent of the threat and its many facets, and how it can damage us personally, we will not be motivated to do something positive and constructive about preventing its effects from harming us and our interests. In considering the various standards of liability with their respective duties and personal responsibilities we become aware of what the law requires of us. And, if we know that and are responsible engineers, we will resolve to do our best to measure up to what the law—through these new standards—requires. If we make such a resolution, we shall have taken a major step in preventing products liability. Although our attention so far may have been directed toward other aspects of the problem; our theme right along has been prevention.

As important as personal dedication and commitment to fulfilling the law's requirements are, they can take us only so far in assuring that our companies and our companies' products remain insulated from the threats of products liability. In an organization, we are members of a team and while each individual team member must be knowledgeable and committed to the right things, there also must be *team* strategies and tactics directed toward the goal of avoiding products liability lawsuits and damages.

This requires teamwork of the highest order and it also requires new organizational policies, new activities, new approaches, new attitudes and outlooks and new ways of doing old things. Since no two companies are alike, no two strategies or organizational approaches will be alike. So, it will be necessary for us to deal in generalities.

At this point, a number of manufacturing executives will question the need for any major change in what they are already doing. Most manufacturing executives would not consciously jeopardize their company's financial stability through totally disregarding the products liability threat. While practically every manufacturer is aware of the potential for problems, far too many see their products in an unrealistic light as being virtually flawless and absolutely safe to use.

Many manufacturers *feel* that they are not exposed to liability—either because they are convinced they make quality products or because they have established a product safety program of some kind or they are relying upon insurance, legal counsel or, most likely, some combination of all of these. Nevertheless, recent history of products liability litigation shows that even so-called "quality" products may be subject to liability; that insurance is only a partial answer, at best; that legal counsel rarely play a dominant role in liability prevention; and many product safety programs founded on good intentions, but with inadequate appreciation and understanding of the legal environment, miss the mark.

Or, perhaps a firm has not had any products liability claims; perhaps its low-risk products are not likely to be involved in injury-causing occurrences; and perhaps it does make well-engineered products. Admittedly, a company with little or no history of products liability claims, and that makes inherently safe products having limited propensity for injury, does not have need for as intensive a program as a manufacturer of products that incur significant risks of injury. This is a matter of judgment, but judgment based upon full understanding of the liability threat, the legal requirements and a correct assessment of the company's exposure and risks.

Considering the complex web of judicial and statutory requirements that has been spun around manufacturers in recent years, becoming more intricate and unforgiving all the time; it is foolhardy to ignore these issues, no matter how immune to products litigation the company may appear. From the few examples given in preceding chapters, it should be evident that there are just too many pitfalls, legal traps, standards, rules and regulations—not to mention aggressive trial lawyers—out there, to not maintain a formal program of products liability awareness and loss prevention. Questions over costs of prevention should not be a consideration because the financial risks in *not* having a program are so overwhelming. Liability prevention is not the place for cost-cutting.

Also, the threat is too extensive and potentially damaging to trust its avoidance to intuition. It is difficult to understand how responsible company management, once made aware of the magnitude of the threat, can continue to operate without some kind of formal policy and liability prevention program.

This chapter is devoted to basic elements of effective products liability prevention. In the next chapter we will look at what it takes to make the whole thing work. This does not imply that individual executives, managers or engineers are immune to being named as defendants in products lawsuits. At the moment, the major threat facing industry is lawsuits aimed at companies. They are the ones with financial resources and insurance coverage. As Willie Sutton put it, *"that's* where the money is." Therefore, manufacturing companies are primary targets. So our emphasis will be upon how companies can avoid products liability.

What is good for a company is also good for everyone, both collectively and individually, in that company. The most basic benefit is job security. Also, we all want to be on a winning team. But an effective team is always more than the sum of its individual members. It takes individual skill, dedication and resolution to win *plus* coordination of these individual ingredients into a concerted, holistic program to do this job.

Top Management's Personal Concern

The first thing to consider, then, is how to integrate the collective skills and dedication of individuals into a monolithic force that will keep the company and its products out of court and prevent its financial resources from being diverted into social-service channels for compensating victims injured by its products. This is clearly an issue that requires top management attention. And it takes a good deal more than lip-service endorsement of platitudes and posting safety slogans around the plant. The day when these were an acceptable response is long past.

Direct personal involvement of top management is essential in any worthwhile products liability prevention activity for a number of reasons. One is that such a program is vital to the firm's long-term survival. Secondly, an effective prevention program must include every person and function in the company. Such extensive involvement and need for company-wide coordination that crosses departmental and divisional boundaries can only be properly controlled from top level management. Also, depending upon the company's products and its markets, preventive measures may require changes in corporate philosophy in product design, communication, or documentation. These, too, should be top management decisions.

Finally, there is an increasing trend toward holding top management personally responsible for product-related statutory violations, with criminal penalties including jail terms for officials of offending companies. The law is increasingly imposing criminal sanctions upon corporate executives for what it considers flagrant violations and unconscionable disregard of statutory requirements designed to protect the public from product hazards. Note these comments of the former Chairman of the Consumer Products Safety Commission:

> Whereas corporations can pay civil penalties, people who work for corporations pay criminal penalties. I am personally inclined in a criminal proceeding to seek out the Board Chairman or Corporate President, in addition to other officials, because I believe they are in the best position to assure corporate compliance with CPSC regulations.[1]

Because it is necessary that products liability prevention concepts pervade the entire organization and become a way of life, there are disadvantages in making "the program" the focus of attention. Ideally, prevention practices should so intimately involve each activity, decision and operation in the company that no one thinks of them as part of some special program, drive or movement that happens to be in vogue at the moment. It is up to each company to set its own goals and institute preventive practices that meet its own specific needs and to implement those that are necessary by whatever method works best for that company.

Whatever method it chooses for implementation, it is important for a top management committed to products liability prevention to state its commitment in the form of written policy. The formal document has its own purposes and advantages, but the strongest reason for written policy is that it forces top management to express its commitment in concrete terms that will be read and understood by others within the company. The "policy" document should be concise, but comprehensive. As a minimum it should clearly state the purpose or objective of the company's liability prevention (or product safety) policy and it should establish authority for its implementation.

Beyond that, it may describe major responsibilities of each department, guidelines for coordinating the effort and relevant organizational matters. The whole idea of written policy is for top management to translate its mental and visceral commitment into specific, meaningful corporate action and standards, with authority for making it happen and controls for assuring its effectiveness.

There are advantages in having key department executives personally participate in developing the policy and preparing its statement. These would include those responsible for product conceptualization and development, product design and engineering, production, purchasing, marketing, sales and advertising, service and customer relations, and legal counsel. Such involvement serves a number of purposes.

It convinces key managers of the firmness of the company's commitment, it secures their endorsement through direct participation in preparing the policy document and it assures communication of its content to those responsible for carrying it out. Such an exercise is often best accomplished in a group session at some location remote from the plant and away from interruptions and distractions. It would be well at the same time to establish organizational structures and procedures for implementing the policy, specific tactics, program costs, budgets and audit procedures.

Get Everyone Involved

The importance of covering *every* operation in the company cannot be over-emphasized. Many products lawsuits stem from simple, even foolish and seemingly insignificant errors or oversights. The magnitude of loss from product failure sometimes is far out of proportion to the magnitude of error that caused it. At the time they occur, many "errors" may not have seemed to be errors at all but well-meaning solutions to production problems threatening schedules or delivery dates. For example, substitution by a conscientious production-line foreman of an apparently equivalent component or part for another.

To be effective, the products liability prevention program must cover all operations, all skills and all people. The program's management must anticipate the additional time and expense it will take to implement new or revised procedures and it should adjust productivity goals and production quotas accordingly. The program's requirements must be translated to all employees in specific terms of assigned responsibilities. Vague generalities won't do.

Also, employees should be made aware of the needs and reasons for whatever changes must be made in the way they had been doing things. This awareness will result in better morale and cooperation and willingness to implement new practices and procedures, as well as endorsement of what the company is trying to accomplish. Primary production goals should be oriented toward meeting products liability prevention targets instead of numbers of finished products shipped out the door. Productivity will benefit from effective implementation of liability prevention measures. But it can be elusive when pursued for its own sake. And there should be some way for assuring conformance to the program's objectives and for recognizing and rewarding achievements.

Not all prevention practices apply to every firm. Even so, the magnitude of the task of products liability prevention and the number of practices and precautions and need for documentation that do apply to a given firm may seem overwhelming. But like any major project, all elements need not, and cannot, be tackled at once. Each firm must set its own priorities consistent with its own organization and liability exposure. Top management commitment to producing safe products and avoiding liability is an essential first step but it must be followed by realistic goals and objectives, a do-able program and reasonable timetable. Creation of awareness of products liability and implementation of a prevention program is largely an educational process, and it will take time.

Peters and Waterman offer helpful comments on implementing extensive programs in response to major corporate commitments. Among the successful companies cited in their survey, *In Search of Excellence*, they found that an effective way to get people to respond was through "incrementally acting [their] way into a major commitment." They say, "only if you get people *acting*, even in small ways, the way you want them to, will they come to believe in what they're doing."[2] Following this theme, these authors cite benefits of "building momentum by accumulating small successes." When the task is so overwhelming it is difficult to know where to begin, it is advantageous to focus not on obstructions but on discrete tasks that everyone can agree on and that are easy to do; not on plans and programs, but upon tackling the easiest and ready targets.[3]

Every firm that is a target for products lawsuits has some obvious vulnerable practice or product characteristic that can be defused right away, usually with little objection or difficulty. That is a good place to begin. Then pick another, and keep on doing that until the most vulnerable areas have been eliminated. In the process, everyone will have learned about products liability prevention, it will seem less formidable, and the firm will be well on its way to a more secure financial future.

At the outset, it must be understood that no program will guarantee a manufacturer immunity to products claims. Existence of a corporate policy and liability prevention program with its standards and controls does not absolve a company of liability for product injuries. But it does give the manufacturer a firm footing for negotiating early and favorable settlements of claims for product injuries, should they occur; and it can significantly reduce the number of claims that are filed.

Also, the program should not be expected to pave the way for turning out perfect products with zero defects. These are noble-sounding goals but it is unrealistic to insist upon perfection. Not only is such a quest out of practical reach but it is unattainable at any price.

William D. Ruckelshaus, former administrator of the Environmental

Protection Agency, in addressing environmental safety and attainable goals, is quoted as saying, "I'd like the American people to understand the difference between reasonable safety and zero risk. One is achievable, the other is fantasy."[4] The law does not demand perfect, flawless and foolproof products,[5,6] but it does expect them to be reasonably safe to use and free of concealed hazards.

TARGETS, GOALS AND SCOPE OF THE EFFECTIVE PROGRAM

Be Realistic and Practical

It may sound like a truism, but one of the most important ingredients of a company's program for avoiding products liability is good judgment. It means setting realistic goals; a prevention program with procedures, standards and an organization for implementing it that are reasonably consistent with the company's liability risks and exposure; and firm commitment supported by adequate funding and resources for the long run.

No two companies are alike. Some are large; some are small. Some make products that are likely to be involved in products lawsuits; while others' products are less susceptible. Some are profitable; others are in financial difficulty. Some deal with intensely competitive product lines with small profit margins; some do not. But products liability affects them all to some degree. None of them can afford to ignore it. Nevertheless, preventive measures will differ significantly from company to company. It is as important to not over-react as it is to not under-react; not to over-spend as it is to not under-spend.

This is where judgment comes in. It is ability to correctly identify a company's exposures and weaknesses and to choose preventive measures that will reduce them in a cost-effective manner. It cannot be an isolated one-time exercise, but an on-going need that must be considered at every turn in the road and tick of the clock.

Assessing Liability Exposure

It is difficult to imagine a manufacturing company that has been in business for any length of time without some knowledge of its liability exposure. It is fairly obvious. It can be deduced from a review of its claims history and record of lawsuits and occurrences of product failures (whether involving injuries or not) and from how insurers view the company. Is products liability coverage available and affordable? If so, have premiums remained stable or gone out of sight in recent years? What is the company's record of statutory violations (OSHA, FDA, CPSC, etc.)? What is the frequency and substance of user or consumer complaints and service comments? What has been the experience of others in the same business or industry? These are but a few of the indicators that might be considered in assessing products liability exposure and need for preventive action.

Since legal requirements are never static but changing all the time, any useful liability exposure assessment must not stop with these indicators, but should include review of all relevant statutory requirements and trends of court cases in your own and other jurisdictions involving products similar to yours. A review should also be made of competitive products' construction methods and materials and any use of safety features, devices or fail-safe designs that represent technological advancements and state-of-the-art improvements that a court and jury might consider safer for the user and the public.

What other manufacturers do can create legal safety standards for products as surely as enactment of statutory requirements. It is not a healthy position to find that, although your product meets all relevant statutory and industry safety standards, it does not incorporate safety-related state-of-the-art advancements that have been made by competitors or that are known in the field.

Liability exposure is also a function of the product itself and assessment of it must be made in addition to review of other factors. A good place to start is with customer or user expectations. Has the company—through its advertising, brochures, product datasheets, packaging, or other means—led users and potential purchasers of its products to expect realistic performance? Is the pricing structure consistent with the product's quality and performance and what the user might expect on the basis of the price? Would any kind of product failure possibly cause personal injury? How probable is its occurrence and how serious would it be? What are the company's policies on handling user complaints?

If it is a new product, has a well-documented design analysis been made of the product? Are specifications for its materials, parts and components, processing, assembly and inspection procedures adequate to identify defective items that could lead to failures and injuries? Are labeling, warnings and user instructions adequate? How about risks of harm from foreseeable misuse or abuse? Is there possibility of injury associated with its container or packaging, or disposal of the product or its container, when it has been consumed or is discarded? A thorough appraisal of the product along these lines, with reference to the legal requirements outlined in earlier chapters and in the cited references, will indicate if there is exposure to liability.

These are some of the considerations a manufacturer might use in determining its exposure and what the scope of its liability avoidance or prevention program should be. At this stage, these might be informal assessments and they do not require sophisticated p primary purpose is to give the manufacturer some insight potential and to provide a basis for determining the scope c program and its emphasis.

If the manufacturer is a large well-established compa

reputation that projects an image of stability and prosperity, it automatically *is* a target for products liability suits, and this is largely irrespective of its products and their characteristics. For such a company, a formal and comprehensive prevention program is a virtual necessity. The same is true for any manufacturer that makes products that have characteristics with a high probability of injury—even if the product cannot be made safer and all requirements for warning and instructing users of its characteristics have been met. Both companies are targets for products lawsuits, although for different reasons; therefore, both need to have formal well-organized and effective prevention programs.

Three Lines of Defense

Products liability prevention programs are not only useful in avoiding products claims and lawsuits, but also for minimizing effects and damages of claims and lawsuits that may be inevitable. The best program is one whose procedures accomplish both.

The first line of defense, of course, is to prevent claims and to keep claims that are filed from developing into lawsuits. The second line of defense is to have a strong position from which to negotiate early and favorable settlement of lawsuits. A third line of defense, related to the second, is to be able to win lawsuits that for some reason cannot be settled at an early stage and eventually do go to trial.

All three lines of defense have been considered in the various preventive procedures and techniques described in this chapter. At first, some may seem heavily detailed and extensive and require excessive documentation for simply assuring that the product is not defective. Keep in mind, though, that product "defectiveness" in the legal sense does not refer only to products that break or fail. Also, many of the measures discussed will be useful in defending a lawsuit or in negotiating a settlement. Details needed for negotiating a favorable settlement or defending a lawsuit must be obtained *as* the product is conceived, developed and produced; it's much too late to try to reconstruct them once a lawsuit is underway.

Not every weapon in our arsenal of products liability defense is used in front-line combat. There are many avenues of attack open to the opposition. This requires intelligent, well-developed defensive strategies, an extensive and versatile arsenal of expertly-maintained implements with people trained in their tactical use. It is not a battle confined to generals or corporate management, nor is it limited to one branch of the service. Every department is critically needed and everyone in the company is an indispensable warrior.

Unfortunately, this war is never over. Victory in one battle or campaign against one foe does not mean that you are winning. There are many foes out there. Repeated and consistent victory, however, will tell the foes that your defenses are strong and not readily breached. This is a reputation well worth having. You can be assured that there will always be firms that will choose to disregard products liability and take no preventive or defensive action against it. Let your opponents attack them. Even if, because of your financial strength or characteristics of your products, you are a primary target for products lawsuits, you can live in relative peace once the world of plaintiffs' attorneys knows you are no match for them.

Scope

Even a cursory review of elements of liability prevention programs will suggest a similarity to elements of other systems quality standards.[7] The similarity should not be surprising, because quality standards should be the same whether the motivation is simply to make a product that does not fail or to make a product that does not fail so that its failure does not injure someone. Many elements are identical and the various published quality standards are excellent starting points for establishing a prevention program or for evaluating an existing one against some standard.[8-12]

One of these standards gives this description of requirements for development of a safety program (see reference 9):

> A total program shall be developed in which design analyses, studies, and testing will identify system performance limitations, failure modes, safety margins, and critical operator tasks. All known facets of safety optimization including design, engineering, education, management policy and supervisory control shall be considered in the identifying and eliminating or controlling hazards. System safety management and engineering shall be integrated with other management and engineering disciplines in the interest of an optimum system design. Procedures for development and integration of the system safety effort shall be applied across the managing activity/contractor interface to assure a system safety program consistent with overall system requirements.

Although military systems are the primary application contemplated for the standard this excerpt was taken from, it applies to any engineered product and its development activity. Note the definition of "system" given in the MIL standard:

> A composite, at any level of complexity, of personnel, materials, tools, equipment, facilities, and software. The elements of this composite entity are used together in the intended operational or support environment to perform a given task or achieve a special production, support or mission requirement.

In some respects, products liability avoidance programs involve additional considerations, particularly new requirements imposed by recent common law court decisions and the trend toward using the law as a mechanism for satisfying the social need for economic redistribution in compensating victims of product injuries. In other words, existing published quality standards are essential in any quality program; but there is more to liability prevention than adherence to one or more existing standards aimed at other needs. For example, quality control (QC) is *an element* in products liability prevention, but the two are not synonymous.

There may be a strong urge to "solve" the product liability prevention problem by merely assigning that function to an existing department. But this will not involve everyone in the firm. The prevention program must cover all activities that relate to the product and involve everyone who has any responsibility in any way for the product or its components or who come into contact with the product. The entire product cycle must be considered, from conception to disposal—literally everything "from the cradle to the grave."

For our purposes here, we will consider seven broad classifications or activities that relate to practically every product. These are:

> Conception, planning and design
> Engineering
> Purchase and procurement
> Production
> Packaging
> Sales, promotion and advertising
> Service and customer relations

A review of this list shows a customary activity, Inspection and Quality Control (or Quality Assurance), missing. This is not an oversight and it is not missing. In effective products liability prevention, quality assuring responsibility cannot be conveniently disposed of by creating a separate, discrete function and naming it "Quality Control" or something similar. In today's climate product quality is everyone's responsibility. The Japanese have proven this to our embarassment.

Accordingly, every employee having any responsibility in the company should be concerned with product quality. To this end, management should not make things too convenient for employees to discard "rejects" or to blame the inspection department for flawed products. It may take a little organizational pruning and improvement in communication to make the plan work, but the rewards in developing an organization intolerant of rejects can be significant.

In the remainder of this chapter we will consider each of these seven activities one-by-one and products liability prevention measures, practices and procedures that apply. Prevention techniques will differ with the product and company, and some products will require their own custom-made procedures and practices. But the general guidelines given and the references cited will at least provide basic tools to get the reader headed in the right direction.

CONCEPTION, PLANNING AND DESIGN

Review Corporate Traditions and Policies

Seeds of a firm's products liability woes can be sown and germinate well before anything materializes that resembles a product. Often, they are planted innocently and unintentionally. Frequently, the source of difficulty is a well-rooted, and even cherished, practice or tradition that is easy to overlook and difficult to weed out.

These might be product design styles; traditional emphasis upon some characteristic of the product or preferred use of material; preoccupation with technology that once was innovative but now obsolete; fixation upon marketing methods and positioning concepts, sales and advertising techniques that once were instrumental in the firm's early business success and have remained unchanged over the years; and other manifestations of fossilized "corporate style" or business approach. Some practices that are blindly perpetuated "because that's the way the company does it" and are never questioned can create liability problems through failing to acknowledge their legal implications in today's litigious climate.

It is essential for a firm to frankly and *objectively* assess its operations methods in a search for these kinds of possibly harmful attitudes, practices and traditions. The assessment should include a review of basic product policies. Perhaps, because of changing social values or statutory requirements, the company's product line has become highly vulnerable to products lawsuits. Materials or constituents that once made a product reliable and gave it features preferred by customers may now be considered hazardous. Asbestos, formaldehyde, and polychlorinated biphenyls (PCBs) are examples.

Consequences of foreseeable misuse and abuse of the product that once seemed too bizarre and far-fetched to worry about may now require warnings or even redesign. Some products may represent such extreme exposure to products liability (particularly if of questionable utility) that they may have to be extensively modified or, perhaps, dropped altogether. Sales and promotion techniques that had been so successful in the past may constitute express warranties that make the company a guarantor against injuries and *absolutely* liable.

The list of possibilities is endless. Respected corporate policies and traditions that have long been sacred to the firm may constitute a spawning ground for attitudes and practices that can manifest themselves as product characteristics or even a corporate posture that makes the firm needlessly vulnerable to liability.

Pre-Design Guidelines and Conceptualization

Product "defects" can originate in the thought process of the researcher or designer, or in unrealistic goals set by top management that lie unchallenged by others. A particular approach to a new product or improvement of an existing one may be clearly preferred over others on technical or economic grounds but commit the program to a high-risk track. As a development program gathers momentum with increasing technical success and deeper financial commitment, a point is reached when it becomes psychologically too late for correcting built-in deficiencies. This situation can make future liability losses a virtual certainty. Once the product has been released to market, attempts to cure defects inherent in the design may be futile, with a recall campaign the only recourse. This can prove a costly and damaging alternative to eliminating the problem in the design stages.

Sometimes the "defect" may lie in the questionable usefulness of the product's concept itself. Perhaps, even if all the design and market objectives for the product can be realized, the product may be conceptually flawed, representing a risk of injury that outweighs its usefulness or social benefits. If so, it would be considered an "unreasonably dangerous" product. Attempts to neutralize this characteristic through disclaimers, warnings or other such measures would be worthless. Choice of a particular material, additive or constituent that has hazardous potentials under certain conditions (for example, when it is burned after being discarded) can also lead to legal problems if a non-hazardous alternative is available. Many of these choices are made in early phases of product conceptualization and set the stage for future difficulties. Those responsible for making such design choices *must* be knowledgeable about products liabilty.

Consequently, liability prevention must include everyone, including the research scientist, theoretical physicist, polymer chemist, physical metallurgist and others engaged in even so-called "basic" studies. There is a temptation to isolate these people from liability concerns because their activities seem so remote from the actual product that is sold. Isolating them can be a mistake. In some respects, these people need clearer understanding of the threat of products liability and its requirements for prevention than others in the organization since their decisions in design and formulation of new products can incur liability.

We must not forget that "*design* defectiveness" can be a most infectious and fatal malady—so much more damaging to a company than the isolated "odd-ball" product having a manufacturing flaw that somehow gets past the inspection department, is sold and hurts someone. This is another reason for being especially vigilant during conceptualization and design stages and for assuring that people having this responsibility are among the most knowledgeable in the company on products liability matters.

Their knowledge must extend beyond technical capability and understanding of legal requirements and statutory regulations. It must include information on the intended market for the product and its sales projections; details on prospective users (in contrast to those of the immediate purchaser, as the two may be different) and use environment; range of unintentional but probable uses that may be made of the product; risks associated with the product's use and misuse; cost constraints and profit margins that will be applied to manufacturing and sale of the product; and history of failure rates and resulting injuries and liability claims for it and similar products having similar characteristics and sold in similar markets.

Design Considerations

Revised Priorities and Design Criteria. From strictly a technical standpoint, product design is largely unaffected by liability prevention requirements. That is, engineering concepts and mechanical analyses, application of physical laws, mathematical relationships, and the "nuts-and-bolts" procedures used to transform mental images into working models, remain the same as before products liabilty became a factor.

But *something* about the design process must change if the firm's products are to succeed in today's litigious climate—where "success" means more than customer acceptance and profits earned for the company through product sales. "Success" today must also include that ability of the company to *keep* its profits, to assure that they won't be taken away in the form of damages and its resources taxed and depleted by plaguing lawsuits, headaches over recall campaigns and frustrations of an avalanche of regulatory paperwork triggered by defective or hazardous products.

The change needed is more one of mental attitude and perspective than of practice. Although design *techniques* may not be affected, the designer's priorities must be. And so must his standards. For a product design to survive in today's environment, the designer must reorient his thinking toward the law's requirements and take them into account at each stage of the design process and in evaluating tradeoffs and compromises. In specific terms, this means that the designer must give more weighty consideration to the user: the user's physical and mental abilities, the user's needs and expectations for the product and motivations for purchasing it, the user's attitude and the user's environment.

Products liability is not an inanimate, cold and impersonal legalistic concept. It is an obligation toward *people*. The duty to exercise due care in designing and manufacturing a product is a duty to *people*. It is *people* who purchase and use products. It is *people* who are injured by them and *people* file claims for damages and are plaintiffs in products lawsuits. So, the designer's first consideration in designing products that will satisfy today's legal standards should be people—in particular, the purchaser and user of the product and others who will come into contact with it.

"People information" the designer needs is of two kinds. One is understanding about human factors in general; the other is information about purchasers and users of the product. The first kind of information is found in various reference sources under the heading of "human factors engineering" or "ergonomics" and, sometimes, "human engineering."[13-17] Although human factors may not receive the attention it deserves in engineering curricula, recent developments in the law have made it a required subject for the product designer.[18]

Information on user profile, or characteristics of the average user of the product or similar products may be available within the company from its sales and service departments and from a study of marketing data, customer complaint or warranty card files. If it is a new product and a competent market analysis was done, the firm's marketing people should have detailed information on the projected user or customer.

Also, there are more standards now than there ever were before and many of the new standards are imposed *from outside* the company, through government regulations, developments in common law and changing industry custom. Many of these have been developed independently of industry's traditional standards-making organizations. Others have evolved within industries as uncodified standards in answer to the need to increase product safety. Some of these standards, like government regulations, are precise and fairly easy to know and follow. Those that result from judicial decisions and industry practices can be more obscure, subjective, elusive and imprecise.

Previous chapters outlined some of the new standards that must be considered during the design process. It is the personal responsibility of the designer to understand them and what they require. It is as much his responsibility as is knowledge of the ASME Boiler and Pressure Vessel Code for the mechanical engineer designing a pressure vessel. It is foolish and wasteful for a firm's design engineers to ignore these new standards and depend upon the QC department, the product safety coordinator or even legal counsel, to take care of any deficiencies that may arise through failure to consider them. Such dependence upon others is not clever delegation of unfamiliar and disagreeable tasks to specialists more familiar with them but, in the eyes of plaintiffs' attorneys, neglect of personal duty and repudiation of professional responsibility.

The new standards dictate criteria the designer should apply in judging adequacy of design. They affect such decisions as choice of material; method of joining; source of materials, parts, components and their grade; as well as production methods and inspection techniques—in fact, every step in the design process. Special attention must be given to suitability of materials and concepts for the intended service, expected performance and operating conditions. The higher the expected performance, the more adverse the operating conditions and the more unusual the service requirements; the more must design be supported by calculations, computer models, prototype tests and evaluations of materials and components under simulated and actual service environments.

The new standards also require greater emphasis upon product reliability and freedom from defects. This does not mean the designer must strive for products that will never wear out or that are idiot-proof; nor does it call for insisting upon "zero-defects" or other unreasonable or impracticable goals.

There is really nothing wrong with striving for zero-defects as long as everyone involved is realistic and maintains a cost-effective outlook. In fact, a defect-free product should *be* the goal. But problems can arise when a rigid zero-defects policy leads to inconsistencies and unreasonable adherence to practices that are not in the best interests of the company; practices that amount to majoring in the minors and minoring in the majors.

Before a firm gets carried away with formulating policies that demand perfection, it should examine its products for obvious flaws in the light of current legal standards. Frequently, there are one or more fairly obvious flaws in a product or its concept that represent or could develop into a hazardous situation for the user or others. Often, these obvious flaws can be eliminated at little cost or effort; and these should be corrected. But, as the seriousness of identified flaws and the potential hazards they represent diminish, and costs of their elimination rise; a point is reached where it becomes impracticable to insist upon eliminating every conceivable flaw. Where that point is will vary with the product, its purpose, its users and a host of other variables. It is not a place for applying formulas, handy rules-of-thumb or for blindly insisting upon unreasonable and unattainable goals or perfection. Again, it is a matter for engineering judgment.

To place what we have been talking about into proper context, it may help to cite an illustration of how good engineering has reduced a common everyday hazard to relatively safe levels. Donald Mackay of the CPSC offers this example:

> The safety record of the electrical products industry is remarkable when you reflect on the thought that every man, woman and child in this country is exposed to the silent, yet potentially fatal, power of electricity several times each day.... Yet, of all accidental deaths occurring each year, it is interesting to note that only about *one* percent are due to electrical shock. It is also worth noting that the annual electrical death rate per million people in the U.S. has dropped from 6.3 in 1950 to 5.6 in 1970, even in the presence of greater electrical usage and more electrical products.[19]

Mackay is not saying that electrical products represent zero risk but that their designers (motivated by competition and the need for consumer acceptance of their products to design out hazards) have done a remarkable job of minimizing hazards, and continue to do so. And it has been done in a cost-effective manner. Shock hazards of electrical consumer products have been decreasing even as their complexity and performance have been increasing; yet, costs of these products are still well within reach of the average U.S. consumer. It's not zero-defects, but an enviable record just the same.

The designer must make every effort to design safety *into* the product. This is done through using fail-safe or inherently safe concepts whenever possible. If it is not possible to eliminate all hazards, and the value and existence of the product are such that they outweigh its risks, then the hazard should be controlled through protective devices and features. Safety in use is not the only consideration, but also safety in service and maintenance, and for the life of the product. Hazards that cannot be designed out of the product must be protected by guards, interlocks or other means. Reliance upon warnings, or assuming that the hazard is obvious and therefore need not be controlled, are not viable substitutions in today's legal environment for eliminating the hazard or guarding against it.[20,21] Safety features essential for avoiding product use hazards must be incorporated into design of the product and not left off and offered as additional-cost options or accessories.

Product safety arrived at through designer's intuition is not enough. Safety concepts in product design must be confirmed, tested and proven in actual use situations and the results well-documented. Safety concepts and features should reflect current technology and failure occurrence data. Practices that were adequate a decade or two ago could well be out of date today.

Beyond this, the designer must take into account capabilities and limitations of those who will make, assemble, inspect and service the product. This is necessary to avoid specifying a design susceptible to manufacturing errors, one that testing and inspection procedures will be unable to adequately evaluate or that cannot be safely maintained. The designer must be familiar with reliability and failure rate data for all parts and components. He must understand the fundamentals of product failure and be able to assess probable effects upon the product, its user and surroundings of accident, misuse, inattention, carelessness, abuse, and other intervening events, environments and combinations of events and circumstances.

By any yardstick, this is heavy and formidable responsibility! Fortunately, others faced with similar "impossible" tasks have devised methods and techniques for coping with it. Although many of the techniques available to the product designer for handling this job were developed for purposes other than products liability avoidance, most had product integrity and reliability as objectives.

One technique that had its origin in the 1950s for improving reliability of military hardware is the *formal design review*, described in the next section. This technique, and others that are mentioned, are not the only ones. Those included, with examples and references to more detailed descriptions, are given to illustrate methods that have been used successfully in improving product reliability and, more recently, as liability prevention procedures.

Design Reviews. Practically every company has, in one form or another, consciously or not, used design reviews for assessing product developments. Even small organizations recognize the importance of having people knowledgeable in specific aspects look over what its designers propose before committing resources to a new or modified product. Whether the proposed concept represents a major innovation or minor modification, success of the company's products concerns everyone, and every department and function has an interest in it—personal interest as well as company interest.

Every designer should acknowledge the need for input from others as no designer, design department, individual or discipline can know everything about every product. The information designers need somehow must be made available during the design process, and the earlier the better. Since product design almost always boils down to a series of compromises or tradeoffs, only those interests directly influenced by these compromises can adequately assess their implications and consequences.

While this need for input and interdisciplinary communication may be undisputed, the form it takes and its communicative effectiveness vary widely. Unfortunately, many design reviews (when conducted formally at all) are little more than perfunctory "show-and-tell" exercises. Questions or comments that may be interpreted as criticism or call for action that would tend to delay getting the product into production usually are unwelcome and politically undesirable. Too frequently, everyone is expected to go along with what is presented and already "cast in concrete." This kind of design review is ineffective and practically worthless; not only as a design tool but as an aid in avoiding products liability.

Design reviews can be cost-effective means for resolving potential problems with a product at the earliest possible stage and, therefore, for expediting its development, production and release. Their value extends well beyond usefulness in liability prevention. It may be of interest that formal design reviews are mandatory for National Aeronautics and Space Administration (NASA) contractors and other federal agencies.[22-24]

Jacobs[25] sees the design review as "primarily a formal system forcing the different technical disciplines to communicate ... [and which] stabilizes and matures the design ... "

According to Boquist,[26]

> The Formal Design Review is a scheduled, systematic review and evaluation of the product design by personnel not directly associated with its development, but who, as a group, are knowledgeable in and have a responsibility for all elements of the product throughout its life cycle.

Our interest is upon benefits of design reviews in liability avoidance. Other benefits will become evident. Timing of the review, its participants, content and emphasis will, of course, differ from one product to another and from one firm to another. Some fundamentals are common to nearly all.

Design reviews should be regarded *as an aid* to the designer and, when properly implemented, save time and money as well as provide other tangible corporate benefits. The review session must not be, or appear to be, strictly a forum for calling the designer or design department to account for their activity. While designers play a key role in the design review, all attendees are participants, not merely passive observers. Potential for personality conflict is obviously high and the utmost in management skill and diplomacy is required of the one who chairs the design review board.

The intent must be to *assist* the design process; to furnish essential information to designers to enable them to intelligently choose alternatives and make right decisions; to allow them to appreciate potential problems that may crop up later during inspection, manufacturing or servicing the product; and to obtain the collective drift of thought and sense of other disciplines. The importance of evaluating the product design through others' eyes is evident in the following description by Boquist of the prime objective of a Formal Design Review:

> [It] is to communicate and measure achievement towards an optimum product design from the standpoint of performance, total cost, safety, reliability, producibility, environmental effects, maintainability, service-ability, human factors, customer needs and expectations, pertinent legislation and litigation, including personal injury, property damage, and environmental damage.[27]

The design review does not shift responsibility for design of the product off the shoulders of designers. The review is merely a consultation or advisory session for their benefit and edification. Nor is the design review a substitute for conscientious design effort. Its value is only as good as the knowledge, preparation, dedication and willingness to help of its participants. Through this participation, knowledgeable people representing a range of disciplines can identify product characteristics likely to incur liability and offer guidance for further development.

To realize maximum benefit from a design review, particularly for liability avoidance, its scope must cover every aspect of the product.[28] This means, in addition to the physical product itself, everything delivered to the customer in, on, or with the product. This includes instructions, user and maintenance manuals, diagrams and installation details, labels, tags, nameplates, warnings, shipping containers, packaging and packing materials, accessories, spare parts, field assembly, warranties, guarantees, sales literature, post-sale documents, service and repair operations.

This range of subjects requires active design review participation of representatives from every company function involved, including engineering, quality and reliability assurance, purchasing, manufacturing, tooling and production planning, marketing, sales, advertising, service, cost analysis, data and risk management, legal counsel, specialists, consultants and other representatives from inside and outside the company. All functions need not attend every review session. It all depends upon the product, whether it is an entirely new product or a modification, and stage of the product's development. Experience shows that about ten participants is the maximum effective number for a design review board. Small companies will necessarily work with fewer individuals.

Jacobs[29] offers guidelines on the desired makeup of the design review board. Its individuals should be qualified engineers having at least the level of technical competence in their respective fields as that required of the designer. They should be able to independently assess the design on its merits without prejudice or emotional involvement. They should have the personal respect of the designer and others of the review team, be objective and constructive and able to accept as well as offer suggestions and criticism.

Design reviews may be conducted at any stage of the product's development that seems necessary or appropriate. Ordinarily, three or four are used at milestones in the development, or just before making major decisions or financial commitments on the product. Traditional ones are (a) Preliminary or Conceptual Design Review, (b) Intermediate Design Review, and (c) Final Design Review. There may be a Manufacturing or Producibility Design Review, (before the Final Design Review) and there may be a First Article Design Review conducted just before committing the product to mass production. Others may be called for, including an Installation or Product Improvement Design Review held in conjunction with field erection or assembly of large complex projects.

The Preliminary Design Review is conducted just before formulating the design. Its purpose is to review various requirements, specifications, proposed functions, markets and legal constraints. It offers everyone concerned an opportunity to identify and bring to light any real or perceived flaws in the product concept. It does this at a time when changes and tradeoffs are readily made with minimal expense. The review session results in various action items being assigned to participants having the particular expertise to answer or resolve and these must be followed up by the review board chairman or coordinator to assure that the designers receive the input information and in time to incorporate it into the design.

The Intermediate Design Review reflects the established product design and is held just before detailed production drawings are made. If the product is complex, it may be useful to conduct separate design reviews on sub-systems; then, combine outcomes of individual sessions in one session representing all sub-systems.

The Final Design Review is conducted just before the design is released to manufacturing. By this time, production drawings and material lists are complete and questions over process flowcharts and production tooling drawings have been resolved. Throughout these reviews, all agreements, decisions, discussion topics, disposition of action items and resolution of disputes should be well-documented along with their reasoning and rationale.

Like all techniques, it is important to avoid placing too much emphasis upon the review process and mechanisms themselves. For this reason, it is best to resist pressures to establish fixed and rigorous schedules and procedures that apply across-the-board to all products. The "tools" should be made to suit the need.

Comprehensive checklists can expedite the reviews, help keep discussions on target, assist in documenting the review process and in conducting the followup. Sample checklists in the cited references can serve as guidelines for preparing ones suited to specific products, organizations and needs.[30-31] In view of the large number of items to consider and diversity of disciplines involved, it is recommended that design review participants be assigned, ahead of time, checklist topics within their respective fields of expertise. In this way, everyone understands what is expected and participants have an opportunity to come prepared with answers or factual information for discussion.[32,33]

Analytical Techniques. *"Systems" Concepts.* Since World War II, with increasing complexity of engineered components and their interaction with one another, traditional principles of intuitive reasoning have become grossly inadequate for assessing reliability of engineered systems. Added to the engineering burden has been an increase in physical, social, economic, political and legal uncertainty that affects technical decisions, standards, criteria and judgment. Determining which one of an array of possibilities is "the best" alternative has become increasingly difficult. The *systems approach* was developed in response to this need for better tools and techniques for making objective analyses of increasingly complex problems. It is worth some of our time in this discussion of liability avoidance.[34-38]

Systems approach merely provides a logical framework for inserting all available information, including data as well as seasoned experience, judgment and intuition of decisions makers, technical people, management and others, as an aid in making decisions. The value of its methodical stepwise analysis lies in its ability to make the decision maker think about the right things. It cannot tell the decision maker the right thing to do, but it does make him enumerate alternatives and ask himself what he is trying to achieve. It gives him a precise statement of what he needs to know to make a rational decision.

Whether they are mathematical, physical, or graphical; systems analysis models are really not much different from mental models we use in solving problems. The significant difference is that systems analysis models are explicit. This makes them easier to manipulate and construct as comprehensive descriptions of the real world than subjective models. Considering, then, complexities associated with attempting to integrate engineering practices and the increasing number of new product standards with liability prevention strategies, it is not surprising that systems analysis techniques have found broad use as tools in evaluating design adequacy.[39]

A number of analytical variations have been proposed and used, particularly for complicated products; but all are either inductive or deductive. Inductive analysis assumes possible states or conditions of *subsystems* or *components* and then considers effects of these parts on the whole. Two inductive methods discussed here are Failure Modes and Effects Analysis (FMEA) and Hazards Analysis.

Deductive analysis works the opposite way. It assumes a state or condition of the *whole* or *system*, or an event, and then proceeds to identify conditions of parts, components and subsystems that could bring about that system state or event. Fault Tree Analysis (FTA) is a deductive method. Analytical techniques also may be qualitative or quantitative, depending upon the stage of development and availability of data from previous experience with the product or similar ones involving similar hazards.

These techniques should be regarded strictly as tools to assist the design process. From a technical viewpoint, they probably need not be applied to every product design decision, but only when intuitive methods are inadequate; when product or system complexity exceeds the capability of the human mind to grasp the array of apparently viable and competing alternatives and use scenarios, all with their own value functions. Even when intuitive reasoning seems adequate, there are advantages to using formal analytical procedures.

One advantage is that their use offers greater assurance that the designer does not overlook critical variables. Other advantages are that when used intelligently to supplement the designer's judgment, analytical methods not only save time but furnish a documented record of the design process and rationale for the various choices and tradeoffs that must be made. Such documentation can be indispensable as a communication tool during in-house design reviews in identifying a product's weaknesses and vulnerabilities to liability claims; in determining the best approach for production, testing and inspection; and as evidence during litigation for demonstrating that the product's design was arrived at through systematic, logical and objective procedures.

Analytical methods are not substitutes for common sense or good judgment. Their value and usefulness depend heavily upon the quality and validity of input data and available information. No analytical procedure can compensate for deficiencies in data or information.[40,41]

The following descriptions of a few of the more widely used techniques are given to acquaint the reader with their existence and usefulness as liability prevention tools. The information is not meant to be comprehensive or exhaustive, for an entire volume could be devoted to each technique. It is recommeded that the reader consult the references and develop a sufficient working knowledge of these techniques to be able to apply them to specific products within his own firm. Such trial use, starting at first with simple situations, will demonstrate their value and help develop skill in applying them to more elaborate products. This capability, like most others, is acquired through actual experience.

Hazards Analysis. Much engineering knowledge has been derived from failures, and failure analysis continues to be an important source of engineering information. But with the growing cost and complexity of engineered systems, we have become increasingly intolerant of failures; mostly because of their serious and far-reaching consequences. Considering the level of technical knowledge of most engineering disciplines today, availability of reliability data, analytical tools and techniques; there really is little excuse for product and system failures.

Nevertheless, time and budget constraints and, sometimes, ignorance, dictate short-cuts, design compromises, use of inferior processes, materials and components, and decisions to by-pass established engineering procedures and ignore available data, guidelines and specifications. A competent and rational engineering design approach will acknowledge advantages in making the product right the first time. Thoughtless frenzy to rush a design from infancy into production before it is ready can furnish an inside track to expensive failure analysis, product recalls and devastating litigation.

It is preferable to substitute *hazards analysis* (at the design stage) for failure analysis (after the product is in production and on the market). Engineering is always less costly than litigation. An increasing number of firms are being convinced of the wisdom of this and finding hazards analysis valuable in liability prevention.

Hazards analysis techniques have been given various names, depending upon the stage of the product's gestation at which they are conducted and the organization conducting them. Our interest here is primarily upon hazards analysis during the conception, planning and design stage. Often, such analysis is referred to as Preliminary Hazards Analysis. Its purpose is to identify hazardous conditions inherent in the product and to determine resulting effects and likelihood of harm from potential accidents.

Lambert[42] describes three steps in Preliminary Hazards Analysis, with its major goal being to prevent accidents of the kind that have occurred in identical or similar systems or products. The first step in the analysis is to identify elements of the product or its functions that are inherently dangerous. These hazardous elements may be categorized as either hazardous energy sources (for example, fuels, explosives, pressure vessels, moving machinery, falling objects) or hazardous processes or events (for example, corrosion, fire, electric shock, leaks, moisture, pressure, radiation, chemical replacement or mechanical impact).[43]

The second step identifies "triggering" events[44] that can transform a hazardous element into a hazardous condition and, in turn, into a potential accident. These events can be conditions, circumstances or undesired faults within the product or system.

The third step is to identify preventive measures. These may be either corrective or contingent in nature. A corrective measure would be a change in design, procedure or performance objectives; contingency action would be use of protective systems (for example, interlocks, guards, redundant systems, fire suppressors, emergency cooling systems, explosion arrestors).

Hammer[45] identifies seven steps in Preliminary Hazards Analysis and includes a review of past experience with similar products, a review of performance requirements, operating environments, and possible methods for eliminating or controlling the hazards, an analysis of methods for restricting damage in the event of loss of control of the hazard, and a determination of how these steps will be accomplished, and by whom.

MIL-STD-882A offers a number of guidelines in using hazards analysis in controlling product or system hazards.[46] These include:

1. A review of pertinent standards, specifications, regulations, design handbooks and other sources of design guidance.

2. Elimination or control of hazards identified by analyses or related engineering efforts including selection of necessary but potentially hazardous materials for optimum safety characteristics.

3. Isolation of hazardous substances, components and operations from other activities, areas, personnel and incompatible materials.

4. Minimizing personnel access and exposure to hazards during operation, maintenance, repair or adjustment.

5. Minimizing hazards for excessive environmental conditions.

6. Designing to minimize human error during operation and support of the system.

7. Controlling hazards that cannot be eliminated.

8. Protecting power sources, controls and critical components for redundant subsystems by physical separation or shielding.

9. Providing suitable warning and caution notes in assembly, operations, maintenance and repair instructions, and stan-

dardized distinctive markings on hazardous components, equipment, or facilities to ensure personnel and equipment protection.

10. Incorporating crashworthy design features in all man-rated systems to minimize severity of personnel injury or damage to equipment in event of a mishap.

11. Reviewing design criteria for inadequate or overly restrictive safety requirements, with recommendations for new design criteria supported by study, analyses or test data.

The same military standard gives the following order of preference for satisfying system safety requirements and resolving identified hazards:

1. Design for minimum hazard (design to eliminate hazards; if impossible, control hazard through design selection.)

2. Use safety devices to control hazards that cannot be eliminated or controlled through design selection.

3. Use warning devices when neither design nor safety devices can effectively eliminate or control identified hazard.

4. Use procedures and training to control the hazard where it is impossible to eliminate or adequately control a hazard by other means. This may include certification of personnel proficiency for safety-critical tasks.

It is clear that before effective hazards elimination or control measures can be devised and implemented, the designer must have a fairly complete understanding of the hazards themselves. And this requires a hazards analysis with input from as broad a cross-section of engineering disciplines and interests as it is possible to obtain. Its formats may differ. They may take the form of a narrative, a matrix chart or logic model, and may be qualitative or quantitative. Figure 5-1 illustrates a common simplified matrix chart format for a number of fairly obvious technical hazards.

Whatever its format, the purpose is always the same: to identify safety-critical aspects, to evaluate hazards associated with the product and identify the best safety design/approach.[47] Identified hazards may be in components, interfaces between components or other subsystems, environmental effects, use or service procedures, related facilities or in safety-related equipment or features.

Hammer[48] recommends that *initial* hazards analysis should be qualitative, with no attempt to consider probabilities, balancing of costs and risks. Its objective should be to identify product hazards with the goal of eliminating them. It is only after all attempts at elimination have been exhausted that the designer should proceed to quantitative techniques with their occurrence

Figure 5-1: Preliminary Hazards Analysis
(Sample Format for Series of Unrelated Hazards)

Condition or Hazard	Cause of Hazard	Category of Hazard	Consequences of Hazard	Corrective Measures and Comments
Embrittlement of high-strength steel pressure vessel	Hydrogen introduced into steel through faulty welding practice	I	Catastrophic fracture of vessel with explosive release of stored energy causing personnel injuries and property damage	Use welding consumables free of organic constituents and moisture and appropriate for vessel alloy
Ruptured fuel line	Fatigue failure from mechanical vibration of internal combustion stationary engine supporting rigid metal fuel line	I	Explosion and engine compartment fire, injury to personnel, property damage	Use flexible fuel line; relocate attachment point to avoid resonant frequency; use material having better fatigue life; re-route line away from ignition source
Electric shock	Personal contact with high-voltage charged capacitors while adjusting contactors inside protective enclosure	I	Potential for electrocution of service personnel	Install power interlock switch on service access door of enclosure with grounding contactor to discharge capacitors upon opening door; relocate contactor adjustment to eliminate need for enclosure access
Stress-corrosion cracking of stainless steel nuclear reactor cooling system	Presence of chlorides in reactor coolant	I	Vessel fracture and/or leakage with radioactive contamination, exposing personnel to radiation with resulting injury and system shutdown	Eliminate chlorides from coolant; use higher alloy resistant to chloride stress-corrosion; produce compressive stresses in walls of vessel exposed to coolant; anticipate leakage potential and keep personnel from area
Aircraft control cable failure	Cable deteriorated by acid leaking from storage battery	I	Loss of aircraft rudder and elevator control; unavoidable crash of aircraft; death of occupants; extensive property damage	Redesign and/or relocate battery compartment; modify battery to eliminate electrolyte leaks
Poisonous gas	Hydrogen cyanide generated by reaction with cleansers of electroplating residues on plated assemblies	I	Workers become seriously ill, potential for fatalities	Do not use acidic cleansers to remove residues of cyanide-containing plating solutions; conduct cleaning operations inside protective exhausting hoods
Unprotected rotating blade on portable power saw	Lower blade guard fails to return to protecting position after use (defective guard return spring)	II	Severe personal injuries (cuts, lacerations, amputations) from unexpected blade exposure	Use stronger spring of better material; redesign spring attachment method; redesign guard to make failure to return more obvious

frequencies, probabilistic or relativistic magnitudes of risks, costs and associated tradeoffs.

Hazards assessment has several basic elements. First, the hazard (the condition, or event) must be identified. Secondly is its cause. This would include circumstances producing or aggravating the hazard. Next, consequences, or result of the hazard's existence, should be determined. Finally, are corrective or preventive measures or actions that might be taken to avoid harm or damage. Besides these primary elements, others may be included, depending upon the product, its complexity, the level of understanding of its hazards and their possible consequences.

From strictly a practical and technical standpoint, hazards analysis may follow any convenient format and procedure. But, for purposes of liability prevention (including litigation defense), it is desirable that analytical procedures be formal, rigorous and, most of all, well-documented. Complete documentation will also materially benefit in-house design activity, review discussions and other communication, and expedite development of subsequent products.

Fault Tree Analysis. Fault Tree Analysis (FTA) and Failure Modes and Effects Analysis (FMEA) have different emphasis and are complementary. It is advantageous to use both methods in evaluating a product. Although they are design tools, primarily, they can and should be applied at various stages along the product development cycle. This will reveal effects of changes in the product that may become necessary after its design has been released. Of the two methods, it is usually preferable to conduct FTA first, as this affords a better perspective of products liability and pinpoints areas needing priority attention.

FTA is a deductive logic model that represents, in a graphic schematic format, various combinations of possible conditions that can lead to the "fault" or undesired event. The analysis comprises two basic activities: construction of the diagram or "fault tree," and its evaluation. Its purpose is to model "system" conditions (or characteristics of the product's operation or effects of its use) that can produce or cause the undesired event. This is done to identify causal relationships between events that result in product or system failure as a result of interactions of hardware, environment and people. The analytical process recognizes that major product, process or system hazards are frequently brought about by a *combination* of relatively minor deficiencies, environmental circumstances and human error that converge unfortuitously to trigger the devastating event. Victor Bignell says "The causal web is wide."[49]

The designer first identifies various undesirable events that could conceivably result from intended and non-intended use of the product, including foreseeable misuse and abuse. These may be available from hazards analyses, conducted previously. Some of the events could have serious consequences in causing injury and possibly death of the user or others. Some may not cause personal injury but could cause property damage, including damage to the product itself; while others might simply cause the product to stop working or cease to be useful, without harming anyone or anything. It is desirable to identify all of these because, in the process, other faults often are revealed. Primary emphasis, of course, is upon events that are the most damaging or detrimental, or least desirable.

FTA starts with the adverse event (or injury-producing occurrence) and works backward through "the system"—from effects to causes. As usually depicted in graphical format, the accident, system failure, catastrophe or undesired event is shown at the top of the diagram, and this event is linked below by event statements and logic gates to more basic fault events. The "tree" results from the branches of sequences of events and system conditions (spreading laterally and downward) that can produce the "top event." See the illustrative example in Figures 5-2 and 5-3.

The analysis concerns itself strictly with identifying system conditions, elements or faults that can lead to a given unwanted event or occurrence. There may be a number of such events that are conceivable for a product, and each would have its own "fault tree" with its event statements and logic gates. The listed references describe procedures on how to construct and evaluate fault trees, both qualitatively and quantitatively.[50-59] Since FTA can involve complex mathematical relationships, particularly when dealing with products having many components and subsystems, it is advisable to learn the procedures using simple and familiar product examples.

Failure Modes and Effects Analysis. From a logic standpoint, this technique is the reverse of FTA. FTA is a true *analysis* in that it focuses on an unwanted effect, then breaks it down into various causative elements. In contrast, Failure Modes and Effects Analysis (FMEA) is really a *synthesis* since it starts with a product's elements and evaluates their respective contributions to some product hazard.[60-65]

Emphasis of FTA is upon events and product faults or conditions that cause those events; FMEA emphasis is upon individual components. FTA works from the "top" down, FMEA works from the "bottom" up. "Top" and "bottom" refer not only to tabular worksheets customarily used with these methods but also to the product's assembly order, with "bottom" being the lowest level of assembly and progressing "upward" to higher or more complete assembly levels.

In its most basic form, FMEA considers each part and item of a product. These are entered in a sort of inventory sheet or tabulation that lists dominant and other failure modes of each part, along with consequences resulting from occurrence of each failure mode. Obviously, FMEA of such an extent requires a detailed concept of the product. This is another reason it is usually done at a later stage in the design process. Nevertheless, FMEA need not be so rigorous an exercise to be useful. It is often desirable to make an informal "cut" at an early conceptual stage listing components that *are*

Figure 5-2: Simplified Fault Tree for Portable Electric Power Saw

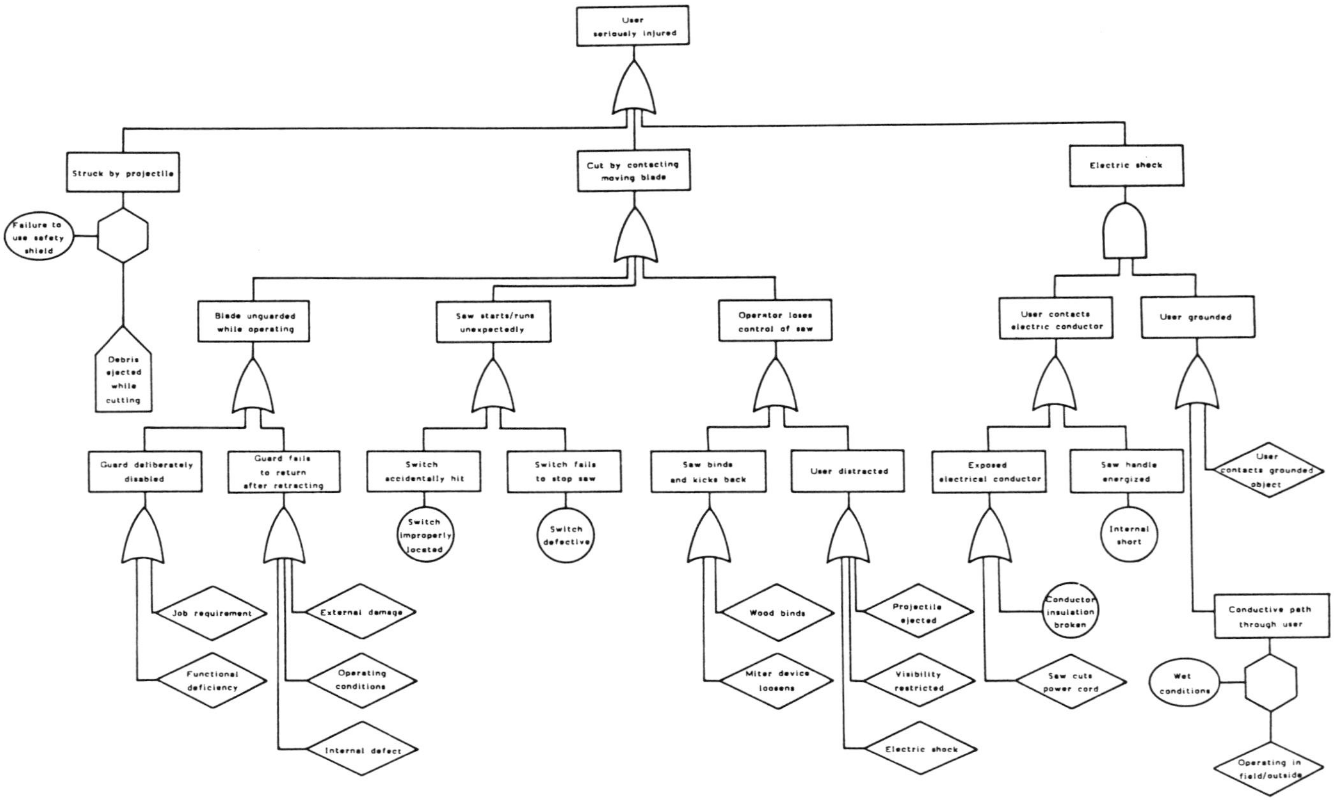

Figure 5-3: Fault Tree Symbols and Significance

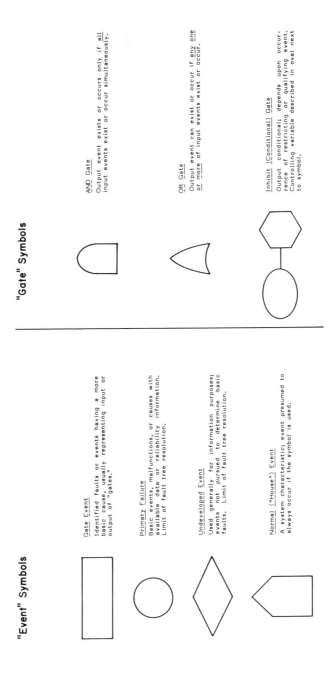

"Event" Symbols

Gate Event
Identified faults or events having a more basic cause, usually representing input or output of "gates."

Primary Failure
Basic events, malfunctions, or causes with available data or reliability information. Limit of fault tree resolution.

Undeveloped Event
Used generally for information purposes; events not pursued to determine basic faults. Limit of fault tree resolution.

Normal ("House") Event
A system characteristic; event presumed to always occur if the symbol is used.

"Gate" Symbols

AND Gate
Output event exists or occurs only if all input events exist or occur simultaneously.

OR Gate
Output event can exist or occur if any one or more of input events exist or occur.

Inhibit (Conditional) Gate
Output conditional; depends upon occurrence of restricting or qualifying event. Controlling variable described in oval next to symbol.

known to be required or confining consideration to the sub-system level. See the sample format in Figures 5-4 and 5-5.

Extent of application of these analytical "tools" is entirely up to the judgment of the designer as is stage of the design process at which they are used. Once the designer becomes familiar with the techniques and realizes the benefits and advantages of using them, their use can become second-nature and more of a subconscious engineering sense and an aid to intuition in evaluating alternatives and modifications.

As commonly used, FMEA is done progressively on entire systems, subsystems, then components and items within each component listed by serial number or identifying code. Along with listing each part or item, the FMEA table could contain details such as possible failure modes and their probabilities; symptoms of failure or impending failure; consequences of failure, rated by criticality indices; precautions or practices to reduce failure probability; and other useful information. It is important to realize that, to be significant or to constitute "failure" in the context of the FMEA, a part need not fracture or be defective in the usual sense. It may be an undesirable condition, situation, or event that could produce a hazard or lead to some unwanted event.

Once the FMEA tabulation is completed, criticality of components may be evaluated based upon the probability and seriousness of part failure or severity of its consequences. From this, it is possible to identify major hazards and establish priorities and measures for correcting them.

There are a number of ways that the tabular data may be represented. Some prefer graphical formats and, for complex productions and systems, computer programs may be developed to assist in analyzing the data, assessing effects, arriving at decisions to remedy certain effects to minimize revealed hazards and in checking effectiveness of remedies.

As with FTA, usefulness of FMEA techniques extends beyond the immediate design process. It can be a valuable product assessment tool whenever part substitution or production change is necessary. Like FTA, it is a communication aid for everyone involved with the product and constitutes a historical record of the rationality of decisions made during the design, development and manufacture of the product.

A word of caution: documentary evidence of FTA, FMEA and other analytical techniques can boomerang and be damning to the company during litigation if resulting hazard indications are not diligently followed through and corrected, or if reasons for not doing so are not satisfactorily explained and similarly documented.

At the moment, use of these or other analytical design methods is optional. However, it is likely that their very existence, along with availability of sophisticated computer procedures for representing and interpreting their results, may create a state-of-the-art of sorts (perhaps even an implicit "standard" for assessing product safety).[66]

Figure 5-4: Failure Modes and Effects Analysis for Portable Electric Power Saw
(Partial, Sub-Systems Level)

Sub-system	Description & Function	Failure Mode	Failure Cause	Failure Result	Consequences of Failure	Hazard Severity Category	Hazard Probability Level	Precautions to Minimize Failures
Internal wiring	Connects switch and motor to source of electric power	Breakage, fraying	Deterioration from heat and lubricant; mechanical flexing	Energized saw housing and handle	Electric shock to user; user distracted causing loss of control of saw, possibly leading to injury	I	B	Use heat-resistant electrical insulation; re-route wiring; design to avoid overheated motor and connections. Use oil-resistant electrical insulation; seal lubricants to avoid leakage. Double-insulate all wiring. Use non-conductive housing and handle
Power cord	Supplies electric power to saw	Breakage, fraying	Cut with saw. Accidental damage. Cord used to lift saw.	Insulation breaks. Interrupts power	Electric shock to user. Replace cord	I	C	Connect cord to saw at location minimizing exposure to blade. Use strong, hard, double-insulated sheathed power cord. Reinforce connection to saw. Give safety warning against lifting saw by cord; give cord repair/replacement information
Power switch	Turns saw on and off	Turns saw on when accidentally contacted. Does not turn saw on or does so intermittently. Does not turn saw off	Age, wear, deterioration of contacts. Electrical short in switch. Switch too accessible, improperly located	Saw does not run, or runs continuously, or runs unintentionally	Manual attempt to rotate blade results in serious injury. Serious injury when saw starts unintentionally	II	C	Use better quality switch and components. Relocate switch to less vulnerable location; require full digital depression to turn on saw
Lower blade guard	Covers cutting edge of blade; a support for saw and protects supporting surfaces	Fails to return to guarding position after cut. Fails to retract during cut. Interferes with blade and use of saw	Return spring broken. Debris clogs return path. Damaged pivot pin/hinge. Bent guard or housing. Excessive blade exposures; improper placement	Unguarded saw blade. Problems prompt manual correction, or removal or disabling guard	Serious injury from contacting blade or when rotating blade contacts another object	II	B	Use strong, solid materials; robust pivot assembly, quality spring having adequate force to overcome friction of pivot assembly and debris buildup. Keep blade path cavity clear of protrusions, roughness, to prevent debris accumulation. Warn against removal of guard or wiring it back or attempts to correct jamming or malfunctioning while saw is running. Design guard mechanism to make its return or failure to return obvious
Saw housing	Supports motor, gearbox, shaft, provides handle	Fracture and separation	External impact, dropping, internal defects, thermal degradation, bolt thread stripping	Case/housing comes apart, and exposes blade	Electric shock. Serious injury from loss of control of saw during operation, serious injury	II	D	Use impact-resistant material; inspect to assure free of cracks, pores and defects. Assure integrity of threaded connections; use lockwashers and thread sealants to minimize loosening

Figure 5-5: Qualitative Hazard Severity and Probability Rankings

Hazard Severity Categories*

- Category I - Catastrophic. May cause death or system loss.

- Category II - Critical. May cause severe injury, severe occupational illness or major system damage.

- Category III - Marginal. May cause minor injury, minor occupational illness, or minor system damage.

- Category IV - Negligible. Will not result in injury, occupational illness or system damage.

Hazard Probability Levels*

Level	Descriptive Word	Specific Individual Item	Fleet or Inventory
A	Frequent	Likely to occur frequently	Continuously experienced
B	Reasonably Probable	Will occur several times in life of an item	Will occur frequently
C	Occasional	Likely to occur sometime in life of an item	Will occur several times
D	Remote	So unlikely, it can be assumed that this hazard will not occur	Unlikely to occur but possible
E	Extremely Improbable	Probability of occurrence cannot be distinguished from zero	So unlikely, it can be assumed that this hazard will not occur
F	Impossible	Physically impossible to occur	Physically impossible to occur

*Adapted from reference 9 at 11-12.

A manufacturer facing allegations of design defectiveness in a products lawsuit and who failed to apply these, or similar design tools *that could have revealed product faults before the design was finalized*, may well find itself in an extremely weak defensive predicament. It might not be difficult for a plaintiff attorney to find an expert witness who will explain to the court that "responsible" manufacturers use such analytical techniques and that, if they had been used (implying that *if* the manufacturer had cared enough about safety to take the time to use them), the plaintiff would not have been injured by the product. Note how a plaintiff attorney regards benefits from using FMEA and computer analyses to assess potential product failures or faults: "You only get product reliability out of product liability."[67]

Difficult Decisions

As useful as analytical techniques can be for identifying product hazards and evaluating a design, techniques do not make decisions. They are merely tools for assisting the decision maker. The one making decisions may be the principal design engineer, or design manager, or someone else; but *some* individual or group must weigh the data, information and facts and, through exercising judgment, make decisions that will determine what the product and its characteristics will be. And these decisions determine whether the product will be profitable or a source of products litigation with its attendant problems and losses.

The decision maker almost always faces a dilemma. Despite all the facts at hand, the product's hazards cannot always be eliminated. The boundary separating concepts for "reasonably safe" products from those for "foolproof" or "accident proof" products can, at times, seem blurred and not well defined. How safe is "reasonably safe?" Costs become a dominant issue. Management can become irritated and impatient over attempts to eliminate identified hazards that, while foreseeable, can appear remote; especially when production schedules are at stake. Pressures for getting the product out of the design stage and on into production increase. If the product is ever to become a reality, compromises and tradeoffs must be made.

This is where understanding of the forces that shape products liability law is indispensable. It can be a reliable guidepost for choosing a path through the bewildering, sometimes conflicting, and dangerous maze of "incommensurable" demands, requirements and standards. Unfortunately, there are no absolute gauges, quantitative minima or maxima, or established tolerances.

Subjective criteria for making technical decisions are largely foreign to the engineer, for he is accustomed to quantifiable standards. Yet, as we saw in the previous chapter, there *are* standards and criteria for assisting the designer, although they may not be as precisely definitive, quantitative and predictable as we might want them to be. When confronted with the necessity of choosing which approach of an array of possibilities is best for the product and company, the designer would do well to step back from the specialized technical intricacies of the product itself and evaluate the tradeoffs from a distance or from the viewpoint of a generalist. For a moment, ignore the trees and get a glimpse of the forest.

One of the evaluations that should be made at this stage is to consider the likelihood of or propensity for the product to contribute to one of four principal causes of product-related injury: (a) failure of material, (b) human error, (c) adverse product characteristics, and (d) unusual service requirements or environmental conditions. This is the place to carefully "think-through" the use of the product with these four possibilities in mind and under circumstances of both intended use and reasonably foreseeable misuse and abuse.

Whether intentionally or unintentionally, a designer dictates circumstances, events and operations that are beyond the immediate scope of product design activity. These include product functions, features and operating principles, choice of materials, methods or construction, performance capability and limitations, economic constraints and these, to varying degrees, influence the market, customer and user, and the use environment. For these reasons, the product designer plays a key role in products liability and its avoidance. When carried out correctly and conscientiously it is not an easy job.

To minimize liability exposure for the product, the designer should become acquainted with every available design tool, analytical technique and evaluation procedure, and master their use, because requirements are getting tougher all the time.

Difficulties and conflicts of demands have always been a way of life for the design engineer. The specific nature of the problem may differ with the product, its related technology and state-of-the-art, but it is always virtually impossible to "have everything" and avoid compromises and tradeoffs. Consider the following description of the dilemma of a ship designer written over two centuries ago:

> For ships, we have to fear an infinity of bad qualities of the greatest consequence, which we are never sure of being able to remove, without understanding the theory.
>
> To possess this theory in all its extent seems to exceed the power of the human understanding. We are obliged therefore to content ourselves with a part of this vast science; that is, with knowing sufficient of it to give to ships the principal good qualities, which I conceive to be:
>
> 1. That a ship with a certain draught of water should be able to contain and carry a determinate loading.
>
> 2. That it should have a sufficient and also determinate stability.
>
> 3. That it should be easy to the sea, or its rolling and pitching not too quick.
>
> 4. That it should sail well before the wind, and close to the wind; and work well in windward.
>
> 5. That it should not be too ardent (a ship's tendency to turn to windward) and yet come easily about.
>
> Of these qualities one part is at variance with another; it is necessary therefore to try to unite theory and practice, that no more is lost in one object than is necessary in order to secure another, so that the sum of both may be a maximum.[68]

Computer Technology in Product Design

In contrast to the problems and array of conflicting requirements facing today's product designer, the ship designer's dilemma seems relatively insignificant. Now, as then, it is most important that the designer *recognize* the dilemma and be aware of all the qualities, variables and requirements he must deal with. But, fortunately for today's designer, there are resources to assist in this design activity that his predecessors never even dreamed about.

Whether we fully realize it or not, a revolution in design techniques has been going on for the past decade or more. Considering the vast increase in product design criteria demanding tradeoffs and compromises that defy human reasoning, it is difficult to imagine how product manufacturers will survive these demands without the assistance that computer technology is making available. The field known as computer-aided design (CAD) is projected to be a $2.3 billion market by the end of 1984, representing a 35% growth over 1983.[69,70]

In considering the effect of these developments upon product design, we first must appreciate the increased availability of information that new data base management programs afford. Through modem (telephone) links, they give the designer access to large bodies of information on such subjects as hazardous chemicals, materials properties and data, patents, technical publications, specifications and standards, government regulations, court decisions and legal digests, product injury data banks, and much more.

This places up-to-date information literally at the fingertips of designers and others involved in product development decisions. The mere *availability* of such state-of-the-art information is creating standards that plaintiff attorneys will increasingly use against defendant manufacturers. Therefore, no effective liability avoidance activity can afford to overlook the broadening availability of data upon which to design a product or to evaluate its potential for harm or injury.

Systems analysis design and evaluation techniques (FTA and FMEA, for example) can be burdensome to perform manually. However, these procedures may be accomplished, and with greater reliability and accuracy, using computer programs. Intricate fault tree models covering complex engineering systems that defy manual analysis may be performed with computers that provide graphical records of the results.

CAD programs make it possible for a designer working with interactive graphics displays to create and modify designs and perform numerous iterations with greater accuracy and confidence and in shorter time than ever before. Capabilities of such systems include drafting, lettering, dimensioning, isometric and wireframe imaging. More advanced systems can perform three-dimensional solids modeling, robot kinematics, and layouts.[71-79]

Computer technology offers product designers revolutionary new tools that not only significantly improve the quality of the information needed for intelligent design, but they also establish necessary data bases for computer-aided manufacturing (CAM), robotics, and automatic test equipment (ATE) programming. These capabilities enable the designer to more reliably integrate all pertinent information and available data into designs that optimize performance, safety and manufacturing requirements.

Besides this, they are compatible with systems analytical techniques and allow iterations to be made along with modifications to adjust to new data and required performance features. The result is a better balance among product performance, quality, safety and cost factors; a shorter gestation period, which means the new product gets to the market faster; and higher profit margins.

ENGINEERING

Transforming "Paper" Concepts into Hardware

Admittedly, product design *is* engineering. But it is useful in discussing liability prevention to make a distinction between steps comprising design activity and those that integrate drawings, specifications, flowcharts, procedures and recommendations—the "paper product"—into a practical plan of how it all can be transformed into hardware that fulfills design objectives. This transformation phase, or "engineering," may run concurrently with design activity.

Engineering does not duplicate the design process but devises means for carrying out its recommendations. In transforming a design into a tangible product, engineering establishes production feasibility, identifies locations of actual or potential conflict that require design modifications, checks interaction of components and operating tolerances, and assesses reasonableness of the product concept. More importantly, perhaps, engineering verifies that the product, manufactured of real components and materials using standard processes and available workforce, not only satisfies design performance criteria but will also be able to survive the scrutiny of a court and jury and their (that is, society's) safety standards and expectations.

That evaluation examines the product's adequacy for intended use as well as foreseeable misuse and abuse. It determines if mandatory contractual and government standards and codes are met (and preferably exceeded) and if the product's quality is consistent with voluntary trade practices, industry standards and the firm's own quality guidelines. It verifies that specified materials and components are adequate for intended service *and* non-intended but foreseeable overloads, use and environments. It pays particular attention to hazardous characteristics that may be associated with its existence, use or misuse and determines if these could have been eliminated or reduced at reasonable cost. And it confirms that safety features are as effective as they might be and reflect good current practice and state-of-the-art.

It is better to voluntarily impose critical evaluations on the product yourself, at the design and engineering stages, than to have it done for you later by unsympathetic experts retained by attorneys for an injured plaintiff. Again, specific steps taken at the product engineering stage to minimize liability exposure will differ with the product, its function and market.

All too often, product engineering finds that "paper" designs are not feasible within applicable cost or availability constraints. Sometimes this is not obvious at first. It is not because the design is deficient but because the real world is unpredictable. Commercial materials and constituents are always variable to some degree, usually are contaminated by other things to some extent, and it is not inconceivable that they may be mislabeled or even misrepresented. So it is imprudent to rely upon representations, sales claims or unconfirmed data on performance or quality.

It is usually not the gross mistakes or blatantly exaggerated claims that cause trouble for product manufacturers. These are obvious and easy to catch. It is subtle differences in quality or performance characteristics from that assumed, cumulative effects of using materials or components supplied within tolerance but that lie at extremes of the acceptable range, or synergistic combinations of maximum or minimum values that become unexpectedly detrimental. The first thing usually checked when difficulty arises is whether components or materials are what was specified and within spec. When this is verified, frustration sets in. Under pressure, even ordinarily rational people (including competent engineers) faced with such a dilemma, frequently take refuge in Murphy's Law, and end up "resolving" the problem by making ill-advised concessions to original product goals and performance objectives.

Problems over inadequacies of materials or constituents seldom stem from conscious vendor misrepresentations or sales "puffery" but originate elsewhere. For example, many designers regard tabulated engineering data on materials—including "handbook data"—wholly reliable and beyond question. Yet, even if the information was developed under valid conditions, it may apply to a limited range of compositions or conditions. This is seldom evident from the tabulations.

Similarly, suitability of materials for applications may be expressed in handbooks and datasheets in terms of resistance to corrosion in various media, properties at high or low temperatures, or characteristics such as machinability, formability, weldability, mechanical strength, ductility, fracture toughness, or physical properties. However, such indications are generally based upon observations made for one composition and lot and a single set of conditions, and do not consider effects of combinations of conditions. The materials used and conditions of the evaluation that the data were based upon may not resemble those being contemplated by the product designer.

For these reasons, product engineering must confirm that specified materials, parts, components and production processes are available and possess the properties and characteristics contemplated, desired and required. Deficiencies inevitably come to light, but this is the time and place to find them; not after the product is in production and a customer discovers them—perhaps through an unfortunate injury.

When changes and substitutions become necessary during the engineering stage, decisions should not be made unilaterally but should involve the original designers. They must assure that apparently necessary changes are, in fact, required and will not introduce other adverse effects. There are examples where a "solution" to one problem became a cause of an even more insidious problem. Recall how flame-retardant chemical, "tris" (2,3-dibromopropyl) phosphate, used to reduce risks of injury to children from clothing fires, was later identified as a carcinogen.

Evaluating the New Product

Besides identifying deficiencies in components and constituents, the engineering phase must critically evaluate the *complete* product and compare its operation and performance against standards established by designers and others. A major question is how to confirm that materials, parts, components, production methods and other planned operations and activities required to make the product and prepare it for shipment to the customer are what was intended and needed.

The answer is that there really is no substitute for experience or actual tests. There are just too many variables, many of them beyond the knowledge and understanding of the designer and engineer, to do anything else. Besides, in the long run, actual testing can be the lowest cost, fastest, most effective and reliable method. And it is easiest to document, explain and defend, as one might have to do some day in court.

Remember that courts will not consider, or care about, excuses that there was not enough time to run in-house verifying tests; that everyone "assumed" the material or component was what was ordered or represented; that there was no indication the product would be incompatible with its operating environment; that there was no way that some cleverly devised safety feature could malfunction in actual use; that the additional cost of testing would cut the profit margin unacceptably; or that the sales department had made firm delivery commitments to customers making it impossible to conduct pre-production tests.

Courts expect manufacturers *to know* about their products, potentially harmful effects and hazards of their use, that some misuse or abuse is foreseeable, and that the product would respond predictably to given environmental conditions, age, or use.[80,81] There is only one way to really know these things and that is to test for them.

While it is desirable to conduct formal instrumented tests and derive quantitative data from them, this cannot always be done. But this should not deter attempts to answer questions or make confirmations. Tests need not be complicated or sophisticated to be valid. You are not preparing a scientific treatise or doctoral dissertation but simply confirming suitability of some material or component for use in some manner. It is often readily and directly evaluated. Any competent engineer with practical experience, solid understanding of fundamentals, resourcefulness and imagination should be able to devise simple and straightforward tests to provide the needed indications.

Of course, not every material, part and component of every product must be tested. It's a matter of engineering judgment. It is up to the engineer to be knowledgeable about the existence and validity of test data and applicability to the product or situation at hand. It is only when there are gaps in available information, when there are enough differences in operating conditions between available data and the application in question, or there are doubts about how *this* product will respond to *these* conditions, that tests should be run.

All results of all tests, along with complete details on how they were set up and run, and why, must be documented. This goes for both good results and bad results, expected outcomes and unexpected "flukes." If nine out of ten tests are "successful" but one fails, that failure must not be disregarded but probably should get the most attention. That one failure, even if it is one out of a hundred or more, may provide more valuable information in avoiding liability than all those successful tests.

Documentation has the obvious benefit of verifying that tests were done and demonstrates that the product manufacturer was responsible and cared about performance of his product, its reliability and safety. Another benefit is that if tests are conducted in an orderly and organized manner (as they should be) and details and results well-documented, they constitute a valuable technical base for designing subsequent products and evaluating their materials and components.

Product tests cannot be run without pilot-scale or prototype products to test. These should be constructed from materials and under conditions, standards and tolerances closely simulating those of actual production. Any necessary deviation from actual production conditions must be recognized and taken into account in evaluating the outcome of the tests.

All tests should be run with a "control" sample, part or product. The control sample is one whose characteristics are known and test response is predictable. It may be a component or previous version of the product for which there is considerable experience. Or, it may be a competitor's product with known behavior. Test samples and their control sample should be run at the same time and under identical conditions; otherwise, significance of test results will be in doubt.

An important consideration in conducting product tests is assurance that the tests duplicate the most demanding conditions encountered in actual use. There is little value in subjecting a product to conditions not representative of what the product will face in actual service. It is as undesirable to err in the direction of higher severity as it is toward lesser severity, as the first is wasteful and can prompt needless over-design while the other gives a false sense of security and incurs unknown liability exposure.

Correct balance is probably best achieved through restricting the amount of testing under simulated or accelerated conditions in favor of actual field experience. Admittedly, this is not practicable for many kinds of products. However, it is worthwhile to make every attempt to get experience with the product in actual use situations and environments. Some success can be achieved in the laboratory but the results are not as relevant as those obtained from actual use.

An effective supplement, if not an alternate, to laboratory testing complete products is actual field evaluation. This may take a number of forms. One possibility is to monitor response of the product while in use by other "captive" corporate divisions. However, even if the product is one that can be used by this other group, it is not always a politically acceptable arrangement because other divisions of the company may resent being looked upon as "guinea pigs" or a test bed. This can cause results to be biased and questionable. Another possibility is to arrange tests by a "friendly customer." This is perhaps more readily done with industrial and business products than with consumer products, but other "test market" approaches have been successful with consumer products.

Through such arrangements a manufacturer might provide a free supply, or use of the product, in return for the privilege of monitoring its use and response. Data may be continually recorded by instrumentation, periodically observed by individuals or through disassembly and laboratory inspection of the product after some given period of operation. Such observations should be supplemented with personal opinion surveys of actual users or operators, using checklists, questionnaires or survey forms prepared by or in consultation with product design and engineering groups.

Extent of product testing depends upon the product and its design precedents, risks associated with its existence or use, and severity of harm that could result from its failure or malfunction. For certain classes of critical products having a high-risk potential these factors may dictate need for an extensive series of evaluations of a large number of product prototypes in a variety of use situations and environments, and may require long-term determination of total life expectancy.

Products of less critical consequences will not require such extensive testing. This is where engineering judgment comes in and where previous operating experience and industry history for the same or similar products can provide useful guidance. Such information can indicate previously disclosed weaknesses and their consequences, failure frequency and corresponding injury statistics, and can assist in establishing what tests should be run, their duration and pertinent aspects. New products without accumulated operating history or test data obviously must be evaluated more thoroughly than others for which there are experience and information.

As part of the product testing program, it is also worthwhile to make spot-recalls of production products from the field for evaluation. This might be done on unfailed products taken from various use environments, and should *always* be done on failed products, particularly those that caused damage or injury and whether litigation is involved or not.

Testing of established products may not seem likely to provide information applicable to entirely new products not yet marketed. But very few products and concepts are so new that they have no precedents. Practically all "new" products have predecessors and materials with similar functions that can provide useful test data and information.

In evaluating new models of existing products where previous features have been up-dated or up-graded, availability of data on products that have seen actual field use is virtually a must. Someone has said that manufactured products, like children, assume a life all their own once they "leave home." Therefore, no designer or product engineer should be content to live without feedback intelligence from the field.

This information may come from examining recalled product samples, through reports from service and sales representatives or customer complaints. The important thing is that the company provides a mechanism for collecting this information and relaying it back to product designers and engineers. This practice has clear advantages for all products, and relevance of the collected information is not limited to those in development.

Remember Human Limitations

In any product testing, adequate attention should be given to human factors, particularly when tests are run in conjunction with liability prevention programs.[82-85] Frequently, complex machine tools, intricate control consoles or other sophisticated equipment demand a level of mental aptitude, alertness, manual dexterity or coordination that exceeds the capability or capacity of the average user.

Accident analyses have shown that while operation of complex equipment may be safely carried out *under normal circumstances*, distractions or loss of concentration by the user or operator can seriously impair one's capability to cope with the situation. A temporary lapse of attention to details can trigger a series of cascading events that very quickly become impossible to reverse or overcome, and terminate in an accident, serious injury or disaster.

Accounts of industrial accidents attributed to "operator error" and aircraft disasters likewise attributed to "pilot error" tend to imply incompetence, negligence, incapacitation or inadequate training. Yet, investigations often reveal that those in control are experienced and competent. Such inconsistencies between conclusions and supporting facts sometimes can be explained through human factors engineering systems analysis.

Findings often show that *design* of the system, equipment or operating procedure did not adequately take human limitations into account. In other words, operating requirements simply expected too much from the user for consistently safe operation under all conditions. The design deficiency may lie in incorrect assumptions for human response time to alarm or warning indications, in overly optimistic expectations of mental capacity or manual dexterity, in failing to anticipate effects of internal or external distractions, or any number of such built-in deficiencies.[86]

A manufactured product, system or equipment may be *technically* perfect, but if its interface with the human who must operate it is deficient in some way that can make it hazardous to use, then the product's design must be considered flawed. However, distinctions are not always drawn during litigation. Nevertheless, plaintiffs' attorneys are becoming knowledgeable about human factors engineering and we can expect them to increasingly apply its principles in products liability litigation. Consequently, product design engineers would do well to make a special effort to become acquainted with this increasingly important field;[87] for, unless it is understood and its concepts applied at the design and engineering stages, it may have to be faced later in court.

Comprehensible Instructions Are Part of the Product

There are other tasks to attend to during the engineering phase of a product's development. One of them is to assure that manuals covering the product's installation, operation, maintenance and service are comprehensible to the intended reader and are complete and clear. They should educate the user both on the product's capabilities and performance as well as its limitations. Hazardous aspects must be prominently, lucidly and unambiguously described and include remedies and recommendations on action to take in the event the hazards are disregarded. Besides manuals, the format, content and location of warning labels, nameplates, tags and other appropriate information must be established and the items prepared.

An increasingly common shortcoming with user instructions, operating and maintenance manuals is their incomprehensibility. The trouble lies not in lack of intelligence of the user or reader. The problem is that the writer of the manual often fails to realize that technical terms and industry jargon familiar to him may be meaningless to the user or reader.

New technology brings with it new language, and designers of hi-tech products must either carefully explain new terms to customers or use terms customers are familiar with. This goes for industrial products, business products and professional products, as well as consumer products. A product user can be an expert in his field and still be totally unfamiliar with terminology of the industry that manufactured the product and those operating manuals he must be able to comprehend to safely use the product.

For these reasons it is highly desirable, and practically essential for some products, for a manufacturer to "test" its operating and service manuals, in addition to its products. This is done through selecting individuals representative of the typical customer or product user, but having no expertise or knowledge within the field of technology of the product, and observing their ability to comprehend key points in the manual; particularly an understanding of details critical to safe operation of the product, system or equipment. Such tests often reveal unanticipated difficulties and frustration of users failing to grasp information that the manual's writers thought would be readily understood.

Information, descriptions, warnings and written procedures so obscure that the average user can understand them only with difficulty or not at all cannot be regarded as effective and, therefore, do not really satisfy communication standards prescribed by regulations and other requirements.

Computer-Aided Engineering

As products become more sophisticated and complex, and performance expectations increase and cost constraints tighten, the need for more thorough engineering analyses becomes more critical. Yet, marketing and delivery requirements often limit the amount and depth of engineering that can be done. Computers do not eliminate need for thorough engineering; this does not change. But what they do is allow engineering analyses to be performed faster, more thoroughly and more reliably.

For example, computer programs can be used to supplement (and sometimes replace) time-consuming physics and mathematical analyses with theoretical computer models. They can augment standard tests and evaluations of actual prototypes and reduce need for extensive full-scale testing. Computer-Aided Engineering (CAE) can help the engineer obtain key information earlier in the product's development. It can help accommodate and realize more product performance objectives and goals with fewer compromises. It offers clearer insight and more complete understanding of the operation and interaction of complex systems. And it can furnish a basis for developing troubleshooting guides and logic diagrams to enable faster and more effective field service.

Anything that can be done to improve product quality and reliability will lessen a firm's liability exposure. Also, there is increasing need to integrate external factors into a product's design and engineering activities. Among other things, this includes information on dangerous characteristics of constituents and materials, and failure experience with similar products. Computers can make such information readily accessible.

These capabilities give manufacturers having such support systems not only a competitive edge[88] in shortening development time and in achieving highly cost-effective product performance, but also in defending their products against liability claims. Besides this, they may also create design and performance standards for the entire industry that others may be forced to follow.

PURCHASE AND PROCUREMENT

Verifying Quality

The procurement function is the gate that admits everything that goes into the product. It is important to assure that only the right items get through. Even in the absence of motivations like products liability, there are compelling reasons for keeping a close check on the quality of incoming materials and components.

Estimates are that the dollar value of purchases in nearly every company amounts to half or more of its sales revenues.[89] Expenditures of such magnitude require diligence to assure that the money is well spent and what is bought will satisfy the need that prompted its purchase.

Products liability prevention involves the entire spectrum of the purchase and procurement function. In addition to traditional purchases—consumables, materials, supplies, parts, components and sub-assemblies—it also includes such things as purchases of production tooling and equipment, testing and inspection instruments, associated computer hardware and software, and outside services.

Most companies are selective of which incoming products they inspect, check or verify. "Standard" materials like screws, wire, paint and angle iron may not require it but solid-state electronic controllers would. The decision boils down to whether the purchaser can confidently use and rely upon the purchased item without in-house confirmation or verification. There are no hard-and-fast rules, as suitability depends upon many things. Therefore, it is up to each purchaser or specifying engineer to determine how much verification of incoming purchases is necessary or affordable.[90]

At one extreme would be 100% acceptance of everything at face value, a willingness to use the items as-bought without any checking. Costs of inspection of incoming material certainly would be low, but expense of frequent production stoppages and a high number of rejects would soon outweigh this apparent cost advantage. The other extreme of checking everything is also prohibitive. A proper balance must be struck and someone must decide which items to test or check, how it should be done and to what standard.

Critical components (as identified in a FMEA, for example) should be tested before being assembled into the product. But how much testing is enough, what kind should be done, and should each item or only representative samples be checked?

It does not take much thought along these lines, or experience with in-house testing of purchased items, to realize that sole reliance upon such inspections for assuring product quality is, at best, a losing game. It has become almost a truism that quality cannot be inspected in, but must be *built* in. So we must start early in the procurement cycle if we want to assure some predictable level of quality in incoming purchases.

We cannot simply drop this whole matter into the laps of purchasing people, as they cannot be expected to know what quality or performance is required for each one of a wide array of products, materials and services. They need definite guidance from designers and engineers. This is a vital communication link that must be maintained. Some management authorities even advocate having the purchasing department report to engineering and production.[91] The scheme has merit.

Assurance of obtaining the desired quality in purchased materials begins at the design stage. Custom-manufactured components that are critical to the safe and successful operation or life of the product will require the most thought and attention; non-critical standard production items, the least. It is one thing to specify quality and performance characteristics in purchase specifications, and tolerances on drawings. It is another to consistently obtain them in actual components at reasonable cost and with realistic delivery schedules. For this reason among others that we will discuss, it is almost always best to keep product designs simple, using standard off-the-shelf parts, components and established manufacturing processes, as much as possible.

A good many products liability problems stem from inconsistencies between what designers specify and what is available. Unavailability of specified items requires substitutions and changes in specifications; or it may call for design modifications and engineering changes that frequently mean revised production schedules. When pressures mount and schedules are strained it is tempting to approve substitutions of *apparently* equivalent, although unproven, alternates. When it is found that substitutions do not perform as expected or as needed, it is usually too late for special ordering or custom-manufacturing of the proper items originally specified. Thus, through failure to anticipate possible supply problems early in the development, the stage is set for more problems down the road.

Of course, not every component is critical to safe use of the product but many are and others are indirectly related. Criticality of each item in the product should be known and established in an FMEA criticality analysis during the design stage. This information will provide a firm basis for procurement guidance later on and will flag which items must receive priority attention. Good communication between design, engineering and procurement departments can alert procurement people early to the criticality of certain items and the possibility of long-lead-time for delivery. This will minimize the need for frantic last-minute substitutions of potentially inferior or questionable components. Timely design reviews can do much to avoid these hassles.

As part complexity, criticality, performance requirements and expectations increase, more attention must be given to its purchase specification, definition of acceptance criteria, and vendor selection. It is not unusual to discover as the design approaches maturity that high-performance items or those representing advanced technology are not commercially available. Options facing the engineering department then are: (a) request redesign to accommodate the characteristics of what is available, (b) make the component in-house, or (c) transfer the technology needed to make the part to an outside supplier to enable it to meet design requirements. Any of these options can prove costly and prohibitively time-consuming at this late stage. This is another reason for making every effort to anticipate unusual requirements early in the design process.

Regardless of where the part is made or who makes it, performance of critical components must be verified before they are assembled into the product. Verification may be done in the vendor's plant or in the product manufacturer's (purchaser's) plant.[92] But quality must be checked by appropriate and sufficiently discriminating methods and the results documented.

Procurement and Acceptance Standards

It is the responsibility of designers and engineers to establish purchase specifications for materials, parts and components, even if another group prepares the actual document and puts it into the prescribed format. The job of the procurement people amounts to a good deal more than placing orders. They should find the source that offers the best item for the money and satisfies the requirements. The source should be dependable, financially stable, reputable, and able to deliver as promised, when promised, and willing to stand behind its products.[93] Beyond that, and perhaps most importantly, procurement people must assure that the designers' requirements are effectively expressed and communicated to vendors and suppliers and the proper contractual documents prepared.

As in all such transactions, there are legal issues involved. In the absence of specific written purchase contract provisions, most of them are covered by the Uniform Commercial Code (UCC). It is well to note that product warranty rules differ with classifications of purchaser, such that commercial purchasers cannot expect the liberal warranty provisions the law extends to purchasers of consumer products. This difference reflects differences recognized by the law in the presumed knowledge of the product between commercial or professional users and the public.

In matters of products liability exposure, vendors and suppliers are not immune to claims of injury or damage arising from defective purchased components. However, the manufacturer of the finished product containing the component is probably the most vulnerable link in the chain; as in most jurisdictions today it is responsible for verifying fitness for use of its purchased components.[94-96] If the product manufacturer is not financially sound and insured and, therefore, not a good prospect for recovery of damages and the supplier of the component is considered a better prospect, then the supplier might have the greater liability exposure.

In specifying parts, components and ingredients for a product, it is advantageous whenever possible to purchase to existing industry standards.[97] These are readily available and understood, are widely used, and most manufacturers are familiar with their requirements and provisions. Keep in mind, though, that these standards constitute *minimum* requirements (a "floor" not a "ceiling") and for certain applications they may not be sufficiently demanding. Design requirements that exceed those of published standards can be easily added as addenda to the basic standard through negotiation and written agreement between purchaser and supplier.

The value of purchasing to industry standards does not lie solely in liability avoidance, although there may be some indirect benefit. The greatest benefit is to simplify matters and to establish a baseline for communication between buyer and seller and for assessing quality and performance of product components.

Consequently, purchasing to industry standards does not eliminate the need for in-house inspection and verification but it does facilitate purchase procedures and contractual agreements. It also simplifies design specifications. It is vastly easier to specify in a single-sentence statement that a given purchased item shall be manufactured in accordance with the requirements of an applicable ANSI or ASTM standard than it is to attempt to re-define and re-state the requirements yourself. Even if this could be successfully done, the vendor would consider the rewritten specification a special requirement and it would probably carry a surcharge to cover the vendor's additional effort and expense to read, comprehend and confirm that these "special" requirements can be met.

Competent individuals from all segments of industry and disciplines donate countless hours of their time that is literally worth millions of dollars annually to prepare and update thousands of voluntary consensus standards covering most engineering materials and a wide spectrum of manufactured products and components. It is just plain foolish to ignore this vast resource of useful and timely information.

Besides these advantages, purchase of materials and parts to existing industry standards provides ready-made acceptance criteria for in-house evaluation of incoming materials. Most standards not only specify compliance requirements but also describe evaluation methods, procedures and testing apparatus, as well as criteria for measuring compliance. This greatly simplifies in-house acceptance testing. If specific needs exceed requirements of the standard, it is not difficult to modify the standard testing procedures to verify compliance.

The Goal of Purchasing and Procurement

The goal of the purchase and procurement function—in addition to its traditional role of locating vendors and ordering specified materials and services—is to make these things available in a timely manner to the company with minimal need for quality verification and determination of compliance with specified standards. The key to achieving this goal lies in the competent preparation of adequate design specifications and in maintaining effective communication between purchasing people and design engineers.

This is much easier said than done. For complex products with hundreds and even thousands of parts and items to specify, order and inventory, in the face of the need to decrease product gestation time while product performance requirements increase; ability to maintain effective communication diminishes drastically. Efforts to communicate by traditional means are found to conflict with other goals that are more clearly tied to productivity and profits. Consequently, they tend to be stifled.

It is to overcome these apparently insurmountable obstacles that computer-integrated manufacturing (CIM) techiques are being developed.[98] Material resource planning, sometimes called manufacturing requirements planning (MRP), software programs are proving helpful in reducing inventories, improving communications and decreasing overall costs.[99] The field is rapidly changing and procurement people should maintain an active awareness of its developments.

PRODUCTION

Profitable Products or Litigation Instrumentality?

As important as design, engineering and procurement functions are in laying groundwork for avoiding products liability, it is on the production floor where the actual product comes into being—a product that will either survive the rigors of the real world, and be profitable, or one that will expose the company to costly litigation. Production converts all that has preceded it—designs, specifications, drawings, descriptions, process and manufacturing sequences, and engineering analyses—into tangible hardware and parts, and those parts into products.

If preceding steps have been competently taken and working drawings, instructions and production/process schedules are complete, correct and unambiguous, production difficulties will be minimal. Yet, there always are inconsistencies between what was thought to be feasible and what actually can be done; between expected tolerances and those that the process can achieve; between presumed response of specified materials and components and that observed in delivered items; and between projected production rates and product completion schedules and those actually attained.

These kinds of situations that arise during production are where many products liability problems originate. This is because, now, the heat is on, production schedules and quotas are at stake, product orders probably are already in hand with customers expecting delivery, and the firm needs the cash flow that will be generated by product sales. Presumably, engineers have "blessed" the product design, the materials, components and manufacturing processes, implying there is nothing that can go wrong.

Any discrepancy reported by the production department now will be looked upon with suspicion and as fabricated excuses for missing production targets. There is, therefore, strong motivation to avoid reporting problems, particularly those that seem insignificant. The temptation is to resolve the difficulty on the shop floor, often at the shift foreman level. And this may take the form of opening tolerances, speedup of some machine or process, eliminating some apparently redundant finishing step, substitution of an "equivalent" part for the specified one that is out-of-stock or is causing production stoppages, or by-passing some seemingly unnecessary quality verification bottleneck.

Such occurrences are difficult to control and practically impossible to audit and identify. But they can be minimized. The posture of management toward production foul-ups, productivity incentive payments and missed schedules can affect the willingness of production people to report discrepancies and problems. If the production incentive wage system or employee performance ratings are adversely affected by "making waves"— even if it is an honest attempt to point out difficulties or potential problems—then employees will be reluctant to report them. Production workers will shrug them off and ignore them as not being part of their job or concern.

This is another reason why liability prevention is everyone's job. But it does no good for everyone to be in tune with liability avoidance procedures when management fails to realize that wage incentive and labor practices can create a climate inconsistent with carrying out an effective liability prevention program.

Other manufacturing difficulties can originate in the engineering phase, where overly optimistic assumptions made about production capacity, worker skill or response, or facility capability can lead to unattainable production expectations. Such things as hostile attitude toward the product or some manufacturing procedure, or attempts by workers to overcome discomfort or perceived workplace hazards, have seriously degraded the quality of parts produced without anyone becoming aware of their existence or consequences until much later. Manufacturing sequences or tolerances that seem unreasonable and unjustified to production workers may be the source of serious difficulties. Other problems can arise when production engineers specify procedures that cannot be achieved by existing equipment, processes or skill levels.

Much of this kind of difficulty can be avoided. There are several ways to do it. One is through closer and more active participation and involvement of manufacturing people during design reviews and engineering phases. More rigorous adherence to manufacturing procedures specified by design and engineering, and insistence upon no unauthorized part or material substitutions, or changes in process or equipment operating parameters, will also help.

Opportunity for product problems stemming from unapproved substitutions or changes is multiplied many times in a plant of a vendor or subcontractor producing components for a product manufacturer. These can be minimized through careful vendor selection, good engineering liaison, thorough and periodic auditing of the vendor's operations and effective testing of delivered components.

Recognizing Importance of Human Factors

Perhaps the single most important precaution in assuring against adverse production changes is to maintain effective communication with those directly responsible for operations. If workers know why certain tasks must be performed in a specified way, it is more likely that they will carry them out as directed. Also, production and assembly drawings should be clear and unambiguous. If standard working drawings are complex, they might be supplemented with pictorials and exploded isometrics. Perhaps supervision is spread too thin for line workers to get decisions or answers to questions.

Periodic departmental meetings, including the lowest skill levels, where workers have an opportunity to bring up problems or difficulties in producing components to the required specifications and to air their opinions in a constructive climate, can have favorable impact on employee morale and contribute significantly to improving communication at the production floor level.

Manufacturing and assembly operations frequently place too much responsibility upon unskilled workers, sometimes requiring decisions and judgment well beyond their capability. It is surprising how well many workers respond to responsibility beyond their innate capacity. However, such reliance represents high risks that can lead to trouble when pressures mount, when complexities overwhelm their limited understanding, or when experienced workers are absent and are replaced by others less familiar with the job.

Decision-making responsibility of production workers must be consistent with their capabilities and training. If it is not, workers having necessary skills should be used, or the operation modified to require lesser skills or changed to suit the skill level. This can be accomplished through semi-automated procedures, use of color-coded markings, digital readouts, visual/aural indicators, go/no-go gauges, microprocessor-assisted controls, non-symmetrical or polarized mounting lugs or bolt spacings to assure correct assembly, and any number of other techniques.

Operations and critical processes that require specific skills should not be compromised through using inadequately trained people. Critical tasks performed by workers without industry-recognized qualifications, licenses or other credentials—particularly if it can be established that they are substituted for economic reasons—expose the firm unnecessarily to products liability. Where special skills are needed but for which there are no industry-recognized standards, the firm should provide or arrange formal training that will provide and assure the necessary skill, with proficiency confirmed through test scoring and well-documented course curricula.

Hiring policies, job assignments, and advancements to higher skill levels and greater responsibility should be based upon objective performance and competence standards, reviewed periodically. Requirements for each skill level and grade should be clearly described in accurate and current job descriptions that reflect assigned tasks.

In recent years there has been significant progress in the discipline that has become known as "human factors engineering" or "ergonomics." We touched on it briefly in discussing product design where it is important to take into account human limitations of prospective users. These concepts also apply to manufacturing processes and can affect a manufacturer's liability.

Production processes, assembly operations, testing and inspection procedures all should be established and reviewed with these concepts in mind.[100] It should be done not only because it will make life easier in the long run, but also because ergonomics is rapidly becoming part of the state-of-the-art of manufacturing. Product failure traced to human error that could have been avoided through awareness and application of these concepts could leave a defendant manufacturer far out on a limb in attempting to defend outmoded production methods.

Materials, Parts and Components

No matter how carefully a product's constituents are specified and purchased, in-house verification of their quality and suitability for intended use is still required. This dictates the need for some means of segregating tested and approved from rejected and untested material to insure against mix-ups. It is also desirable to provide a method for identifying lots of incoming material, particularly items critical to the safe and successful functioning of the product.

An important advantage of identification is that it makes it possible to trace material to its origin. Traceability has generally been considered essential only for critical federal government purchases for weapons components, defense and aerospace systems. But the increase in performance requirements and customer expectations for most products, along with heightened awareness of products liability, have made traceability virtually indispensable today for most product elements and components.

Recent developments in microprocessor technology in conjunction with magnetic tape, the Universal Product Code (UPC "bar code") and laser scanner make identification, data storage, retrieval and traceability a fairly straightforward process. It has become readily implemented and compatible with existing data processing installations[101-103] and essential input for CIM systems.

Since there is an obvious economic limit to the extent incoming materials can be inspected, the manufacturing firm needs some guidance on testing priority and its intensity. Such decisions should be based upon criticality considerations derived from FMEA studies and other product life and performance data. Obviously, the more critical the part or component is to the safe operation of the product, the more discriminating the inspection should be; the more intensely and thoroughly it should be inspected; and the more samples individually evaluated.

Besides criticality of the part, other criteria influencing the decision to inspect should include degree of reliability or confidence in the component to function. This might be based upon previous history or industry experience, or simply lack of it. Processes or operations that are notorious for faults or deficiencies or that depend heavily upon worker skill and competence also call for greater vigilance and thoroughness in inspection.

Any testing called for by government regulation, the work contract, or other requirement must be done. Care should be taken to assure that all testing equipment and instruments are properly calibrated and calibration certificates are current. A lack of regulated or contracted testing requirements should not prompt a manufacturer to conclude that testing need not be done, however. Demonstrations of a responsible attitude toward product safety through development and use of special in-house testing equipment and procedures could have a strongly favorable influence upon a court in defending a products lawsuit.

Testing is done at various levels of product assembly. Once the more fundamental elements such as raw materials and standard items have been verified to be as specified, they move on to be incorporated into the manufacturing system as process feedstock or as parts of sub-assemblies. Since manufacturing operations change the physical or chemical form of raw materials and ingredients, it is necessary to verify proper response in these operations. This verification should check both correctness of the process and control parameters as well as condition of the processed material or part. Operations that have been known to incur liability through inadequate process control or inherent variability have been heat treating, coating processes, drying or baking operations, welding, brazing and soldering and chemical reactions.

As lower component or product elements are combined into sub-systems, their ability to properly interact with other elements or components must be checked, along with effectiveness of the combining operation itself, which may be mechanical, electrical, chemical or thermal. Testing should not stop with successful response of sub-assemblies but must include evaluation of the total or complete product. Sub-assemblies must be connected to one another, operation of one successfully-tested component can influence the functioning, output or life of another through vibration, radiation, thermal effects, leakage or some other condition. So it is essential to verify that the fully-assembled and complete product performs as intended.

Computer-Aided Manufacturing

Before leaving the subject of material and quality verification in production, it is worth noting the rapid developments in computer and microprocessing technology that have taken place in recent years and are revolutionizing industrial operations. Advancements in lasers and computer/microprocessing are being applied to virtually every aspect of manu-facturing—from process and machine control, metrology, surface inspection, chemical analysis and compositional verification, hardness testing, metal-lurgical analysis, non-destructive evaluation (NDE) and many others. These advances in Computer-Aided Manufacturing (CAM) are making traditional control and inspection methods obsolete; as they are faster, more accurate, more reliable and less labor-intensive.[104-106]

A key concept that is emerging is substitution of *process control* for product testing.[107] That is, if the manufacturing process is adequately monitored and controlled, theoretically there will be no product rejects and no need for traditional testing of finished products. In actual practice, zero rejects may be impractical to achieve, regardless of the degree of process control exercised. Nevertheless, there is much to be said for stressing process control. It is obviously more efficient to make the product right than to tolerate substandard processes that produce some percentage of flawed products and rely upon inspection (with compromised acceptance standards devised to accommodate the flaws) to identify acceptable products and unacceptable ones that either must be fixed or thrown away.

We read much about robots and the "automatic factory" that seems pure fantasy. Some of it may be. However, computer technology is developing at such a rate that the day is fast approaching when these fantasies may become reality.[108-111] Computer-integrated manufacturing (CIM) is, today perhaps, more philosophy than working hardware. But its goals are worth some thought; for CIM looks to the *integration* of design and engineering with manufacturing planning, manufacturing process control, factory automation, and testing and inspection or monitoring.[112,113]

Systems are now in use where design data bases may be transferred to manufacturing and where, besides finished drawings, they provide machine setup information and geometry verification data for preparation of programs for numerically-controlled (NC) or computer-numerically-controlled (CNC) manufacturing operations.

We have already briefly mentioned developments in computerized procurement and inventory control, and MRP, with its potential for greater efficiencies in materials handling and quality verification.

Automated testing and inspection is being used for many traditionally manual operations, with more being added every day.[114] These systems provide data printouts with test results, already documented and readily made a part of a product's profile or data base. These systems enable testing of more samples with increased statistical confidence and greater probability of detecting manufacturing defects. They are more discriminating, so that defects or out-of-tolerance tendencies once too subtle to detect are now revealed. Since many of these quality control procedures may be incorporated into real-time, on-line, production operations, they offer opportunity to correct deviations from standards before they become rejectable.

In the plant itself, computer information management systems permit better traceability of a product and its components, no matter how numerous or complicated they are. This capability offers better control, higher levels of confidence, and faster resolution of problems when they do occur. Beyond the plant, they enable more detailed records of product destination together with information on customer and user profiles. Such information and short retrieval time are becoming essential for many high risk products in facilitating regulatory compliance in issuing hazard advisory or recall notices.

For the moment, however, most manufacturers must be content to live with what have been called "islands of automation" that must be bridged and interconnected before further progress is made. These "islands" represent equipment of different manufacturers, with different computer codes and languages and incompatible data base management systems. A CIM network requires compatibility of these with one another, clear and intelligible links between CAD and CAM, and the necessary hardware and software to tie it all together.[115,116]

As formidable as these hurdles may seem, realization of the goals may not be far away. Pilot flexible manufacturing systems (FMS) already are in operation.[117,118] Artificial intelligence systems capable of coordinating a large number of problem diagnoses, process controls and manufacturing operations are being developed.[119,120] Robotic equipment with visual and tactile sensor capabilities with voice recognition and response systems are making headway.[121-126] And "supercomputers" capable of tying it all together are becoming available.[127-129]

The implications of all this to products liability are not difficult to discern. Such methods allow better control and monitoring of manufacturing operations, and more parts and samples to be checked at lower cost. They permit use of more discriminating tests with greater reliability, and afford a direct readout and machine-documented record of the test and its results.

As these automated testing and control procedures become widely used they will constitute the state-of-the-art in manufacturing process control and inspectability. Manufacturers who continue to rely upon functional, although obsolete, equipment and methods having inferior response can face a difficult time explaining why they chose to ignore new and available technology for assuring product quality.

It is here, and in other areas of manufacturing, where the most compelling "standard" may not be a government regulation but rapid advance in some technology that could enable a manufacturer to assure a higher quality and safer product. What competition does about implementing this new technology could well establish a new industry standard that could be used by an aggressive plaintiffs' attorney in a products liability lawsuit. This is just one more reason for keeping abreast of technological developments that, in any way, are relevant to the product, its design, manufacture or inspection.

PACKAGING

Its Scope

It is easy to become preoccupied with the product and regard packaging as an afterthought—little more than a box, container or promotional gimmick. As insignificant as packaging may seem to be, a large number of products lawsuits are brought over some characteristic of product packaging. Even a cursory look at products-related litigation will show its importance. It is apparent in today's judicial decisions and in the evolution of products liability law over the past several decades.

Packaging technology (and it has become sufficiently sophisticated to be called a "technology") involves a number of disciplines such as mechanical and chemical engineering, physics, toxicology, economics, transportation logistics, mathematics and computer science. And it's big business. As long as a decade ago, annual expenditures in this country for packaging were estimated at nearly $25 billion[130] and it has been growing steadily.

A product manufacturer should assess design and suitability of the package with the same care used for the product being packaged. In the eyes of products liability law, the package *is* a product in its own right and can incur liability, even when the packaged product may not. This means that design, engineering, specification preparation, manufacturing and testing of the package must be as thorough and competently done as that for the product.

Considering the broad array of products being handled and moved by every conceivable means, there is understandably a maze of rules and regulations that deal with packaging requirements, many of them dictating minute—often apparently conflicting—details. Among the principal regulators of product packaging are the FDA, U.S. Department of Commerce, U.S. Postal Service, Interstate Commerce Commission (ICC), the Federal Trade Commission (FTC), U.S. Coast Guard, various carrier regulating bodies, the military services, municipal fire departments, bureaus of weights and measures, and bridge and tunnel authorities. Besides such regulations, there are numerous industry consensus standards that apply to the entire spectrum of packaging. ASTM, alone, lists well over a hundred individual packaging standards.

These standards and regulations usually specify *minimum* requirements. Again, these requirements constitute a "floor" and not a "ceiling" on capability, endurance or performance. A manufacturer's packaging quality standards should exceed these minimums and suitability of its packaging confirmed by its own field tests. As with product regulations, compliance does not confer immunity to legal claims or liability; but failure to comply may be regarded as lack of due care. Whether or not this deficiency is relevant to the immediate liability issue, non-compliance with legislated regulations could weaken defense arguments and make it difficult to refute an injured plaintiff's allegations that the manufacturer was irresponsible in its manufacture, marketing and distribution of the product in question.

Product packaging has several functions. The most obvious one is to contain, cushion, protect and preserve the product between its point of manufacture and final destination, and perhaps throughout its useful life and beyond. Another function is to communicate or convey information in the form of instructions, specifications, guarantees, descriptions, and warnings. Through shape, color, texture and other design feature or characteristic, the package also serves as display medium and sales tool to motivate the prospect to buy the product. For some products, the package is used as a dispenser and even a measuring device. Besides these functions, packaging plays a key role in product distribution to enable effective conveyance from manufacturer to user or consumer.

Because of the intimate association of the product with its packaging, and its dependence upon it, these functions can become a basis for liability action. In the following sections we will consider liability aspects of concern to product manufacturers.

Physical Considerations

Faulty containment can take a number of different forms, each with its own set of consequences. Simple breakage of the container with loss of a harmless product is probably the least damaging kind of containment deficiency. Liability may be involved but not necessarily a classical products liability action where container defectiveness leads to personal injury or property damage. However, if rupture of the container allows a hazardous product to be released, potential for personal injuries and damages can far exceed the incidental costs of product loss. Even a product, ordinarily harmless in itself, when allowed to leak or escape from its container, can cause serious damage to other materials, products, people or property.

Another form of containment defect that ruptures the container could permit contamination of the contained product by moisture, dust, insect or vermin infestation, or other foreign matter. A bizarre and widely publicized occurrence a couple of years ago illustrates the possible extent of product contamination caused by what may be termed a containment "defect" that exposed a manufacturer to liability. It involved susceptibility of containers of pain remedy capsules to opening and deliberate contamination with cyanide—apparently by a psychopathic killer—then closing again, without external evidence of tampering.[131-133]

These incredible events and the series of "copycat" occurrences that followed them raise many legal questions of extent of liability of the product manufacturer or packer/distributor. There are no clear-cut answers.[134] Key questions are: Was poisoning of the capsules through criminal intervention reasonably foreseeable? Did the manufacturer owe consumers of its product a duty to protect them from irrational acts of senseless murderers?[135] Nevertheless, public outrage over these incidents and series of resulting deaths, plus the demoralizing fear and recognized potential for widespread damage from such product tampering, led to rapid enactment of FDA regulations for tamper-resistant (and tamper-evident) packaging for a broad class of pharmaceutical and health-care products.[136,137]

A more common but equally serious problem of somewhat similar nature has been the ease with which children could open containers of prescription and over-the-counter drugs and other potentially harmful household products. Public intolerance of these needless injuries and deaths to children unable to understand the risks and dangers from toying with attractively colored and packaged products led to the "child-resistant" seals and lids that today defy and frustrate even many adults.

Besides offering reliable containment, protection and preservation of the product, containers should not react with the product they contain. A reaction might dangerously contaminate the product without any external evidence of its occurrence. Such contamination by the container might not make the product a hazardous material, but may ruin it. It may cause it to lose its properties which, when relied upon later, may lead to damage or harmful consequences. Depending upon the product and the container material, interaction between a product and its container may deteriorate the container and cause it to leak, rupture or explode.

A product's container or package must be able to withstand the handling, transportation and storage that are not only normally expected but reasonably foreseeable as the product makes its way from the manufacturer's plant to its warehouse, followed by transportation to a wholesaler's or distributor's warehouse, from there to a retailer or supplier and eventually to the consumer or user. There may be a number of transportation segments with delays or storage in-between, in all kinds of weather and environmental conditions, and handling may be rough and severe. Yet, the contained product must not be adversely affected.

Once the packaged product safely reaches its point of use or consumption, it still is not "home-free" as far as liability risks are concerned; for there is potential for liability exposure in disposal of the used product, its containers and packaging material. Over a decade ago, it was estimated that manufacturers in this country purchased 50 million *tons* of packaging materials alone.[138] This included cardboard and paper, wood, glass, plastics, various metals and many combinations. Some of this is, no doubt, recycled today; but much of it is not. Not all such materials are hazardous but a surprising number of them can be.

In a recent estimate of the *hazardous* waste disposal problem in this country, Congressman James J. Florio (D.1st-N.J.), author of the Superfund legislation, said: "Incredibly, American industry now produces one metric ton of hazardous waste for every man, woman and child in this country each year." He indicated its cost to the government was expected to exceed $12 billion by the end of the 1990s.[139]

A prominent environmentalist, in an indictment of industry for its apparent lack of concern over the disposal problem said this, and it is pertinent to our subject here:

> Nothing "goes away;" it is simply transferred from place to place, converted from one molecular form to another, acting on the life processes of any organism in which it becomes, for a time, lodged. One of the chief reasons for the present environmental crisis is that great amounts of materials have been extracted from the earth, converted into new forms, and discharged into the environment without taking into account that "everything has to go somewhere." The result, too often, is the accumulation of harmful amounts of material in places where, in nature, they do not belong.[140]

"Hazardous" wastes include process effluents, unuseable by-products, and substances from sources other than discarded packaging. But a vast portion of these wastes, and many of our environmental hazards, are traceable to materials that, in broad terms, originate with the manufacture and distribution of products, whether they are discarded containers, packaging, unused or spent product or process residues, or even the worn-out product itself.[141]

The legal rationale that enables victims injured by products to penetrate the "deep pockets" of manufacturers for compensation can equally apply to victims injured by discarded products and disposed product-related materials that harm those who inadvertently come into contact with them. Legal issues that govern liability for such incidents include the manufacturer's recognition of expected and reasonably foreseeable disposal hazards and its duty to warn of the hazard in explicit terms, with instructions for disposal that will eliminate or drastically reduce the likelihood of injuries from improperly disposed products or product-related materials.[142,143]

Marketing Functions

Communications. In addition to containing, protecting and preserving the product, packaging has become a primary medium for product marketing. One packaging consultant described the marketing unity of the product/package in these terms:

> For the modern packager—industrial, consumer, or institutional—the product and the package are always closely allied and often almost synonymous subjects. Since marketing itself has but one ultimate objective—to sell products (packages) at a profit—packaging plays a unique dual role of object and tool in the selling process.[144]

This "unique role" of packaging demands the careful attention of the manufacturer to its products liability implications. The nature of the product and its market dictate both the need for communication and its content as well as limits to its format. While much attention in recent times has been given to the advertising impact of a product's packaging; the label and other information written on or accompanying the package have a much larger role to play than that of promoting the product or positioning its image and that of the company in the minds of prospective customers. An increasing number of products lawsuits are decided strictly upon what was or was not printed on the package, container, label, tag, instruction sheet or manual.

"Defectiveness" of a product frequently hinges upon a user's expectations. The information that serves as a basis for much of the user's expectations comes from the manufacturer in the form of advertising claims and descriptions and other information contained on or within the product. Therefore, it is important for the manufacturer to critically review information aimed at customers and prospective buyers to determine if it is providing facts and information that are sufficiently objective to enable the purchaser or user to evaluate the product's suitability for satisfying his needs.

As products become increasingly sophisticated, the gap in understanding between manufacturer and user also increases. It is up to the designer of the product package and writer of the instruction sheet or manual to bridge this gap and educate the user sufficiently to enable safe use of the product. This means that the information should be accessible, well-organized, comprehensive, and easy to follow.

It should be complete enough to cover all aspects of the product that have a bearing on safety, including its suitability for specific purposes, instructions on storage and handling, unpacking, installation, use, maintenance and repair, service, and directions for disposal. Any related codes or regulations covering its existence or use should be described. This is not the place to let concerns over product appeal and corporate image detract from the completeness, accuracy and clarity of the message.

Besides giving factual information on capability of the product and level of performance to be expected, the information should warn of risks and dangers inherent in its use or existence. It should outline precautions for use under normal and even unusual but foreseeable conditions with clear descriptions and explanations of possible consequences that may result from failure to observe the precautions. And the information should include descriptions of remedial action in the event the precautions are not followed and an injury occurs. If use of the product involves other materials or conditions that may be hazardous, these too should be foreseen and warned against.

Hazards analysis and FMEA should identify all adverse consequences of usual and unusual use, including abuse and foreseeable misuse—from the moment the product leaves the manufacturer's plant until the time it is consumed or destroyed in disposal. And the information accompanying the product should reflect the findings and determinations of those analyses.

Legal requirements stem from a common law obligation of a product manufacturer to provide users and others with adequate warning of risks and hazards associated with the product and instructions for its safe use.[145] It is important to understand that all this presumes that the manufacturer has taken every possible action and precaution to design out all danger associated with the product and that its utility outweighs any risk that its use may incur.

While duty to warn is critically important for relevant products, it is equally important not to rely upon warnings as a mechanism of escape from products liability. Warnings and instructions are not always observed, read, heeded or understood. Court debates over adequacy of a warning after someone has been injured by the product may prove inconclusive and an expensive lesson in the value of eliminating the hazard in the first place.

A products lawsuit based upon failure to warn may proceed upon negligence or strict liability grounds. However, failure to warn may seem to be closely tied to a manufacturer's behavior and not some product quality or characteristic. Accordingly, it would seem to be clearly a negligence action. Nevertheless, strict liability concepts have so pervaded the recent law that in many jurisdictions failure-to-warn cases are essentially strict liabilty actions.

A few words of clarification will show how this occurs. There are a number of elements to prove in an action for negligent failure to warn. As with other negligence actions, there must be a duty to warn. Duty to warn exists when a manufacturer knows, or should know, of danger in the use of his product. Whether a manufacturer *should* know of dangerous characteristics depends upon the product, its ingredients and obviousness of the danger to expected and foreseeable users.

Yet, some jurisdictions hold to a concept where such knowledge, whether or not it is reasonably available or "knowable," is *imputed* to the manufacturer, holding it responsible for properly acting upon such knowledge.[146] That is, where a product contains toxic ingredients, the manufacturer is expected to know of its potential danger and, therefore, to warn of it.[147] In a recent comment, legal scholars had this to say about knowledge imputed by the court:

> The imputation of knowledge is, of course, a legal fiction. It is another way of saying that for purposes of strict liability the defendant's knowledge of the danger is irrelevant.[148]

Legal fiction or not, courts expect manufacturers to know their products' dangerous characteristics and this creates a duty to warn users of these characteristics and the consequences of ignoring them. Note the rationale of a recent New Jersey decision:

> Fairness suggests that manufacturers not be excused from liability because their prior inadequate investment in safety rendered the hazards of their product unknowable. . . . Defendants have argued that it is unreasonable to impose a duty on them to warn of the unknowable. Failure to warn of a risk which one could not have known existed is not unreasonable conduct. But this argument is based on negligence principles. We are not saying what defendants should have done. That is negligence. We are saying that defendants' products were not reasonably safe because they did not have a warning. Without a warning, users of the product were unaware of its hazards and could not protect themselves from injury. We impose strict liability because it is unfair for the distributors of a defective product not to compensate its victims. As between those innocent victims and the distributors, it is the distributors—and the public which consumes their products—

which should bear the unforeseen costs of the product. (*Beshada v. Johns-Manville Products Corp.*)[149]

Need to warn of dangerous characteristics extends to all expected or reasonably foreseeable handlers and users. If a manufacturer fails to warn of danger and an expected user is injured, the manufacturer may be held liable, whether the user was or was not the immediate purchaser. However, if the manufacturer gave adequate warning of the danger in the original sale, subsequent users would probably have no cause for action for failure to warn against the product manufacturer. It is all a matter of the product, how it is marketed, the danger involved, and knowledge of the expected user.

A need or duty to warn springs from a dangerous condition of the product. While it is conceivable that every product might have capability for inflicting harm, this does not create a duty to warn of possible injury.[150] At the other extreme, products that are *obviously* dangerous (such as knives, guns, saws, razors, axes, dynamite, motorcycles) do not create a duty to warn of danger if the nature of the product is such that possibility of harm is apparent to the average person. Generally, it is concealed hazards that create duty to warn.[151] And the question of concealment depends, again, upon the product, the danger, and the background and understanding of the user.

The substance, content and format of the warning should be sufficient to protect the product user from harm.[152,153] This means that, for some particularly dangerous products, considerably more than a few words of advice may be required and may call for a clear and unambiguous description of the specific risk and consequences from failure to heed the advice. The duty to warn goes beyond a few cryptic words on a cautionary label, but includes instructions and directions on how to use the product to avoid harm or injury, whatever it takes.

Normal use or handling of a product may not be dangerous, but if some unusual, but foreseeable, use or method of using the product does create a hazard, the manufacturer has a duty to warn of it. For example, it is not normal for one to use a hammer to strike another hammer; yet it is foreseeable that a user might do so. Because of the necessary hardness of steel hammer striking surfaces, such impact of one hammer upon another is likely to result in sharp flying metal fragments being chipped off. These have been known to cause serious personal injury. Therefore, manufacturers have a duty to warn of this danger from abnormal but foreseeable use.

Preparation of written information accompanying a product must not be left solely to the discretion of technical writers, graphic arts or sales departments. This responsibility should lie with competent engineering professionals following the same liability avoidance guidelines as used for product design and engineering. These activities should proceed while the product is being developed and not be an afterthought. It is not a haphazard task that can be left to whims of individuals but should be subject to design reviews and receive the same attention accorded the product itself. Warning formats have received considerable attention by courts and these and other available guidelines and information dealing with effective signal words, internationally understood symbols or pictograms, prominent coloring and markings, should be consulted.[154-161]

We have already mentioned some of the legislation dealing with manufacture, sale and use of hazardous substances that creates specific duties to warn and how failure to comply with their provisions can constitute negligence and evidence of lack of due care. Manufacturers, dealers, or merchants whose activities involve products within the purview of legislated statutes must conform to those provisions. However, in the light of strict liability principles that examine the product and its defectiveness—in exclusion of considerations of the manufacturer's conduct—a manufacturer's liability avoidance measures must go beyond that.

There are hundreds of product categories not regulated by legislation or covered by industry standards. Such lack of regulation or standards does not absolve manufacturers of such products of a legal (common law) duty to warn of known or discoverable hazards and dangers.

The question of disclaimers often comes up in discussions of legal implications of written communication by a manufacturer aimed at the buyer or user of the product. In an attempt to find an "easy way out" of the liability trap, many would like to believe that they may conveniently avoid the problem through a written disclaimer somewhere on the package or product.

These statements made to limit or avoid liability are usually buried within the warranty. While appearing to promise benefits, the warranty statement often has the opposite effect. It has been said that "what the large print giveth the fine print taketh away." Courts have long been unsympathetic to attempts to place the unwary purchaser at an unequitable disadvantage.[162]

Consequently, it is risky to view disclaimers as a loophole for avoiding products liability. Courts declare void or simply ignore disclaimers that they consider unconscionable, inequitable or in violation of public policy or safety. Secondly, liability for negligence or statutory violations is unaffected by disclaimers. And disclaimers offer no defense in a strict liability action.

Nevertheless, the Uniform Commercial Code (UCC) does permit their use in limiting liability for implied warranties of fitness, provided they are conspicuously displayed and carry specific wording.[163] In general, disclaimers carry more legal weight in commercial transactions, such as between a manufacturer and an industrial user, or where bargaining is carried out on equal footing. The commercial status of the user carries a presumption of experience and knowledge adequate to comprehend the disclaimer and to judge fitness of the product for specific and intended purposes.

Disclaimers on consumer products aimed at unknowledgeable users who do not understand the product or cannot readily judge its fitness for specific purposes would be less effective in avoiding liability for product deficiencies. There are no clear-cut rules on disclaimers. Their effectiveness and legal validity depend upon the nature of the product, the knowledge and status of the product user, and the kind of liability being disclaimed.[164]

It makes a great deal of difference if a manufacturer is attempting to avoid liability for personal injury caused by a consumer product, or disclaiming commercial loss from an industrial product. The first would probably be considered unconscionable and in violation of public policy; while the latter might be entirely valid. Each situation must be evaluated on its own set of facts. Competent legal advice is essential before making decisions on using and depending upon written disclaimers on a product or its packaging to limit liability.[165]

The most frequent cause of action under the category of marketing-related factors is failure to warn or give adequate warning of risks and unavoidable hazards associated with use of the product. Another marketing aspect, discussed below, that can incur liability is making unwarranted or unsupportable claims of product performance, safety, reliability and suitability for particular use, service or environment.

Sales and Promotion. Since the days when the "cracker barrel" and generic products gave way to brand names, marketers have appreciated the value and promotional impact of the package as an advertising medium. This is most evident in point-of-purchase displays of consumer products, health-care formulations and prepared foods. There are very few products that do not take advantage of the potential opportunity a package offers for promoting that product, another product or service, or the company's image.

It is an effective opportunity because the message is often directed to a "captive" customer, consumer or potential user—one already attracted to the product, or who has already bought it and, therefore, is a prime prospect for repeat purchases or purchase of similar or related products.

Because the package or its accompanying literature may not be regarded as true media advertising, the message conveyed through packaging sometimes does not receive the firm's full scrutiny with regard to legal implications that the message deserves. Yet, what is said via product packaging can carry more weight than any other promotional communication because it accompanies the product, is generally read by the actual user, is probably read more intensely and is communicated nearer to the time of use of the product than any other.

Since its message is intended to be read by the actual user of the product, and the user expects it to be factual, correct and able to assist him in determining the suitability of the product for its intended purpose; the manufacturer is under an obligation to take special care to avoid misleading or ambiguous statements or implications.

There is a built-in conflict of interests here. On the one hand the manufacturer (or distributor, packager or promoter) of the product wants to make the most of the opportunity to create a wholly positive and favorable impression for the product and its manufacturer or promoter, and, perhaps, generate interest in and desire for another sale. At the same time, liability considerations (including the need to comply with legislated codes, standards and regulations) demand truthful, comprehensive and adequate communication of any risks in use of the product, harmful side-effects, and a clear and frank warning of inherent dangers.

As inconsistent as the two objectives may be, it is essential that liability issues are not compromised in favor of maintaining a positive image or overstressing benefits. It is far preferable to "go overboard" in truthfulness and detail about some risk associated with normal use or foreseeable misuse than to soft-pedal these matters for the sake of an upbeat image and risk the adverse publicity over user injuries, damages and resulting litigation.

It is important to keep in mind that what is conveyed through the product's packaging to the prospective customer or user as affirmations of fact can create express warranties in the eyes of the courts. These can have the legal effect of *guarantees* against harm or injury caused by the product and can make the manufacturer or promoter of the product a virtual insurer. Today's products liability law is difficult enough for a manufacturer to avoid without risking financial loss through carelessly-made claims on packages, instruction sheets or other communication directed to and intended to be read by the product's purchaser and user.

These reasons, added to those mandated by regulations or other requirements, make it essential for the manufacturer to include promotional statements or claims within the ambit of all design reviews and hazards analyses to assure that nothing is said or implied that could expose the firm to liability.

SALES, PROMOTION AND ADVERTISING

What You Say Can Be Used Against You

Most of our discussion so far has dealt with liability incurred by products that somehow are defective. Such defectiveness could arise in a number of ways, but liability generally comes from an inherent design deficiency or manufacturing defect. It could also come from failure to conform to some regulation or standard enacted to reduce the risk of harm from the use or existence of manufactured products.

Here we deal with issues that can impose liability upon a manufacturer for products that are *not necessarily defective*. What manufacturers say in advertisements or promotional statements have a way of returning to haunt them through creating express warranties or in incurring strict liability for misrepresentation. These are usually unintentional, and the misrepresentations need not be fraudulent or negligent, but they can make the manufacturer a guarantor against harm or injury from its products. Also, the law imposes what are known as "implied" warranties of fitness that come into being with the sales transaction. What is said during sales negotiations can affect these warranties and the liability exposure that goes with them.

Advertising prepared and paid for by manufacturers has been increasingly used by plaintiffs' attorneys as a weapon against manufacturers to defeat them in court.[166] Promotional statements have even been the instrumentality for imposing punitive damages against defendant manufacturers. It is ironic for a manufacturer to find that its legal difficulties are directly caused by something it carelessly or thoughtlessly said, and paid substantial sums to say, and that the problems caused are largely unrelated to the quality of the product itself.

Virtually all liability brought about through product promotion stems from difficulty in properly balancing two inherently conflicting interests. At one hand is a desire to stress a product's positive aspects and benefits. On the other is the legal need for conservatism in making claims and for conforming with requirements for warnings of hazards and risks in the product's use.

A manufacturer has a basic legal obligation to see to it that products it places on the market are fit for the "ordinary purposes for which such goods are used."[167] This is known as a warranty of merchantability "implied" (by law) through the act of selling the product.

Beyond this implied warranty, a manufacturer can incur a legal obligation in an implied warranty of "fitness for a particular purpose."[168] This one deals with representations the seller might make to the buyer. The warranty comes into being when the buyer relies upon the skill, judgment and superior knowledge of the seller in selecting a product for a specific purpose or use, and where the seller is aware that the buyer is relying upon his representations and skill. The degree of reliance and weight that the buyer might be justified in giving the seller's representations are influenced by the firm's reputation, the corporate image it projects through its advertising, trade marks and other credibility factors.

A desire to motivate prospective customers to buy a particular brand or product of a particular manufacturer leads the manufacturer to make promises, claims and other statements that can create legal obligations even beyond warranties implied by law. Such statements are not only those that accompany the product, as discussed in the previous section, but may be made by a diversity of means and media: newspapers, magazines, display ads, radio, television, direct mail, computer marketing, and through direct contact with sales personnel.

These can create obligations that are greater than those legally implied through sales transactions, and are known as *express* warranties. They are created when the seller makes the buyer a promise or other affirmation of fact that relates to the goods and is a bargaining point or sales inducement in the transaction. Such conditions create an express warranty by the seller that the goods are as promised or represented (even as represented by a sample submitted to the buyer).[169] It does not matter if the seller did or did not know, or whether he should have known, that his representations of fact were not true. That is, validity of the express warranty and liability for it do not hinge upon misrepresentation. If the affirmations made are incorrect, they expose the seller to liability for any damage that occurs through relying upon them.

Express warranties are not necessarily a bad thing. They have become an indispensable asset and sales tool in convincing prospective customers of a product's quality through demonstrating a manufacturer's confidence in its products and commitment to stand behind them. It does this through specific actions it promises to take in the event something goes wrong with the products it sells. The manufacturer can choose the degree of commitment it makes. However, when it makes a commitment to back its products (thereby establishing a warranty) it must comply with applicable federal regulations (the Magnuson-Moss Warranty Act, for example) and any state (the UCC or modifications of it) or local regulations that may apply.

There can be no objection to a manufacturer's desire to stand behind its products, as this certainly is to be encouraged as strategy in avoiding liability.[170] What we are concerned with are *unintentional* warranties that a company might make in the course of promoting its products that commit it to some action that it does not care to take, is beyond its capacity to assume, or could invalidate its insurance coverage.

Create Realistic Expectations

The crux of liability problems that may result from promotion, sales or advertising lies in the effect of this activity upon the buyer's motivations. Promotional statements are deliberately made to induce a prospect to buy, and he won't do that if he does not believe what is said. So, the statements must be convincing. There is no harm in motivating prospective purchasers to buy products. Trouble comes when the basis for motivation departs from reality; through making promises that the product cannot fulfill, citing performance that is beyond its capability, or representing facts that lead the user to expect a level of operation or safety beyond what the product can perform.[171]

It is easy to see how a perfectly satisfactory product can become a dangerous one when a purchaser is led to reasonably believe that it can do more than it was intended to do. If the seller somehow (even innocently) misleads the purchaser to believe and expect a level of performance that the (even flawless) product cannot deliver, the seller can be strictly liable for the consequences.

With spreading use of consumer expectation tests[172] in products liability litigation, an increasing number of manufacturers are being held liable for failure of their products to live up to expectations generated by advertisements.[173-177] This can be particularly relevant in today's advertising-oriented business world where sales and marketing people operate on the notion that consumers do not buy "products" and "things" but *benefits*, or fulfillment of expectations. Consider this explanation by a leading marketing authority:

> The "purpose" of the product is not what the engineer explicitly says it is, but what the consumer explicitly demands that it shall be. Thus the consumer consumes not things but expected benefits—not cosmetics, but the satisfaction of the allurements they promise; not quarter-inch drills, but quarter-inch holes; . . . not low-cal whipped cream, but self-rewarding indulgence combined with sophisticated convenience.[178]

In the same vein, Charles Revson of Revlon, the cosmetics manufacturer, said, "In the factory we make cosmetics. In the store we sell hope."[179] The most effective advertising and promotional campaigns for *all* products, whether they are for consumer, business, professional, or industrial markets, promise benefits and satisfactions of wants. This is what sells.

Customers are "conditioned" to expect increasing benefits and fulfillments by our apparently insatiable need for perpetual industrial growth through increasing product sales. Sometimes we get carried away and the "conditioning" is overdone. This contributes to liability and consumerism crises that now are pressing us from all sides. A direct-marketing consultant commented a few years ago:

> We have made the monster of consumerism that haunts us all. We have, through negligent or deliberately poor practices, begged for the wild legislative reaction that is causing problems for us now, and which will ultimately contribute to further inflationary pricing by those of us who survive, brought on by the cost of doing business according to the regulations and guidelines being laid down for us at nearly all levels of government.[180]

How Promotional Representations Incur Liability

Not all promotional statements create express warranties that lead to liability. According to the UCC[181] and the Restatement,[182] what can incur liability are "affirmations of fact" concerning the character or quality of the product that are justifiably relied upon by the product buyer but, because they are wrong, misleading or misrepresented, cause physical harm. One example of this is assurance by a sales representative that a product complies with some industry or military specification, code or standard when, in fact, specific qualification tests were never run and certification cannot properly be given.

The law professes to allow for a certain measure of "sales talk" or what it refers to as "puffery."[183,184] That is, promotional communication made as an inducement to buy but that does not amount to affirmations of material fact. Within this category might be personal opinions and preferences of the sales representative, citations of test results, and broad commendations accorded the product in indicating, for example, that the product is "the best on the market for the price." Since law is imprecise, it is not always easy to know what the court will regard as sales talk and what it will call representation of material fact.

It really cannot be more definite because such determination depends upon characteristics of the product being offered, status of both prospective user and offerer or promoter, and nature of the statement made and circumstances surrounding it. It is conceivable that the same words made about one product to one prospect would be obvious sales talk, but when made about another product, to another prospect, would be considered statement of material fact.

Usually though, it is not the obvious examples that generate problems. It is the "gray areas" between noncontroversial extremes that cause the issue to wind up in court. Frequently liability problems arise when the promoter is simply "making talk" and either is unaware of potential legal implications or does not believe that what he is saying will be taken seriously and relied upon to his or her employer's detriment.

Credibility of those making the statement also enters into the picture. Do they *hold themselves out to be* experts especially qualified by position, education or training to comment and advise on the product's performance, suitability for particular uses, or its safety characteristics? Subtleties of personal demeanor, dress, mannerisms and vocabulary can create impressions of professional competence and authority that may not be accurate or true and can lead the hearer or prospect to rely upon what is being said as material and incontrovertible fact.

The practice by some companies of referring to their sales people as "engineers," engineering specialists, or a variety of other professional-sounding credible titles when, in fact, they have no formal qualifications or credentials warranting them, sets the stage for liability problems—perhaps from several directions.

Liability Prevention Through a Trained Sales Force

The moral in all this is that company policy should require that, before their implementation, all advertising copy, product claims, promotional strategies and sales pitches are formally prepared, reviewed and approved in-house by those acquainted with liability issues and competent to make a critique.

Further, it should insist that sales, marketing and other communications adhere strictly to approved statements and product claims. This means that promotional claims should be founded upon actual test data and information objectively derived from reliable sources. This is particularly important when commenting upon suitability for some unusual or demanding application, aggressive environment or combinations of conditions for which there is limited precedent or experience. Such statements should be well-supported by test results obtained under conditions that precisely duplicate or closely simulate those planned by the user. Any differences should be clearly explained.

Product suitability claims should not be based on opinions, wishful thinking or reckless extrapolations of existing data. The basis for all advertising claims must be well-documented, in detail, and these files kept up-to-date and readily available or retrievable. Besides this, test methods and procedures used to generate the data should reflect accepted industry practices and state-of-the-art, including verified calibration of all equipment and instrumentation traceable to applicable standards.

Adequate sales training will include comprehensive and rigorous instruction in products liability implications with emphasis upon strict adherence to the firm's policies and published statements on product performance and other characteristics. Sensitivity of these issues to liability exposure makes it advisable to include role-playing practice sessions with active participation of all sales people followed by critiques by legal counsel or others knowledgeable in products liability matters. This will instruct in proper sales approach and disciplined responses to prospect inquiries, develop good habits in dealing with potentially troublesome issues, and indoctrinate in fundamentals of products-related liability and its avoidance.

The scope of potential liability exposure through promotional avenues is broad. The obvious example is in giving incorrect or exaggerated data on assurance of suitability of products unsuitable or inadequate for the application; particularly where life and limb are at risk. But there is much more to it than this. Statements giving an unwarranted sense of security, implying freedom from hazard or risk, or need for maintenance or precaution in use are also high on the list of potentially damaging kinds of promotion.

Descriptors like "harmless," "absolutely safe," "indestructible" and "waterproof," "shatterproof," "fireproof" or "bulletproof" are invitations to trouble. Encouragement through ads to abandon ordinary prudence and "live it up" with the product, or urging users to acquire a macho image through engaging in potentially dangerous activity with implications of apparent safety, have had costly outcomes for some manufacturers.

The promotional "statement" or affirmations of fact need not be in words to be damaging. Advertising photographs, television commercials, and sales demonstrations all prove the old proverb that "one picture is worth a thousand words" and, with similar eloquence, can incur liabilty exposure. If normal use of the product is hazardous and requires personal protection or use of guards, safety clothing or other precaution; then promotions or demonstrations showing the product in use *must* include them, even if they detract from product appeal. Otherwise, the observer may be led to expect that with *this* product, they are unnecessary.

While it may be promotionally tempting to demonstrate a product, in the hands of experts or stuntmen, surviving bizarre conditions of use and performing astounding feats to convince prospective users of a product's durability; it is risky business from a products liability viewpoint. Children, especially, are easily enticed by demonstrations and convincing media presentations. Promotions aimed at creating a demand at this level should be conceived, planned, reviewed, prepared and presented with utmost care.

There has been much criticism of broadened rules of legal discovery that gives adversaries in lawsuits access to a firm's records and manufacturing procedures, test and inspection data to support a plaintiff's allegations of lack of due care, indifference to public safety or other deficiencies. Yet, manufacturers sometimes overlook the fact that advertisements and radio and television commericals can provide adversaries with their best obtainable evidence. These are literally "broadcast" publicly to the world by the manufacturer itself and, in many cases, have been the dominant force in convincing a court and jury of the validity of a plaintiff's claims.

It should be evident that there is potential for conflict within the company over liability implications of promotional policies and practices. If handled improperly and indiscretely, sales people will allege that their hands are tied over mangement's paranoia and preoccupation with products liability matters. When and if management are told that decreasing sales revenues are the outcome of the promotional restrictions prompted by liability concerns, there will be backlash that could cripple the liability prevention program.

For these reasons, it is important *not* to formulate liability prevention policies unilaterally. If this is done, it can stir up resentment by sales people (and others)—with all the problems that go with it. This is one more reason why a prevention program *must* be diplomatically coordinated with everyone in the company, and management policies on these matters drawn up with endorsement of *all* key operating executives.

A prerequisite to all of it, however, is familiarity with products liability issues, knowledge of workable avoidance strategies, and an objective appraisal of risks inherent in various options for coping with the products liability threat. Establishing such a basis through education of key people on these matters can be the single most important step, and probably the most difficult one, in developing a successful and effective liability prevention program.

Use Advertising to Avoid Liability

As potentially damaging as promotional statements can be in exposing a firm to products liability, there is also a positive side to it. Advertising, sales and promotion can be constructively used to educate the prospect, the user and the public on product safety, to demonstrate proper use of products, and to create an image of responsible concern and awareness of the rights of consumers and product users to safe products, and to capture the public's confidence.

In the long run, this approach will do the company more good than attempts to joust with windmills of consumerism and other social forces that have gained a foothold. Corporate management would do well to consider adopting and drafting affirmative statements defining its policies on constructive promotional strategy and customer relations and urging their company-wide adoption and implementation. Acknowledged existence of such policies could go far in defusing potentially damaging liability problems at an early stage.

There are significant liability avoidance benefits in having a policy and program for educating the product user and the public. This is particularly relevant for products and product lines involving technology that is new and unfamiliar. The more knowledgeable people are, the more realistic and objective will be their expectations of product performance and awareness of risks in its existence and use. Many liability claims arise from ignorant misuse of a product based upon faulty expectations.

While it is essential to avoid making statements that will create false impressions about the product, it is equally important to make every reasonable effort to acquaint prospective users and consumers with the technology and state-of-the-art. This can be done through any number of routes, including articles and announcements to news media, reprinting of published magazine pieces, and other informational channels besides through paid advertising and promotions. These steps can materially assist in decreasing product-related harm and, therefore, in reducing the number of liability claims.

SERVICE AND CUSTOMER RELATIONS

Scope And Relevance to Liability Prevention

In its *Final Report*[185] the National Commission on Product Safety said:

> [T]he greatest promise for reducing risks resides in energizing the manufacturer's ingenuity... The law has tended in recent years to

place full responsibility for injuries attributable to defective products upon the manufacturer . . . But beyond his liability for damages, a producer owes society-at-large the duty to assure that unnecessary risks of injury are eliminated. He is in the best possible position to know what are the safest designs, materials, construction methods, and modes of use. Before anyone else, he must explore the boundaries of potential danger from the use of his product. He must be in a position to advise the buyer competently how to use and how to maintain and repair the product.

This restates the axiom that the most effective way to avoid products liability is to eliminate causes for claims. This requires that care and vigilance of the manufacturer continue all the way from product conception through giving instructions for its disposal. This not only is reasonable and prudent; it is the law.

So far in our discussion of liability prevention we have covered various aspects dealing with design, production and sale of the product. Not long ago, responsibility of the manufacturer would have ended with the sale. Not so today. The manufacturer's *duty* now extends well beyond the sale to assuring safe use of the product for virtually its entire life.[186] This is heavy responsibility because of the breadth of today's marketing activity.

Customer service covers many facets of interfacing with purchasers and users of one's products. For our purposes, we will confine attention to product safety and liability avoidance considerations. There is likely to be some question over liability of the one furnishing the service connected with the product, and whether the servicer or the manufacturer of the product used in the service is liable when harm results.

Our interest, however, is confined to responsibility of a product manufacturer for harm caused by its products. Liability for negligent or incompetent performance of services is outside the scope of our subject of products liability. Nevertheless, there is an area of overlap where a product is used in the performance of a service and harm or injury occurs.

The application of products liability law in such cases generally hinges upon whether the product was dangerous and defective. If so, the one providing the service could be held strictly liable for using the defective product.[187] However, the strict liability rule has not been extended to professionals where service is the dominant characteristic of the transaction.[188,189]

Our interest is directed toward the manufacturer of the product and whether the product is safe or unsafe to use. *If it is adjudged safe*, but harm occurs because of negligent application, the manufacturer would not be held liable. Harm resulting from use of a defective product can impose liability upon the manufacturer and, in some jurisdictions, upon the user of the product in providing the service.

A product manufacturer's primary concern in the area of customer service is with three elements.[190] One is instruction and advice given through literature (instruction manuals, for example) or personal training on how the product should be installed and used to prevent harm and injury. The second is to advise customers and users on procedures for service, maintenance and correcting defects or other difficulties with the product that may be hazardous. This would include providing physical facilities for handling such problems. And thirdly, is a system established by the manufacturer allowing traceability of its products through serial and model numbers or other identifying notations to their distributors and, for certain particularly hazardous products, even to their ultimate users or consumers.

Legal requirements imposed both by common law and government regulations make it essential for the manufacturer to have definite policies and provisions for these elements. They should be based upon information from hazards analyses and other studies conducted during development of the product and from other sources, such as reports from the field and experience with similar products. Whatever the product, its weaknesses, vulnerability and specific needs for continued safe and trouble-free operation, the manufacturer should know what they are and provide them to customers and users. The manufacturer must anticipate customers' needs for answers to inquiries, access to service facilities and availability of replacement parts, instructions and for resolution of complaints.

These activities should not be viewed strictly as a legal obligation and overhead expense that is to be curtailed wherever possible. Manufacturers are only beginning to realize what has been known and practiced by the most successful businesses all along, that you can't do enough for customers.[191-194] Effective customer service should be regarded as an investment in future sales and enhanced public relations, in addition to benefits in preventing liability.

The Customer—A Primary Resource for Information

Besides needs of customers for information and guidance for proper and safe use of products, a manufacturer can never have enough information about its own products. So, it is a two-way street. A manufacturer has added incentives that go beyond legal requirements for maintaining an effective customer service program. Even in the absence of liability avoidance motivations, a manufacturer must understand how its products are used, how they perform, and what users' impressions are of them. This is especially so for new products or those that have been redesigned or modified. Without a good grasp of such facts a manufacturer's business cannot remain viable. Products conceived, designed and marketed solely upon in-house information tend to be like "hot-house" vegetables; they get by in a pinch but, because they somehow lack the appeal and quality of the real thing, consumers tend to shun them if they have a choice.

Most successful products depend upon product information and intelligence from the field—specific facts and comments from the actual purchaser and user. Without this feedback, a manufacturer cannot hope to completely satisfy the need that prompted the product's development or to fulfill the purchaser's expectations.[195] (We are presuming here that the product is made in response to *customer* needs and not manufacturer's needs.)

While the customer is a dependable source of information in any marketing venture, his input is virtually indispensable to products liability prevention programs. Even the most imaginative designer or engineer cannot conceive of the array of situations facing products in the real world. Products have a way of finding their own niche and making their own way after they leave the hands of the manufacturer or seller. It is said they assume a life all their own. Unfortunately, it may not be what the designer intended or anticipated.

Designers are often appalled at how their products are commonly abused and mistreated. All the well-planned hazards analyses, design reviews and in-plant tests and evaluations cannot accurately predict how products will respond in the hands of actual users. In-house studies are needed, but they must be supplemented and tempered with intelligence from the field. The company must provide means for collecting and handling it, as well as policy for doing so.

Ordinarily, we tend to think of product information as dealing mostly with sales statistics, market share, customer preferences and competitive advantages. Too often, manufacturers presume that since they followed accepted practices and standards in designing, manufacturing and testing the product; and since they have confidence in their people and operations; their products can do no wrong. They become preoccupied with market statistics, sometimes remaining blind and oblivious to other issues of perhaps greater significance.

We need product information from the field to effectively evaluate adequacy of design; suitability of testing and inspection procedures and packaging; and adequacy of safety features, warnings, and instructions. We need to know if our sales, promotion and advertising are consistent with the product's performance and characteristics, and if consumer expectations are realistic or if we somehow misled them to expect features, capability or safety beyond what the product can deliver. These are difficult, if not impossible, to determine in-house; however, the required information is available to every manufacturer, and its benefits far outweigh the costs of collecting and assessing it.

Even if a manufacturer takes no definite steps to solicit field information, it becomes available anyway through customer complaints, user inquiries, sales records, service reports, returns for credit and allowances, and warranty records. This does not mean that the information is in a readily useable form or that it is always effectively used.

A mechanism must be provided for coordinating and assembling what becomes available from these and other sources, for digesting it and learning what it has to say. This takes management commitment to organize a clearinghouse and develop policies and procedures for making best use of the information. With little additional expense, the company's customer relations activity can become a source of key information that will help it make better and more profitable products and do so while substantially reducing liability exposure.

The product manufacturer should recognize the value of direct and personal contact with purchasers and users of its products. Sales and service people routinely have such contact. But, unless they are made aware of the need for collecting the information that can be derived from these contacts and feeding it back to the company, much of the potential value of the contacts can be lost.

The place to start in recovering these values is in training sales and service people. They must be made aware of what kind of information the company needs from its customers and product users and why it needs it. Besides that, the company should prepare standardized checklists or information feedback forms to assist in collecting the right information and to assure that it is complete and sufficiently detailed to be useful.

Checklist format and content will depend upon the product, its characteristics and complexity, its applications and potential hazards in its use or existence. Field representatives, also, should be familiar with products liability fundamentals. Without sensitivity to certain issues, they could miss the significance of information critically important in avoiding liability.

Obviously, they should be technically qualified, fully knowledgeable about the product, how it works and limits of its capacity or capability. They should know how it should be installed, serviced and maintained, consequences of misuse and attempts to "soup it up" to make it put out more than the manufacturer designed it to.[196] They should understand safety features and functions to assure that they are in place and being used properly. And they should be sufficiently familiar with liability aspects to advise the product user—on the spot—of any obviously hazardous practice or condition that should be corrected to avoid harm, damage or injury.

Complaints: Early Warning

Complaints require special attention in that they signal something is wrong with the product or its user's expectations.[197,198] A complaint is a clear message that there is dissatisfaction over the product or its purchase. In a complaint, a customer has taken a definite step on his own to advise the firm of a problem. Complaints usually are constructive, are made in good faith and seek only to correct a real deficiency. No single source probably offers more useful product intelligence than customer complaints.

They should not be treated lightly but followed up promptly, positively and personally. Policies or practices that give the customer an impression of being ignored, shuffled about and treated as an annoyance or forced to communicate with what amounts to a "machine" will quickly frustrate and lead to legal claims. Litigation is increasingly viewed as an appealing alternative for dissatisfied customers who have attempted the complaint route only to get a "run-around" by inconsiderate policies and mindless telephone monitors.

Product manufacturers should realize that it takes a considerable level of dissatisfaction over a product for a purchaser to lodge a complaint with a company. Often, a few dollars spent to resolve the complaint can save thousands in legal fees and defense costs. It has been said that complaints are an inexpensive source of market research. They are more than that today, as they are advance warning of liability potential.

Investigating Occurrences Having Liability Potential

It is to the product manufacturer's advantage to make every effort to resolve all customer complaints as expeditiously as possible. Those that involve product failures, defective products, damage, harm, injury, "near-misses," and even business interruption and lost income, demand priority attention. This is so regardless of the amount of reported damage or apparent seriousness of injury.

When these factors are involved the company should, without delay, notify its legal counsel and insurance carrier and thoroughly investigate the matter. Sufficient detail should be obtained to determine who, what, where, how, when and why and to establish roles played by the product, user, conditions or environment of use and any other circumstances involved.

If investigation reveals a defective product, it is essential to determine its cause and correct it. The defect may be a manufacturing flaw, the result of misuse, or design deficiency. A product may be defective because of insufficient warnings or instructions, faulty packaging, improper installation, inadequate service or maintenance, or over-selling. For these reasons, assessment of the product involved should follow broad products liability guidelines and not be restricted to traditional defectiveness criteria, as the "defect" may lie outside the physical product itself.

Information from the investigation must be communicated back to the manufacturer where there should be qualified and trained individuals, and an organized facility with standardized procedures for handling it. These people should see to it that the problem is resolved and that pertinent facts get the attention of those within the company who are responsible for assuring that steps are taken to avoid recurrences.

At first, the cause and area of responsibility may not be immediately obvious; as raw facts may require further analysis, technical study, and diagnosis by specialists. Also, meaningful determinations may require more facts than were available from the investigation itself.

This indicates the desirability of making every effort to gain possession of the failed, defective or faulty product and any other items or materials (or at least samples of them) that in any way may be involved in the occurrence. This will assist the engineering staff in making valid assessment of the cause and in taking corrective action. If circumstances lead to litigation, having the failed product in hand, with results of an investigation *made soon after the occurrence*, can give the manufacturer a significant edge in negotiating early and favorable settlement.

The information the manufacturer derives from such an investigation and study can have other benefits. It may reveal incorrect or substandard material that was not disclosed during in-house tests. It may show that existing inspection procedures are not discriminating enough or are not checking certain aspects. It may reveal that the product is unexpectedly sensitive to combinations of environments or conditions of use. Users may be pushing the product beyond reasonable and intended limits. Perhaps there is risk in its use that previously escaped detection. Operating instructions may be ambiguous about a critically important point. There are any number of useful things that may be discovered in product failure investigations.

Coping with the Information Avalanche

The information that must be handled in customer-relations activity is of many kinds and varies with the product. The manufacturer is responsible for preparing instruction manuals covering everything—from unpacking, setting up and installation, trial operation, verification of proper operation, how to add accessories and connect to other systems, how to service and maintain the product, to what to do if it does not work as it should.

As product innovations, improvements and modifications are made, they must be incorporated into instruction and service manuals. Besides this customer information, are needs for parts lists, component breakdowns, disassembly and reassembly diagrams and procedures, shop manuals with recommended practices for service, repair and maintenance. These, too, must reflect current production models and recommendations.

All of this means that the manufacturer must have accurate records on its products and their constituents to enable traceability back to basic production operations and sources of materials. This requires identification of products (and even their components) by serial number, model, production date, run, control or batch number—sometimes even to the shift and line it was made on—and their ultimate destination. For complex products and those having high risk potential, it is becoming indispensable for the manufacturer to know the name and location of the user. To complicate matters, the user may not be the original purchaser.

As product complexity, potential risks and performance expectations increase, and with them the likelihood of product problems and related complaints; it is evident that public relations and customer service, handled properly and responsively, could become an overwhelming burden. For this reason, among others, the company must stay current with developments in use of computers for record keeping, retention and retrieval.

Difficulty in handling the volume of facts and data does not excuse and should not deter the firm from taking responsible action in collecting product information, assessing it, and using it for prompt resolution of potential safety or liability problems. Fortunately for the product manufacturer, as products have grown in complexity and liability exposure, so also has development of data processing technology to provide systems for handling large amounts of information.

Availability and accessibility to countless product details are indispensable in complying with regulations dealing with various aspects of product safety. Some of the regulatory agencies that require a manufacturer to have such information include the CPSC, NHTSA, FDA, EPA, OSHA, FTC, DOE and others—some at the state and municipality level. As an example, note the following requirement of the Consumer Product Safety Act, paragraph 16(b):[199]

> Every person who is a manufacturer, private labeler, or distributor of a consumer product shall establish and maintain such records, make such reports, and provide such information as the Commission may, by rule, reasonably require for the purpose of implementing this Act, or to determine compliance with rules or orders prescribed under this Act. Upon request of an officer or employee duly delegated by the Commission, every such manufacturer, private labeler, or distributor shall permit the inspection of appropriate books, records and papers relevant to determining whether such manufacturer, private labeler, or distributor has acted or is acting in compliance with this Act and rules under this Act.

Requirements for Mass Communication

Product safety regulations create incentives for manufacturers to voluntarily institute product traceability and records-keeping systems and safety assurance programs. In the event that a marketed product is found by a regulatory agency to constitute a "substantial product hazard" or similar risk, a manufacturer will need an effective product information system to respond to claims by these agencies.

We frequently consider product problems as isolated events involving a single product and occurrence that are relatively simple to correct. However, things suddenly get immensely more complicated when there is an epidemic of failures, when well-documented studies reveal that an entire production or model run, or even the whole product line, is affected. This can expose the manufacturer and others in the marketing chain to liability across a broad front and even threaten viability of the firm and others involved with the product. This is when a well-staffed and effective customer relations and liability prevention staff with adequate data processing capability pays off.

Through news media, all of us have been made aware of the vast increase in recent years of large-scale product difficulties with their massive recalls. We read almost daily of product recalls and releases of notices of some hazardous aspect of a product. These are expensive undertakings and require difficult management decisions. Many of them are mandated by regulatory agencies, but they are usually preceded by opportunities for the manufacturer to review claims of a product hazard and to respond to the claim. Others may be initiated by the manufacturer itself.

It is to the manufacturer's advantage to take the initiative when it discovers a product hazard or potential hazard. Depending upon the product and governing regulations, a manufacturer has a legal obligation to give the regulating agency timely notice of its findings and its strategy for handling it.

In general, it is important that the action taken is prompt and effective in eliminating the hazard. Intensity of the action required depends upon the product, type of user, and nature and degree of the hazard. Often, it is desirable to first issue advisory notices to customers and users of the product to prevent further use or to explain precautions and other steps necessary to eliminate the hazard. This may be followed by more detailed instructions on corrective measures on disposition of the product, its repair or replacement.

These kinds of measures and needs for widespread communication require a previously prepared plan, system and organization for carrying them out. It is too late to defer development and implementation of customer advisory and recall procedures until a product hazard is discovered.

Understandably, there is considerable debate on effectiveness of product recalls and other mass communication attempts to minimize harm from products proven to be or thought to be hazardous. The longer the product has been on the market, the more difficult it is to reach users with the communication, and the less effective they probably are.

Manufacturers are prone to evaluate the need for a product recall using a cost-benefit analysis: Is it less costly to forego a recall and take a chance on adverse lawsuits (possibly covered by insurance) than to conduct a recall with its questionable effectiveness and possibly avoid some lawsuits? Other less tangible factors and risks enter the picture, however.

One is what effect a firm's decision not to recall a dangerous product would have upon a court's inclination toward imposing punitive damages (not ordinarily covered by insurance) for failing to take timely and responsible action to minimize harm. Another is what effect failure to recall would have upon liability insurance coverage, its premiums, and the company's reputation.

Then, too, regulations may not give the manufacturer much of an option. The manufacturer may contest the decision by the regulatory agency only to lose anyway. This merely adds to expense of the recall, besides placing the company in a position of being found irresponsible in delaying action which, if taken earlier, might have averted occurrences of harm and injury caused by the product.

Like so much of products liability, there are no easy, clear-cut answers to handling customer relations, advisory notices and product recalls. But it is helpful if *all* products liability-related matters are handled by the same office or company coordinator. In this way a company's response to any given occurrence or threat of this nature is likely to be more consistent with its basic policies and reflect good conservative judgment than if each product-related problem were treated as an entirely new event ("brushfire" strategy).

It is to the company's long-term benefit to cultivate a reputation for manufacturing safe, high-quality products and for caring about the safety and welfare of its customers and the public at large. A well-documented record of such behavior, policies, and practices, in itself, can have material benefit in minimizing lawsuits and damages.

REFERENCES

1. Simpson, R.O., former Chairman of the CPSC, quoted by David M. Natelson in *Quality Assurance—A Primary Management Tool for Products Liability Prevention*, Proceedings PLP-77E at 57, Product Liability Prevention Conference, Hasbrouck Heights, NJ (August 22-24, 1977).
2. Peters, T.J., and Waterman, R.H. Jr., *In Search of Excellence* 74, Warner Books Edition (1982).
3. *Id.* at 119-55.
4. Shabecoff, P., *Cleaning Up the E.P.A. Vocabulary*, The New York Times, p. 16, col.1 (June 13, 1984).
5. *Evans v. General Motors Corp.*, 359 F.2d 822 (U.S. Court of Appeals, Indiana) (1966).
6. *Jamieson v. Woodward & Lothrop*, 101 App.D.C. 32, 247 F.2d 23, *cert. den.* 355 U.S. 855, 2 L.Ed.2d 63, 783 S.Ct. 84 (1957).
7. Peach, R.W., *ANSI/ASQC Guide for Quality Systems*, PLP-80 Proceedings 71, Product Liability Prevention Conference, Washington, DC (September 22-24, 1980), IEEE Catalog No. 80CH1582-6, Library of Congress 78-641548.
8. MIL-Q-9858A, *Quality Program Requirements* (16 December 1963) including Amendment 1 (of 7 August 1981).
9. MIL-STD-882A, *System Safety Program Requirements* (28 June 1977).
10. ANSI Std. Z1.8-1971 (ASQC Standard Cl-1968), *Specification of General Requirements For A Quality Program*, American Society for Quality Control, Milwaukee, WI 53203.
11. ANSI/ASQC Z1.5-1979, *Generic Guidelines for Quality Systems*, American National Standards Insitute, New York, NY 10018.

12. *Handbook & Standard for Manufacturing Safer Consumer Products*, U.S. Consumer Products Safety Commission, June 1975 (Revised May 1977), available from Supt. of Documents, U.S. Govt. Printing Office, Washington, DC 20402.

13. McCormick, E.J. and Sanders, M.S., *Human Factors in Engineering and Design*, Fifth Edition, McGraw-Hill Book Co. (1982).

14. Hammer, W., *Handbook of System and Product Safety*, Prentice-Hall, Inc. (1972).

15. Mihalasky, J., *The Human Element in Products Liability*, Proceedings PLP-77E at 11-17, Product Liability Prevention Conference, Hasbrouck Heights, NJ (August 22-24, 1977).

16. English, W., *Human Factors Engineering—A Neglected Art*, PLP-80 Proceedings at 95-103, Product Liability Prevention Conference, Washington, DC (September 22-24, 1980), IEEE Catalog No. 80-CH1582-6, Library of Congress 78-641548.

17. Greenberg, M., *The Human Elements of Product Liability*, Proceedings PLP-73 at 147-52, Product Liability Prevention Conference, Newark, NJ (August 22-24, 1973), IEEE Catalog No. 73-CH0814-4PLP.

18. Philo, H.M., 1 *Lawyer's Desk Reference* 118, 6th ed., The Lawyer's Co-Operative Publishing Co., Rochester, NY 14694, and Bancroft-Whitney Co., San Francisco, CA 94107 (1979).

19. Mackay, D.R., *Voluntary Industry Actions*, Proceedings PLP-77E at 29, Product Liability Prevention Conference, Hasbrouck Heights, NJ (August 22-24, 1977).

20. Philo, H.M., and Rine, N.J., *The Danger Never Was Obvious*, 1 Journal of Products Liability 12-19 (1977).

21. *Micallef v. Miehle Co., Div. of Miehle-Goss Dexter, Inc.*, 39 N.Y.2d 376, 384 N.Y.S.2d 115, 348 N.E.2d 571 (1976).

22. NHB 5300.4 (1A) *Reliability Program Provisions for Aeronautical and Space System Contractors* (1970), Supt. of Documents, U.S. Govt. Printing Office, Washington, DC 20402.

23. MIL-R-27542, *Design Review Standard*.

24. MIL-STD-882A, *supra* reference 9.

25. Jacobs, R.M., *The Technique of Design Review*, PLP-79 Proceedings at 79-94, Product Liability Prevention Conference, New York, NY (October 22-24, 1979), IEEE Catalog No. 79CH1512-3R, Library of Congress 78-641548.

26. Boquist, E.R., *Tutorial on Formal Design Reviews*, PLP-73 Proceedings at 75-84, Product Liability Prevention Conference, Newark, NJ (August 22-24, 1973), IEEE Catalog No. 73CH0814-4PLP.

27. *Id.*

28. S.44, 98th Cong. 1st Sess., Sect. 2(6), (1983).

29. Jacobs, R.M., *Design Review*, PLP/75 Proceedings at 49-59, Product Liability Prevention Conference, Newark, NJ (August 19-22, 1975), IEEE Catalog No. 75CH0986-OR.

30. Boquist, E.R., *supra* reference 26, and Hammer, W., *supra* reference 14 at 113.

31. *Product Liability Portfolio* 65, Business Research Publications, 87 Terminal Dr., Plainview, NY 11803 (1977).

32. Boquist, E.R., *supra* reference 26.

33. Victor, J.E., *Design Review—What's It About, How Used for Designing a Safe Product*, PLP-74 Proceedings at 211-13, Product Liability Prevention Conference, Newark, NJ (August 21-23, 1974), IEEE Catalog No. 74CH0911-8R.

34. Ramo, S., *Cure for Chaos*, David McKay Co., Inc., New York, NY (1969).

35. English, J.M., ed., *Cost-Effectiveness—The Economic Evaluation of Engineered Systems*, University of California Engineering and Physical Sciences Extension Series, John Wiley & Sons, Inc. (1968).

36. Rudwick, B.H., *Systems Analysis for Effective Planning—Principles and Cases*, John Wiley & Sons, Inc. (1969).

37. Cleland, D.I. and King, W.R., *Systems Analysis and Project Management*, McGraw-Hill Book Co., Inc. (1968).

38. Johnson, R.A., Kast, F.E. and Rosenzweig, J.E., *The Theory and Management of Systems*, McGraw-Hill Book Co. (1967).

39. Hammer, W., *supra* reference 14 at 62-250.

40. Gottfried, P., *Product Risks: Prediction Techniques*, Proceedings PLP/75 at 25, Product Liability Prevention Conference, Newark, NJ (August 19-22, 1975), IEEE Catalog No. 75CH0986-OR.

41. Gibson, S.B., *Hazard Analysis and Risk Criteria*, 14 Loss Prevention 11-17, American Inst. of Chem. Engrs. (1980).

42. Lambert, H.E., *Fault Trees for Decision Making in Systems Analysis*, Lawrence Livermore National Laboratory, Livermore, CA 94550, UCRL-51829 (October 9, 1975).

43. *Id.* and Hammer, W., *supra* reference 14 at 113-15.

44. Bignell, V., Peters, G. and Pym, C., *Catastrophic Failures*, Second Printing (revised), The Open University Press, New York, NY (1978).

45. Hammer, W., *supra* reference 14 at 111.

46. MIL-STD-882A, *supra* reference 9 at 10.

47. *Id.* at 13.

48. Hammer, W., *supra* reference 14 at 88.

49. Bignell, V. et al, *supra* reference 44.

50. Henley, E.J. and Kumamoto, H., *Reliability Engineering and Risk Assessment* 44-108, Prentice-Hall, Inc. (1981).

51. Roberts, V.L. and Jones, P.L., *Analytical Techniques in Product Safety*, 4 Journal of Products Liability 67-93 (1981).

52. Mundel, A.B., *Failure Modes and Effects Analysis As A Means of Product Liability Prevention*, Proceedings PLP/75 at 61, Product Liability Prevention Conference, Newark, NJ (August 19-22, 1975).

53. Lambert, H.E., *supra* reference 42.

54. Browning, R.L., *Use a Fault Tree To Check Safeguards*, 12 Loss Prevention 20, Amer. Inst. of Chem. Engrs. (1979).

55. Prugh, R.W., *Application of Fault Tree Analysis*, 14 Loss Prevention 1, Am. Inst. of Chem. Engrs. (1980).

56. Brandell, J.L., *The Fault Tree Analysis Technique*, Proceedings PLP/75 at 79, Product Liability Prevention Conference, Newark, NJ (August 19-22, 1975).

57. Kohansedgh, F., *Computerized Fault Tree Analysis at Duke Power Company*, 2 Journal of Products Liability 21 (1978).

58. Gottfried, P., *Qualitative Risk Analysis: FTA and FMEA,* PLP-73 Proceedings at 101, Product Liability Prevention Conference, Newark, NJ (August 22-24, 1973), IEEE Catalog No. 73CH0814-4PLP.
59. Roberts, V.L. and Jones, P.L., *supra* reference 51.
60. Marpet, M., *FMEA-FTA—Qualitative Analysis Used in PLP*, Proceedings PLP-77E at 91, Product Liability Prevention Conference, Hasbrouck Heights, NJ (August 22-24, 1977).
61. ANSI/ASQC Z1.5-1979, *supra* reference 11, Roberts, V.L. and Jones, P.L., *supra* reference 51, and Mundel, A.B., *supra* reference 52.
62. Dudley, R.H. and Heldack, J.M., *PLP Planning in a Multinational Corporation*, PLP-80 Proceedings at 1-17, Product Liability Prevention Conference, Washington, DC (September 22-24, 1980), IEEE Catalog No. 80CH1582-6, Library of Congress 78-641548.
63. Hammer, W., *supra* reference 14 at 148-59.
64. *Design Analysis Procedure for Failure Modes, Effects and Criticality Analysis (FMECA)*, SAE Aerospace Recommended Practice ARP926 (15 September 1967).
65. Greene, K., *Failure Mode, Effects and Criticality Analysis*, PLP-79 Proceedings at 55, Product Liability Prevention Conference, New York, NY (October 22-24, 1979), IEEE Catalog No. 79CH1512-3R, Library of Congress 78-641548.
66. Pearsall, G.W., *Risks, Decisions and Product Safety*, 5 Journal of Products Liability 219 (1982).
67. Philo, H.M., 2 *Lawyer's Desk Reference* 503-08, 6th ed., The Lawyer's Co-Operative Publishing Co., Rochester, NY 14694 and Bancroft-Whitney Co., San Francisco, CA 94107 (1979).
68. From *A Treatise on Ship-Building* (1775).
69. *IBM's Grand Design To Become A Force In The Factory*, Business Week 142C-142J (May 7, 1984).
70. Foundyller, C.M. and Jenkins, B.L. (eds.), *CAD/CAM Computer Graphics*, Daratech, Inc., P.O. Box 410, Cambridge, MA 02238 (Fall Edition 1983).
71. Besant, C.B., *Computer-Aided Design and Manufacture*, American Society for Quality Control, Milwaukee, WI 53203 (1983).
72. Krouse, J.K., *What Every Engineer Should Know About Computer-Aided Design and Computer-Aided Manufacturing*, Marcel Dekker, Inc., New York, NY (1982).
73. Taraman, K.S., *CAD/CAM: Meeting Today's Productivity Challenge*, American Society for Quality Control, Milwaukee, WI 53203 (1980).
74. Rodenberger, C.A., Herndon, C.F., Majors, S.O., and Rogers, W.A., *The Average $100,000,000 Design Engineer*, Mechanical Engineering 36-42 (July 1983).
75. *Learning CAD/CAM*, Mechanical Engineering 42-45 (May 1983).
76. *Plugging Process Plant Designs Into The Computer*, Mechanical Engineering 26-31 (August 1984).
77. *Speeding Up The Revolution In 3-D Computer-Aided Design*, Business Week 90F-90G (March 5, 1984).
78. Fong, H.H., *Interactive Graphics And Commercial Finite Element Codes*, Mechanical Engineering 18-25 (June 1984).
79. Zecher, J.E., Lehman, N.W., Graves, M.T., and Brown, C.W., *Developing A*

Desktop Computer-Based Three-Dimensional Modeling System, Mechanical Engineering 50-61 (November 1983).

80. *Freund v. Cellofilm Properties, Inc.*, 87 N.J. 229, 432 A2d 925 (1981).

81. *Beshada v. Johns-Manville Products Corp.*,90 N.J. 191, 442 A2d 539 (1982).

82. Hammer, W., *supra* reference 14 at 182-223.

83. Mihalasky, J., *supra* reference 15.

84. English, W., *supra* reference 16.

85. Greenberg, M., *supra* reference 17.

86. *Berkebile v. Brantly Helicopter Corp.*, 462 Pa. 83, 337 A.2d 893 (1975).

87. McCormick, E.J. and Sanders, M.S., *supra* reference 13.

88. *Business Is Turning Data into a Potent Strategic Weapon*, Business Week 92-98 (August 22, 1983).

89. Juran, J.M., *Quality Control Handbook* 10-2, Third Edition, McGraw-Hill Book Company (1979).

90. Bacon, L., *How to Assess the Risks When Specifying New Products*, Consulting Engineer 94 (June 1981).

91. Townsend, R., *Up The Organization* 142, Fawcett Crest Edition (1970).

92. Juran, J.M., *supra* reference 89 at 10-23.

93. *Vendor Evaluation Check List*, Quality Management & Engineering 14 (August 1971).

94. *McPherson v. Buick Motor Co.*, 217 N.Y. 382, 111 N.E. 1050 (1916).

95. American Law Institute, *Restatement (Second) of the Law: Torts*, Section 400, American Law Institute Publishers, St. Paul, MN (1965).

96. *Ford Motor Co. v. Mathis*, 322 F.2d 267 (Fifth Cir. 1963).

97. Hendron, J.A., *Why Use A Code for Fabrication?*, Mechanical Engineering 26 (January 1975).

98. Patterson, W.P., *The Software Solution*, Industry Week 93 (September 17, 1984).

99. Grondstra, J.W. *Automatic Inventory Data Acquisition* at 973-76, in Proceedings of the First International IFIP Conference on Computer Applications in Production and Engineering, CAPE '83, (E.A. Warman, ed.), North-Holland Publishing Co., New York, NY (April 25-28, 1983)

100. McCormick, E.J. and Sanders, M.S., *supra* reference 13.

101. *Bar Codes Improve Industrial Efficiency, Productivity, and Records Keeping*, Mechanical Engineering 50 (April 1983).

102. Pilgrim, A., *Bar Codes in Industry*, Quality 14 (October 1983).

103. MIL-STD-1189, *Military Standard, Standard Symbology for Marking Unit Packs, Outer Containers, and Selected Documents*, 1982-505.022 (2431), available from U.S. Government Printing Office, Washington, DC 20402 (4 January 1982).

104. Rohan, T.M., *Quest for Quality*, Industry Week 29 (April 30, 1984).

105. Chandler, H.E., *Hybrid Technology*, Metal Progress 9 (May 1984).

106. Chandler, H.E., *New Directions in Testing and Inspection Technology*, Metal Progress 49 (May 1984).

107. Faber, M., *Trends in Data Aquisition*, Test & Measurement World 57-64 (October 1984).

108. Chouinard, S. and Malpiel, C. (eds.), *Factory of the Future*, Test & Measurement World 31-133 (December 1983).

109. Vlietstra, J., *Computer Applications in Technology—Opportunities and Prob-*

lems at xvii-xxiii, in Proceedings of the First International IFIP Conference on Computer Applications in Production and Engineering, CAPE '83, (E.A. Warman, ed.), North-Holland Publishing Co., New York, NY (April 25-28, 1983).

110. Hatvany, J., *Dreams, Nightmares and Reality* at 3-10, in Proceedings of the First International IFIP Conference on Computer Applications in Production and Engineering, CAPE '83 (E.A. Warman, ed.), North-Holland Publishing Co., New York, NY (April 25-28, 1983).

111. Moore, J.A., *Instrumentation and Control—Toward The Automated Factory*, Mechanical Engineering 26-32 (October 1984).

112. *A Design Computer That Talks to the Shop Floor*, Business Week 76B-76D (September 5, 1983).

113. Business Week, *supra* reference 69.

114. Chandler, H.E., *supra* reference 106.

115. Zajdel, T.T., *Standardizing Computer Integrated Manufacturing* 18-21, ASTM Standardization News 18-21 (October 1984).

116. Williams, T.J., *Developments in Hierarchical Computer Control Systems As Affecting Industrial Manufacturing Systems of the Future* at 1041-80, in Proceedings of the First International IFIP Conference on Computer Applications in Production and Engineering, CAPE '83, (E.A. Warman, ed.), North-Holland Publishing Co., New York, NY (April 25-28, 1983).

117. Sata, T., *Technology of the Unmanned Operation of the Flexible Manufacturing System* at 1095-1107, in Proceedings of the First International IFIP Conference on Computer Applications in Production and Engineering, CAPE '83, (E.A. Warman, ed.), North-Holland Publishing Co., New York, NY (April 25-28, 1983).

118. Paprocki, J.T., *FMS—Automating The Factory*, Mechanical Engineering 37-43 (October 1984).

119. *Artificial Intelligence Is Here*, Business Week 54-62 (July 9, 1984).

120. *Artificial Intelligence Machines Burst Out Of The Lab*, Business Week 109-112 (October 1, 1984).

121. *Why GM Has Set Its Sights on Artificial Vision*, Business Week 144P-144R (September 24, 1984).

122. Denker, S.P., *Choosing a Vision System That Improves Testing Effectiveness*, Test & Measurement World 192-200 (October 1984).

123. *The U.S. Robot Industry Starts To Come To Life*, Business Week 194AA-194FF (November 14, 1983).

124. Bloznelis, M., Vaitkevicius, H., Meskauskas, A., and Karalius, M., *Robotics Vision Based on Local Detectors* at 1109-14, in Proceedings of the First International IFIP Conference on Computer Applications in Production and Engineering, CAPE '83, (E.A. Warman, ed.), North-Holland Publishing Co., New York, NY (April 25-28, 1983).

125. Toepperwein, L.L., Blackman, M.T., Park, W.T., Tanner, W.R. and Adolfson, W.F., *Robotics Applications for Industry—A Practical Guide*, Noyes Publications, Park Ridge, NJ (1983).

126. Hunt, V.D., *Industrial Robotics Handbook*, American Society for Quality Control, Milwaukee, WI 53203 (1983).

127. *The Battle of the Supercomputers: Japan's All-Out Challenge to the U.S.*, Business Week 156-166 (October 17, 1983).

128. *Supercomputers Are Breaking Out of a Once-Tiny Market,* Business Week 164D-164H (November 19, 1984).

129. *And Now, an "Affordable" Supercomputer,* Business Week 164H-164L (November 19, 1984).

130. Hanlon, J.F., *Handbook of Package Engineering* 1-1, McGraw-Hill Book Company (1971).

131. *A Death Blow for Tylenol?* Business Week 151 (October 18, 1982).

132. Carley, W.M., *Johnson & Johnson Is Hit with First Suit Following Deaths from Poisoned Tylenol,* The Wall Street Journal, 24, Col.2 (Tuesday, October 5, 1982).

133. Hertzberg, D. and Waldholz, M., *Johnson & Johnson Unit Sues 9 Insurers for $117 Million on Tylenol-Recall Cost,* The Wall Street Journal, 4, Col.2 (Wednesday, January 12, 1983).

134. Berg, H.M. and Kosseff, R.A., *Should The Manufacturer Be Held Liable for the Tylenol Murders?,* For The Defense 12 (December 1982).

135. Kaplan, H.L. and Fawcett, R.E., *Components of Manufacturers' Products Liability Based upon Defective Packaging: Foreseeability, Superseding Cause and Federal Presumption,* 7 Journal of Products Liability 119-41 (1984).

136. 47 *Federal Register* 50442 (1982), as amended, 48 *Federal Register* 1706 (1983).

137. 21 C.F.R., Sections 211.132, 700.25 and 800.12 (1983).

138. Hanlon, J.F., *supra* reference 130 at 1-6.

139. Florio, J.J., *Commentary,* Technology & Society 3, New Jersey Institute of Technology, Newark, NJ (Summer 1983).

140. Commoner, B., *The Closing Circle* 40-41, Alfred A. Knopf, New York, NY (1971).

141. Jackson, L.P., *Waste Disposal: A Modern Day Pandora's Box,* ASTM Standardization News 24-27 (August 1983).

142. *Browlee v. Louisville Varnish Co.* 641 F.2d 397 (Fifth Circuit, 1981).

143. *Hall v. E.I. DuPont de Nemours & Co.,* 345 F.Suppl. 353 (D.Ct., N.Y. 1972).

144. Fladager, V.L., *Packaging as a Marketing Tool,* in Handbook of Modern Marketing 16-3 (V.P. Buell, ed.) McGraw-Hill Book Company (1970).

145. American Law Institute, *supra* reference 95 at Sections 402 A (Comments j and k) and 402 B.

146. *Freund v. Cellofilm, supra* reference 80.

147. *Beshada v. Johns Manville, supra* reference 81.

148. Keeton, W.P., Owen, D.G. and Montgomery, J.E., *1983 Case and Statutory Supplement to Products Liability and Safety Cases and Materials,* 23 (footnote 3), The Foundation Press, Mineola, NY (1983).

149. *Beshada v. Johns Manville, supra* reference 6.

150. *Jamieson v. Woodward & Lothrop, supra* reference 6.

151. Walk v. J.I. Case Co., 36 A.D.2d 60, 318 N.Y.S.2d 598 (1971).

152. *Williams v. Caterpillar Tractor Co.,* 149 So.2d 898 (1963).

153. Dorris, A.L. and Purswell, J.L., *Warnings and Human Behavior: Implications for the Deisgn of Product Warnings,* 1 Journal of Products Liability 255-63 (1977).

154. Ross, K., *Legal and Practical Considerations for The Creation of Warning Labels and Instruction Books,* 4 Journal of Products Liability 29-45 (1981).

155. *Product Liability Portfolio, supra* reference 31 at 23-26.

156. Sales, J.B., *The Marketing Defect (Warning and Instructions) in Strict Tort Liability* 7-35, D.R.I. Monograph No. 2, Duty To Warn And Other Current Issues, Defense Research Institute, Chicago, IL 60611 (1980).
157. Dreyfuss, H., *Symbol Sourcebook*, McGraw-Hill Book Company (1972).
158. Federal Hazardous Substances Act, Public Law No. 86-613, Sect. 17, 74 Stat. 380 (1960); *as amended*, 80 Stat. 1305 (1966); *as amended and renumbered*, Sect. 18(b) (2), 83 Stat. 190 (1969); *as amended*, 90 Stat. 510 (1976).
159. Poison Prevention Packaging Act, Public Law No. 91-601, Sect. 1-9, 84 Stat. 1670-74 (1970), 15 U.S.C. 1471-76.
160. Feldman, J.A., *Pharmaceutical Product Labeling—What Does the Future Entail?*, Proceedings PLP-77E at 121-27, Product Liability Prevention Conference, Hasbrouck Heights, NJ (August 22-24, 1977).
161. Sperber, P., *The Strategy of Product Labeling for Loss Prevention*, 1 Journal of Products Liability 171-82 (1977).
162. *Henningsen v. Bloomfield Motors, Inc.*, 32 N.J. 358, 161 A.2d 69 (1960).
163. Uniform Commercial Code (UCC), Uniform Laws Annotated (Master ed. 1976), Sections 2-316 and 2-719.
164. Prosser, W.L., *Handbook of the Law of Torts* 655-56, 4th Ed., West Publishing Co., St. Paul, MN (1971).
165. McGill, J., *Warranties: What They Are and How They Can Be Used in Risk Control*, 2 Journal of Products Liability 105-15 (1978).
166. Hoenig, M., *The Influence of Advertising in Products Liability Litigation*, 5 Journal of Products Liability 321-40 (1982).
167. UCC, *supra* reference 163 at Section 2-314(2) (c).
168. UCC, *supra* reference 163 at Section 2-315.
169. UCC, *supra* reference 163 at Section 2-313.
170. *Product Warranties and Servicing—Responsive Business Approaches to Consumer Needs*, Office of Consumer Affairs, U.S. Department of Commerce (October 1980), available from Superintendent of Documents, U.S. Government Printing Office, Washington, DC 20402.
171. *Getting Rid of the Bugs*, Time 68 (October 3, 1983).
172. American Law Institute, *supra* reference 95 at Section 402 A, comment i.
173. *Baxter v. Ford Motor Co.*, 179 Wash. 123, 35 P.3d 1090 (1934).
174. *Rogers v. Toni Home Permanent Co.*, 167 Ohio St. 244, 147 N.E.2d 612 (1958).
175. *Pritchard v. Liggett & Myers Tobacco Co.*, 295 F.2d 292 (3d Circuit 1961).
176. *Greenman v. Yuba Power Products, Inc.*, 59 Cal.2d 57, 27 Cal.Reptr. 697, 377 P.2d 897 (1963).
177. *Leichtamer v. American Motors Corp.*, 424 N.E.2d 568 (Ohio Sup. Ct. 1981).
178. Levitt, T., Professor, Harvard Business School, Cambridge, MA.
179. Ross, N., *Why Do People Buy? Product Satisfies*, a book review, Direct Marketing 62 (April 1975).
180. Maxon, J.W. Jr., *An Insider's View: We Made the Monster of Consumerism*, Direct Marketing 52 (January 1973).
181. UCC, *supra* reference 163 at Section 2-313.
182. American Law Institute, *supra* reference 95 at Section 402 B.
183. UCC, *supra* reference 163 at Section 2-313(2).
184. American Law Institute, *supra* reference 95 at Section 402 B, comment g.
185. National Commission on Product Safety, *Final Report* (June 1970), Library of

Congress Card No. 76-606753, available from the Superintendent of Documents, U.S. Government Printing Office, Washington, DC 20402.

186. Onan, R.C. Jr., *Postsale Legal Responsibilities of Partsmakers and Systems Sellers*, Metal Progress 59-64 (August 1981).

187. *Newmark v. Gimbel's, Inc.*, 54 N.J. 585, 258 A.2d 697 (1969).

188. *Magrine v. Krasnica*, 94 N.J. Super. 228, 227 A.2d 539 (1967), *aff'd.* 100 N.J. Super. 223, 241 A.2d 637 (1968), *aff'd.* 53 N.J. 259, 250 A.2d 129 (1969).

189. Keeton, W.P., Owen, D.G., and Montgomery, J.E., *Products Liability and Safety, Cases and Materials* 768-805, The Foundation Press, Mineola, NY (1980).

190. *Handbook (CPSC), supra* reference 12.

191. Falvey, J., *So Wrapped Up in Business, We Forget the Customer*, The Wall Street Journal, "Manager's Journal" (May 24, 1983).

192. *Making Service a Potent Marketing Tool*, Business Week 164-70 (June 11, 1984).

193. *What Is Quality? ... Ask the Customer*, Quality 21-22 (February 1983).

194. Peters, T.J. and Waterman, R.H., *supra* reference 2 at 156-99.

195. Sena, R.A., *Sources and Uses of Product Performance Information*, PLP-79 Proceedings at 61-64, Product Liability Prevention Conference, New York, NY (October 22-24, 1979), IEEE Catalog No. 79CH1512-3R, Library of Congress 78-641548.

196. Figgie, H.E. Jr., *The Cost Reduction and Profit Improvement Handbook*, Van Nostrand Reinhold Co., New York, NY (1983).

197. Cohen, D., *Product Complaints And Product Performance*, Proceedings PLP-74 at 113-17, Product Liability Prevention Conference, Newark, NJ (August 21-23, 1974), IEEE Catalog No. 74CH0911-8R.155.

198. *Managing Consumer Complaints*, Office of Consumer Affairs, U.S. Department of Commerce (April 1981), available from the Superintendent of Documents, U.S. Government Printing Office, Washington, DC 20402.

199. Consumer Product Safety Act, Public Law No. 92-573, 92d Congress, S.3419, October 27, 1972, 15 U.S.C. 2047-84; Consumer Product Safety Commission Improvements Act of 1976, Public Law No. 94-234, May 11, 1976; the Emergency Interim Consumer Product Safety Act of 1978, Public Law No. 95-319, July 11, 1978; Public Law No. 95-631, November 10, 1978; Public Law No. 96-373, October 3, 1980; Public Law No. 96-486, December 1, 1980; Public Law No. 97-35, August 13, 1981; Public Law No. 97-258, September 13, 1982; Public Law No. 97-414, January 4, 1983.

6

Making the Program Work

INCENTIVE FOR COMMITMENT

Today's younger generation seems obsessed with the "here and now." It stresses the positive and upbeat, and excludes from its mind things that seem negative or threatening. This does not make threats less threatening or cause them to disappear. Engineers like to see themselves as more informed, realistic, and practical; but we're not always consistent. Like upbeat adolescents we, too, tend to shun threats, particularly those we are not familiar with and take considerable pains to rationalize them away.

Taking action to avoid products liability does a good deal more for a company and its people than accomplish its primary goal of avoiding products liability. It so happens that—even if products liability had never existed—these same steps can improve a company's productivity, increase profits, strengthen its organization and morale of its workforce, and enhance its image.

When you get right down to it, the basic management procedures for avoiding products liability are the very ones that well-run companies have followed right along to keep productive, profitable and healthy. Responsible executives have always insisted that their companies make quality products that are safe. They have always cared about customers' well-being and have made it their business to know about and comply with regulations. Consequently, their products liability losses have been minimal.

Sound, responsible management practices backed by engineering professionalism go a long way in avoiding liability losses. But nothing is static, and what once was responsible management may no longer be adequate. It

232

is essential, then, for management to keep pace with changing social values, attitudes and requirements.

The liability threat facing industry today requires some reorientation of traditional management practices and attitudes, greater vigilance in some of our activities, and shifts in emphasis—even for well-run firms. Need for readjustment becomes more urgent and acute for certain kinds of products having greater risks and potential hazards than others. Nevertheless, the additional practices and organizational realignment needed for coping with the products liability threat will only make a good effective company better and more effective.

A company whose management is alert to the changing world about us, including consciousness of the need to avoid products liability claims, and establishes policies and programs that will minimize its liability exposure, will create a highly impregnable two-sided shield.

On the one side, it will drastically reduce the primary cause of claims against the company: unsafe or hazardous products. It will thereby reduce financial losses prompted by the need to pay damage claims.

Secondly, its liability prevention program will build a solid foundation of proven and documented quality, care and responsible concern of the company and its management for the safety of its products. This will enable it to negotiate early and favorable settlement of claims that may be filed against it. But the benefits do not stop there. For the company that can avoid products lawsuits and their damages through confidently marketing safe products cannot help but win in the marketplace, as well.

Instead of being an irritating threat to company management, products liability requirements can be the motivating force needed for implementing policies and measures that will pay impressive dividends. Not only will they help avoid financial difficulties of needless lawsuits, but they can be the incentive to build the sound footing needed for virtually limitless growth and a profitable future in a fast-moving industrial world.

Ingredients for an effective liability prevention program will, of course, vary somewhat with the company, its products and markets. But there are six basic elements that virtually every program must have:

People	Information
Organization	Risk Management
Documentation	Audits

WHAT IT TAKES

People

A Proper State of Mind. The reminder to involve everyone in the company in liability prevention is not merely a boring plea for rallying around the corporate banner and cause; but an absolutely essential requirement. And it takes more than just "involvement."

Among eight basic principles Peters and Waterman cite as helping America's best-run companies stay on top, Number Four is "Productivity through people—creating in *all* employees the awareness that their best efforts are essential and that they will share in the rewards of the company's success."[1] They note "respect for the individual" to be a pervasive theme in excellent companies,[2] making them "truly unusual in their ability to achieve extraordinary results through ordinary people."

Such respect works two ways. In one way it helps the company achieve its business objectives. In another way, respect for the individual does not stop with employees but extends to customers and users. It shows in the quality of its products, sales policies and willingness to stand behind its products.

Even the finest of tools, equipment and plant facilities will have little effect on product quality and avoidance of liability if employees' attitudes are not right. This is the key to making quality products and to the firm's profitability:

> Quality is about 99.8% state of mind. It's attention to "trivia" and the presence of persistence—not magic—that lead to excellence. . . . The issues . . . are customer courtesy, product quality, customer service, regular innovation and regular experimentation.And the providers of these things are *all* the people in the organization—not just a select few.[3]

In our consideration in the previous chapter of seven classifications of activity involved in development, production and marketing of manufactured products, it became evident that responsibility for products liability avoidance could not be delegated to one office or group and then forgotten. The task must be considered an on-going *personal* responsibility of everyone in the company. In products liability, everything the company does affects everything else. Not only "quality," is a state of mind, but liability avoidance—the larger picture—also is a state of mind.

Mere perfunctory compliance with rules and regulations won't do it. Laws and regulations are only the outward manifestation of an inner attitude or spirit that pervades society. It is this attitude that lies at the root of products liability law. Before we can attempt to cope with its requirements, we must comprehend its origin—why it developed as it did and why it did so now. In analyzing it, we come to realize that we are not dealing with predictable and docile nuts and bolts but with unpredictable and sometimes stubborn human attitudes, ideals, and emotions.

Unless we understand this, and adjust our attitudes to these new values, we will find ourselves attempting to play our own tune in some long-abandoned key as the world about us—while we were not listening—has not only changed keys and tunes, but the drumbeat as well.

Although we are coping with elusive forces, intangible concepts, and an intricate web of social values, it does not mean that liability avoidance strategies cannot be tangible, definite and precise. Procedures discussed in the previous chapter are practical measures. They must involve every person and activity. Such involvement does not just happen, but must be planned and organized; people must be trained and kept informed about what is going on; and, like any important activity, there must be procedures for assuring that the program is working and accomplishing its objectives.

Need for Training Never Ends. Everyone that comes into contact with the product or its components during its development, manufacture and marketing influences the company's liability for that product. This is why everyone must know how to do his part to avoid liability. That knowledge does not come through issuing policies or management edicts, but through training.

Before training can start, however, it must be clear to all that liability avoidance for *this* company is not a fad but is here to stay; that top management, and the ones who sign the paychecks, evaluate performance and approve promotions and pay increases are 100% behind it. There should be no doubt that there is solid, unswerving commitment. Right down the line of management hierarchy, people must understand that they are being held accountable by their superiors for how they respond to the company's liability prevention guidelines and prescribed procedures. They must be convinced that it is part of their job and that their quality of response will be reflected in performance evaluations. Attempts to train employees in new methods or approaches will not yield much return unless they know the program is "for real."[4,5]

Training content, at least at the operational level, will differ little from accepted standards of care for making quality products; for that is the primary goal. With increasing decision-making responsibility, training content will require additional consideration on matters of record-keeping, inspection and other practices. Details of the training program will depend upon the product, its constituents and associated manufacturing operations. Also, as an employee's customer contacts increase, other issues come into play; so that the content for training production people in liability avoidance is different from that for training sales people.

What this means in establishing training programs is that each manufacturer must determine its potential for liability exposure and identify those activities and operations most susceptible. FMEA and other analytical procedures can assist in this. Once primary sources for potential liability problems have been identified, training the people involved in those operations or activities can center upon avoiding these difficulties.

It all cannot be accomplished at once. Determination of training needs is a continuing iterative process. It should begin with the most liability-sensitive aspect of the company's products or operations and do all it can to assure that its people know how to minimize these problems. Once that is under control, it can consider the next most liability-sensitive product, part or activity and attend to that, and so on. Training and orientation are never over, however; because new regulations and standards, new products with new potential for liability, and the simple fact that people need reminding, all make liability avoidance training a never-ending activity and responsibility.

Organization

Start with Constructive Policy. The importance of a formal policy on liability prevention and its endorsement by all operating executives has already been discussed. The policy should reflect commitment by top management to make safe products. But it should go beyond that to include strategic steps in a plan for implementing the policy.

There are two possible directions that liability avoidance policy can take. One is negative and antagonistic. It takes the position that products liability law is flawed and unfair, that product manufacturers should not be looked upon as the source of financial compensation for product-related harm and injuries. Usually, management that takes this tack believes in its products, is confident they are "safe," resists regulatory efforts and does its best to deflect them from its organization, and lobbies for tort reform. Its policy is to rely heavily upon liability insurance and look to its legal counsel for defensive tactics to blunt effects of lawsuits and to minimize damage awards.

Such a position on products liability does not require significant changes in operating practices (except as mandated under threat of fines by OSHA or other government agencies), as it does not embrace the notion of constructive prevention but hard-nosed resistance. Through this stance, it cannot help but signal to its employees and customers that it is unsympathetic to present concepts of product safety.

A temptation to lean toward such a policy is understandable since it requires less organizational concessions and disruptions and, for a time at least, may appear the less costly and, therefore, the preferable approach to handling the products liability threat. But this position largely ignores recent developments in both common and legislated law, with their shifting burden of proof, changes in public attitude toward product-inflicted injuries, and intolerance of courts and juries to evidence of lack of due care, indifference to product safety and unconcern over public welfare.

The inference is that these are sacrificed by the company for the sake of increased profits. In the eyes of courts, this is irresponsible behavior, and it sets the stage for awarding punitive damages.[6,7] Management policies that endorse this approach are inevitably more costly, in litigation expenses alone, and can lead to massive judgments that can seriously undermine the company's financial position, if not destroy it. All available evidence shows that this is *not* the better approach for the company's long-term well-being.

The other direction management and its liability prevention policies may take is that advocated by this book. Its philosophy is positive and poles apart from the other view. While it does not necessarily endorse recent developments in products liability law, it acknowledges its evolution as an outgrowth, and an inevitable product, of changing attitudes toward human rights. It sees this change being prompted, in part, by our expanding technology and society's bewilderment and failure to comprehend it. This has led to growing disenchantment over ability of technology to solve mankind's ills, if not a conviction that it is the cause of many of them.

Although these forces may not be altogether irreversible, this position on products liability anticipates no significantly diminished trend toward yet greater demands on the manufacturer in the foreseeable future. Besides this, it concludes that the best way to avoid products liability problems is through eliminating the cause of liability claims by making quality products that are safe to own and use. Minimized liability woes is but one advantage of this position, as the policies and practices needed for making quality products are the same ones that make the company and its operations more efficient and more profitable.

Other considerations also influence policy on products liability avoidance and what the company will do to implement that policy. One is the nature of its products, its customers and the propensity its products have for litigation. Before embarking on an ambitious program, management should evaluate its liability potential, just as it does other risks and ventures. This should be done carefully, factually and objectively. Its conclusions should not be based upon intuition or other subjective criteria. Such assessment should be re-done periodically, as the law is changing all the time and, with it, a manufacturer's liability exposure.

Whichever approach management adopts, its choice should reflect a realistic assessment of its liability exposure based upon all available facts, including its own litigation history and that of other firms in the same industry or those making and marketing similar products with similar risks. These are decisions each company must make for itself, for no two will be alike. In fact, the situation can differ from division to division within the same company. Management policies and its liability prevention implementation plan should recognize and reflect these differences for most effective use of resources.[8]

Coordinating Company-Wide Effort. The need for an *organized* approach is self-evident. There is too much at stake to adopt and issue a policy statement, then leave it to chance that it will be carried out. The size and nature of the organization needed to do the job will differ with the company, its products and markets. The Institute for Civil Justice of The Rand Corporation, in an excellent work on corporate responses to products liability regulation,[9] summarizes its findings on the most effective product safety organizations (or liability prevention team):

> A lean product safety organization that clearly has the ear of the CEO and good working relations at various levels of the firm is likely to be much more effective than a highly visible unit that establishes procedures but clearly lacks either the resources to impose them or, even more disastrous, the support of the firm's top officers when such support is necessary.

Effectiveness of the liability prevention organization (whether it is a committee, team, or individual) lies in its thorough understanding of and ability to work with all operations within the company. And it must have sufficient backing and management clout to carry it off. There are clear advantages in having this function report to top management.

Its responsibility must be broad, yet specific. It should cover everything from R&D, through design and development, prototype testing and manufacturing, to packaging, labeling, preparing user instructions, advertising, sales and service—a tall order. Obviously the product safety or liability prevention organization cannot do this job all by itself, but it must be a coordinating function. Each department manager must be responsible for liability aspects that impinge upon his own operation.

The product safety coordinator (or group) should assure that management's policies are communicated, understood and carried out on the department level. It should keep abreast of products liability law and regulations, assessing their impact upon the company and its operations, and passing this information along to those involved. It should serve as liaison with legal counsel, the insurance carrier and other outside specialists and consultants.

It should play an active role in design reviews, product failure analyses, investigations, and resolution of claims. It should regularly keep management advised on the status of its activities, developments in both technical and legal fields that could affect the company's liability exposure, and recommend procedures for more effective administration of its prevention program.

Again, tasks and responsibilities of the product safety coordinating function should be clearly spelled out in guidelines covering its purpose, specific duties and responsibilities, expected achievements, and necessary qualifications.[10,11] Likewise, there should be written job descriptions covering the principal coordinator and all members of his staff, team or committee.

Since this function requires broad working knowledge of many corporate operations, the product safety coordination group should be interdisciplinary in background and represent a range of expertise and interests. The principal coordinator should be a generalist, respected for being competent, fair and diplomatic in interfacing with all divisional and company groups.

Documentation

What To Write and What Not To Write. At every stage of developing, manufacturing and marketing a product where decisions affect a company's liability—and that includes virtually every decision and action—adequate documentation is an essential ingredient of the liability prevention program. Designs, calculations, analyses and their results, codes and regulations, compliance verifications, and all precautions, tests and inspections carried out can fulfill their liability prevention role only if a record that they were done, and their results, were documented. Individually, they have limited value; but taken together, and over a period of time, they are strong evidence of a company's consistent and responsible behavior. Such a record can be a bulwark of defense in a lawsuit, and a firm basis for bringing about early settlement of disputes.

Despite the strong case that can be made for keeping complete records there is, unfortunately, another side to the record-keeping story. That is, liberalized rules of discovery (see earlier discussion of discovery in Chapter 4) make virtually everything in a manufacturer's files "discoverable," or open to the scrutiny of opposing attorneys, in a lawsuit. Discovery processes have been characterized as "witch hunts" or "treasure hunts," depending upon which side of the litigation proceedings you are on.

This is because the object of the search usually is not merely a manufacturer's records or design data proving regulatory compliance or lack of it. The prize for a plaintiffs' attorney is what is often referred to as a "smoking gun"—something that will convince the court of the manufacturer's blatant disregard for danger in its products. It may be as simple as an inter-office memo from an engineer to his superior or another engineer. It could have been an informal handwritten note commenting on some weak point or questionable condition in the product.

All too frequently, however, the trophy turns out to be a memo written to document a previous verbal statement that went unheeded, was brushed aside, or was overruled. In writing the memo, the irritated engineer is not only emphasizing his position and opinion and reasons for it but, perhaps more significntly, is attempting to exonerate himself from future blame should the condition lead to trouble. This familiar tactic, which has been called the "save-your-hide" syndrome (or words to that effect) often pervades an organization, like a malady. Before long, everyone is doing it as an instinctive twich of self-preservation.

While it is easy to criticize those engaging in this practice, it is probably unfair to do so. Most often the practice stems from inept management that creates a climate of distrust of one's superiors, of the company's management, and of possibly everyone else in the operation. It is deplorable when professionals feel so frustated in their failure to communicate with management that they must resort to this approach. It is a warning signal that management, if alert to the problem as it should be, should heed, as it is a symptom of an unhealthy organization.

Returning to the liability implications of such memoranda and other communications records, these somewhat informal statements critical of decisions or company policies on products carry much weight in court. They can seriously undermine a firm's ability to defend itself in a products lawsuit. They are particularly damning if they point out a deficiency that goes uncorrected or unresolved (but could have been resolved at minimal cost) and later becomes the cause of a plaintiff's injury.

To be damaging, the memo or written statement need not be a criticism. It may simply state a consensus agreement to curtail testing, to use inexpensive (and possibly unproven, but believed adequate) substitutes, or to take some well-meaning shortcut to getting the product to market. Or, it may be a record of some such agreed-upon action that could be interpreted by a court as indifference to a hazard or unwillingness to spend a small sum of money that could have made the product safer. It is not so much *what* is said but *how it appears in court*, with the court having benefit of 20/20 hindsight, that really matters.

Statements made to document affirmative decisions to correct deficiencies, but that somehow do not get corrected, can be most damaging. Such records suggest that the deficiency was considered low priority by the company. The point will be sure to be exploited to the hilt by an aggressive attorney for a plaintiff injured because the problem went uncorrected.

This means that, along with every documented decision to perform some step that could have liability implications, there must be a built-in check, or audit, to confirm that it was actually done. If such a decision cannot, for good reasons, be carried out, it is important that these facts, with complete rationale, are thoroughly explained and well-documented to avoid potentially incriminating loose ends.

Innocent-appearing informal product correspondence containing frank statements or opinions about the firm's products and safety practices can do harm. Yet, at the same time, manufacturers *must* keep good factual records. Some regulating agencies, like the FDA, CPSC and NHTSA, mandate it. Without discriminating control over what goes into the company's files (meaning files maintained by each employee as well as master files), the manufacturer is subject to difficulties it may not deserve. As unwieldy as document files may be to control, it must be done. It is another reason why everyone in the organization should develop the habit of frequently asking himself how whatever he says or does today might look tomorrow to a court and jury.

Without legal guidance, engineers may at first have difficulty in determining which statements are potentially damaging and which are not. This requires sensitivity and instinct that can be, and should be, developed.

As a first step, assistance of legal counsel (and possibly insurance representatives) should be enlisted to go over, with senders and recipients, all files that even remotely deal with the company's products or services. This includes meeting agendas, minutes, informal inter-office memos and field reports. Potentially damaging and even questionable material should be purged from the files and reasons for this action carefully explained to the people that generated it and those who received and filed it. The objective is to develop awareness of the potential for harm to the company and sensitivity to the issues involved so that employees will not continue to generate these kinds of files.

A company can do much to develop record-keeping practices and procedures that will assist in creating documents that are beneficial and essential and minimizing those which can be damaging during discovery processes. The liability prevention coordinator should study the firm's communications requirements and develop recommendations for making the most efficient use of forms and what should be written, and what should not be written but communicated verbally. Communication forms should be designed for ease of use, should not allow room for ambiguous interpretations of entries, should effectively accomplish their purpose and make the information readily referenced, retained and retrievable.

Computerized Information Management Systems. When liability prevention and regulatory requirements are added to the already-existing paperwork burden, the problem of records storage, retrieval and management becomes an unmanageable nightmare. For manufacturers of "regulated" high-risk products, like pharmaceuticals, drugs or health-care products, costs of facilities for filing and storing hard (paper) records to adequately maintain the required documentation can be prohibitive. Alternative methods must be used, and data processing technology has reached a stage of reliability and cost that makes computerized systems indispensable in managing these records.

Although a revolution in data and information processing has been underway for some years,[12] little has been said about its impact upon products liability issues. But its effects can be profound. Since information handling is so crucial to products liability prevention, as well as to litigation defense, the subject deserves some attention.

Right now, computer technology exists, and is in use, for establishing and maintaining a system capable of documenting a complete profile on each product made and sold.[13] This is not widely done, or need be done for many products; but it *can* be done, if necessary.

Such a system could include updated documentation of relevant standards and regulations, conceptual and design data including results of mathematical and systems analysis studies, complete summaries of design review deliberations and decisions, purchase and procurement criteria and records, component design with complete breakdown part-by-part, drafting records including all modifications with machine-readable programs used for manufacturing the part, assembly sequences including time and location, manufacturing and process schedules with printouts recording actual conditions, inspection and test standards and measured data showing statistical reliability, product-related correspondence, sales and distribution information, field reports and customer files.

Presently-available methods for managing such information can take a number of forms. For relatively small volumes of information, the computer disc has remarkable accuracy and capacity for its size. However, the information usually must be transcribed from hard copy; although data collection forms and systems could be made where the data are entered directly into computer memory for subsequent transfer to magnetic discs for archival storage.

Other state-of-the-art systems are microfilm images of paper documents.[14,15] These are indexed on each film reel and addressed by microprocessor control. Indexes are stored in a computer memory and document retrieval is through an on-line computer interface that locates the desired document in a few seconds and displays it on a screen. Ready conversion of the displayed image to a photocopy, if desired, can be made available.

More sophisticated "electronic filing" systems convert information into digital electronic impulses or signals that may be stored on microfilm, magnetic tape or on optical discs.[16-18] It is claimed that one 12-inch optical disc is capable of storing the equivalent of text appearing in over 15 years of daily newspapers.[19] Although optical discs are read-only memory devices and are intended primarily for archival storage, laser beam scanning allows random access of any stored information on the disc in a fraction of a second.

What does it all mean to product manufacturers concerned with avoiding products liability? There are a number of implications. First, computerized information management systems afford unprecedented availability and accessibility to design, performance and failure data that may be used in designing and upgrading products. Rather than being viewed merely as new "industry standards" that can be used against the company in a lawsuit, these developments should be considered a boon to help it make safer and more dependable products. Secondly, they enable a company to improve its profile files on each product—from conception to delivery, and even beyond if necessary. And they can keep similar information on customers.

Possessing improved information on materials, design and engineering, manufacturing processes and their control, sales, distribution, and users, can benefit the company; in general, as well as its liability prevention activity. It can be particularly valuable in investigating product failures, pinpointing causes in defending lawsuits, and in conducting recall campaigns—should that ever become necessary. On top of that, availability of better and more timely information can help management in auditing its operations, assessing profitability, and identifying where and how improvements can be made.[20]

Information

A Legally-mandated "Graduate Course". Effective business management has always required information. There must be information on needs of prospective customers and clients and how much they are able and willing to pay to fulfill their needs. There must be information on how to meet these needs through making and selling products or providing services. Unless information is available on what the competition is doing, and on customer preferences and demographics, there might not be a viable market for the contemplated product or service.

During the last several decades, government has intensely involved itself in just about every segment of a company's business, and its managers must understand these requirements and regulations. Management must therefore spend increasing amounts of its time collecting and digesting information. This need has always existed but, in recent years, change has become more frequent, and issues have grown more complex and interrelated, making it increasingly difficult to keep up with developments affecting business—to get enough of the right kinds of information.

One of the causes for the products liability *crisis* has been failure of industry to recognize changes in society's attitudes toward human rights, growing distrust of technology, and intolerance for injuries that technology causes or appears to cause. As we saw earlier, groundwork for all of this was being laid for several decades and, while it was going on, virtually no one was aware of the possible extent of its consequences.

The probable reason for this is that products liability is itself a product of the many converging forces already discussed. No one could have foreseen their convergence or its outcome. Now, it all can be logically explained as we review its history, after the fact.

And the process is not over, by any means. It is still going on, and what happens each day—in industry, in courts and legislatures, and in the world of the consumer and product user—can have profound effects upon our businesses and whether they will continue to be profitable and even survive. Therefore, if we would be responsible managers and engineers, we must not only comprehend the climate we find ourselves in and the demand it makes of us today, but we must be able to evaluate implications of changes we observe.

With experience in monitoring these events and trends, we can learn to predict with some confidence how it all might affect us tomorrow. This, of course, goes for all aspects of business, not only products liability. But products liability is a special case in that technical people, who have been accustomed to working under fairly static rules in a stable legal environment, have suddenly found themselves in a climate where new rules and responsibilities have supplanted old comfortable ones. It is this sudden, and unprecedented, need for a new kind of information—information about *legal* standards and responsibilities that can drastically affect our technical activities—that we are addressing here.

Early chapters of this book gave a capsule view of the origins of products liability law. The purpose was to develop understanding of the winds that have forced us onto the course we are now on. It is absurd to believe that industry and business deliberately steered onto it. Since these winds have not abated, but are still blowing, we cannot afford to remain complacent and smugly satisfied with our limited knowledge about how we got to where we are. For, what really matters most to us is where we are headed.

None of us can foretell the future, but we can sense momentum and accelerations—changes in driving forces. And we can discern trends in the legal climate from reading the newspapers. This is probably the most we can do. But it is not all that unreliable. Therefore, we should at least try to discern our direction and not leave destiny to chance. We may not be able to stop the wind from blowing, but we need not despair and take our hands off the helm because there is a storm going on.

Having agreed that the intelligent thing to do is to become and stay informed about products liability matters, we must consider where the information might come from and how we can get it. Unfortunately, engineering schools failed to discern the approaching advent of products liability as much as did business schools and executive suites of our largest corporations.

Even today, with this problem on industry's very doorstep, products liability and its prevention are subjects still not found in engineering curricula.[21] There are a few noteworthy exceptions where engineering institutions have pioneered extension programs and founded seminars on products liability prevention.[22] Our technical societies, with all their stated dedication to humanities in the curriculum and professionalism in engineers, are doing little more than issuing industry news items on the subject now and then in their journals. But, again there are exceptions that are providing useful service.[23]

In contrast to the disappointingly few sources for information on products liability, the business press contains a considerable volume of information on it. Almost no issue of a national business publication over the past few years has been without some mention of it. However, their emphasis is upon occurrences, recounts of lawsuits, damage claims and their adverse effects upon afflicted companies and industries—in short, their interest is in news. These accounts have some limited value in keeping us aware of the problem, but they do next to nothing to offer information on how to avoid it or its consequences. Without such guidance, news articles on the devastating effects of products liability will only create paranoia. As always, knowledge is its only cure.

Despite lack of concerted effort to educate engineering professionals about products liability, every engineer should consider such knowledge a legally-mandated "graduate course." Since the subject deals with matters and issues concerned with the technology/society interface and the engineer's related professional responsibilities, such knowledge represents a higher level of engineering, and professional development in the fullest sense.

In a way, it is far too late in our technological evolution for the engineering community to begin now to give thought to hazard potentials and social implications of what they do and make. But better now than to continue relegating these matters to low priority and then paying the consequences in legal damages. Education in products liability matters should not be viewed as optional or elective. The law imposes non-delegable responsibility upon the engineering professional to design products that do not harm their users or others who come into contact with them.

At the moment, it is usually the impersonal corporation that pays damage claims, but all this may change.[24-28] Whatever tack the law may take toward individual liability, in today's world it must be considered dereliction of employee responsibility for an engineer to shun matters of product safety, presuming that "the company" will pay for any deficiencies caused by the engineer's irresponsible attitude and behavior.

As trite as it may sound, the basic prerequisite for becoming knowledgeable enough about products liability issues to effectively avoid lawsuits and damages is a proper attitude. Readjustment of personal values is needed, not only to acknowledge the influence (and dominance) of social forces and need for professionalism, but also with respect to engineering practices consistent with them. The readjustment can only come about through a positive outlook, willingness to listen to society's side of the story in an effort to try to understand its fears and apprehensions, and dedication to concern for the welfare of human beings.

Needed Information and How To Get It. The information the engineer needs for developing an understanding of products liability and a capability for avoiding it has three principal elements.

One is appreciation of the forces that brought about the litigious situation facing industry today. The second is sufficient breadth of knowledge to be able to actively maintain an awareness of relevant developments now underway and to intelligently monitor and evaluate them. And third is working knowledge of the "tools" of liability prevention.

Bear in mind that we are not talking here about "legal" training or law school curricula. Those have a different intent and purpose, namely counselling and advocacy. The goal here, simply, is to learn how to avoid products liability. This is best accomplished through learning how to eliminate injury and damage claims. It is not "playing lawyer" any more than personally caring for one's health is "playing doctor."

Lawyers are essential in the conduct of business, but prevention of products liability is not their responsibility; nor can it be. It must be the *engineer's* job—the personal responsibility of every professional who, on a daily basis, makes the decisions that directly influence the liability associated with products and services. This does not mean, of course, that lawyers cannot or should not assist in the prevention process. They should be one of the primary sources management looks to for information and guidance.[29,30]

Appreciation of the circumstances that led to products liability and its associated problems may be readily gained from the growing number of excellent legal texts, commentaries, journal and review articles, and restatements on the subject.[31-39] Although intended for the legal profession, these are highly readable and stimulating for any professional. An occasional encounter with unfamiliar terms and phrases is easily resolved through consulting a comprehensive law dictionary.[40,41] Most of the leading texts are available from law school bookstores or from lawbook distributors.

Perusal of these books will show heavy reliance upon common law. That is, the practice of citing decisions of appellate courts, or courts of final authority, for every point being made. These are decisions on actual cases made by state supreme courts, federal courts and the U.S. Supreme Court. Such decisions are broadly cited in studies of law because *they are the law*, at least in the immediate jurisdiction of their decision, or until they are superseded or overruled by a subsequent decision. Thorough reading of texts and commentaries on products liability tort law will give the engineer a good foundation for understanding what is going on in the field.

As informative as commentaries and textbooks are, they offer retrospective analyses of past events; consequently, they have limited usefulness in maintaining an up-to-date view of what is daily occurring in products liability law. Different sources are required for monitoring current developments. This is the province of reporter, newsletter, and looseleaf services.[42-47] The latter provide periodic updating through insertion of newly published pages to replace superseded ones.

For a subscription fee, publishers of these services send (weekly, bi-weekly, or monthly) reports, digests of noteworthy legal decisions, summaries (and even full texts) of regulations and federal legislation, and descriptions of industry voluntary standardization activity. Case reporting services contain full texts of court decisions.

Some sources, like *The Federal Register*[48] covering rules and regulations of federal agencies, may be found in public libraries. Others are usually subscribed to by in-house legal counsel of larger firms, law offices and law libraries.

Before attempting to locate cases or information on specific subjects in a law library, it is advisable for those unfamiliar with formats and procedures to consult guides to locating the law in law libraries,[49-52] or have someone familiar with them help in getting started.

As an initial step in that direction and in locating the various case references cited throughout this book it may be helpful to note that most legal citations to published court decisions, legal textbooks, commentaries, digests and law reviews follow the same format. That is, the case name (or name of the author of the textbook or article) is listed first, then the title of the work, followed by the volume number, name of the title and the volume, and page number—in that order.

For example, for the citation "377 Pacific 2nd 897," the case would be found in a law library among the Second Series of the Pacific regional reporters (published by West Publishing Co.) on page 897 of Volume 377. Similarly, for the citation "74 Michigan Law Review 1257," the article would be found in the law review section of a law library, where the Michigan Law Review is filed, by locating Volume 74 and turning to page 1257.

"Tools" for liability avoidance vary with the manufacturing organization, its products and markets. The previous chapter outlined the range of general techniques and procedures. A primary need is familiarity with regulations affecting the firm, its products and markets.[53] Copies of the regulations and any addenda and modifications should be obtained and read. These are available from the *The Federal Register* (if a federal regulation), from reporting and listing services subscribed to by law libraries, from the regulatory agency itself, or through the firm's legal counsel.

Also important is information on the materials and ingredients that go into the product, their hazardous propensities and those of the product itself. Again, in addition to the company's own data base, there are numerous sources for this information,[54-59] with some publishers offering weekly or biweekly reports and updates on developments.[60-62] Computer access to data bases of such information from remote terminals through telephone modems is becoming increasingly available on a subscriber and time-share basis.

Other information that should be obtained and studied is failure or injury data collected by the company or by others in the industry. Trade organizations, technical societies, government agencies, newsletter or subscription services, and reports of legal decisions or actions by regulatory agencies are other sources for information.

Competitors' literature and samples of their products should be obtained and studied to learn of others' practices and safety features that could be innovative, effective and establish a new plateau of state-of-the-art. The engineer should also keep up-to-date in industry practices and trade customs. These set standards (although informal ones) that a court can use in evaluating a defendant's products. It is unhealthy to find your product or company practice obsolete with respect to current industry safety practice, even if the product complies with all published codes, regulations and standards. Such information is available from trade or business literature and periodicals.

Besides published information needed to evaluate a product and its liability potential, the engineer should develop an understanding of analytical procedures and systems techniques, including use of computers to augment computations, prototype evaluations and product tests. Up-to-date information on automatic test equipment, computerized manufacturing methods and process control, and management of data banks should be made available to all those responsible for design, engineering and production operations.

Admittedly, information needs for an effective liability prevention program can appear overwhelming, and are increasing every day. Considering that everyone in the organization is probably burdened with daily demands of the job itself, it is difficult to find time to deal with these additional requirements.

Some of the task of collecting and digesting the information can be assumed by the prevention program coordinator or his office. They could also arrange for intensive indoctrination sessions, workshops and seminars conducted by specialists, consultants or legal counsel. Conferences on the subject held several times each year at various locations around the country can be another source of help.

Risk Management

An Integrated Approach. No one likes to take risks that could have harmful consequences. Frequently, more cautious individuals choose to forego opportunities for financial gain or some apparent benefit because they judge the risks, or possibility of losses exceeding gains, too great. They feel more comfortable being conservative. But we do not always have a choice. All businesses are full of risks. A risk-free business cannot exist. So, it is not a matter of deciding to take or not to take risks, as they "go with the territory," and are implicit in operating a business. It is more a question of choosing risks, trading off one for another. In other words, *managing* or *controlling* risks.

Risks involve unknowns. Once unknowns become known, decisions become easier to make as the risk either disappears or diminishes considerably. Therefore, risk management is largely a task of resolving unknowns, or gathering intelligence information that removes all or part of the unknown, and then deciding which risks are preferred over others. If we decide that some risk is altogether intolerable, we can take steps to trade that risk for one or more lesser risks that are more acceptable. Or we might take action that permits us to accept *some* of that risk. It is all a matter of tradeoffs and compromises and is very complex. Yet, we deal with such risks on a personal basis many times each day. We do it so often it becomes spontaneous and we seldom think about it.

Consistently prudent responses to these encounters and events is regarded as sound judgment. In fact, it is that human ability to predictively respond prudently and reasonably to the myriad risks in life that constitutes the basis for negligence law, with its "reasonable man" standard. It is a useful standard because most people—even those uneducated in law— have little difficulty in judging what, for a given set of circumstances, is or is not "reasonable" conduct. Courts use juries comprised of average citizens, not those trained in legal matters, to decide cases. Usually, attorneys prefer untrained lay-persons for jurors because they can be expected to respond as reasonable individuals without biases and prejudices that may be present in the minds of those having formal training in the issue at hand.

But effectiveness and responsible decision-making in business environments require more skill and ability than the spontaneous reactions we make to the relatively simple every-day risks and confrontations. The decision process model may be essentially the same, but there are more unknowns, more uncertainty, more risks and, usually, more serious consequences in business decisions. These are more difficult to make because of the economic uncertainty that overshadows it all. And economics— profitability and return on investment—is the kingpin of business enterprise.

Then there are complex interactions, where everything we do affects everything else, that make it impossible to apply plain common sense and logic to business decisions. Also, in recent years, there has been an increase in the need to consider issues and factors that defy attempts at quantification; factors like human rights, social values and environmental impact. The complexity of it all has created a perpetual dilemma for which there often is no one "best" solution.

So far in our discussion of products liability, its threats, risks, and procedures for minimizing it, we have largely concentrated on that one problem. But, in the real world of a manufacturing business, products liability is only one of many problems and risks. It is, of course, pointless to concern oneself with exposure to products liability when the plant is closed because of a labor dispute, because there is no longer a market for the product, or because a fire has destroyed it all. A skillful manager has the sense to know what the priorities are and to appreciate that a business without customers having needs, or capacity to make products or provide services to satisfy those needs, has no real need to worry about liability exposure. This is one extreme, perhaps.

It is at the other extreme where need for skill in risk management is more acute. The need is greatest in successful businesses that are so preoccupied with meeting production and sales quotas and filling orders that there is no time to consider *all* the risks the business is facing. Astute managers resist the temptation to become so preoccupied with some matters, that at the time appear extremely urgent, that they fail to monitor other, less evident but perhaps equally critical ones. They, somehow, have ability to juggle all the issues at once, giving each one a fast but discriminating evaluation, and subtle trajectory adjustment, to keep everything well-balanced, coordinated, and in its proper place.

This is the context within which mangement must consider the need for products liability prevention. It is simply one more issue to juggle—as much a mistake to become preoccupied and paranoid over it as it would be to ignore it. It must be factored into the company's operations and considered along with the rest of it. By this, we mean intelligent and simultaneous balancing of all the company's interests, values, costs and risks.

At the beginning of this chapter, we reviewed how liability avoidance measures had broad benefits for a company, beyond the immediate benefit of helping to avoid liability. And we noted how they had to involve everyone in the company. When viewed in this light, it becomes evident that liability prevention fits easily into a firm's risk management program; for every step needed to avoid products lawsuits will have a constructive and positive effect upon other activities and operations.

That is, it makes the tradeoff decisions easier to make. It is not a question of diverting funds from constructive programs into a questionable "sink hole" but one of readjustment of priorities and values such that across-the-board emphasis is upon quality, product safety and reliability. And this cannot help but relieve other problems while avoiding products liability. Without such reorientation, liability prevention can become an expensive and irritating burden when attempted to be grafted-on or merely super-imposed upon an existing rigid and unyielding system.

With a proper integrated approach, the firm's liability avoidance program will blend in with each activity, eventually becoming a part of it. Manage-ment will evaluate its exposure and the possible consequences along with its other risks and strategies for controlling them. Depending upon its products and their risks of liability exposure, management may elect to modify its formulations, its processes, its packaging, or its marketing strategies. Perhaps it will find its risks with a product of questionable utility are too great and the product must be withdrawn from the market.

Whatever course management takes on its multitude of variables, its decisions should be the result of an orderly and systematic process of choice and not made through default.[63-65] The complexities of today's manufacturing industry demand use of all available decision-making tools. This includes reliable data bases, ready access to them, and procedures for analyzing the information and applying it to the deliberations at hand.

The previous chapter described various analytical techniques for evaluat-ing product designs for injury-producing propensity or their liability risks. These same methods may be used for evaluating broader risks and for assisting decision-making processes covering the spectrum of management's concerns.[66-68]

Risk-Sharing, The Role of Insurance. A common, but flawed, impression is that a simple "solution" to products liability and its exposure risks is an insurance policy. This over-simplified impression is not confined to manufacturing managers and others concerned with running products businesses, but also is found in landmark court decisions:

> [T]he burden of losses consequent upon use of defective articles is borne by those who are in a position to either control the danger *or make an equitable distribution of the losses* when they do occur. (*Henningsen v. Bloomfield Motors, Inc.*)[69] (emphasis added)

> The cost of an injury and the loss of time or health may be an overwhelming misfortune to the person injured, and a needless one, *for the risk of injury can be insured by the manufacturer and distributed among the public as a cost of doing business.* (*Escola v. Coca Cola Bottling Co. of Fresno*)[70] (emphasis added)

It would, indeed, relieve much of manufacturers' products liability problems if they could truly *shift* all such losses over to insurers, as many would like to believe they can. Unfortunately, such presumed perpetual availability of insurance coverage is a myth and probably always will be. What stands in the way of it is the unalterable fact that insurance companies are organized and run, like all businesses, to make a profit. To do so they must assure that income through payment of premiums exceeds what it costs to run the business, which includes settling claims and defending lawsuits against clients who pay premiums. To assure this, the insurance company writes an insurance "policy"—a legal contractual document—that very carefully and succinctly spells out limits of its obligation.

Through years of insurance underwriting and associated court decisions for disputes between insurers and others, plus the recent sharp increase in products liability claims and damage awards, the writing of insurance policies has become a finely-honed art.[71-73] It is not a place for laymen to attempt to fathom the extent of their own coverage and assess their own risks. There are intricate limitations, exclusions and conditions, plus coverage definitions, that have tightly-interpreted meanings that very narrowly define what the policy covers and does not cover.[74-77]

The task of evaluating options of products liability insurance coverage and benefits is a very difficult one and requires skill, experience and training in a field that most manufacturing executives do not have. Accordingly, purchase of insurance (all insurance, as liability coverage usually is a segment of broader coverage) should be made with careful consideration of what is being bought and how it affects the company's total liability exposure.

As a first step, management must have an accurate assessment of its liability exposure from its products and other business activities. It should have this even apart from insurance considerations as a baseline for organizing its liability avoidance program. Having established the extent of its exposure, it must decide how much of it is acceptable. That is, how much it considers it can self-insure (or even ignore until a claim is filed). Then, through discussions with knowledgeable experts or insurance consultants (not necessarily sales agents or brokers), it should determine what amounts of its exposure may be covered by insurance and for what cost.

Inevitably, there will be gaps or coverage that either is unavailable or too costly. Gaps left uncovered will be "covered" by the company itself; either through an in-house self-insurance fund or through cooperative agreements with other industry members or some other arrangement. Even if a policy is written by an insurer, there will be deductibles and various limitations and exclusions that limit coverage. These gaps are borne by the "insured." So, the net effect is a *sharing* of risks.

Products liability costs ordinarily outside limits of the standard policy include damages for injuries traceable to design deficiencies, difficulties that arise from contractual obligations assumed by the insured, punitive damages, expenses of product withdrawal from the market or recall, and loss of property owned by the insured. Depending upon the product, the manufacturer's and its industry's loss history and other factors affecting the risk and considered by the insurance underwriter in offering coverage and setting rates; these coverages sometimes can be purchased separately as policy endorsements.

But the risks and their costs that may be shared to some extent with insurers are but a part of the total cost of disposition of products claims and of defending lawsuits. Manufacturers' costs that are almost never covered by insurance include expense and time lost in claims investigation; retrieval, examination and interpretation of files and records; conferences with attorneys and insurance adjusters; and costs incurred in discovery processes, replying to interrogatories, preparing for and attending depositions and testifying in court. Besides this are policy deductibles, verdicts beyond policy limits, and costs of loss of goodwill and company reputation and losses associated with the internal disruption and need to divert corporate resources away from mainstream operations.

Then, once a company has experienced an insurer-defended lawsuit, it can expect other costs. These might include higher premiums for the same or less coverage brought about through risk reassessments by underwriter audits, higher deductibles and lower policy limits, increased and broader exclusions, and perhaps policy cancellation altogether.

The moral to all this is that liability insurance is but one means for sharing and helping to control liability risks. *It does not prevent claims* and their many non-insurable costs. Nevertheless, considering the magnitude of risk involved in manufacturing products in today's litigious climate it is not only prudent, but essential, to have good liability insurance coverage. But it must be purchased intelligently with full awareness of its limitations, what risks remain and must be covered by the company, and its coverages and exposures reevaluated periodically.

Since an insurer has as strong incentives as anyone for products liability prevention, it can be a valuable ally and source of information to a company in its prevention program. The insurer not only has incentives to minimize losses but also has extensive experience. It has resources in personal expertise in liability prevention, statistical data and helpful literature.[78] It has developed claims-handling procedures, plans and strategies that work and it can advise its clients in minimizing claims and costs of responding to claims and defending lawsuits. A manufacturer should make use of this source of assistance.

It is well to keep in mind, however, that while an insurer's incentives for minimizing losses do coincide with those of the product manufacturer; its primary goal of making a profit can—in event of an occurrence—conflict with interests of the insured. That is, it is an insurer's underlying objective to avoid paying for losses. So it may dispute coverage and attempt to deny responsibility. There are many contractual loopholes that an unwary manufacturer may not appreciate but that claims investigators are keenly aware of. Therefore, in the event of a claim, the firm's legal counsel should be relied upon to guide management in every step, including how to deal with the insurance company and in making the necessary timely reports of occurrence and in fulfilling other contractual obligations.

Auditing

Need for Monitoring Program Effectiveness. There is far too much at stake for management to assume that its liability prevention policy and directives for implementing it will automatically result in a smoothly operating program. Besides, necessary company-wide involvement, and pervasive effects of liability avoidance practices upon virtually all activities, require active monitoring. This is not only to assure that the program is accomplishing its goals, but that in doing so it is not introducing other problems and difficulties.

Since each company has its own set of needs and liability exposures, it must tailor-make its prevention program fit its requirements. As any designer knows—whether it is a suit of clothing, a complex electronic circuit, or a liability prevention program—such tasks require many iterative steps that are largely trial-and-error exercises to achieve a smoothly functioning unit or system. A liability prevention program is definitely not a system that can be declared into existence—simply wound-up—then left to run all by itself.

It is essential for management to provide a means for evaluating each step of its liability prevention program as well as its overall effects. Such evaluations or assessments, or audits, are common in accounting and are particularly necessary in assuring effectiveness of liability prevention activity. The very nature of the program, in affecting every activity and person in the company, requires a means for accommodating all safety-critical operations, for collecting audit responses in an orderly manner, and for maintaining a clear and intelligible record of results.

Approach and Procedures. A good starting point for the audit is with high-risk activities, product components and materials susceptible to failure and likely to cause injury or harm, and similar sensitive operations. These are priority items for audit to assure that the program, its strategies and procedures are working as intended and expected, and that too much attention is not being given lesser critical aspects at the sacrifice of the most sensitive ones.

Checklists have been widely used in conducting products liability audits and assuring that important aspects and functions are not overlooked.[79] Checklists are used not only for identifying specific items to audit, but also for establishing scope of the audit itself.[80] This can be determined through reviewing hazard analyses and other data and information derived during design stages.

Audit information need not be generated from scratch for each operation and activity. Output information already available from inspections and other surveys and evaluations during design, production and marketing the product may simply be plugged into the audit machinery. It will save time if the information system is devised to anticipate these and other needs for retrieval.

While the most liability-sensitive factors in the company's operations must be thoroughly scrutinized, attention should not be confined to them. Each of the seven broad classifications of activity noted in the previous chapter should be covered, with emphasis upon the more critical aspects of each for that company. Specific mechanics and procedures will vary with the company and its own set of potential liability problems, but a number of considerations apply to all.

For example, it is to be expected that everyone will resent being audited. So, it is important that the need for it, procedures used and its timing are understood, agreed upon and endorsed at least to the divisional management level. Their recommendations for minimizing disruption and any demoralizing effects should be sought and followed as much as possible.

Constructive aspects of the audit should be emphasized instead of using the exercise as a tool for uncovering personal shortcomings and program deficiencies. Everyone involved should be made to realize that the primary goal of the audit is to assure continued effectiveness of the company's liability prevention program—that it is accomplishing what it is supposed to accomplish while maintaining optimal operating efficiency and productivity.

As with financial audits, these audits also should be conducted by people not directly connected with the prevention program or the manufacturing operations—that is, they should be conducted by outsiders. They should be engaged by, and report to, top management and be familiar with the company, its products, manufacturing methods, markets and liability exposure.

Audit records and reports should be sufficiently documented to measure effectiveness of the prevention program and to furnish evidence of management's conscientious commitment to manufacturing safe, quality products. However, if entries identify poor practices, ineffective methods or product deficiencies, they can prove damaging in the event of a lawsuit. Such reports are discoverable and can be used by a plaintiffs' attorney to attempt to convince a court and jury (through the firm's own recorded facts and admissions) of the company's failure to eliminate product hazards despite its verbal commitment to product safety.

Therefore, the format of the audit's working documents, checklists and reports deserves careful scrutiny and judicious wording to avoid having records of deficiencies that can be used against the company. With a little forethought, the format of these documents and checklists can be devised to avoid damaging statements or admissions of internal problems.[81] Before they are used and made part of the company's information system, the firm's legal counsel should review and approve them.

DEFENSE-PLANNING

Anticipate The Inevitable Claim

Whatever adverse occurrence we want to avoid—fire, flood, burglary, mechanical breakdowns—the prudent approach is to make every reasonable attempt to prevent it. Yet, we cannot complacently rely upon preventive measures alone. We take every precaution to prevent fires from starting as they can destroy property and lives; but we do not stop with preventive measures. We install automatic sprinkler systems, fire and smoke alarms and monitors, fire escapes, and plan evacuation routes. We conduct fire drills and purchase firefighting and resuscitation eqiuipment.

These are defensive measures. They do not take the place of prevention. We know that regardless of how careful we are or try to be, now and then a fire starts. It is for this dreaded, but possible, eventuality that we are willing to pay for fire alarms and firefighting equipment.

So it must be for products liability. Because the threat is so potentially devastating to a company, we cannot afford to stop at prevention. We must realize that even the best prevention program will be unable to prevent all claims; that once in a while a defective product will slip through even the best system and a claim will be filed. The more preparation a company makes for that inevitable claim, the better it will be able to promptly resolve it. Not only will it help minimize damages but also costs of prolonged settlement negotiations or defense of a lawsuit.

Here, again, a positive attitude is the catalyst for marshalling an effective defense. It must be founded on belief that products liability *losses* are not inevitable, although a few claims may be. *A claim is not a verdict.* The objective is to resolve disputes or claims at the earliest possible stage and prevent them from becoming lawsuits.

It is essential that those concerned with formulating liability prevention policy and its implementation understand that each incident, occurrence and case is unique. No two are ever exactly alike, even if the offending product and occurrence seem the same.

Since each situation is different from all others, apparently subtle differences between facts can have major influences upon the outcome. Even in strict liability cases, there are a number of elements that the plaintiff must prove; for without them he has no case. Proof of negligence claims is even more difficult for the plaintiff. And a decision by one jurisdiction on one set of facts does not mean that another court and jurisdiction will decide the same way on apparently identical facts.

There always will be differences, and these offer opportunities for defense. Each allegation by the plaintiff, each issue raised, each item of evidence presented, each statement made and fact uncovered, offers defense an opportunity. A claim against the company is no occasion for losing hope and capitulating to the opponent's allegations or to regard it as an inevitable loss to be paid out and letting it go at that.

Aim for Early Settlement

Although it is the million-dollar jury verdicts that get the most publicity and create the impression that all claims inevitably lead to lawsuits and massive verdicts; most products liability claims are settled by the parties before a verdict, or even before a trial.

A 1979 study examined characteristics of closed products liability claims for which payment and expenses exceeded $100,000. Figure 6-1 shows the stages of these cases where settlement was made (that is, where the claim was closed). These are of significant interest because, although claims of this magnitude represent only about 1% of all products liability *claims*, they account for about half of the total products liability *payments.*[82]

Note that nearly 70% of these claims were settled before trial. Another 17% or so were settled during the trial, before the verdict. Only about 13% of these claims for which a suit was filed reached a court verdict.

These figures reflect the desire by all parties (defendant, insurer, plaintiff and judicial system, alike) to settle claims without resorting to a full-scale trial. While prevention and liability defense effort should conservatively proceed on the assumption that every dispute can end up in court, the fact

Figure 6-1: Products Liability Closed Claims Costing Over $100,000
(Stage Where Claim Was Closed)

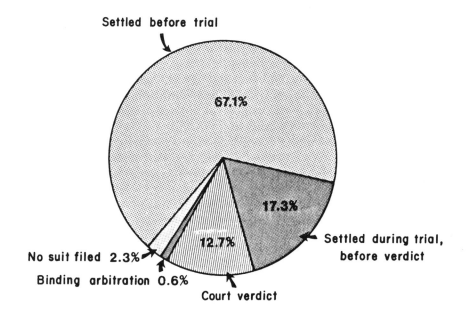

Settled before trial

67.1%

17.3%

12.7%

Settled during trial,
before verdict

No suit filed 2.3%

Binding arbitration 0.6%

Court verdict

Data: Alliance of American Insurers

remains that most claims are settled out of court. Therefore, the manufacturer's defense strategies should be directed toward building a basis for
bargaining clout for reaching early and favorable settlement. The objective
is to gain a "winning hand" early in the game.

Negotiations are going on during all stages of a products dispute. There are
exchange and review of facts, evidence and arguments of both sides.
Through it all, both sides do their best to guess how the court and jury will
apply the law and decide the case based upon this set of facts and
circumstances. Frequently, the amount a plaintiff is willing to accept in
settlement is a function of the thoroughness and competence of the
defendant's preparation—preparation that possibly began long before the
plaintiff ever came into contact with the defendant's product.

Strong evidence of responsible conduct, and care in making and testing
the product, can force the plaintiff's attorney into a risk-benefit analysis of
his own to determine whether it is in his client's best interest to settle for a
certain, but modest, sum early in the game; or to risk losing even that
through holding out for more through a trial. Deliberation of this question

(on both sides of the dispute) is not over until either a settlement is agreed upon or a verdict is announced.

Organized Defense Effort

As there are advantages in having a products liability coordinator, committee or team, there also are advantages in having a litigation defense task force. For a small manufacturer or one with minimal liability risks, it may require only a few people with part-time responsibility. In larger firms or those manufacturing products with greater risks, there could be a full-time staff.

Its success depends upon accessibility to product information, familiarity with the range of operations of the company, and thoroughness of its preparation. If the group is to be effective, all organizing and preparation must be done well before there is an occurrence or filed claim. The task force should be staffed with both technically and legally trained people familiar with the design, production and marketing of the product, as well as management's policies, regulatory requirements and other relevant standards. They should be able to maintain a good working relationship with the liability prevention or safety coordination group and have full and un-restricted access to all relevant data bases and in-house technical expertise.

The task force should be able to anticipate probable product failure mode or occurrence scenarios and their legal consequences, and to devise an approach and operating plan accordingly—complete with comprehensive checklists, delegation of tasks and staff assignments, and a realistic budget. Scope of strategic elements should include its own information system and access to other company systems; capability for ready traceability of materials and product components through purchase records, manufacturing logs, inspection and test data, and product sales and distribution information. It should include a complete product failure/occurrence investigation facility, litigation expertise and support, and capability for maintaining awareness and skill in new litigation methods and trial concepts.

The mission of the defense task force begins long before the litigation process. In fact, one of its objectives is to avert litigation. Its effectiveness hinges upon ability to respond promptly to *occurrences* and reports of occurrences. It cannot afford to wait until a claim is filed. This means that it should monitor customer complaints, product failure reports (whether there is resulting harm or injury or not) and field service logs. While every report of dissatisfaction over the product cannot be investigated, some require it. It is up to the judgment of the task force to identify those with potential for trouble. This requires knowledge of the product and its uses and levels of risks associated with it. These will, of course, vary with the product.

Many potentially serious products claims and lawsuits might have been averted if someone at the manufacturing company had heeded and looked into the first reports of a problem. The company must recognize the need, and provide for, a distant early warning system to monitor product occurrences and make every attempt to quickly learn the pertinent facts and, as necessary, promptly resolve the problem.

In the context of products liability, we tend to think of "occurrence" as meaning an isolated product failure. But we cannot so limit our concept of it. Consider the widescale consequences of occurrences in recent years of product tampering, spills and leakage of harmful chemicals, injuries from birth control devices, and the need for massive product recalls. These dramatic events become news items that receive extensive media coverage. How manufacturers of these products respond can have a profound effect upon public opinion and outcome of subsequent legal action.

Therefore, the company's litigation avoidance and defense people must address these possibilities, especially if the firm manufactures products having widespread risk potential. The company should have a detailed advance plan for prompt action to, first of all, limit the spread of damage and to minimize its harmful effects. There is usually no time for calling meetings of corporate committees to assess the situation, plan strategies and work out solutions to make it all go away. It can be a situation where hours and even minutes count, and what is done in the brief interval following a disastrous occurrence (or discovery) can be highly significant to the company's future.[83]

Second in importance to limiting scope of the problem is the need for responding calmly, coherently and positively to the press, consumer action, environmentalist and other groups. This is when a friendly working relationship with local and national media can pay off.[84] This requires prior cultivation of their interest in the firm's operations, in its concern for the community and education of the public to acquaint it with the company and its products. Anything done before an occurrence to project a positive company image will pay dividends in the days, months and years to follow.

While this activity may traditionally be a public relations function, technical and legal ramifications make it necessary to involve the litigation avoidance and defense teams, even to the point of identifying a specific spokesperson to deal with legally sensitive subjects. The role of the public relations function is to develop good relationships *before* oocurrences and disasters. The litigation avoidance and defense teams can supplement this role through providing accurate technical facts and other details as necessary to assure that a correct, consistent and unified front, as favorable to the company as possible, is continually presented.

Investigating Product-Related Occurrences

The company's task force should be continually prepared to investigate and collect evidence from the moment of a product-related occurrence. It is particularly desirable to get possession of the failed product and any other physical items related to it and the occurrence. The sooner all this is done, the better. The investigation must cover a broad spectrum of activity. The checklist of Appendix A was prepared by the Products Liability Committee of the International Association of Insurance Counsel to provide practical guidance in investigating and preparing products liability cases and is reprinted with their permission.

It is clear from a review of this checklist that the investigation must not confine itself to technical issues, but include interviews of witnesses and anyone else having information about the product, the occurrence or event. And it must establish the conditions surrounding the occurrence and any information on history of the product that could have had some effect.

Analysis of product failures and accident reconstruction are demanding tasks that require a combination of skills and solid background of practical experience, plus well-honed intuition.[85-88] The firm's task force should have this expertise, either through in-house employees or outside consultants familiar with the company, its operations and products. Also, it should have portable investigative equipment and facilities and be fully trained in their use and in gathering facts and data from on-site field locations.[89-98]

Litigation Assistance

The rise in number and seriousness of products liability cases and increase in product sophistication and complexity have made the need for outside expert assistance—in evaluating evidence and in giving legal testimony—virtually indispensable. Note this theme in the following excerpt from a trial guidebook[99] prepared for practicing attorneys handling products lawsuits:

> Trial practice today has been labelled by many as the age of the expert. This is particularly appropriate in products liability cases, because expert testimony is almost always important and generally indispensable ... [I]t is reasonably inferrable that a products liability case will become a battle of experts, with the trier of fact [the jury, generally] having to not only comprehend, but also to resolve, inevitably conflicting expert testimony.

It is likely that the product-related incident, occurrence or event will involve more than one technical discipline or a field outside that of in-house expertise. This requires assistance of outside experts to guide the manufacturer's defense team in their investigation and later, perhaps, to guide legal counsel in preparing its case. Again, the sooner after the occurrence that these experts are retained and become involved and acquainted with the problem and have an opportunity to examine the evidence, the better all around.

Experts should not be regarded merely as expert *witnesses*, where their function is confined to issuing statements, giving opinions during discovery proceedings or testifying in court. This is but one function. There are many circumstances and steps in investigating a products case that require on-going availability of expertise relevant to the product or occurrence.[100,101] It is not a time for cutting corners or penny-pinching a limited budget.

Selection of the right expert or experts is critically important to the successful outcome of the case and it should be given careful consideration.[102] Besides possessing required technical competence, the defense task force and legal counsel should find the expert personally comfortable to work with. It is desirable to avoid choices that will lead to personality clashes or conflicts that generate friction within the team.

There are, of course, two kinds of experts that the company must deal with—its own experts and those of the opposition. There will be opportunities for questioning the plaintiff's experts and these occasions should be well-planned and discussed thoroughly with the defendant manufacturer's experts.[103]

There are various personal preferences in selecting technical experts. While there can be no hard-and-fast rules that fit every situation, it is advisable to retain the best available expert, do it early in the case, and insist that the expert confine his opinions to his specific field. It can weaken one's case to use the general-practice expert or "hired gun" who professes knowledge of many fields and frequently testifies on a wide range of topics and products.

Depending upon the product and the case, it can also be useful to engage an expert having direct hands-on experience in the field involved. Often, such a practically-oriented expert is more readily understood by a jury, is accorded more credibility, and therefore has more clout than a pure theoretician.

As financial stakes in products cases have grown, so also has sophistication of techniques for preparing a case and evaluating its strengths and weaknesses. Use of microforms has become commonplace in the storage and retrieval of case and legislative law and regulations.[104,105] Computerized data bases of court decisions and legislated and regulatory law, as well as technical data, are increasingly accessible through on-line computer terminals and modems.[106-113] All this improves access to both technical information and law, and makes it possible to evaluate facts, issues and probable legal position in a very short time.

Besides accessibility of current information, social psychologists are studying juror profiles and response mechanisms.[114] Important cases are increasingly "tried" in dry-runs before a full complement of mock jurors and judges. Their results are analyzed by experts in behavioral science to assist attorneys in every aspect of the trial, from juror selection, to witness appearance and response, attorney demeanor, approach and presentation of evidence and persuasive arguments.[115-116]

Firms manufacturing and marketing products having significant liability potential should keep aware of these developments and its defense task force should make provisions for implementing them should its risk assessments and litigation prospects warrant it. It is a fast-moving field, with newer and more effective tools becoming available nearly every day. No product manufacturer can afford to ignore it.

REFERENCES

1. Peters, T.J. and Waterman, R.H., Jr., *In Search of Excellence* 156, 165, Warner Books Edition (1982).
2. *Id.* at 238-39.
3. Peters, T.J. and Pascarella, P., *Searching for Excellence, The Winners Deliver on Value*, Industry Week 61-2 (April 16, 1984).
4. Feigenbaum, A.V., *Total Quality Control*, Third Edition, McGraw-Hill Book Co., New York, NY (1981).
5. Karabatsos, N.A., (ed.), *Training: A Key to Quality*, Quality 23-38 (May 1984).
6. Owen, D.G., *Punitive Damages in Products Liability Litigation*, 74 Michigan Law Review 1257 (1976).
7. Owen, D.G., *Problems in Assessing Punitive Damages Against Manufacturers of Defective Products*, 5 Journal of Products Liability 341-99 (1982).
8. Bass, L. and Weis, P., *The Safety and Liability Audit: Applying System Safety Analyses to Management*, 6 Journal of Products Liability 227-36 (1983).
9. Eads, G. and Reuter, P., *Designing Safer Products, Corporate Reponses to Product Liability Law and Regulation* 151, Report No. R-3022 ICJ, The Rand Corporation, The Institute of Civil Justice, 1700 Main Street, P.O. Box 2138, Santa Monica, CA 90406 (1983).
10. *Product Liability Portfolio* 7-22, Business Research Publications, 87 Terminal Drive, Plainview, NY 11803 (1977).
11. Manuele, F.A., *Product Safety Program Management*, 2 Journal of Products Liability 97-104 (1978).
12. Patterson, W.P., *Corporations in Crisis*, Industry Week 57-62 (March 5, 1984).
13. *Managing Records*, Quality 54 (January 1982).
14. Personal communication with L.A. Thompson of Business Imaging Systems, Eastman Kodak Co., San Francisco, CA (January 1983).
15. Personal communciation with E. Severson of File Management Systems, 3M Company, St. Paul, MN (February 1983).
16. *STC'S Headstart In Optical Memories*, Business Week 106A-106B (October 3, 1983).
17. *Electronic Files for the Paper Flood*, Business Week 88A (August 23, 1982).
18. Hill, B., *Optical Memory Systems in Digital Memory and Storage* 273-89 (W.E. Proebster, ed.) F. Vieweg, W. Germany (1978).
19. Published product announcement, Hitachi America Ltd., San Francisco, CA (September 1983).
20. *Office Automation Restructures Business*, Business Week 118-30 (October 8, 1984).
21. Flores, A., *Engineering Ethics in Organizational Contexts: Monsanto Co.,* in

Designing for Safety: Engineering Ethics in Organizational Contexts (A. Flores, ed.) Rensselear Polytechnic Institute, Troy, NY (1982).

22. The New Jersey Institute of Technology (formerly Newark College of Engineering), Newark, NJ initiated, organized and financially supported the highly regarded and informative series of Product Liability Prevention (PLP) Conferences that provided an effective forum for exchange of information for engineers, attorneys, legislators, manufacturers and representatives of regulatory agencies. Others that have contributed significantly to an understanding of products liability for engineering professionals through organizing seminars and symposia have included the University of Wisconsin (at Milwaukee and Madison) and The University of California at Los Angeles.

23. The American Society of Safety Engineers (ASSE), American Society for Quality Control (ASQC), American Society for Testing and Materials (ASTM), and American Society for Metals (ASM), have organized and sponsored conferences, seminars, courses and/or publications on product safety and liability prevention.

24. Simpson, R.O., *supra* reference 1 of Chapter 5.

25. Consumer Product Safety Act, *supra* reference 41 of Chapter 4.

26. Fogle, F.D., *Personal Liability of Engineers*, Proceedings PLP-77E at 129-36, Product Liability Prevention Conference, Hasbrouck Heights, NJ (August 22-24, 1977).

27. *Florida Electric Firm, 3 Executives Charged in Toxic-Dump Case*, The Wall Street Journal p.32, col.3 (October 28, 1983).

28. Taylor, R.E., *U.S. Increases Prosecutions of Polluters*, The Wall Street Journal 30 (October 27, 1983).

29. Ross, K., *The Role of Attorneys in Product Liability Prevention*, 6 Journal of Products Liability 1-6 (1983).

30. Dauer, E.A. and Kolmar, J.R., *Lawyers' Roles in Products Liability Prevention for the Small Business Client*, 7 Journal of Products Liability 31-48 (1984).

31. Keeton, W.P., Owen, D.G., and Montgomery, J.E., *Products Liability and Safety, Cases and Materials*, The Foundation Press, Inc., Mineola, NY (1980).

32. Prosser, W.L., *Handbook of the Law of Torts*, Fourth Edition, West Publishing Co., St. Paul, MN (1971).

33. Kionka, E.J., *Torts In A Nutshell*, West Publishing Co., St. Paul, MN (1977).

34. Noel, D.W. and Phillips, J.J., *Products Liability, Cases and Materials,* West Publishing Co., St. Paul, MN (1976).

35. Noel, D.W. and Phillips, J.J., *Products Liability In A Nutshell*, Second Edition, West Publishing Co., St. Paul, MN (1981).

36. Hursh, R.D. and Bailey, H.J., *American Law of Products Liability*, Second Edition (6 volumes, with periodic supplements), The Lawyers Co-Operative Publishing Co., Rochester, NY 14694 and Bancroft-Whitney Co., San Francisco, CA 94107 (1974).

37. Frumer, L.R. and Friedman, M.I., *Products Liability* (4 volumes), Matthew Bender, New York, NY (1975).

38. Schreiber, S. and Rheingold, P., *Products Liability—law, practice, science,* Practicing Law Institute, New York, NY (1967).

39. American Law Institute, *Restatement (Second) of the Law: Torts*, American

Law Institute Publishers, St. Paul, MN (1965).

40. *Black's Law Dictionary*, 5th ed., West Publishing Co., St. Paul, MN (1979).

41. *Ballentine's Law Dictionary*, 3d ed., The Lawyers Co-Operative Publishing Co., Rochester, NY 14694, and Bancroft-Whitney Co., San Francisco, CA 94107 (1969).

42. *Product Safety & Liability Reporter*, The Bureau of National Affairs, Inc., 1231 25th Street, N.W., Washington, DC 20037. Annual subscription fee provides binders and weekly reports.

43. *Product Liability Trends*, The Research Group, Inc., P.O. Box 7187, Charlottesville, VA 22906.

44. *Products Liability Reporter*, Commerce Clearing House, Inc., 425 13th Street, N.W., Washington, DC 20004.

45. *Consumer Product Safety Guide*, Commerce Clearing House, Inc., 425 13th Street, N.W., Washington, DC 20004.

46. *Product Liability Newsletter,* Leader Publications Inc., 111 Eighth Avenue, New York, NY 10114.

47. *Products Liability Law & Litigation Report*, Law & Business, Inc., 655 Valley Road, Clifton, NJ 07013 (monthly newsletter).

48. *The Federal Register*, U.S. Government Printing Office, Washington, DC 20402.

49. Cohen, M.L. and Berring, R.C., *How To Find the Law, 8th Ed.*, West Publishing Co., St. Paul, MN (1983).

50. Cohen, M.L. and Berring, R.C., *Finding The Law*, an abridged edition of *How To Find the Law, 8th Ed.*, West Publishing Co., St. Paul, MN (1984).

51. Stromme, G., *Basic Legal Research Techniques*, Revised Fourth Edition, The Research Group, Inc., American Law Publishing Service, San Mateo, CA (1979).

52. *A Uniform System of Citation*, Thirteenth Edition, The Harvard Law Review Assn., Cambridge, MA 02138 (1983).

53. *Index to Government Regulation*, The Bureau of National Affairs, Inc., 1231 25th Street, N.W., Washington, DC 20037.

54. *NIOSH Registry of Toxic Effects of Chemical Substances* (RTECS), GPO Stock No. 017-033-00399-8, available from Superintendent of Documents, U.S. Government Printing Office, Washington, DC 20402.

55. Gross, P. and Braun, D.C., *Toxic and Biomedical Effects of Fibers*, Noyes Publications, Park Ridge, NJ 07656 (1984).

56. *Patty's Industrial Hygiene and Toxicology*, 3d ed., (3 volumes), John Wiley & Sons, New York, NY (1978-1982).

57. Landrock, A.H., *Handbook of Plastics Flammability and Combustion Toxicology*, Noyes Publications, Park Ridge, NJ 07656 (1983).

58. Sittig, M., *Handbook of Toxic and Hazardous Chemicals and Carcinogens—* Second Edition, Noyes Publications, Park Ridge, NJ 07656 (1985).

59. Worobec, M.D., *Toxic Substances Controls Primer*, The Bureau of National Affairs, Inc., 1231 25th Street, N.W., Washington, DC 20037 (1984).

60. *Chemical Regulation Reporter*, The Bureau of National Affairs, Inc., 1231 25th Street, N.W., Washington, DC 20037. Annual subscription fee provides binders and weekly reports.

61. *Chemical Substances Control*, The Bureau of National Affairs, Inc., 1231 25th

Street, N.W., Washington, DC 20037. Annual subscription fee provides binder and biweekly bulletins.

62. *Environment Reporter*, The Bureau of National Affairs, Inc., 1231 25th Street, N.W., Washington, DC 20037. Annual subscription fee provides binders and weekly reports.

63. Rinefort, F.C., *Cost-Benefit Analysis: A Useful Tool for Products Liability Prevention*, PLP-79 Proceedings 137-42; Product Liability Prevention Conference, New York, NY (October 22-24, 1979) IEEE Catalog No. 79CH1512-3R, Library of Congress 78-641548.

64. Henley, E.J. and Kumamoto, H., *Reliability Engineering and Risk Assessment*, Prentice-Hall, Inc., Englewood Cliffs, NJ 07632 (1981).

65. Bartfeld, C.I., Selman, V. and Selman, J., *Risk Assessment for Product Liability Prevention*, PLP-80 Proceedings 123-27, Product Liability Prevention Conference, Washington, DC (September 22-24, 1980) IEEE Catalog No. 80CH1582-6, Library of Congress 78-641548.

66. Moghissi, A.A., *Risk Management—Practice and Prospects*, Mechanical Engineering 21-23 (November 1984).

67. Paustenbach, D.J., *Risk Assessment . . . And Engineering in The 80s*, Mechanical Engineering 54-59 (November 1984). (The reader is also referred to several other articles on risk assessment in the November 1984 issue of Mechanical Engineering with specific emphasis upon offshore oil and gas operations, regulation of nuclear power plants, ecology, cancer, highway travel and EPA regulation of chemical compounds.)

68. *Loss Prevention and Control*, The Bureau of National Affairs, Inc., 1231 25th Street, N.W., Washington, DC 20037. Annual subscription fee provides binder and biweekly bulletins.

69. *Henningsen v. Bloomfield Motors, Inc.*, 32 N.J. 358, 161 A.2d 69 (1960).

70. *Escola v. Coca Cola Bottling Co. of Fresno*, 24 Cal.2d 453, 150 P.2d 436, in concurring opinion by Justice R. Traynor (1944).

71. Harvey, W.B., *Products Liability Insurance Coverage*, 31 South Carolina Law Review 718-55 (1980).

72. McGeough, T.J. *Insurance Coverage for Products Liability* in *Products Liability: Practical Defense Problems* 39-48, DRI Monograph, Volume 1972, No. 9, Defense Research Institute, Inc., Chicago, IL (1972).

73. Kennedy, L.E., *Insurer's View of Products Liability Problems—A Practical Approach*, DRI Defense Practice Seminar, New Orleans, LA, Products Liability Defense Coursebook El-Ell, Defense Research Institute, Inc., Chicago, IL (January 18, 1979).

74. *Insurance Litigation Reporter*, Litigation Insurance Group, 425 Brannan Street, San Francisco, CA 94107.

75. Veal, H.K., *Product Insurance Coverage—When Is an Occurrence?*, 1 Journal of Products Liability 149-55 (1977).

76. Ghiardi, J.D. and Kircher, J.J., *Insurance Against Punitive Damages*, in DRI Monograph, "Occurrence" and Other Insurance Coverage Issues, at 20-44 (D.J. Hirsch and E.M. Soeka, eds.) Volume 1982, No. 2, Defense Research Institute, Inc. 750 North Lake Shore Drive, Chicago, IL 60611 (1982).

77. *Insurance: Complex Problems in Law and Practice*, Course Book No. CB-78-1, DRI Seminar, Reno, NV, Defense Research Institute, Inc., 750 North Lake

Shore Drive, Chicago, IL 60611 (1978).

78. *Product Safety and Liability Loss Control Handbook*, Alliance of American Insurers, Loss Control Dept., 20 North Wacker Drive, Chicago, IL 60606 (1979).

79. Corley, G.W. and Brown, F.X., *Auditing—A Product Liability Prevention Tool*, PLP-78 Proceedings 45-56, Product Liability Prevention Conference, Philadelphia, PA (August 21-23, 1978) IEEE Catalog No. 78CH1370-6R.

80. *Id.*

81. Ross, S.S., *Assuring Good Information for Managing Product Liability Prevention*, PLP-80 Proceedings 77-81, Product Liability Prevention Conference, Washington DC (September 22-24, 1980) IEEE Catalog No. 80CH1582-6, Library of Congress 78-641548.

82. *Highlights of Large-Loss Product Liability Claims* 6, Alliance of American Insurers, 20 North Wacker Drive, Chicago, IL 60606 (1980).

83. Reagan, C.R., *When Disaster Strikes, Be Prepared*, The Wall Street Journal, "Manager's Journal" (January 9, 1984).

84. Barry, R.A., *Crisis Communications—What To Do When the Roof Falls In*, Business Marketing 96-100 (March 1984).

85. Kingston, C.R., *Forensic Science*, ASTM Standardization News 8-15 (April 1973).

86. Lement, B.S. and Ferrara, J.J., *Accident Causation Analysis by Technical Experts*, 5 Journal of Products Liability 145-60 (1982).

87. Thunder, J.M., *Defending Product Liability Matters: Procedure and Evidence Concerning The Preservation of Physical Evidence*, 6 Journal of Products Liability 185-99 (1983).

88. Peters, G.A., *The Expert's Inside View of Product Liability*, 1 Journal of Products Liability 20-26 (1977).

89. ASTM E860-82, *Standard Practice for Examining and Testing Items That Are or May Become Involved in Products Liability Litigation*, American Society for Testing and Materials, Philadelphia, PA 19103 (October 1982).

90. Thornton, J.W., *Product Failure Analysis—Methods and Sources*, in Products Liability, Practical Defense Problems II at 62-65, Volume 1976, No. 1, Defense Research Institute, Inc., 750 North Lake Shore Drive, Chicago, IL 60611 (1976).

91. Rinaman, J.C. and Perritt, H.F.., *Preparation and Trial of Products Liability Cases,* in Products Liability, Defense of A Products Case (1978 Supplement) at 25-41, Volume 1978, No. 5, Defense Research Institute, Inc., 750 North Lake Shore Drive, Chicago, IL 60611 (1978).

92. Spencer, J.H., *A Proper Products Liability Investigation*, PLP-80 Proceedings 33-39, Product Liability Prevention Conference, Washington, DC (September 22-24, 1980) IEEE Catalog No. 80CH1582-6, Library of Congress 78-641548.

93. Pearsall, G.W. and Shepard, M.L., *Materials Failures and Their Analysis*, 1 Journal of Products Liability 65-80 (1977).

94. Dean, R., *Preparation of an Engineering Report in the Product Liability Case—A Legal Perspective*, 3 Journal of Products Liability 73-84 (1979).

95. Unterweiser, P.M. and Cubberly, W.H. (eds.), *Case Histories in Failure Analysis*, American Society for Metals, Metals Park, OH 44073 (1979).

96. Naumann, F.K., *Failure Analysis, Case Histories and Methodology*, American Society for Metals, Metals Park, OH 44073 (1983).

97. *Source Book In Failure Analysis*, American Society for Metals, Metals Park, OH 44073 (1974).

98. *Metals Handbook*, 8th Edition, Volume 10, *Failure Analysis and Prevention*, American Society for Metals, Metals Park, OH 44073 (1975).

99. Day, D.H. (ed.), *Products Liability Trial Notebook*, Defense Research Institute, Inc., 750 North Lake Shore Drive, Chicago, IL 60611 (1983).

100. Dombroff, M.A., *Prepare and Present Your Expert Witness,* For The Defense 15 (August 1984).

101. Reilly, T.J., *The Technical Expert: A Resource for Assistance* (Parts One and Two), For The Defense 28-30 (August 1983), For The Defense 28-30 (September 1983).

102. Philo, H.M., 1 *Lawyer's Desk Reference*, 6th Edition, *Cumulative Supplement to Volume I* at 15-402 (March 1984).

103. Danner, D., *Expert Witness Checklists*, The Lawyer's Co-Operative Publishing Co., Rochester, NY 14694, and Bancroft-Whitney Co., San Francisco, CA 94107 (1983).

104. *Guide to Microforms in Print*, Meckler Publishing, 520 Riverside Ave., Westport, CT 06880.

105. Tseng, H.R., *Complete Guide to Legal Materials in Microform*, University Publications of America, Frederick, MD (1976); annual supplements, AMCO International, Staten Island, NY.

106. LEXIS, a service of Mead Data Control, includes the full text of all current federal and state appellate court decisions and limited retrospective coverage. It now also includes the *United States Code* and some state statutes, administrative and regulatory material. LEXIS is a registered trademark of Mead Data Control.

107. NEXIS, also a service of Mead Data Control, is a library containing the full text of many general and business news publications and major wire services (includes *American Banker, Washington Post, Business Week, Newsweek, U.S. News and World Report* and others). NEXIS is a registered trademark of Mead Data Control.

108. WESTLAW, the computerized legal research service of West Publishing Company closely follows the company's National Reporter System. It now offers headnotes and full texts of current federal and state appellate court decisions, with retrospective coverage being continually added. The WEST-LAW system also offers data bases which include *Black's Law Dictionary, Dow Jones News/Retrieval Services, Forensic Services Dictionary,* and *Comprehensive World Patent Index*. WESTLAW is a registered trademark of West Publishing Company.

109. COMPENDEX, a digital data base version of the *Engineering Index Monthly*, provides abstracts of technical articles from journals, monographs, standards and reports. COMPENDEX is a registered trademark of Engineering Information, Inc., 345 East 47th St., New York, NY 10017.

110. METADEX is a data base offering *Metals Abstracts, Metals Abstracts Index*, and *Alloys Index*, from January 1966 to the present. Details are available from Metals Information, American Society for Metals, Metals Park, OH

44073 or DIALOG Information Services, Palo Alto, CA. METADEX is a registered trademark of the American Society for Metals.

111. MDF/1 (Metal Data File) offers access to numerical data on mechanical and physical properties and specifications of metals and alloys. Details are available from Systems Development Corporation, Santa Monica, CA. MDF/1 is a registered trademark of Systems Development Corporation.

112. Cohen, M.L. and Berring, R.C., *supra* reference 50 at 504-523.

113. *Directory of Online Databases*, Vol. 5, No. 3 (Spring 1984), Caudra Assoc., Inc., 2001 Wilshire Blvd., Santa Monica, CA 90403.

114. Litigation Sciences, *Believers in a Just World: The Perfect Jurors?*, For The Defense 8-11 (December 1982).

115. Litigation Sciences, *Behavioral Insights: The Effective Use of Witnesses*, For The Defense 27-29 (April 1983).

116. Litigation Sciences, *The Social Psychology of Persuasion*, For The Defense 11-16 (April 1984).

7

What Lies Ahead?

GUIDEPOSTS TO THE FUTURE

Today's motivations for avoiding products liability hinge upon what we think will happen tomorrow. There is little use in committing resources and effort to a major program and reorientation of our people if the perceived need for doing so could be a fleeting fad. No company can afford to play guessing games with its assets. So, every decision a company makes must be supported by solid evidence that each expenditure and activity will accomplish its objective and that there are good reasons for giving it priority over other worthwhile competing causes.

Commitment to products liability prevention is no different from any other commitment; although it should, perhaps, be evaluated more objectively and thoroughly than other activities and programs. This is because products liability prevention is so pervasive in its effects upon everything—how the company thinks, how it views itself, how it operates, how its products perform and are positioned in the marketplace, and more. And it must be a long-term commitment. It's not easily turned off and on to suit climatic idiosyncrasies. These decisions cannot be made hastily or under pressures of the moment, but with painstaking thoughtfulness and an unrestricted view of the future and the company's role in it.

Before any steps are taken to minimize products liability, a company must have an accurate assessment of its liability exposure and whether it is apt to change. These liability risks, like all others, should be evaluated systematically and, preferably, with help of legal counsel. Previous chapters have shown the many facets that must be considered; as products liability can come from various directions and in different forms.

The classic case of a missing bolt (manufacturing defect) causing product failure with resulting harm or injury is but one way a product may be defective and incur liability for its maker. The manufacturer faces liability from contractual "defects," or warranties unconsciously made; from failure to warn of hazards from normal use and even from abnormal use and foreseeable misuse; and from failure to comply with some government regulation—to say nothing about consequences of ignorance of industry safety standards and practices, subtle design "flaws" and advertising that promises performance the product cannot deliver.

The manufacturer must fully comprehend the risks coming from all these directions before it can determine the extent of its actions to reduce these risks, to accept them, or perhaps share them with an insurer. All risks are unknowns, but major decisions affecting the future course of a company's operations and that have to do with non-technical issues are particularly difficult to make. While none of us can predict the future, we are far from being lost at sea without a compass or other navigational aids. We are, in fact, surrounded by guideposts. While all are not 100% reliable, many are reliable enough that it would be a serious mistake to ignore them. Besides guideposts, we are not without our own senses that tell us that there are forces, largely outside our control, propelling us, our companies and industries in definite directions. No manufacturer can, for very long, remain oblivious to the government regulations affecting most of the details of operating that business. Not all deal with products liability issues, but many of them do, either directly or indirectly. It does not take much sensitivity or knowledge of law to detect these forces and to discern how they are vectoring the company.

Then there are "climatic" indicators. It has been frequently said that we live in a litigious climate. There are reasons for this. We have considered some of them, and have noted that the manufacturer is a prime target for products litigation and why it is. We saw that our products litigation system is really machinery for transferring funds from deep pockets of industry into the pockets of "helpless" individuals who in some way have been personally harmed by manufactured products.

It is an awkward system. It uses the law, with its traditional function of regulating human conduct, to bring about a socially-desirable purpose of economic redistribution. A most indirect scheme and, from the manufacturers' viewpoint, unfair; but that is how it evolved. Certainly, there are critics of it and there are frequent recommendations for a better system.[1] But this one, with all its faults, is functioning. It is doing the job it is supposed to do, and it is unlikely that it will soon be supplanted by another system. This one is too well-rooted for major modifications to be made in it overnight. Until drastic changes uproot this system, we must learn to live with it. Nevertheless, change is inevitable, and everyone affected by the system should develop an awareness of what is happening in this field and make an effort to monitor the changes and learn to interpret them.

Probably the best barometer we have for monitoring legal climate is the daily newspaper. Virtually no issue of a major daily paper in this country over the past decade or so has been without some indication that a manufacturer can use in assessing both its present and future products liability risks. Newspapers are useful because they reflect social attitudes, values and judgments. And this—*public policy*—is what feeds the root system of all products liability issues.

In an earlier chapter we outlined nine factors that contributed to the precipitation of a products liability crisis some years ago (these are still critical to the vitality of some high-risk industries). These factors were not isolated events that have now faded into oblivion. They are existing, ongoing trends that are still here and readily accessible for inspection, study and analysis.

It is not a bad idea, therefore, for everyone responsible for products liability avoidance to make it a habit to regularly maintain a personal file of clippings of newspaper, business publication and journal articles dealing with products liability issues. Even a casual review of these clippings from time to time will give a valuable indication of these trends, and others, that may influence a particular industry or product manufacturer. Such awareness, when supplemented with knowledge of products liability issues and periodic monitoring of newsletters or reporting services, and even reading of pertinent case law, will provide guidelines as reliable as any available today anywhere.

Remember, nothing about the law is once-and-for-all fixed and settled. It is a growing, changing *organism* and, by its very nature, it cannot remain static. Concepts that form the basis for today's products liability law did not come into being with a stroke of a legislator's pen or an epic judicial pronouncement, but took decades to evolve. They are still evolving. Once we know what these concepts are and how they developed to where they are today; we can monitor their changes and trends and come up with a fairly reliable understanding of how our own companies, operations and products can be affected.

Development of such ability also can provide useful market intelligence, for it offers those who possess it a significant competitive advantage. As trends become evident to the firm that actively monitors them, it can fine-tune its operations and product line accordingly, and even set the pace for the industry. This will help it to lower costs through avoiding the need for making major corrections at the last minute on a crash basis.What is even more beneficial, it will help the company avoid products liability and its costs.

It is worth mentioning here that the alert manufacturer will recognize that the close relationship between social values and products liability issues offers an opportunity to influence these trends. Admittedly, there is so much inertia in the products liability system that the influence of one manufacturer, or even an entire industry, may not be measurable for some time, if ever. Nevertheless, public policy and sentiment *can* be influenced, and changed; but it takes effort, dedication, patience and long-term commitment. It's not impossible to turn public sentiment around, to reverse—or at least slow-down—some of the trends that are making life (and profitability) so difficult today for many manufacturers.

But it takes education. It may be done in various ways—through advertising, public relations and through making safe and reliable products. It may be a formidable task but, if industry does not do it, it will not get done and conditions may worsen. If every manufacturer would do what it could to reverse the spread of social skepticism and distrust for technology, in time the trend could be changed. And it would pay dividends in decreasing products liability risks and their damages.

TORT-REFORM PROSPECTS

One of manufacturing industry's responses to products liability has been to lobby for "a change in the law." This is understandable and, from a manufacturer's viewpoint, logical. But we have seen that *products liability law* is not one discrete enactment or regulation that is easily rescinded. It is an amalgam of thousands of common law decisions, legislative acts, government agency regulations, local ordinances, and commercial business codes and standards. It is a general *body* of law that has been evolving for decades.

Some of it, like common law decisions, generally applies only to the state jurisdiction where the leading case was decided and, perhaps, others adopting the concept. Other legal bases, like regulations of federal agencies, are national in scope. Nevertheless, most companies today sell products nationally and, therefore, come under the jurisdiction of all state laws. While it may seem reasonable to want to change the law of products liability, it is much easier said than done. For, the law is really a social philosophy that permeates our way of life.

But, even if there were a single control somewhere that could switch products liability law on and off, no one would want to turn the whole thing off. Even the manufacturer most critical of products liability law is also a consumer and user of products who expects a certain level of quality, reliability and safety in those products. Should they fail and cause injury of his employees or damage to his operations, that manufacturer-user would expect there to be available a forum for hearing his complaint and administering a remedy. That forum would be a court and, without products liability law, there would be no remedy. We would be back to the days of the old English courts with their system of writs where there was no remedy for a wrong if that wrong did not correspond to some available writ.

While this may be oversimplification of the issues, the fact remains that none of us, and no company, is an island unto itself. Manufacturers of one product are users and consumers of many others. We all wear many hats. One day, as defendant in a lawsuit, I may be a manufacturer deploring products liability law; tomorrow, I may be an injured plaintiff looking to have the court right a wrong done to me through someone else's defective product. The difficult part of the question of reforming products liability law is to decide which part of it to discard and which to keep, and who should decide. Products liability law does, indeed, take on a character that varies with the side of the courtroom you happen to be on.

The thrust of the initial movement for tort reform centered about availability or, perhaps more correctly, affordability of products liability insurance or ability of a manufacturer to share its risks with insurers.[2] The sharp rise in damage claims and adverse verdicts in the 1970s created an unstable insurance market,[3] with insurers having little actuarial experience to draw upon. Rates were set largely by guesswork and everything was chaotic. Many manufacturers of high-risk products were left uninsured. This is what prompted the reported "crisis."

By now, however, the products liability insurance market has stabilized somewhat. Manufacturers have the option through the Risk Retention Act of 1981 to create self-insurance pools,[4] or can elect to share their risks with insurers at acceptable costs through applying high deductibles or through limiting their insurance purchases to "excess" coverages. Some choose to self-insure altogether. Nonetheless, even though there is a semblance of insurance stability in some sectors of the manufacturing industry, manufacturers of high-risk products still face considerable uncertainty and are living in an atmosphere just short of panic.

Since the Interagency Task Force on Products Liability was organized and the model state products liability statute drafted,[5,6] there has been a noticeable shift in rationale for reform of products liability law.[7] Whereas, initially, it centered upon availability and/or affordability of insurance coverage; it is now more concerned over adverse consequences of certain recent court decisions.

The basic motivation is still to resolve uncertainty and this has been the driving force behind recent legislative proposals. Unfortunately, drafting the model statute did little more than muddy the legal waters. A few dozen states have adopted portions of it but, to the product manufacturer marketing nationally, state enactments merely changed a few colors in the "crazy-quilt" of state products liability laws.[8,9] The manufacturer marketing products in all 50 states, with their differing liability standards, must base its product standards upon the law of the strictest state, and this can change frequently.

Greatest concern today among product manufacturers is over the potential implications of several recent court decisions which, if widely followed in other states, could have damaging consequences. In general, these are concerns over spread of "market share" theories, questions over length of "safe useful life" of a product (or the need for statutes of limitation or "repose"), legal standards and definitions for design defectiveness, admissibility of evidence of subsequent product modification, failure to warn of "unknowable" hazards, and the apparent indiscriminate increase in punitive damage awards, among others.[10-12] No doubt, this list of "most-concerned" subjects will change, depending upon directions future appellate court verdicts take.

During the past several years, there have been a number of federal legislative proposals for reform of products liability tort law.[13] Most of them have been fashioned after the model state statute that was drafted in an attempt to provide a baseline for unifying products liability rules across the states and thereby reduce uncertainty. The bills also proposed to restore "fairness" to products liability law through provisions covering many of the subjects of most current concern to manufacturers.

The most recent proposal at this writing is the Product Liability Act (S.44) proposed by Senator Robert W. Kasten, Jr. (R-Wisc.).[14] The bill became available on September 12, 1984 for Senate floor action but failed to be considered before the session adjourned. Since its provisions have broad support and represent a direction that future legislation, if enacted, could take; a copy of this bill is included in Appendix B.

The proposed Act would govern "any civil action brought against a manufacturer or product seller for loss or damage caused by a product" and would supersede any state law on matters covered by the Act.

It continues a strict liability standard for products unreasonably dangerous in construction or manufacture (*manufacturing* defects) but reverts to a negligence (or fault) standard for defective *design* or failure to warn.[15] It provides that the court (not the jury) determine amounts of punitive damages that may be awarded. The bill also contains various other provisions covering product misuse and alteration, comparative responsibility, evidentiary matters and definitions.

Critics of the proposed legislation have pointed out some inherent difficulties with it. One long-standing criticism of federal tort reform is that tort law is fundamentally a common law subject, traditionally a responsibility for states to administer. The recently proposed federally-enacted legislation establishes rules the states must follow, thereby undermining states rights. Critics also point out the difficulty in proving negligence cases and see the bill, with its negligence standard for design defectiveness, as a major step backward in providing injured victims a remedy. Understandably, consumer groups and plaintiffs' attorneys are among its strongest critics.

Supporters of the bill emphasize its benefits in regulating interstate commerce by providing uniform products liability law to replace the patchwork of 50 states' laws.[16,17] They also point to "fairness" aspects of the bill in requiring a finding of fault before imposing sanctions upon a manufacturer for defective design. They cite this provision as intrinsically fair as opposed to the current trend in a number of jurisdictions that finds the manufacturer liable for little reason other than that its products injured someone, which amounts to absolute liability.

Yet, in actual practice, enactment of legislation that calls for application of negligence principles for design defects does not represent as fundamental a change as it might seem at first. We saw in Chapter 4 that the law had gravitated toward strict liability principles mainly to relieve injured plaintiffs of procedural and evidential burdens of sustaining a claim.[18] But these devices did not, and could not, change the fact that in an action alleging defective *design* the plaintiff is questioning not the product itself but the designer's conduct—an issue squarely within the province of negligence law and its fault principle.

All things considered, federal enactment of a Product Liability Act similar in provisions to S.44 may not result in much of a change in products liability law for the manufacturer. Besides, it is not known how state courts will interpret various issues on which the legislation is silent. When in doubt over legislative intent, state courts will probably conform to previously-established concepts. Room for such state interpretation is provided for in the summary of the Act as presented to the Senate in January 1983[19] where it stated that "State law is superseded *to the extent the Act addresses an issue*" (emphasis added).

Also, it is difficult to foresee how passage of a federal Act along the lines of the S.44 draft proposal will have any long-lasting effect in deterring society in its relentless drive to secure compensation for product-related injuries. The roots of this notion go deep, are embedded in human rights and interwoven into the fabric of today's social attitudes and values. Federal products liability legislation may have an initial stabilizing influence, but it probably will not constitute a major retrenchment in tort law.

IS "NO-FAULT" INSURANCE THE ANSWER?

Since tort reform legislation may not prove to be the panacea for products liability that so many hope for, it is worth briefly reviewing other solutions that have been suggested from time to time. One is "no-fault" or social insurance.[20-22] It is a resilient concept and, while it may seem to represent a drastic change in products liability litigation, there are precedents for it.[23,24] Besides precedents for substituting a no-fault insurance system for adversary proceedings that, at considerable expense, seek to establish fault in the defendant to allow the injured plaintiff to be compensated; our tort system has, in fact, been moving on its own steadily toward such a system.

Consider development of the concept of strict liability. Its intent was to make it easier for injured victims to recover damages from presumably wealthy manufacturers. Strict liability, by definition, is liability imposed without the need for proving fault. This works quite well for *manufacturing* defects, where everyone can generally agree that the offending product is defective and compensation is justified. However, the strict liability concept causes problems over *design* defects, which must relate back to the conduct of the manufacturer. Recall that the proposed tort reform legislation (see Appendix B) retains a strict liability standard for *manufacturing* defects but reverts to a negligence (or fault) standard for design defects.

Much of the clamor for tort reform has stemmed from attempts by plaintiffs' attorneys to convince courts to expand the ambit of liability of product manufacturers to virtually assure that all plaintiffs injured by manufactured products are compensated. That is really their goal and they have said so. As we pointed out earlier, the adversary legal system has become a clumsy and inefficient mechanism for accomplishing this goal. Advocates of a no-fault insurance system for products liability are quick to point out the fact that the major amount of damage awards "won" by plaintiffs go to their attorneys, insurance investigators, expert witnesses and all the others who make their living by the adversary system.[25] The suggestion is, simply, to cut out the "middlemen."

Critics of a compulsory no-fault system for handling products-related injuries say that, like workmen's compensation, it would force a victim to accept a compromise, a predetermined (and usually inadequate) compensation in return for waiving rights to sue. They point out that this constitutes a loss of human rights to pursue claims in a court of law—rights that took decades to be recognized. (Some of this criticism might be avoided through an elective system). Furthermore, they cite that a no-fault system would eliminate the censuring function of law and its "therapeutic effect" upon manufacturers to produce safer products.[26]

However, supporters of the no-fault approach claim that the present tort system is not a deterrent to irresponsible manufacturers.[27] They indicate that a manufacturer's decisions affecting product safety are often made through a risk-benefit judgment where costs of safe products are balanced against expenses of litigation. If projected costs of making safer products exceed estimates of cost of insurance and products litigation, the product user gets an inferior product to use at his peril.

In a no-fault system, the manufacturer would, indirectly, pay for all product-related injuries through a form of compulsory insurance. The manufacturer would be motivated to produce safe products since its insurance rates would reflect its claims record. No-fault supporters cite the improvement in workplace safety that accompanied passage of workmen's compensation laws earlier in this century when manufacturers had similar incentives to reduce out-of-pocket costs.

Considering that our present tort system and some of its recent court decisions tend to lead to essentially a system of no-fault insurance; it is surprising that the concept has not been promoted more vigorously. Perhaps it is because manufacturers are convinced that pending federal tort reform legislation will be the solution.

Adoption of a no-fault basis may begin, as has been suggested,[28,29] with applying a no-fault standard for minor, undisputed and "routine" products cases. This would reserve the present adversary system for complicated cases where responsibility is sharply disputed or where damages are extensive. If the no-fault system proves effective for some classes of products cases, it may be extended to others. It seems probable, if products liability law continues its present plaintiff-favored course, that some form of no-fault insurance will eventually be adopted.[30]

PERSONAL LIABILITY

Early law was almost entirely concerned with conduct of the individual. Conduct and behavior—whether proper or improper in the eyes of the law—are personal attributes. The instrumentality of personal harm often was inanimate—knives, clubs, guns, dammed water, fire, a collapsing wall or building, sometimes escaping wild animals. Today, it may be a chemical substance, an automobile, or other manufactured product. But all these are traceable to human control, or the lack of it, in establishing liability.

Tort liability has always been concerned with human conduct. It is difficult to know at what point in the development of law inanimate and impersonal corporate entities, or companies, became acceptable substitutes for human beings as defendants in legal actions. It is possible that it began when organizations, representing interests of a group of people, were first called upon to answer for harm.

We noted previously that early industry enjoyed virtual immunity from tort action because industrial activity was considered indispensable to the community, for improving the quality of life, providing jobs and wages, and progress of civilization. In time, this immunity wore off. Yet, the willingness of courts to substitute the *corporate* "person" for human beings who control it is a compromise wherein the responsible individuals, shielded by a corporate shell, retain personal immunity to legal action.

Notwithstanding this immunity of sorts that has been enjoyed by corporate executives and managers; individual proprietors or those providing professional services have not been so immune. Nonetheless, courts have generally confined liability of engineers and other professionals to negligence, or malpractice, actions:

> [T]he vast body of malpractice law, presumably an expression of the public policy involved in this area of health care, imposes upon a dentist or physician liability only for negligent performance of his services— negligent deviation from the standards of his profession. (*Magrine v. Krasnica*)[31]

> [T]hose who sell their services for the guidance of others in their economic, financial, and personal affairs are not liable in the absence of negligence or intentional misconduct. . . Those who hire [expert professionals] are not justified in expecting infallibility, but can expect only reasonable care and competence. They purchase service, not insurance. (*Gagne v. Bertran*)[32]

Despite these limitations, professional malpractice claims (based upon negligence) have risen sharply in recent years. The potential for professional liability has become significant, particularly for medical practitioners, architects, consulting engineers in private practice, attorneys, and even marriage counsellors and clergymen. A detailed treatment of professional liability is beyond the scope of this book; however, the concerned reader may consult the references cited at the end of this chapter that summarize the issues involved.[33-38] Our immediate interest is in personal liability of individuals—executives, managers and engineers—who are responsible for manufactured products as employees of a company.

Throughout our discussion, the "product manufacturer" (the manufacturing or distribution or sales *company*) has been the focus of our attention. This is because virtually all products lawsuits have named companies, or corporate entities, as defendants. There are various reasons why this is so. The main one is that companies are expected to have financial resources for adequately compensating injured victims (and for making the time and effort of their attorneys worth while). For these reasons, primarily, they are the obvious targets.

The manufacturer is the undisputed creator of the product, the one clearly responsible for its existence, its design, features, and other characteristics. Besides being the one paid for making the product and selling it, the manufacturer makes public claims for it through advertising and other promotional channels. Also, since the design, production, marketing, sales and service of a product is a team effort, it is so much easier to name the "team" (the impersonal company) as defendant.

Nevertheless, it is a mistake to assume that the individual executive, manager, supervisor or engineer—within the corporate organization—is immune from liability. By *today's* practice, it is improbable (but not impossible) for the individual employee to be named a defendant in a products liability lawsuit. But this situation may be temporary. It is important to realize that an organization does not make decisions or products. It is the *people* within that organization that make it work and that are responsible. The public is becoming increasingly conscious of this fact.

Not many years ago it was unheard of for a company executive to be personally charged with offenses committed by or in the name of the company. Yet, we are all aware of examples in recent decades where company officials have been personally fined, and some of them jailed, for price-fixing and other violations of federal law. Most federal regulations that establish standards for personal and public safety (for example, the CPSA, FDA, EPA, OSHA and others) carry provisions for charging responsible individuals of companies with *criminal* violations for non-compliance. The following comments, already noted in Chapter 5, bear repeating in this context:[39]

> Whereas corporations can pay civil penalties, people who work for corporations pay criminal penalties. I am personally inclined in a criminal proceeding to seek out the Board Chairman or Corporate President, in addition to other officials, because I believe they are in the best position to assure corporate compliance with . . . regulations.

This is not merely an opinion of a federal official, it is law. Note the following excerpt from a 1975 decision by the United States Supreme Court in a strict liability action against the president of a national retail food chain for an FDA violation by one of its divisions:

> Thus . . . the cases . . . reveal that in providing sanctions which reach and touch the individuals who execute the corporate mission—and this is by no means necessarily confined to a single corporate agent or employee—the Act imposes not only a positive duty to seek out and remedy violations when they occur but also, and primarily, a duty to implement measures that will insure that violations will not occur. The requirements of foresight and vigilance imposed on responsible corporate agents are beyond question demanding, and perhaps onerous, but they are no more stringent than the public has a right to expect of those who voluntarily assume positions of authority in business enterprises whose services and products affect the health and well-being of the public that supports them. (*United States v. Park*)[40]

This, and other recent court decisions against corporate officials and managers, could be the beginning of a trend for plaintiffs and courts to be not content with monetary compensation and occasionally, punitive damages from the corporate treasury; but to seek out executives of companies responsible for the offensive act and charge them personally with criminal conduct.[41-45] Courts have not yet been inclined to impose criminal charges upon individuals employed by the manufacturing industry for injuries from defective products, per se, although there has been a dramatic rise in punitive damage awards against companies.[46] It appears to be only a matter of time before courts impose criminal sanctions upon executives for conscious and negligent disregard of the public safety.

Even as this is being written, news headlines are carrying reports of more than 2,000 deaths, and some 150,000 injuries, in what is being called the world's worst chemical disaster. Lethal gas leaking during the night from an American-owned pesticide plant in Bhopal, India, blanketed the city, affecting nearly a quarter-million people.

Reports are that immediately after the occurrence Indian authorities confiscated company records and arrested the plant manager on charges of "culpable homicide through negligence."[47-50] When the firm's U.S. chairman arrived in the country a few days later, he and two officials of the Indian subsidiary were also arrested and charged with "negligence and criminal corporate liability" and "criminal conspiracy." They were later released on bond.[51]

Less than two weeks before the India disaster, 452 people were killed and 4,248 injured when a liquefied natural gas (LNG) plant in Mexico exploded, forcing evacuation of 100,000 nearby residents from the Mexico City suburb.[52]

The tone of the news reports and commentaries on these incidents echoes the fear, grief and anger over human tragedies caused by what the uninformed and bewildered public perceive to be a well-meaning technological monster that has run amok.[53-55] As expressed by one news commentator,

> Human progress came up against human frailty . . . a modern parable of
> the risks and rewards originally engendered by the Industrial Revolution:
> Frankenstein's wonder becoming Frankenstein's monster.[56]

It is not difficult to understand why some groups feel that payment of fines or damages by wealthy corporations is not an effective deterrent to prevent personal injuries and widespread tragedies. Should such public sentiment intensify and spread, company executives, managers and even responsible engineers are likely to be increasingly named as defendants, not only in civil cases, but in criminal actions as well.

No one employed by industry and, certainly, no engineer worthy of the title, can remain complacent over such incidents and the increasing hostility in some quarters of our society toward technology. As said at the outset, each of us has a *personal* duty and responsibility to assure that whatever we do, make or say does not hurt other people. There has always been a moral duty to do so but, in addition to that, there is now legal duty. Besides this fairly obvious need, we must also be sensitive to the emotional response of the uneducated and unsophisticated members of society and attempt to appreciate their real or perceived fears of technology.

Some commentators and behavioral analysts feel that development of nuclear weapons triggered the public sentiment that is running against industry and technology today.[57-59] The existence of such implements of mass destruction made it clear to everyone, perhaps for the first time, that man's technology had reached the point where it was capable of destroying civilization as we know it. Whether this is or is not the reason for increased apprehensions over technology is immaterial to us now. The fact is that this fear and disillusionment are all around us and we, as responsible professionals—engineers, managers, and industrial executives—are at the focal point of it.

It is time for informed technologists to recognize how our climate has changed and to determine what we must do about it. It is, in every sense of the word, critical to the livelihood and career of each one of us.

There is, of course, no question in minds of thinking people that the civilized world is better off because of advancements wrought by technology. Yet, like all things, there is a price to pay. It is easy to glibly accept this when we and our families are, for the moment, safe from its effects. But we, too, quickly begin to question whether its benefits are worth the price when its costs hit us personally, and we demand instant payment.

It is equally as wrong to condemn technology as it is to ignore its costs, risks, side-effects and uninformed society's backlash. At the beginning of this book I said that there were no easy solutions to products liability problems. As difficult and complex as its issues are, there is too much to lose to choose to look the other way. We must resolve to face it, learn all we can about it, and realize that what we do and how well we do it will affect other people out there. Once we do that, we will be well on our way to avoiding products lawsuits and their damages. And, in the process, we might even be responsible for restoring some of society's faith in our profession.

REFERENCES

1. Owen, D.G., *Rethinking the Policies of Strict Products Liability*, 33 Vanderbilt Law Review 681 (1980).
2. U.S. Interagency Task Force on Product Liability, *Insurance Report*, U.S. Department of Commerce (1977), available from National Technical Information Service, Springfield, VA 22161.
3. Figures 2-1 through 2-3 (Chapter 2).
4. *The Risk Retention Act*, Public Law 97-45 (September 1981).
5. *A Draft Uniform Product Liability Law*, 44 Federal Register 2996 (1979), and the *Model Uniform Product Liability Act*, 44 Federal Register 62714 (1979).
6. Dworkin, T., *Product Liability Reform and the Uniform Product Liability Act*, 60 Nebraska Law Review 50 (1981).
7. *Unsafe Products: The Great Debate over Blame and Punishment*, Business Week 96 (April 30, 1984).

8. 9 Product Safety & Liability Reporter (Current Report) 951 (December 18, 1981).

9. *State Regulations Rush In Where Washington No Longer Treads*, Business Week 124 (September 19, 1983).

10. Weber, O.J., *Mass Tort Litigation: The Pot Boils Over*, 6 Journal of Products Liability 273-96 (1983).

11. Hirsch, D.J., *Bichler and Sindell: Generic Drug Products and Liability Without Causation*, 6 Journal of Products Liability 253-72 (1983).

12. Walsh, M.W., *Filing of Punitive Damage Claims Is Focus of Increasing Controversy*, The Wall Street Journal, p. 27, col. 4 (November 12, 1984).

13. For examples, see *Congressional Record*, No. 188 - Part II, Vol. 127, 97th Congress, First Session, House of Representatives, H.R. 5261 (December 16, 1981), identical to H.R. 1675 introduced during the 96th Congress; and *Congressional Record*, No. 2, Vol. 128, 97th Congress, Second Session, House of Representatives, H.R. 5214 (January 26, 1982).

14. *Congressional Record*, No. 4 - Part II, Vol. 129, 98th Congress, First Session, Senate, S283, S.44 (January 26, 1983).

15. Robb, G.C., *The Effect of the Proposed Federal Product Liability Act on Current Law Regarding Liability for Defectively Designed Products*, 6 Journal of Products Liability 147-70 (1983).

16. *A Liability Patchwork Congress May Replace*, Business Week 34 (May 31, 1982).

17. *The Quest for Product Liability Reform*, Quality 59 (November 1983).

18. *Barker v. Lull Engineering Co.*, 20 Cal.3d 413, 143 Cal. Rptr. 225, 573 P.2d 443 (1978).

19. *Congressional Record, supra* reference 14.

20. O'Connell, J., *Ending Insult to Injury*, Bulletin No. 67, The University of Illinois Press (1975).

21. Igbokwe, E.M., *No-Fault Insurance and Products Liability: A Proposal for Legislative Review*, 4 Journal of Products Liability 1-10 (1981).

22. Franklin, M.A., *Replacing the Negligence Lottery, Compensation and Selective Reimbursement*, 53 Virginia Law Review 774 (1967).

23. In this connection, review the portions of Chapter 3 that deal with workmen's compensation laws and their effects on society's attitudes toward compensation for product-related injuries.

24. Blum, W.J., and Kalven, H., *Ceilings, Costs and Compulsion in Auto Compensation Legislation*, 1973 Utah Law Review 341.

25. O'Connell, J., *supra* reference 20.

26. Todd, B., *Rebuttal to No-Fault Insurance and Products Liability: A Proposal for Legislative Review by Eric M. Igbokwe*, 4 Journal of Products Liability 333-40 (1981).

27. Calabresi, G., *Optimal Deterrence and Accidents*, 84 Yale Law Journal 656 (1975).

28. White, G.E., *Tort Law in America—An Intellectual History* 235-43, Oxford University Press, New York, NY (1980).

29. O'Connell, J., *An Alternative to Abandoning Tort Liability: Elective No-Fault for Many Kinds of Injuries*, 60 Minnesota Law Review 501 (1976).

30. For a comprehensive summary of the subject of tort reform, see Prosser, W.L., Wade, J.W., and Schwartz, V.E., *Cases and Materials on Torts*, Sixth

Edition, Chapter XXII, "Major Statutory Modifications in Tort Law, Including No-Fault Compensation Systems," 1177-1261, The Foundation Press, Inc., Mineola, NY (1976).

31. *Magrine v. Krasnica*, 94 N.J. Super. 228, 227 A.2d 539 (1967), *affirmed* 100 N.J. Super. 223, 241 A.2d 637 (1968), *affirmed* 53 N.J. 259, 250 A.2d 129 (1969).

32. *Gagne v. Bertran*, 43 Cal.2d 481, 275 P.2d 15 (1954).

33. Seybold, R.M., *Liability of Architects or Engineers to Their Clients*, in *Liability of Architects and Engineers* 3-22 (D.J. Hirsch and A.K. Karpowitz, eds.) DRI Monograph Vol. 1982, No. 1, Defense Research Institute, 750 North Lake Shore Drive, Chicago, IL 60611 (1982). The reader is also referred to the excellent bibliography, dealing with liability of architects and engineers, on pages 52 and 53 of this DRI Monograph.

34. Finster, E.H., *Liability Suit Threat Discourages Engineers*, Consulting Engineer 54-58, 61 (November 1978).

35. Peckner, D., *Products Liability and the Engineer*, Metal Progress 42-46 (September 1977).

36. Fogle, F.D., *Personal Liability of Engineers*, Proceedings PLP-77E at 129-36, Product Liability Prevention Conference, Hasbrouck Heights, NJ (August 22-24, 1977).

37. Freeman, J.A., *Personal Responsibility and Personal Liability*, PLP-78 Proceedings at 89-92, Product Liability Prevention Conference, Philadelphia, PA (August 21-23, 1978), IEEE Catalog No. 78CH1370-GR.

38. Wereszczynski, J., *Professional Liability Strategies*, Consulting Engineer 85-89 (October 1984).

39. Simpson, R.O., former Chairman of the CPSC, quoted by David M. Natelson in *Quality Assurance—A Primary Management Tool for Products Liability Prevention*, Proceedings PLP-77E at 57, Products Liability Prevention Conference, Hasbrouck Heights, NJ (August 22-24, 1977).

40. *United States v. Park*, 421 U.S. 658, 95 S. Ct. 1903, 44 L. Ed.2d 489 (1975).

41. *Lytell v. Hurshfield*, 408 So.2d 1344 (La. Sup. Ct., 1982).

42. Abrams, N., *Criminal Liability of Corporate Officers for Strict Liability Offenses—A Comment on Dotterweich and Park*, 28 UCLA Law Review 463 (1981).

43. Taylor, R.E., *U.S. Increases Prosecutions of Polluters*, The Wall Street Journal (October 27, 1983).

44. Meier, B., *EPA Criminal Unit Gets Police Powers with Right to Arms*, The Wall Street Journal, p. 28, col. 2 (May 3, 1984).

45. *Florida Electric Firm, 3 Executives Charged in Toxic-Dump Case*, The Wall Street Journal, p. 32, col. 3 (October 28, 1983).

46. Figure 2-3 (Chapter 2).

47. The New York Times (December 5 and 6, 1984).

48. Hall, A., *The Bhopal Tragedy Has Union Carbide Reeling*, Business Week 32 (December 17, 1984).

49. Iyer, P., *India's Night of Death*, Time 22-26, 31 (December 17, 1984).

50. Dobrzynski, J.H., Glaberson, W.B., King, R.W., Powell, W.J. Jr., and Helm, L., *Union Carbide Fights for Its Life*, (Cover Story) Business Week 52-56 (December 24, 1984).

51. *Id.* at 24.

52. The New York Times, p. 1, col. 6 (November 20, 1984).

53. The New York Times, pp. 1, 8, 10 (December 7, 1984).

54. Meislin, R.J., *In Devastated Mexican Area, the Anger Persists*, The New York Times, p. 8, col. 3 (December 6, 1984).

55. Hall, A., Recio, M., Cahan, V., and Miles, G.L., *A Backlash Threatening Chemical Makers,* Business Week 60-61 (December 24, 1984).

56. Rosenblatt, R., *All the World Gasped*, Time 20 (December 17, 1984).

57. Broad, W.J., *Risks and Benefits*, The New York Times, p. 10, col. 1 (December 7, 1984).

58. Parisi, A.J., *The Hard Lesson of Bhopal: It Can Happen Again*, Business Week 61 (December 24, 1984).

59. DuPont, R.L., *The Nuclear Power Phobia*, Business Week 14, 16 (September 7, 1981).

Appendix A

Product Liability Investigation Checklist

A. *Identify the Product*
  1. Did Your Client Manufacture the Product?
     (a) Establish chain of distribution or lessor names and addresses (including states of incorporation, sales, manufacturing, etc.) of all organizations and individuals involved, including nature/date(s) of involvement.
        1. Manufacturer
        2. Component parts manufacturers
        3. Assemblers
        4. Wholesalers
        5. Distributors and other intermediaries
        6. Private parties having ownership prior to claimant's contact with the product
        7. Repair/service personnel
        8. Transporters
        9. Jobbers
        10. Retailers
        11. Installers
     (b) For each of the above relationships:
        1. What did they do?
        2. Degree of control exercised or exercisable?
        3. Was package opened?
        4. Documentation of sale (including date & price)
        5. Is sale/manufacture of this product part of business?
        6. Intended market
        7. Volume of production/sales of this type of product
        8. Complaint history:
           —knowledge of problems (defects, failures, dangerous properties)
           —incidence of problems
           —disposition/response to said problems
           —corrective action: what, when, how, how costly, effectiveness
           —litigation/claims (where are the claims files)
           —insurance carriers (their knowledge)
           —inspection and advice provided to the manufacturer by the insurance company's loss prevention personnel
     (c) Where is delivery presumed; where does sale become final?
     (d) Arrival to user in unchanged condition.

  2. Acquire the product (or remains thereof); identify and preserve the same.
     (a) Physical description, color photograph or sketch for identification, including different angles
        1. dimensions
        2. weight
        3. color
        4. shape
        5. identification plates or other identifying numbers or codes
     (b) If a complicated process or equipment is involved, video tape or movies may be taken
     (c) Photos/sketches of surrounding area
     (d) Obtain product label (not a photocopy) to reflect colors used:
        1. Any labeling changes (names/addresses of persons responsible for)
        2. Is labeler the manufacturer?
        3. Any statutory labeling requirements?
        4. What is permanence of label and how is it applied to product?
     (e) Obtain product package, if relevant:
        1. Adequacy for shipment
        2. What is printed on it?
        2. Any Statutory packaging/handling standards?

    4. Is packager the manufacturer?
(f) Guards/safety devices
    1. Were any provided? (sold and delivered with product)
    2. Would they prevent injury?
    3. Are they *now* provided?
    4. Were they physically affixed at time of installation?
(g) Product identification data may be indicative of date of manufacturing; may also be useful in answering design change and chain of control questions:
    1. Serial #
    2. Model #
    3. Lot #
    4. Batch #
    5. Patent #
    6. Names/aliases/brand names
(h) Do not change or lose the product.

B. *Testing of Product*
    1. If an insurance client regularly tests the product prior to turning the investigation over to the attorney, please indicate to them that they should not waive the attorney's right to have further testing done by an additional expert.
    2. If "destructive testing" is necessary and deemed to be appropriate, get agreement from opposing counsel and/or court order. Obtain duplicate product for comparison testing (if necessary).
    3. Arrange for testing by (any or all of the following)
        (a) Manufacturer of the product
        (b) An expert reviewing the product (but not necessarily the designated expert)
        (c) Designated expert

C. *Acquire General Product Data*
    1. Function/utilization of the product
        (a) How it works
        (b) What it is intended to do
        (c) Other *known* uses (common but unintended)
        (d) Other *possible* uses
        (e) How it was being used
        (f) How dangerous is product in normal use?
        (g) Safe alternative(s)
    2. Defectiveness/harmfulness of the product
        (a) Nature/type/description
        (b) When discovered?
        (c) By whom?
        (d) How?
        (e) What was done with this information?
        (f) Probable cause(s) of defect?
        (g) Obviousness?
    3. Product life data
        (a) Age of product?
        (b) Expected life, basis for this
        (c) Effect of time
        (d) Conditions/uses known to shorten life of product or to cause failures
        (e) Effect of the elements on the product
        (f) Maintenance recommendations
    4. Warranties
        (a) Warranty defenses

  —relationship between injured party and purchaser
  —inspection by purchaser before sale
  —course of dealing and usage of trade
  —notice of defect; when; form; content; to whom; waiver

(b) Express warranty
  —What did the seller say to the buyer as affirmation of fact to induce the sale? Be specific.
  —Did buyer in fact rely on this affirmation?
  —Was any description of the goods made part of the basis of the bargain?
  —What did the description of goods say?
  —Was any sample or model made part of the basis of the bargain?
  —Is this sample or model available?

5. Relationship between dealer and manufacturer
 (a) Is there a vendor's endorsement or contract of indemnity?
 (b) Was product in a sealed container?
 (c) Name, address and relationship of dealer selling product (i.e., company branch office or independent sales agent)

6. Makes of components or ingredients involved:
 (a) Identify manufacturer of components or ingredients and specifications, if any, furnished to such manufacturers
 (b) If failure of a component part is indicated, determine the source of the component part, when acquired and installed by assured and obtain copies of any written indemnity agreements between component parts manufacturer and assured

7. Design drawings and design plates, including all the dates of and reasons and/or purposes for any design changes, design criteria and design testing (as related to the product):
 (a) Patents:
  —was any patented process used to produce the product?
  —who holds the proprietary rights to the product?
 (b) Identification of design, including qualifications
 (c) Copies of specification sheets and prints showing design and design modifications
 (d) Obtain description of each improvement made on product designs for safety and protection of the operator
 (e) Name(s) and address(es) of individual(s) responsible for design and qualifications in terms of education, publications, professional society memberships, etc. of individual(s) responsible for design
 (f) Was any outside consultant engaged to assist in the design?

8. Manuals: installation, operation and maintenance; warnings, parts; owners' manual, instructions furnished with product
 (a) Check for updating

9. Quality Control
 (a) Was any risk or hazard analysis performed on the product both before and after manufacture?
 (b) What type of quality control testing is done at the site of manufacture?
  —type of inspection and test conducted, by whom and when?
  —objectives of inspection/test program
  —who are responsible for said quality control program?
  —who are responsible for said quality control problem?
  —is the quality control program the result of any industry/government standards?
  —if test results are negative what, if anything, is done?
  —what is management's feeling with regard to quality control?
  —what is done with defective units identified?
 (c) Are any tests done subsequent to installation of product?

10. Regulations governing product
    (a) State
    (b) Federal
    (c) Industry
    (d) State of the art
    (e) Underwriter Laboratory standards
11. Warnings
    (a) Warnings in literature accompanying product
    (b) Warnings affixed to product by plate or other device
    (c) Warnings affixed to packaging
    (d) Company's experience in this field

D. *Acquire Specific Product Data*
    1. In addition to the general product data mentioned in the previous subsection, specific data and records should be obtained regarding the product which is the subject of the lawsuit in all of the areas mentioned in Section C. In addition, the following should be obtained.
       (a) Date of manufacture of specific product
       (b) When, how and to whom product originally sold
       (c) Subsequent substantial changes to the condition of the product
       (d) Warranty claims made
           (1) If written warranty or guarantee given to customer, obtain a copy of same
           (2) Any disclaimers/limitations of warranty
           (3) Names/addresses of authors
       (e) If product used by claimant, his employer, request information from assured or dealer tracing history of product, including ownership, modifications, condition, repair and complaints as to any malfunction.
    2. Name of Salesmen:
       (a) Did salesman give a demonstration? If so, get the form of the demonstration.
       (b) Is salesman still employed by company? If so, obtain statement.
       (c) If injured party received training in use of the product, what was the exact substance of the course?
    3. Documents incident to sale, including those already listed in contracts, change of orders, telephone memos, invoices, correspondence, any documents relating to installation, maintenance, operation, repair, inspection and complaints, and all advertising and sales literature (pamphlets, brochures, radio-TV, direct mail, newspapers, magazines or trade journals); proposals and revised proposals.
       (a) Where your suspected product is only a part of an assembly or system, determine who sold and recommended the system, and especially who set it up and the establishment of work rules with regard to the operation of the system. Frequently an entirely different entity is employed to furnish safety devices, fail-safes, electrical disconnects, photoelectric cells, et al.
       (b) Date of sale and delivery and name of original customer.
       (c) Determine exact terms and conditions under which product was sold insofar as such terms and conditions are not expressly set forth in above-mentioned documents.

E. *Acquire information with reference to competing products*
    1. Obtain information regarding similar products to establish a general state of the trade or product and alert counsel to potential warnings that competing products may carry.
    2. Obtain advertising and sales literature of competing product.
    3. Obtain competitors' names, addresses and products by brand name.

F. *Investigation of the occurrence itself — who, what, when, where, why and how?*

1. Standard information on the event itself.
   (a) Date
   (b) Time
   (c) Weather
   (d) Names and addresses of witnesses, statements they made at the time of the event
   (e) Description of precisely how the injury occurred, in minute detail (including sketches if appropriate), visual or audio indications of impending trouble
   (f) Was the problem covered in instructions, warnings and warranties?
   (g) The key question: why was the claimant where he was?

2. For accident involving operation of equipment:
   (a) Determine position of claimant (operator) at time of accident
   (b) Determine exact manner in which claimant was utilizing equipment;
   (c) Obtain claimant's prior experience with equipment, including familiarity through cleaning, etc. of moving parts, use and purpose of equipment
   (d) Ascertain whether any instructions were given to claimant prior to accident, including when such instructions were given, by whom, and the substance of the instructions
   (e) Determine whether or not warning plates and guards were in place at time of accident
   (f) If such plates and/or guards were removed prior to the accident, determine when they were so removed, by whom and the circumstances surrounding their removal
   (g) Was claimant guilty of any negligent conduct in method of operation? If so, specify nature of negligence
   (h) Was dealer or manufacturer ever made aware of any alleged defect or malfunction prior to the accident and, if so, obtain names of the individuals making the complaint and to whom the complaint was made, the date or dates when the complaint was made and the surrounding circumstances.
   (i) Was equipment ever serviced or repaired by assured or its dealer prior to accident?
   (j) If repairs and/or service were made, name the repairman, when the repairs were made and the nature of service or repair
   (k) Request copies of any and all records pertaining to service and repairs.

3. Identify and obtain copies of any official investigations:
   (a) Police investigation
   (b) OSHA investigation
   (c) Consumer Product Safety Commission Investigation
   (d) If an industrial accident, the workmen's compensation file
   (e) Recall
   (f) Users' maintenance records
   (g) TV station or newspaper article on the incident or the product.

4. The claimant's knowledge of the product
   (a) Did the injured claimant have exposure to
      —training
      —oral instructions
      —labels
      —brochure
      —what documentation exists for this?
   (b) If product had been altered, did claimant know?
   (c) If the product was worn out, was the claimant aware of it?

5. The injured claimant/plaintiff
   (a) Full name; nicknames; aliases
   (b) Address

(c) Age

(d) Sex

(e) Occupation

(f) Education

(g) Salary

(h) Loss of earnings from injury — income tax returns from prior years

(i) Career objectives

(j) Marital status

(k) Name of spouse, address of spouse, occupation of spouse

(l) Children's names and addresses

(m) Injury; nature; scope; which one(s) (is/are) permanent

(n) Medical history (Complete medical history reviewing medical records in depth to determine whether they refer to any other hospitals or doctors, whose reports and records should also be obtained in an effort to determine whether or not present injuries are the result of pre-existing injuries or aggravation of same.)

(o) Medical documentation of injury

　　(1) Bills, hospital records, doctors' records, prescriptions, prognosis, identify experts

　　(2) Medical personnel involved in treatment of the injury, including nurses, ambulance attendants, physicians, hospitals, passers-by

(p) If injured claimant is a business what are —

　　—opportunities to replace defective products from lost profits, effects on goodwill?

G. *Arrange a Conference with Client at Place of Product Manufacture*

　1. Consider having defense counsel present even if only in the claim state

　2. Coordinate visit with staff counsel or risk manager

　3. Arrange to have present all material previously gathered and have available insured's top level technical personnel

　　(a) Defense counsel should be present so that privilege and work product may be claimed

　4. Have available new product or one similar to it fully assembled and during assembly

　5. Discuss at least the following:

　　(a) Pre-design criteria and design, manufacturing process; compare with competitors

　　(b) The selection and use of raw materials and components

　　(c) Similar claims:

　　　(1) Any interrogatories answered in other litigation

　　　(2) Persons deposed in the litigation

　　(d) Instructions and warnings

　　　(1) This should be coordinated with the hiring of defense counsel. Any preliminary opinions should be verbal — later claim work product,

　　(e) Applicable governmental regulations

　　(f) Speculate on the cause of action; including possible exemplary damage claim

　　(g) Explore packaging or containers

　6. Arrange for expert from company represented and an outside expert (university professor versus active practitioners). Check with company on outside expert they may desire.

H. *Obtaining an Expert*

　1. Decide whether or not an outsider or independent expert is needed or whether someone from the manufacturer or plant is or can be used

　2. Meet and talk with experts

3. Identify through research and cooperation with your defense consultants/expert applicable standards and treaties
4. Visit site of accident if possible with expert.

Appendix B

Product Liability Act

II

98TH CONGRESS
1ST SESSION
S. 44

To regulate interstate commerce by providing for a uniform product liability law, and for other purposes.

———————————

IN THE SENATE OF THE UNITED STATES

JANUARY 26 (legislative day, JANUARY 25), 1983

Mr. BAKER (for Mr. KASTEN) (for himself, Mr. PERCY, Mr. GORTON, Mr. STAF-FORD, Mr. HELMS, Mr. HATCH, Mr. LUGAR, Mr. GARN, Mr. NICKLES, Mr. QUAYLE, and Mr. GLENN) introduced the following bill; which was read twice and referred to the Committee on Commerce, Science, and Transportation

———————————

A BILL

To regulate interstate commerce by providing for a uniform product liability law, and for other purposes.

1   *Be it enacted by the Senate and House of Representa-*
2   *tives of the United States of America in Congress assembled,*

3   SHORT TITLE

4   SECTION 1. This Act may be cited as the "Product Lia-
5   bility Act".

6   DEFINITIONS

7   SEC. 2. As used in this Act—

8   (1) "claimant" means any person who brings a
9   product liability action, and if such an action is brought

2

1   through or on behalf of an estate, the term includes the

2   claimant's decedent, or if such an action is brought

3   through or on behalf of a minor, the term includes the

4   claimant's parent or guardian;

5   (2) "clear and convincing evidence" is that meas-

6   ure or degree of proof that will produce in the mind of

7   the trier of fact a firm belief or conviction as to the

8   truth of the allegations sought to be established; the

9   level of proof required to satisfy this standard is more

10   than that required under preponderance of the evi-

11   dence, but less than that required for proof beyond a

12   reasonable doubt;

13   (3) "commerce" means trade, traffic, commerce,

14   or transportation (A) between a place in a State and

15   any place outside of that State; or (B) which affects

16   trade, commerce, or transportation described in clause

17   (A);

18   (4) "express warranty" means any affirmation of

19   fact, promise, or description relating to a product;

20   (5) "harm" means (A) physical damage to proper-

21   ty other than the product itself; (B) personal physical

22   illness, injury, or death of the claimant; or (C) mental

23   anguish or emotional harm of the claimant caused by

24   the claimant's personal physical illness or injury;

25   "harm" does not include commercial loss;

3

1   (6) "manufacturer" means (A) any person who is

2 engaged in a business to design or formulate and to

3 produce, create, make, or construct any product (or

4 component part of a product), including a product

5 seller, distributor, or retailer of products with respect

6 to any product to the extent that such a product seller,

7 distributor, or retailer designs or formulates and pro-

8 duces, creates, makes, or constructs the product before

9 that product seller, distributor, or retailer sells the

10 product; or (B) any product seller not described in

11 clause (A) which holds itself out as a manufacturer to

12 the user of the product;

13   (7) "person" means any individual, corporation,

14 company, association, firm, partnership, society, joint

15 stock company, or any other entity (including any gov-

16 ernmental entity);

17   (8) "practical technological feasibility" means the

18 technical, medical, and scientific knowledge relating to

19 the safety of a product which, at the time of production

20 or manufacture of a product, was developed, available

21 and capable of use in the manufacture of a product,

22 and economically feasible for use by a manufacturer;

23   (9) "preponderance of the evidence" is that meas-

24 ure or degree of proof which, by the weight, credit,

25 and value of the aggregate evidence on either side, es-

4

1   tablishes that it is more probable than not that a fact

2   occurred or did not occur;

3   (10) "product" means any object, substance, mix-

4   ture or raw material in a gaseous, liquid or solid state

5   which is capable of delivery itself, or as an assembled

6   whole in a mixed or combined state or as a component

7   part or ingredient, which is produced for introduction

8   into trade or commerce, which has intrinsic economic

9   value, and which is intended for sale or lease to per-

10   sons for commercial or personal use; "product" does

11   not include human tissue or organs;

12   (11) "product seller" means a person who, in the

13   course of a business conducted for that purpose, sells,

14   distributes, leases, installs, prepares, blends, packages,

15   labels, markets, repairs, maintains, or otherwise is in-

16   volved in placing a product in the stream of commerce;

17   but does not include—

18   (A) a seller of real property;

19   (B) a provider of professional services in any

20   case in which the sale or use of a product is inci-

21   dental to the transaction and the essence of the

22   transaction is the furnishing of judgment, skill, or

23   services; or

24   (C) any person who—

5

1   (i) acts in only a financial capacity with

2   respect to the sale of a product; and

3   (ii) leases a product under a lease ar-

4   rangement in which the selection, possession,

5   maintenance, and operation of the product

6   are controlled by a person other than the

7   lessor;

8   (12) "product user" means any person, including

9   the claimant's employer, who owns, operates, or has

10   control of a product;

11   (13) "reasonably anticipated conduct" means the

12   conduct which would be expected of a reasonably pru-

13   dent person who is likely to use or become exposed to

14   the product in the same or similar circumstances; and

15   (14) "State" means any State of the United

16   States, the District of Columbia, the Commonwealth of

17   Puerto Rico, the Virgin Islands, Guam, American

18   Samoa, the Northern Mariana Islands, the Trust Terri-

19   tory of the Pacific Islands, and any other territory or

20   possession of the United States.

21   PREEMPTION OF OTHER LAWS

22   SEC. 3. (a) This Act governs any civil action brought

23   against a manufacturer or product seller for loss or damage

24   caused by a product, including any action which before the

25   effective date of this Act would have been based on: (1) strict

6

1 or absolute liability in tort; (2) negligence or gross negli-

2 gence; (3) breach of express or implied warranty; (4) failure

3 to discharge a duty to warn or instruct; or (5) any other

4 theory that is the basis for an award for damages for loss or

5 damage caused by a product. Any civil action brought against

6 a manufacturer or product seller for harm caused by a prod-

7 uct is a product liability action.

8   (b) No person may recover for any loss or damage

9 caused by a product except to the extent that the loss or

10 damage constitutes harm. A civil action for loss or damage

11 caused to a product itself or for commercial loss is not a

12 product liability action, and shall be governed by applicable

13 commercial or contract law.

14   (c) This Act supersedes any State law regarding matters

15 governed by this Act.

16   (d) The district courts of the United States shall not

17 have jurisdiction over any civil action arising under this Act,

18 based on sections 1331 or 1337 of title 28, United States

19 Code.

20   RESPONSIBILITY OF MANUFACTURERS

21   SEC. 4. (a) In any product liability action, a manufactur-

22 er is liable to a claimant if—

23   (1) the claimant establishes by a preponderance of

24   the evidence that—

7

1   (A) the product was unreasonably dangerous

2   in construction or manufacture, as defined in sec-

3   tion 5(a);

4   (B) the product was unreasonably dangerous

5   in design or formulation, as defined in section

6   5(b);

7   (C) the product was unreasonably dangerous

8   because the manufacturer failed to provide ade-

9   quate warnings or instructions about a danger

10   connected with the product or about the proper

11   use of the product, as defined in section 6; or

12   (D) the product was unreasonably dangerous

13   because the product did not conform to an express

14   warranty made by the manufacturer with respect

15   to the product, as defined in section 7; and

16   (2) the claimant establishes by a preponderance of

17   the evidence that the unreasonably dangerous aspect of

18   the product was a proximate cause of the harm com-

19   plained of by the claimant.

20   (b) The claimant must introduce sufficient evidence to

21 allow a reasonable person, by a preponderance of the evi-

22 dence, to make the determinations specified in subsection (a).

23   (c)(1) A claimant may not establish any fact necessary to

24 make the determinations described in subsection (a) by show-

25 ing that the identical issue of fact was determined adversely

8

1 to the manufacturer in another action by another claimant

2 unless both actions were based on harm caused by the same

3 event in which two or more persons were harmed.

4   (2) A manufacturer may not establish any fact necessary

5 to make the determinations described in subsection (a) by

6 showing that the identical issue of fact was determined ad-

7 versely to another claimant in another action against that

8 manufacturer unless both actions were based on harm caused

9 by the same event in which two or more persons were

10 harmed and the claimant is the same as or is in privity with

11 the claimant in the other action.

12   PRODUCT CONSTRUCTION AND DESIGN

13   SEC. 5. (a) A product is unreasonably dangerous in con-

14 struction or manufacture if, when the product left the control

15 of the manufacturer, it deviated in a material way—

16   (1) from the design specifications, formula, or per-

17   formance standards of the manufacturer; or

18   (2) from otherwise identical units manufactured to

19   the same manufacturing specification or formula.

20   (b) A product is unreasonably dangerous in design or

21 formulation if, at the earlier of the time of manufacture or

22 Government certification of the product, a reasonably pru-

23 dent manufacturer in the same or similar circumstances

24 would not have used the design or formulation that the man-

9

1 ufacturer used. A product is not unreasonably dangerous in

2 design or formulation unless—

3   (1) the manufacturer knew or, based on knowl-

4   edge which was reasonably accepted in the scientific,

5   technical, or medical community for the existence of

6   the danger which caused the claimant's harm, should

7   have known about the danger which allegedly caused

8   the claimant's harm; and

9   (2) a means to eliminate the danger that caused

10   the harm was within practical technological feasibility.

11   (c) A product is not unreasonably dangerous in design or

12 formulation if the harm was caused by an unavoidably dan-

13 gerous aspect of a product. As used in this paragraph, an

14 "unavoidably dangerous aspect" means that aspect of a prod-

15 uct which could not, in light of knowledge which was reason-

16 ably accepted in the scientific, technical, or medical commu-

17 nity at the time of manufacture, have been eliminated with-

18 out seriously impairing the effectiveness with which the prod-

19 uct performs its intended function or the desirability, econom-

20 ic and otherwise, of the product to the person who uses or

21 consumes it.

22   (d) A product is not unreasonably dangerous in design or

23 formulation if the harm was caused by an unsafe aspect of a

24 product which was an inherent characteristic of the product

25 and which would be recognized by the ordinary person who

10

1 uses or consumes the product with the ordinary knowledge

2 common to the community.

3   (e) An alternative design or formulation is evidence that

4 a product was unreasonably dangerous in design or formula-

5 tion only if the claimant establishes that, at the time of the

6 manufacture of the product—

7   (1) the manufacturer knew or, based on knowl-

8   edge which was reasonably accepted in the scientific,

9   technical, or medical community for the existence of

10   the alternative design, should have known about the

11   alternative design; and

12   (2) the alternative design or formulation would

13   have—

14   (A) utilized only science and technology

15   which was reasonably accepted in the scientific,

16   technical, or medical community and which was

17   within practical technological feasibility;

18   (B) prevented the claimant's harm and pro-

19   vided equivalent or better overall safety than the

20   chosen design or formula. The overall safety of

21   the alternative design or formula is better than

22   the chosen design or formula if the hazards it

23   eliminates are greater than any new hazards it

24   creates for any persons and for any uses; and

11

1   (C) been desirable, functionally, economical-

2   ly, and otherwise, to the person who uses or con-

3   sumes it.

4   PRODUCT WARNINGS OR INSTRUCTIONS

5   SEC. 6. (a) A product is unreasonably dangerous be-

6 cause of the failure of the manufacturer to provide warnings

7 or instructions about a danger connected with the product or

8 about the proper use of the product if—

9   (1) necessary warnings or instructions were not

10   provided, under subsection (b); or

11   (2) post-manufacture warnings or instructions

12   were not provided, under subsection (c).

13   (b) A product is unreasonably dangerous for lack of nec-

14 essary warnings or instructions if the claimant establishes by

15 a preponderance of the evidence that at the time the product

16 was sold—

17   (1) the manufacturer knew or, based on knowl-

18   edge which was reasonably accepted in the scientific,

19   technical, or medical community for the existence of

20   the danger which caused the claimant's harm, should

21   have known about the danger which allegedly caused

22   the claimant's harm;

23   (2) the manufacturer failed to provide the warn-

24   ings or instructions that a reasonably prudent manufac-

25   turer in the same or similar circumstances would have

12

1   provided with respect to the danger which caused the

2   harm alleged by the claimant, given the likelihood that

3   the product would cause harm of the type alleged by

4   the claimant and given the seriousness of that harm;

5   (3) the manufacturer failed to provide those warn-

6   ings or instructions to the claimant or to another

7   person in accordance with subsection (d)(1); and

8   (4) those warnings or instructions, if provided,

9   would have led a reasonably prudent product user

10   either to decline to use the product or to use it in a

11   manner so as to avoid harm of the type alleged by the

12   claimant.

13   (c)(1) A product is unreasonably dangerous for lack of

14   post-manufacture warnings or instructions if the claimant es-

15   tablishes by a preponderance of the evidence that—

16   (A) after the product was manufactured, the man-

17   ufacturer knew or, based on knowledge which was rea-

18   sonably accepted in the scientific, technical, or medical

19   community for the existence of the danger which

20   caused the claimant's harm, should have known about

21   the danger which allegedly caused the claimant's harm;

22   and

23   (B) post-manufacture warnings or instructions

24   would have been provided by a reasonably prudent

25   manufacturer in the same or similar circumstances,

13

1   given the likelihood that the product would cause harm

2   of the type alleged by the claimant and given the seri-

3   ousness of that harm.

4   (2) A product is not unreasonably dangerous under this

5   subsection if the manufacturer made reasonable efforts to

6   provide post-manufacture warnings or instructions to a prod-

7   uct user or to another person, in accordance with subsection

8   (d)(1).

9   (d)(1) A product is not unreasonably dangerous for lack

10   of either necessary or post-manufacture warnings or instruc-

11   tions if those warnings or instructions were provided to—

12   (A) a person, including an employer, who could

13   reasonably have been expected to assure that action

14   would be taken to avoid the harm or that the risk of

15   harm would be explained to the actual product user,

16   except where those warnings or instructions could be

17   readily attached by a reasonably prudent manufacturer

18   to the product itself in a form which could reach the

19   claimant;

20   (B) the using or supervising expert, where the

21   product involved is one which may be legally used only

22   by or under the supervision of a class of experts. For

23   purposes of this clause, warnings or instructions are

24   considered provided to the using or supervising expert

25   where the manufacturer employed means reasonably

14

1   calculated to make them available to the expert, and

2   this does not require actual, personal notice to the

3   expert; or

4   (C) the manufacturer's immediate buyer—

5   (i) where the product was sold as a compo-

6   nent or material to be incorporated into another

7   product and the claimant was exposed to the com-

8   ponent or material after it was incorporated or

9   converted into another product;

10   (ii) where the product was used in a work-

11   place and there was no practical, feasible means

12   of transmitting warnings or instructions directly to

13   the claimant; or

14   (iii) where the claimant was not an employee

15   of the manufacturer's immediate buyer and there

16   was no practical, feasible means of transmitting

17   the warnings or instructions to the claimant.

18   (2) A product is not unreasonably dangerous for lack of

19   warnings or instructions regarding—

20   (A) dangers that are obvious. As used in this

21   clause, "dangers that are obvious" are those of which

22   a reasonably prudent product user or a person identi-

23   fied in paragraph (1), if applicable, would have been

24   aware without a warning or instruction and dangers

15

1 which were a matter of common knowledge to persons

2 in the same or similar position as the claimant;

3 (B) the consequences of product misuse, as defined

4 in section 10(a)(2), or use contrary to warnings or

5 instructions available to the user or to a person identi-

6 fied in paragraph (1), if applicable; or

7 (C) the consequences of alterations or modifica-

8 tions, as defined in section 10(b)(2), of the product

9 which do not constitute reasonably anticipated conduct.

10 PRODUCT EXPRESS WARRANTY

11 SEC. 7. (a) A product is unreasonably dangerous be-

12 cause it did not conform to an express warranty if—

13 (1) the manufacturer made an express warranty

14 about a material fact relating to the safe performance

15 of the product;

16 (2) this express warranty proved to be untrue; and

17 (3) the failure of the product to conform to the

18 warranty caused the harm.

19 As used in this subsection, "material fact" means any specific

20 characteristic or quality of the product, but does not include a

21 general opinion about, or general praise of, the product or its

22 quality.

23 (b) A product may be unreasonably dangerous for failure

24 to conform to an express warranty although the manufacturer

16

1 did not engage in negligent or fraudulent conduct in making

2 the express warranty.

3   RESPONSIBILITY OF PRODUCT SELLERS

4   SEC. 8. (a) In any product liability action, a product

5 seller other than a manufacturer is liable to a claimant, if the

6 claimant establishes by a preponderance of the evidence

7 that—

8   (1)(A) the individual product unit which allegedly

9   caused the harm complained of was sold by the defend-

10   ant;

11   (B) the product seller failed to exercise reasonable

12   care with respect to the product; and

13   (C) such failure to exercise reasonable care was a

14   proximate cause of the claimant's harm; or

15   (2)(A) the product seller made an express warran-

16   ty, independent of any express warranty made by a

17   manufacturer as to the same product, about a material

18   fact directly relating to the safe performance of the

19   product;

20   (B) this express warranty proved to be untrue;

21   and

22   (C) the failure of the product to conform to the

23   warranty caused the harm.

17

1   (b) The claimant must introduce sufficient evidence to
2 allow a reasonable person, by a preponderance of the evi-
3 dence, to make the determinations specified in subsection (a).

4   (c)(1) A claimant may not establish any fact necessary to
5 make the determinations described in subsection (a) by show-
6 ing that the identical issue of fact was determined adversely
7 to the product seller in another action brought by another
8 claimant, unless both actions were based on harm caused by
9 the same event in which two or more persons were harmed.

10   (2) A product seller may not establish any fact neces-
11 sary to make the determinations described in subsection (a)
12 by showing that the identical issue of fact was determined
13 adversely to another claimant in another action against that
14 product seller, unless both actions were based on harm
15 caused by the same event in which two or more persons were
16 harmed and the claimant is the same as or is in privity with
17 the claimant in the other action.

18   (d)(1) In determining whether a product seller is subject
19 to liability under subsection (a)(1), the trier of fact may con-
20 sider the effect of the conduct of the seller with respect to the
21 construction, inspection, or condition of the product, and any
22 failure of the seller to transmit adequate warnings or instruc-
23 tions about the dangers and proper use of the product.

24   (2) A product seller shall not be liable under this Act
25 where there was no reasonable opportunity to inspect the

18

1 product in a manner which would or should, in the exercise of

2 reasonable care, have revealed the aspect of the product

3 which allegedly rendered it unreasonably dangerous.

4   (e) A product seller is liable for harm to the claimant

5 caused by a product in the same manner as the manufacturer

6 of the product if—

7   (1) the manufacturer is not subject to service of

8   process under the laws of the State in which the action

9   is brought; or

10   (2) the court determines that the claimant would

11   be unable to enforce a judgment against the manufac-

12   turer.

13   COMPARATIVE RESPONSIBILITY

14   SEC. 9. (a) All claims under this Act shall be governed

15 by the principles of comparative responsibility. Comparative

16 responsibility attributed to the claimant's conduct under sec-

17 tion 10(c) shall not bar recovery in a product liability action,

18 but shall reduce any damages awarded to the claimant in an

19 amount proportionate to the responsibility of the claimant.

20   (b) In any product liability action involving a claim of

21 comparative responsibility, the court, unless otherwise agreed

22 by all parties, shall instruct the jury to answer special inter-

23 rogatories (or, if there is no jury, the court shall make find-

24 ings) indicating (1) the amount of damages each claimant

25 would be entitled to recover if comparative responsibility

19

1   were disregarded and (2) the percentage of total responsibili-

2   ty for the claimant's harm to be allocated to each defendant,

3   to any third-party defendant, and to conduct defined in sec-

4   tion 10. For purposes of this paragraph, the court may deter-

5   mine that two or more persons are to be treated as a single

6   person.

7   (c) The court shall enter judgment against each party

8   determined to be liable in proportion to its percentage of re-

9   sponsibility for the claimant's harm, as determined under sub-

10 section (b)(2), unless section 11(a) requires a different result.

11   (d) If a claimant has not been able to collect on a judg-

12 ment in a product liability action, and if the claimant makes a

13 motion within 1 year after the judgment is entered, the court

14 shall determine whether any part of the obligation allocated

15 to a person who is a party to the action is not collectable

16 from such a person. Any amount of obligation which the

17 court determines is uncollectable from that person shall be

18 reallocated to the other persons who are parties to the action

19 and to whom responsibility was allocated and to the claimant

20 according to the respective percentages of their responsibili-

21 ty, as determined under subsection (b)(2).

22 MISUSE, ALTERATION, CONTRIBUTORY NEGLIGENCE OR

23   ASSUMPTION OF THE RISK

24   SEC. 10. (a)(1) If a manufacturer or product seller

25 proves by a preponderance of the evidence that misuse of a

20

1 product by any person other than the defendant manufacturer

2 or product seller and other than the claimant has caused the

3 claimant's harm, the determination in section 9(b)(2) shall re-

4 flect the percentage of total responsibility for the claimant's

5 harm allocable to misuse. Under this subsection, the trier of

6 fact may determine that the harm caused by the product oc-

7 curred solely because of misuse of the product.

8   (2) For purposes of this Act, misuse shall be considered

9 to occur when a product is used for a purpose or in a manner

10 which is not consistent with the warnings or instructions

11 available to the user, or which is not consistent with reason-

12 able practice of users of the product, or when a product user

13 fails adequately to train another person in the safe use of the

14 product, or otherwise provide for the safe use of the product,

15 and that lack of training or the failure otherwise to provide

16 for the safe use of the product was a cause of the claimant's

17 harm.

18   (b)(1) If a manufacturer or product seller proves by a

19 preponderance of the evidence that an alteration or modifica-

20 tion of the product by any person other than the defendant

21 manufacturer or product seller and other than the claimant

22 has caused the claimant's harm, the determination in section

23 9(b)(2) shall reflect the percentage of total responsibility for

24 the claimants' harm allocable to alteration or modification.

25 Under this subsection, the trier of fact may determine that

21

1   the harm arose solely because of the product alteration or

2   modification. The determination in section 9(b)(2) shall not be

3   made if—

4   (A) the alteration or modification was in accord-

5   ance with instructions or specifications of the manufac-

6   turer or product seller;

7   (B) the alteration or modification was made with

8   the express consent of the manufacturer or product

9   seller; or

10   (C) the alteration or modification was reasonably

11   anticipated conduct, and the manufacturer or product

12   seller failed to provide adequate warnings or instruc-

13   tions with respect to that alteration or modification.

14   (2) For purposes of this Act, alteration or modification

15   shall be considered to occur—

16   (A) when a person other than the manufacturer or

17   product seller changes the design, construction, or for-

18   mula of the product, or changes or removes warnings,

19   instructions, or safety devices that accompanied or

20   were displayed on the product; or

21   (B) when a product user fails to observe the rou-

22   tine care and maintenance necessary for a product and

23   that failure was the cause of the claimant's harm.

22

1   (3) Ordinary wear and tear of a product shall not be
2   considered to be alteration or modification of a product under
3   this subsection.

4   (c)(1) If a manufacturer or product seller proves by a
5   preponderance of the evidence that the conduct of the claim-
6   ant involving negligence, contributory negligence, or assump-
7   tion of risk has caused the claimant's harm, the determination
8   in section 9(b)(2) shall reflect the percentage of total respon-
9   sibility for the clamaint's harm allocable to the claimant.
10   Under this subsection, the trier of fact may determine that
11   the harm arose solely because of the conduct of the claimant.

12   (2) For purposes of this Act, conduct of the claimant
13   involving negligence, contributory negligence, or assumption
14   of risk shall be considered to occur—

15   (A) when the claimant, while using the product,
16   was injured by a defective condition that would have
17   been apparent, without inspection, to an ordinary rea-
18   sonably prudent person;

19   (B) when the claimant knew about the product's
20   defective condition, and voluntarily used the product or
21   voluntarily assumed the risk of harm from the product;
22   or

23   (C) when the claimant misused, altered, or modi-
24   fied the product, as those terms are defined in subsec-
25   tions (a)(2) and (b)(2).

23

2   SEC. 11. (a) In any product liability action in which

3   damages are sought for harm for which the person injured is

4   entitled to compensation under any State or Federal workers'

5   compensation law, and in which (1) the sum of the amount

6   paid as workers' compensation benefits for that harm and the

7   present value of all workers' compensation benefits to which

8   the employee is or would be entitled for the harm is greater

9   than (2) the sum of the amount proportionate to conduct de-

10   fined in section 10, the court shall enter judgment against the

11   defendant or defendants determined to be liable in an amount

12   equal to the amount of total damages to the claimant, as

13   determined under section 9(b)(1), less the amount of workers'

14   compensation benefits, as determined under this subsection.

15   If a person eligible to file a claim for workers' compensation

16   benefits has not filed such a claim, or either he or his employ-

17   er has failed to exhaust their remedies under an applicable

18   workers' compensation law, any product liability action

19   brought by the claimant shall be dismissed without prejudice

20   until those remedies are exhausted. The determination of

21   workers' compensation benefits by the trier of fact in a prod-

22   uct liability action shall have no binding effect on and shall

23   not be used as evidence in any other proceeding.

24

1   (b) Unless the manufacturer or product seller has ex-
2 pressly agreed to indemnify or hold an employer harmless for
3 harm to an employee caused by a product—

4   (1) the employer shall have no right of subroga-
5   tion, contribution, implied indemnity or lien against the
6   manufacturer or product seller if the harm is one for
7   which a product liability action may be brought under
8   this Act; and

9   (2) the workers' compensation insurance carrier of
10   the employer shall have no right of subrogation against
11   the manufacturer or product seller.

12   (c) In any product liability action in which damages are
13 sought for harm for which the person injured is entitled to
14 compensation under any State or Federal workers' compen-
15 sation law, no third party tortfeasor may maintain any action
16 for implied indemnity or contribution against the employer or
17 any coemployee of the person who was injured.

18   (d) No person entitled to file a claim for benefits pursu-
19 ant to applicable State or Federal workers' compensation
20 laws or who would have been entitled to file such a claim, or
21 any other person whose claim would be derivative from such
22 a claim, shall be allowed to recover in any action other than
23 a workers' compensation claim against a present or former
24 employer or workers' compensation insurer of the employer
25 or any coemployee for harm caused by a product.

25

2   SEC. 12. (a)(1) If any product is a capital good, no claim

3   alleging unsafe design or formulation as provided in section

4   5(b), or failure to give adequate warnings or instructions as

5   provided in section 6(a), may be brought for harm caused by

6   such a product more than 25 years from the date of delivery

7   of the product to its first purchaser or lessee who was not

8   engaged in the business of selling or leasing the product or

9   using the product as a component in the manufacture of an-

10 other product.

11   (2) As used in this subsection, "capital good" means any

12 product, other than a motor vehicle, or any component of any

13 such product, if it is also of a character subject to allowance

14 for depreciation under the Internal Revenue Code of 1954, as

15 amended, and was—

16   (A) used in a trade or business;

17   (B) held for the production of income; or

18   (C) sold, leased, or donated to a governmental or

19   private entity for the production of goods, for training,

20   for demonstration, or other similar purposes.

21   (b) Subsection (a) is not applicable if—

22   (1) the manufacturer or product seller intentional-

23   ly misrepresented facts about the product or fraudu-

24   lently concealed information about the product, and

26

1   that conduct was a substantial cause of the claimant's

2   harm;

3   (2) the harm of the claimant was caused by the

4   cumulative effect of prolonged exposure to a defective

5   product; or

6   (3) the harm, caused within the period referred to

7   in subsection (a), did not manifest itself until after the

8   expiration of that period.

9   (c) Nothing in subsection (a) shall affect the right of any

10   person who is subject to liability for harm under this Act to

11   seek and obtain contribution or indemnity from any other

12   person who is responsible for that harm.

13   PUNITIVE DAMAGES

14   SEC. 13. (a)(1) Punitive damages may be awarded to

15   any claimant who establishes by clear and convincing evi-

16   dence that the harm suffered was the result of the reckless

17   disregard of the manufacturer or product seller for the safety

18   of product users, consumers, or persons who might be

19   harmed by the product. Punitive damages may not be award-

20   ed in the absence of a compensatory award.

21   (2) As used in this subsection, "reckless disregard"

22   means conduct manifesting a conscious, flagrant indifference

23   to the safety of those persons who might be harmed by a

24   product and constituting an extreme departure from accepted

25   practice. A negligent choice among alternative product de-

27

1 signs or warnings, when made in the ordinary course of busi-

2 ness, does not by itself constitute "reckless disregard".

3 　　(b) The trier of fact, in determining under subsection (a)

4 whether punitive damages should be awarded, shall

5 consider—

6 　　　　(1) the manufacturer's or product seller's aware-

7 　　　　ness of the likelihood that serious harm would arise

8 　　　　from the sale or manufacture of a product;

9 　　　　(2) the conduct of the manufacturer or product

10 　　　　seller upon discovery that the product caused harm or

11 　　　　was related to harm caused to users or others, includ-

12 　　　　ing whether upon confirmation of the problem the man-

13 　　　　ufacturer or product seller took appropriate steps to

14 　　　　reduce the risk of harm;

15 　　　　(3) the duration of the conduct and any conceal-

16 　　　　ment of it by the manufacturer or product seller; and

17 　　　　(4) whether the harm suffered by the claimant

18 　　　　was partly the result of the claimant's own negligent

19 　　　　conduct.

20 　　(c) If the trier of fact determines under subsection (a)

21 that punitive damages should be awarded to a claimant, the

22 court shall determine the amount of those damages. In

23 making that determination, the court shall consider—

24 　　　　(1) all relevant evidence relating to the factors set

25 　　　　forth in subsection (b);

28

1 (2) the profitability of the conduct to the manufac-
2 turer or product seller; and

3 (3) the total effect of other punishment imposed
4 upon the manufacturer or product seller as a result of
5 the misconduct, including punitive damage awards to
6 persons similarly situated to the claimant and the se-
7 verity of other penalties to which the manufacturer or
8 product seller has been or may be subjected.

9 (d) Notwithstanding the provisions of section 14, a man-
10 ufacturer or product seller may introduce relevant evidence
11 of post-manufacturing improvements in defense of punitive
12 damages.

13 SUBSEQUENT REMEDIAL MEASURES

14 SEC. 14. (a) Except as provided in subsection (b), evi-
15 dence of any measure taken after an event, which if taken
16 previously would have made the event less likely to occur, is
17 not admissible.

18 (b) This section does not require the exclusion of evi-
19 dence of a subsequent measure in an action alleging a prod-
20 uct was unreasonably dangerous in design or formulation, if
21 offered to impeach a witness for the manufacturer or product
22 seller who has expressly denied the feasibility of such a
23 measure.

29

1   SEPARABILITY CLAUSE

2   SEC. 15. If any provision of this Act or the application

3   of it to any person or circumstance is held invalid, the re-

4   mainder of this Act and the application of the provision to

5   any other person or circumstance shall not be affected by that

6   invalidation.

7   EFFECTIVE DATE

8   SEC. 16. (a) This Act shall be effective 60 days after the

9   date of its enactment, and shall apply to all product liability

10   actions commenced on or after that date, including any action

11   in which the harm or the conduct which caused the harm

12   occurred before the effective date.

13   (b) If any provision of this Act would shorten the period

14   during which a manufacturer is exposed to liability under this

15   Act, the claimant may, notwithstanding the otherwise appli-

16   cable time period in section 12, bring any such action within

17   1 year after the effective date of this Act.

O

Index